FOURTH EDITION

Java Network Programming

Elliotte Rusty Harold

Beijing · Boston · Farnham · Sebastopol · Tokyo

Java Network Programming, Fourth Edition

by Elliotte Rusty Harold

Copyright © 2014 Elliotte Rusty Harold. All rights reserved.

Published by O'Reilly Media, Inc., 1005 Gravenstein Highway North, Sebastopol, CA 95472.

O'Reilly books may be purchased for educational, business, or sales promotional use. Online editions are also available for most titles (*http://safaribooksonline.com*). For more information, contact our corporate/institutional sales department: 800-998-9938 or *corporate@oreilly.com*.

Editor: Meghan Blanchette	**Indexer:** Judy McConville
Production Editor: Nicole Shelby	**Cover Designer:** Randy Comer
Copyeditor: Kim Cofer	**Interior Designer:** David Futato
Proofreader: Jasmine Kwityn	**Illustrator:** Rebecca Demarest

October 2013: Fourth Edition

Revision History for the Fourth Edition:

2013-09-23: First release

2015-08-21: Second release

See *http://oreilly.com/catalog/errata.csp?isbn=9781449357672* for release details.

Nutshell Handbook, the Nutshell Handbook logo, and the O'Reilly logo are registered trademarks of O'Reilly Media, Inc. *Java Network Programming*, the image of a North American river otter, and related trade dress are trademarks of O'Reilly Media, Inc.

Many of the designations used by manufacturers and sellers to distinguish their products are claimed as trademarks. Where those designations appear in this book, and O'Reilly Media, Inc., was aware of a trademark claim, the designations have been printed in caps or initial caps.

While every precaution has been taken in the preparation of this book, the publisher and author assume no responsibility for errors or omissions, or for damages resulting from the use of the information contained herein.

ISBN: 978-1-449-35767-2

[LSI]

This book is dedicated to my dog, Thor.

Table of Contents

Preface

Java's growth over the past 20 years has been nothing short of phenomenal. Given Java's rapid rise to prominence and the even more spectacular growth of the Internet, it's a little surprising that network programming in Java remains so mysterious to so many. It doesn't have to be. In fact, writing network programs in Java is quite simple, as this book will show. Readers with previous experience in network programming in a Unix, Windows, or Macintosh environment will be pleasantly surprised at how much easier it is to write equivalent programs in Java. The Java core API includes well-designed interfaces to most network features. Indeed, there is very little application layer network software you can write in C or C++ that you can't write more easily in Java. *Java Network Programming*, Fourth Edition, endeavors to show you how to take advantage of Java's network class library to quickly and easily write programs that accomplish many common networking tasks. Some of these include:

- Browsing the Web with HTTP
- Writing multithreaded servers
- Encrypting communications for confidentiality, authentication, and guaranteed message integrity
- Designing GUI clients for network services
- Posting data to server-side programs
- Looking up hosts using DNS
- Downloading files with anonymous FTP
- Connecting sockets for low-level network communication
- Multicasting to all hosts on the network

Java is the first (though no longer the only) language to provide such a powerful cross-platform network library for handling all these diverse tasks. *Java Network Programming* exposes the power and sophistication of this library. This book's goal is to enable you to start using Java as a platform for serious network programming. To do so, this book provides a general background in network fundamentals, as well as detailed discussions of Java's facilities for writing network programs. You'll learn how to write Java programs that share data across the Internet for games, collaboration, software updates, file transfer, and more. You'll also get a behind-the-scenes look at HTTP, SMTP, TCP/IP, and the other protocols that support the Internet and the Web. When you finish this book, you'll have the knowledge and the tools to create the next generation of software that takes full advantage of the Internet.

About the Fourth Edition

In 1996, in the first edition of this book's opening chapter, I wrote extensively about the sort of dynamic, distributed network applications I thought Java would make possible. One of the most exciting parts of writing subsequent editions has been seeing virtually all of the applications I foretold come to pass. Programmers are using Java to query database servers, monitor web pages, control telescopes, manage multiplayer games, and more, all by using Java's native ability to access the Internet. Java in general and network programming in Java in particular has moved well beyond the hype stage and into the realm of real, working applications.

This book has come a long way, too. The fourth edition focuses even more heavily on HTTP and REST. HTTP has gone from being one of many network protocols to almost *the* network protocol. As you'll see, it is often the protocol on which other protocols are built, forming its own layer in the network stack.

There have been lots of other small changes and updates throughout the java.net and supporting packages in Java 6, 7, and 8, and these are covered here as well. New classes addressed in this edition include CookieManager, CookiePolicy, CookieStore, HttpCookie, SwingWorker, Executor, ExecutorService, AsynchronousSocketChannel, AsynchronousServerSocketChannel, and more. Many other methods have been added to existing classes in the last three releases of Java, and these are discussed in the relevant chapters. I've also rewritten large parts of the book to reflect the ever-changing fashions in Java programming in general and network programming in particular. I hope you'll find this fourth edition an even stronger, longer-lived, more accurate, and more enjoyable tutorial and reference to network programming in Java than the previous one.

Organization of the Book

Chapter 1, *Basic Network Concepts*, explains in detail what a programmer needs to know about how the networks and the Internet work. It covers the protocols that underlie the Internet, such as TCP/IP and UDP/IP.

The next two chapters throw some light on two parts of Java programming that are critical to almost all network programs but are often misunderstood and misused: I/O and threading. Chapter 2, *Streams*, explores Java's classic I/O which—despite the new I/O APIs—isn't going away any time soon and is still the preferred means of handling input and output in most client applications. Understanding how Java handles I/O in the general case is a prerequisite for understanding the special case of how Java handles network I/O. Chapter 3, *Threads*, explores multithreading and synchronization, with a special emphasis on how they can be used for asynchronous I/O and network servers.

Experienced Java programmers may be able to skim or skip these two chapters. However, Chapter 4, *Internet Addresses*, is essential reading for everyone. It shows how Java programs interact with the Domain Name System through the InetAddress class, the one class that's needed by essentially all network programs. Once you've finished this chapter, it's possible to jump around in the book as your interests and needs dictate.

Chapter 5, *URLs and URIs*, explores Java's URL class, a powerful abstraction for downloading information and files from network servers of many kinds. The URL class enables you to connect to and download files and documents from a network server without concerning yourself with the details of the protocol the server speaks. It lets you connect to an FTP server using the same code you use to talk to an HTTP server or to read a file on the local hard disk. You'll also learn about the newer URI class, a more standards-conformant alternative for identifying but not retrieving resources.

Chapter 6, *HTTP*, delves deeper into the HTTP protocol specifically. Topics covered include REST, HTTP headers, and cookies. Chapter 7, *URLConnections*, shows you how to use the URLConnection and HttpURLConnection classes not just to download data from web servers, but to upload documents and configure connections.

Chapter 8 through Chapter 10 discuss Java's low-level socket classes for network access. Chapter 8, *Sockets for Clients*, introduces the Java sockets API and the Socket class in particular. It shows you how to write network clients that interact with TCP servers of all kinds including whois, dict, and HTTP. Chapter 9, *Sockets for Servers*, shows you how to use the ServerSocket class to write servers for these and other protocols. Finally, Chapter 10, *Secure Sockets*, shows you how to protect your client-server communications using the Secure Sockets Layer (SSL) and the Java Secure Sockets Extension (JSSE).

Chapter 11, *Nonblocking I/O*, introduces the new I/O APIs specifically designed for network servers. These APIs enable a program to figure out whether a connection is ready before it tries to read from or write to the socket. This allows a single thread to manage many different connections simultaneously, thereby placing much less load on the virtual machine. The new I/O APIs don't help much for small servers or clients that don't open many simultaneous connections, but they may provide performance boosts for high-volume servers that want to transmit as much data as the network can handle as fast as the network can deliver it.

Chapter 12, *UDP*, introduces the User Datagram Protocol (UDP) and the associated `DatagramPacket` and `DatagramSocket` classes that provide fast, unreliable communication. Finally, Chapter 13, *IP Multicast*, shows you how to use UDP to communicate with multiple hosts at the same time.

Who You Are

This book assumes you are comfortable with the Java language and programming environment, in addition to object-oriented programming in general. This book does not attempt to be a basic language tutorial. You should be thoroughly familiar with the syntax of Java. You should have written simple applications. It also wouldn't hurt if you're familiar with basic Swing programming, though that's not required aside from a few examples. When you encounter a topic that requires a deeper understanding for network programming than is customary—for instance, threads and streams—I'll cover that topic as well, at least briefly.

However, this book doesn't assume that you have prior experience with network programming. You should find it a complete introduction to networking concepts and network application development. I don't assume that you have a few thousand networking acronyms (TCP, UDP, SMTP, etc.) at the tip of your tongue. You'll learn what you need to know about these here.

Java Versions

Java's network classes have changed a lot more slowly since Java 1.0 than other parts of the core API. In comparison to the AWT or I/O, there have been almost no changes and only a few additions. Of course, all network programs make extensive use of the I/O classes and some make heavy use of GUIs. This book is written with the assumption that you are coding with at least Java 5.0. In general, I use Java 5 features like generics and the enhanced `for` loop freely without further explanation.

For network programming purposes, the distinction between Java 5 and Java 6 is not large. Most examples look identical in the two versions. When a particular method or class is new in Java 6, 7, or 8, it is noted by a comment following its declaration like this:

```
public void setFixedLengthStreamingMode(long contentLength) // Java 7
```

Java 7 is a bit more of a stretch. I have not shied away from using features introduced in Java 7 where they seemed especially useful or convenient—for instance, try-with-resources and multicatch are both very helpful when trying to fit examples into the limited space available in a printed book—but I have been careful to point out my use of such features.

Overall, though, Java's networking API has been relatively stable since Java 1.0. Very little of the post-1.0 networking API has ever been deprecated, and additions have been relatively minor. You shouldn't have any trouble using this book after Java 8 is released. New APIs, however, have been somewhat more frequent in the supporting classes, particularly I/O, which has undergone three major revisions since Java 1.0.

About the Examples

Most methods and classes described in this book are illustrated with at least one complete working program, simple though it may be. In my experience, a complete working program is essential to showing the proper use of a method. Without a program, it is too easy to drop into jargon or to gloss over points about which the author may be unclear in his own mind. The Java API documentation itself often suffers from excessively terse descriptions of the method calls. In this book, I have tried to err on the side of providing too much explication rather than too little. If a point is obvious to you, feel free to skip over it. You do not need to type in and run every example in this book; but if a particular method does give you trouble, you should have at least one working example.

Each chapter includes at least one (and often several) more complex programs that demonstrate the classes and methods of that chapter in a more realistic setting. These often rely on Java features not discussed in this book. Indeed, in many of the programs, the networking components are only a small fraction of the source code and often the least difficult parts. Nonetheless, none of these programs could be written as easily in languages that didn't give networking the central position it occupies in Java. The apparent simplicity of the networked sections of the code reflects the extent to which networking has been made a core feature of Java, and not any triviality of the program itself. All example programs presented in this book are available online, often with corrections and additions. You can download the source code from *http://www.cafeau lait.org/books/jnp4/*.

I have tested all the examples on Linux and many on Windows and Mac OS X. Most of the examples given here *should* work on other platforms and with other compilers and virtual machines that support Java 5 or later. The most common reasons an example may not compile with Java 5 or 6 are try-with-resources and multicatch. These examples can easily be rewritten to support earlier Java versions at the cost of increased verbosity.

I do feel a little guilty about a couple of compromises necessitated by the needs of space in a printed book. First, I rarely check preconditions. Most methods assume they are passed good data, and dispense with null checks and similar principles of good code hygiene. Furthermore, I have reduced the indentation to two characters per block and four characters per continuation line, as opposed to the Java standard of four and eight, respectively. I hope these flaws will not be too distracting. On the positive side, these compromises have aided me in making this edition considerably shorter (by several hundred pages) than the previous edition.

Conventions Used in This Book

Body text is Minion Pro, normal, like you're reading now.

A `monospaced typewriter font` is used for:

- Code examples and fragments
- Anything that might appear in a Java program, including keywords, operators, data types, method names, variable names, class names, and interface names
- Program output
- Tags that might appear in an HTML document

A **`bold monospaced font`** is used for:

- Command lines and options that should be typed verbatim on the screen

An *italicized* font is used for:

- New terms where they are defined
- Pathnames, filenames, and program names (however, if the program name is also the name of a Java class, it is given in a monospaced font, like other class names)
- Host and domain names (*www.hpmor.com*)
- URLs (*http://www.cafeaulait.org/slides/*)
- Titles of other books (*Java I/O*)

 Indicates a tip, suggestion, or general note.

 Indicates a warning or caution.

Significant code fragments and complete programs are generally placed into a separate paragraph, like this:

```
Socket s = new Socket("java.oreilly.com", 80);
if (!s.getTcpNoDelay()) s.setTcpNoDelay(true);
```

When code is presented as fragments rather than complete programs, the existence of the appropriate `import` statements should be inferred. For example, in the preceding code fragment you may assume that `java.net.Socket` was imported.

Some examples intermix user input with program output. In these cases, the user input will be displayed in bold, as in this example from Chapter 9:

```
% telnet rama.poly.edu 7
Trying 128.238.10.212...
Connected to rama.poly.edu.
Escape character is '^]'.
This is a test
This is a test
This is another test
This is another test
9876543210
9876543210
^]
telnet> close
Connection closed.
```

Finally, although many of the examples used here are toy examples unlikely to be reused, a few of the classes I develop have real value. Please feel free to reuse them or any parts of them in your own code. No special permission is required. They are in the public domain (although the same is most definitely not true of the explanatory text!).

Request for Comments

I enjoy hearing from readers, whether with general comments about this book, specific corrections, other topics they would like to see covered, or just war stories about their own network programming travails. You can reach me by sending an email to *elharo@ibiblio.org*. Please realize, however, that I receive several hundred pieces of email a day and cannot personally respond to each one. For the best chance of getting a personal response, please identify yourself as a reader of this book. If you have a question about a particular program that isn't working as you expect, try to reduce it to the simplest case that reproduces the bug, preferably a single class, and paste the text of the entire program into the body of your email. Unsolicited attachments will be deleted unopened. And please, please send the message from the account you want me to reply to and make sure that your Reply-to address is properly set! There's nothing quite so frustrating as spending an hour or more carefully researching the answer to an interesting question and composing a detailed response, only to have it bounce because my correspondent sent her feedback from a public terminal and neglected to set the browser preferences to include her actual email address.

I also adhere to the old saying "If you like this book, tell your friends. If you don't like it, tell me." I'm especially interested in hearing about mistakes. This is the fourth edition. I've yet to make it perfect, but I keep trying. As hard as I and the editors at O'Reilly worked on this book, I'm sure there are mistakes and typographical errors that we missed here somewhere. And I'm sure that at least one of them is a really embarrassing whopper of a problem. If you find a mistake or a typo, please let me know so I can correct it. I'll post it on the O'Reilly website at *http://bit.ly/java_ntwk_program_errata*. Before reporting errors, please check one of those pages to see if I already know about it and have posted a fix. Any errors that are reported will be fixed in future printings.

Using Code Examples

This book is here to help you get your job done. In general, if this book includes code examples, you may use the code in this book in your programs and documentation. You do not need to contact us for permission unless you're reproducing a significant portion of the code. For example, writing a program that uses several chunks of code from this book does not require permission. Selling or distributing a CD-ROM of examples from O'Reilly books does require permission. Answering a question by citing this book and quoting example code does not require permission. Incorporating a significant amount of example code from this book into your product's documentation does require permission.

We appreciate, but do not require, attribution. An attribution usually includes the title, author, publisher, and ISBN. For example: "*Java Network Programming*, Fourth Edition, by Elliotte Rusty Harold (O'Reilly). Copyright 2014 Elliotte Rusty Harold, 978-1-449-35767-2."

If you feel your use of code examples falls outside fair use or the permission given here, feel free to contact us at *permissions@oreilly.com*.

Safari® Books Online

 *Safari Books Online* is an on-demand digital library that delivers expert content in both book and video form from the world's leading authors in technology and business.

Technology professionals, software developers, web designers, and business and creative professionals use Safari Books Online as their primary resource for research, problem solving, learning, and certification training.

Safari Books Online offers a range of plans and pricing for enterprise, government, education, and individuals.

Members have access to thousands of books, training videos, and prepublication manuscripts in one fully searchable database from publishers like O'Reilly Media, Prentice Hall Professional, Addison-Wesley Professional, Microsoft Press, Sams, Que, Peachpit Press, Focal Press, Cisco Press, John Wiley & Sons, Syngress, Morgan Kaufmann, IBM Redbooks, Packt, Adobe Press, FT Press, Apress, Manning, New Riders, McGraw-Hill,

Jones & Bartlett, Course Technology, and hundreds more. For more information about Safari Books Online, please visit us online.

How to Contact Us

Please address comments and questions concerning this book to the publisher:

O'Reilly Media, Inc.
1005 Gravenstein Highway North
Sebastopol, CA 95472
800-998-9938 (in the United States or Canada)
707-829-0515 (international or local)
707-829-0104 (fax)

We have a web page for this book, where we list errata, examples, and any additional information. You can access this page at *http://oreil.ly/java-network-prgamming*.

To comment or ask technical questions about this book, send email to *bookques tions@oreilly.com*.

For more information about our books, courses, conferences, and news, see our website at *http://www.oreilly.com*.

Find us on Facebook: *http://facebook.com/oreilly*

Follow us on Twitter: *http://twitter.com/oreillymedia*

Watch us on YouTube: *http://www.youtube.com/oreillymedia*

Acknowledgments

Many people were involved in the production of this book. My editor, Mike Loukides, got things rolling, and provided many helpful comments along the way that substantially improved the book. Dr. Peter "Peppar" Parnes helped out immensely with Chapter 13. The technical editors all provided invaluable assistance in hunting down errors and omissions. Simon St. Laurent provided crucial advice on which topics deserved more coverage. Scott Oaks lent his thread expertise to Chapter 3, proving once again by the many subtle bugs he hunted down that multithreading still requires the attention of an expert. Ron Hitchens shone light into many of the darker areas of the new I/O APIs. Marc Loy and Jim Elliott reviewed some of the most bleeding edge material in the book. Timothy F. Rohaly was unswerving in his commitment to making sure I closed all my sockets and caught all possible exceptions, and in general wrote the cleanest, safest, most exemplary code I could write. John Zukowski found numerous errors of omission, all now filled thanks to him. And the eagle-eyed Avner Gelb displayed an astonishing ability to spot mistakes that had somehow managed to go unnoticed by myself, all the other editors, and the tens of thousands of readers of the first edition. Alex Stangl and Ryan Cuprak provided further assistance with spotting both new and lingering mistakes in this latest edition.

It isn't customary to thank the publisher, but the publisher does set the tone for the rest of the company, authors, editors, and production staff alike; and I think Tim O'Reilly deserves special credit for making O'Reilly Media absolutely one of the best houses an author can write for. If there's one person without whom this book would never have been written, it's him. If you, the reader, find O'Reilly books to be consistently better than most of the dreck on the market, the reason really can be traced straight back to Tim.

My agent, David Rogelberg, convinced me it was possible to make a living writing books like this rather than working in an office. The entire crew at *ibiblio.org* over the last several years has really helped me to communicate better with my readers in a variety of ways. Every reader who sent in bouquets and brickbats for previous editions has been instrumental in helping me write this much-improved edition. All these people deserve much thanks and credit. Finally, as always, I'd like to offer my largest thanks to my wife, Beth, without whose love and support this book would never have happened.

—Elliotte Rusty Harold
elharo@ibiblio.org
July 5, 2013

CHAPTER 1

Basic Network Concepts

Network programming is no longer the province of a few specialists. It has become a core part of every developer's toolbox. Today, more programs are network aware than aren't. Besides classic applications like email, web browsers, and remote login, most major applications have some level of networking built in. For example:

- Text editors like BBEdit save and open files directly from FTP servers.
- IDEs like Eclipse and IntelliJ IDEA communicate with source code repositories like GitHub and Sourceforge.
- Word processors like Microsoft Word open files from URLs.
- Antivirus programs like Norton AntiVirus check for new virus definitions by connecting to the vendor's website every time the computer is started.
- Music players like Winamp and iTunes upload CD track lengths to CDDB and download the corresponding track titles.
- Gamers playing multiplayer first-person shooters like Halo gleefully frag each other in real time.
- Supermarket cash registers running IBM SurePOS ACE communicate with their store's server in real time with each transaction. The server uploads its daily receipts to the chain's central computers each night.
- Schedule applications like Microsoft Outlook automatically synchronize calendars among employees in a company.

Java was the first programming language designed from the ground up for network applications. Java was originally aimed at proprietary cable television networks rather than the Internet, but it's always had the network foremost in mind. One of the first two real Java applications was a web browser. As the Internet continues to grow, Java is uniquely suited to build the next generation of network applications.

One of the biggest secrets about Java is that it makes writing network programs easy. In fact, it is far easier to write network programs in Java than in almost any other language. This book shows you dozens of complete programs that take advantage of the Internet. Some are simple textbook examples, while others are completely functional applications. One thing you'll notice in the fully functional applications is just how little code is devoted to networking. Even in network-intensive programs like web servers and clients, almost all the code handles data manipulation or the user interface. The part of the program that deals with the network is almost always the shortest and simplest. In brief, it is easy for Java applications to send and receive data across the Internet.

This chapter covers the background networking concepts you need to understand before writing networked programs in Java (or, for that matter, in any language). Moving from the most general to the most specific, it explains what you need to know about networks in general, IP and TCP/IP-based networks in particular, and the Internet. This chapter doesn't try to teach you how to wire a network or configure a router, but you will learn what you need to know to write applications that communicate across the Internet. Topics covered in this chapter include the nature of networks; the TCP/IP layer model; the IP, TCP, and UDP protocols; firewalls and proxy servers; the Internet; and the Internet standardization process. Experienced network gurus may safely skip this chapter, and move on to the next chapter where you begin developing the tools needed to write your own network programs in Java.

Networks

A *network* is a collection of computers and other devices that can send data to and receive data from one another, more or less in real time. A network is often connected by wires, and the bits of data are turned into electromagnetic waves that move through the wires. However, wireless networks transmit data using radio waves; and most long-distance transmissions are now carried over fiber-optic cables that send light waves through glass filaments. There's nothing sacred about any particular physical medium for the transmission of data. Theoretically, data could be transmitted by coal-powered computers that send smoke signals to one another. The response time (and environmental impact) of such a network would be rather poor.

Each machine on a network is called a *node*. Most nodes are computers, but printers, routers, bridges, gateways, dumb terminals, and Coca-Cola™ machines can also be nodes. You might use Java to interface with a Coke machine, but otherwise you'll mostly talk to other computers. Nodes that are fully functional computers are also called *hosts*. I will use the word *node* to refer to any device on the network, and the word *host* to refer to a node that is a general-purpose computer.

Every network node has an *address*, a sequence of bytes that uniquely identifies it. You can think of this group of bytes as a number, but in general the number of bytes in an address or the ordering of those bytes (big endian or little endian) is not guaranteed to match any primitive numeric data type in Java. The more bytes there are in each address, the more addresses there are available and the more devices that can be connected to the network simultaneously.

Addresses are assigned differently on different kinds of networks. Ethernet addresses are attached to the physical Ethernet hardware. Manufacturers of Ethernet hardware use preassigned manufacturer codes to make sure there are no conflicts between the addresses in their hardware and the addresses of other manufacturers' hardware. Each manufacturer is responsible for making sure it doesn't ship two Ethernet cards with the same address. Internet addresses are normally assigned to a computer by the organization that is responsible for it. However, the addresses that an organization is allowed to choose for its computers are assigned by the organization's Internet service provider (ISP). ISPs get their IP addresses from one of four regional Internet registries (the registry for North America is ARIN (*http://www.arin.net*), the American Registry for Internet Numbers), which are in turn assigned IP addresses by the Internet Corporation for Assigned Names and Numbers (ICANN (*http://www.icann.org*)).

On some kinds of networks, nodes also have text names that help human beings identify them such as "www.elharo.com" or "Beth Harold's Computer." At a set moment in time, a particular name normally refers to exactly one address. However, names are not locked to addresses. Names can change while addresses stay the same; likewise, addresses can change while the names stay the same. One address can have several names and one name can refer to several different addresses.

All modern computer networks are *packet-switched* networks: data traveling on the network is broken into chunks called *packets* and each packet is handled separately. Each packet contains information about who sent it and where it's going. The most important advantage of breaking data into individually addressed packets is that packets from many ongoing exchanges can travel on one wire, which makes it much cheaper to build a network: many computers can share the same wire without interfering. (In contrast, when you make a local telephone call within the same exchange on a traditional phone line, you have essentially reserved a wire from your phone to the phone of the person you're calling. When all the wires are in use, as sometimes happens during a major emergency or holiday, not everyone who picks up a phone will get a dial tone. If you stay on the line, you'll eventually get a dial tone when a line becomes free. In some countries with worse phone service than the United States, it's not uncommon to have to wait half an hour or more for a dial tone.) Another advantage of packets is that checksums can be used to detect whether a packet was damaged in transit.

We're still missing one important piece: some notion of what computers need to say to pass data back and forth. A *protocol* is a precise set of rules defining how computers communicate: the format of addresses, how data is split into packets, and so on. There are many different protocols defining different aspects of network communication. For example, the Hypertext Transfer Protocol (HTTP) defines how web browsers and servers communicate; at the other end of the spectrum, the IEEE 802.3 standard defines a protocol for how bits are encoded as electrical signals on a particular type of wire. Open, published protocol standards allow software and equipment from different vendors to communicate with one another. A web server doesn't care whether the client is a Unix workstation, an Android phone, or an iPad, because all clients speak the same HTTP protocol regardless of platform.

The Layers of a Network

Sending data across a network is a complex operation that must be carefully tuned to the physical characteristics of the network as well as the logical character of the data being sent. Software that sends data across a network must understand how to avoid collisions between packets, convert digital data to analog signals, detect and correct errors, route packets from one host to another, and more. The process is further complicated when the requirement to support multiple operating systems and heterogeneous network cabling is added.

To hide most of this complexity from the application developer and end user, the different aspects of network communication are separated into multiple layers. Each layer represents a different level of abstraction between the physical hardware (i.e., the wires and electricity) and the information being transmitted. In theory, each layer only talks to the layers immediately above and immediately below it. Separating the network into layers lets you modify or even replace the software in one layer without affecting the others, as long as the interfaces between the layers stay the same.

Figure 1-1 shows a stack of possible protocols that may exist in your network. While the middle layer protocols are fairly consistent across most of the Internet today, the top and the bottom vary a lot. Some hosts use Ethernet; some use WiFi; some use PPP; some use something else. Similarly, what's on the top of the stack will depend completely on which programs a host is running. The key is that from the top of the stack, it doesn't really matter what's on the bottom and vice versa. The layer model decouples the application protocols (the main subject of this book) from the physics of the network hardware and the topology of the network connections.

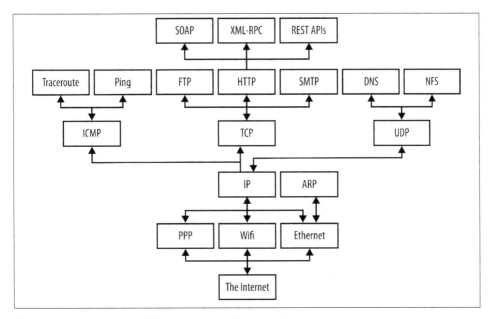

Figure 1-1. Protocols in different layers of a network

There are several different layer models, each organized to fit the needs of a particular kind of network. This book uses the standard TCP/IP four-layer model appropriate for the Internet, shown in Figure 1-2. In this model, applications like Firefox and Warcraft run in the application layer and talk only to the transport layer. The transport layer talks only to the application layer and the Internet layer. The Internet layer in turn talks only to the host-to-network layer and the transport layer, never directly to the application layer. The host-to-network layer moves the data across the wires, fiber-optic cables, or other medium to the host-to-network layer on the remote system, which then moves the data up the layers to the application on the remote system.

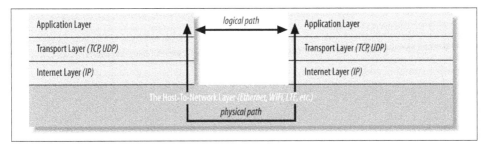

Figure 1-2. The layers of a network

For example, when a web browser sends a request to a web server to retrieve a page, the browser is actually talking to the transport layer on the local client machine. The transport layer breaks the request into TCP segments, adds some sequence numbers and checksums to the data, and then passes the request to the local internet layer. The internet layer fragments the segments into IP datagrams of the necessary size for the local network and passes them to the host-to-network layer for transmission onto the wire. The host-to-network layer encodes the digital data as analog signals appropriate for the particular physical medium and sends the request out the wire where it will be read by the host-to-network layer of the remote system to which it's addressed.

The host-to-network layer on the remote system decodes the analog signals into digital data, then passes the resulting IP datagrams to the server's internet layer. The internet layer does some simple checks to see that the IP datagrams aren't corrupt, reassembles them if they've been fragmented, and passes them to the server's transport layer. The server's transport layer checks to see that all the data arrived and requests retransmission of any missing or corrupt pieces. (This request actually goes back down through the server's internet layer, through the server's host-to-network layer, and back to the client system, where it bubbles back up to the client's transport layer, which retransmits the missing data back down through the layers. This is all transparent to the application layer.) Once the server's transport layer has received enough contiguous, sequential datagrams, it reassembles them and writes them onto a stream read by the web server running in the server application layer. The server responds to the request and sends its response back down through the layers on the server system for transmission back across the Internet and delivery to the web client.

As you can guess, the real process is much more elaborate. The host-to-network layer is by far the most complex, and a lot has been deliberately hidden. For example, it's entirely possible that data sent across the Internet will pass through several routers and their layers before reaching its final destination. It may need to be converted from radio waves in the air to electrical signals in copper wire to light pulses in fiber-optic cables and back again, possibly more than once. However, 90% of the time your Java code will work in the application layer and only need to talk to the transport layer. The other 10% of the time, you'll be in the transport layer and talking to the application layer or the internet layer. The complexity of the host-to-network layer is hidden from you; that's the point of the layer model.

If you read the network literature, you're likely to encounter an alternative seven-layer model called the Open Systems Interconnection (OSI) Reference Model. For network programs in Java, the OSI model is overkill. The biggest difference between the OSI model and the TCP/IP model used in this book is that the OSI model splits the host-to-network layer into data link and physical layers and inserts presentation and session layers in between the application and transport layers. The OSI model is more general and better suited for non-TCP/IP networks, although most of the time it's still overly complex. In any case, Java's network classes only work on TCP/IP networks and always in the application or transport layers, so for the purposes of this book, absolutely nothing is gained by using the more complicated OSI model.

To the application layer, it seems as if it is talking directly to the application layer on the other system; the network creates a logical path between the two application layers. It's easy to understand the logical path if you think about an IRC chat session. Most participants in an IRC chat would say that they're talking to another person. If you really push them, they might say that they're talking to their computer (really the application layer), which is talking to the other person's computer, which is talking to the other person. Everything more than one layer deep is effectively invisible, and that is exactly the way it should be. Let's consider each layer in more detail.

The Host-to-Network Layer

As a Java programmer, you're fairly high up in the network food chain. A lot happens below your radar. In the standard reference model for IP-based Internets (the only kind of network Java really understands), the hidden parts of the network belong to the *host-to-network layer* (also known as the link layer, data link layer, or network interface layer). The host-to-network layer defines how a particular network interface—such as an Ethernet card or a WiFi antenna—sends IP datagrams over its physical connection to the local network and the world.

The part of the host-to-network layer made up of the hardware that connects different computers (wires, fiber-optic cables, radio waves, or smoke signals) is sometimes called the physical layer of the network. As a Java programmer, you don't need to worry about this layer unless something goes wrong—the plug falls out of the back of your computer, or someone drops a backhoe through the T–1 line between you and the rest of the world. In other words, Java never sees the physical layer.

The primary reason you'll need to think about the host-to-network layer and the physical layer, if you need to think about them at all, is performance. For instance, if your clients reside on fast, reliable fiber-optic connections, you will design your protocol and applications differently than if they're on high-latency satellite connections on an oil rig in the North Sea. You'll make still different choices if your clients are on a 3G data plan where they're charged by the byte for relatively low bandwidth. And if you're writing a general consumer application that could be used by any of these clients, you'll try to hit a sweet spot somewhere in the middle, or perhaps even detect and dynamically adapt to individual client capabilities. However, whichever physical links you encounter, the APIs you use to communicate across those networks are the same. What makes that possible is the internet layer.

The Internet Layer

The next layer of the network, and the first that you need to concern yourself with, is the *internet layer*. In the OSI model, the internet layer goes by the more generic name *network layer*. A network layer protocol defines how bits and bytes of data are organized into the larger groups called packets, and the addressing scheme by which different machines find one another. The Internet Protocol (IP) is the most widely used network layer protocol in the world and the only network layer protocol Java understands.

In fact, it's two protocols: IPv4, which uses 32-bit addresses, and IPv6, which uses 128-bit addresses and adds a few other technical features to assist with routing. At the time of this writing, IPv4 still accounts for more than 90% of Internet traffic, but IPv6 is catching on fast and may well surpass IPv4 before the next edition of this book. Although these are two very different network protocols that do not interoperate on the same network without special gateways and/or tunneling protocols, Java hides almost all of the differences from you.

In both IPv4 and IPv6, data is sent across the internet layer in packets called *datagrams*. Each IPv4 datagram contains a header between 20 and 60 bytes long and a payload that contains up to 65,515 bytes of data. (In practice, most IPv4 datagrams are much smaller, ranging from a few dozen bytes to a little more than eight kilobytes.) An IPv6 datagram contains a larger header and up to four gigabytes of data.

Figure 1-3 shows how the different quantities are arranged in an IPv4 datagram. All bits and bytes are big endian; most significant to least significant runs left to right.

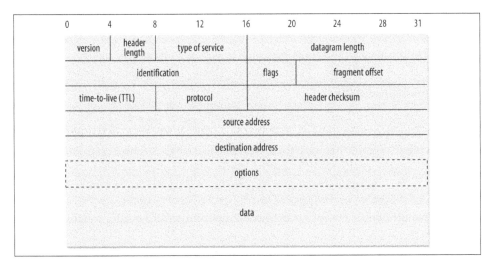

Figure 1-3. The structure of an IPv4 datagram

Besides routing and addressing, the second purpose of the Internet layer is to enable different types of Host-to-Network layers to talk to each other. Internet routers translate between WiFi and Ethernet, Ethernet and DSL, DSL and fiber-optic backhaul protocols, and so forth. Without the internet layer or something like it, each computer could only talk to other computers that shared its particular type of network. The internet layer is responsible for connecting heterogenous networks to each other using homogeneous protocols.

The Transport Layer

Raw datagrams have some drawbacks. Most notably, there's no guarantee that they will be delivered. Even if they are delivered, they may have been corrupted in transit. The header checksum can only detect corruption in the header, not in the data portion of a datagram. Finally, even if the datagrams arrive uncorrupted, they do not necessarily arrive in the order in which they were sent. Individual datagrams may follow different routes from source to destination. Just because datagram A is sent before datagram B does not mean that datagram A will arrive before datagram B.

The *transport layer* is responsible for ensuring that packets are received in the order they were sent and that no data is lost or corrupted. If a packet is lost, the transport layer can ask the sender to retransmit the packet. IP networks implement this by adding an additional header to each datagram that contains more information. There are two primary protocols at this level. The first, the Transmission Control Protocol (TCP), is a high-overhead protocol that allows for retransmission of lost or corrupted data and delivery of bytes in the order they were sent. The second protocol, the User Datagram Protocol (UDP), allows the receiver to detect corrupted packets but does not guarantee that packets are delivered in the correct order (or at all). However, UDP is often much faster than TCP. TCP is called a *reliable* protocol; UDP is an *unreliable* protocol. Later, you'll see that unreliable protocols are much more useful than they sound.

The Application Layer

The layer that delivers data to the user is called the *application layer*. The three lower layers all work together to define how data is transferred from one computer to another. The application layer decides what to do with the data after it's transferred. For example, an application protocol like HTTP (for the World Wide Web) makes sure that your web browser displays a graphic image as a picture, not a long stream of numbers. The application layer is where most of the network parts of your programs spend their time. There is an entire alphabet soup of application layer protocols: in addition to HTTP for the Web, there are SMTP, POP, and IMAP for email; FTP, FSP, and TFTP for file transfer; NFS for file access; Gnutella and BitTorrent for file sharing; the Session Initiation Protocol (SIP) and Skype for voice communication; and many, many more. In addition, your programs can define their own application layer protocols as necessary.

IP, TCP, and UDP

IP, the Internet protocol, was developed with military sponsorship during the Cold War, and ended up with a lot of features that the military was interested in. First, it had to be robust. The entire network couldn't stop functioning if the Soviets nuked a router in Cleveland; all messages still had to get through to their intended destinations (except those going to Cleveland, of course). Therefore, IP was designed to allow multiple routes between any two points and to route packets of data around damaged routers.

Second, the military had many different kinds of computers, and all of them had to be able to talk to one another. Therefore, IP had to be open and platform-independent; it wasn't good enough to have one protocol for IBM mainframes and another for PDP-11s. The IBM mainframes needed to talk to the PDP-11s and any other strange computers that might be lying around.

Because there are multiple routes between two points, and because the quickest path between two points may change over time as a function of network traffic and other factors (such as the existence of Cleveland), the packets that make up a particular data stream may not all take the same route. Furthermore, they may not arrive in the order they were sent, if they even arrive at all. To improve on the basic scheme, TCP was layered on top of IP to give each end of a connection the ability to acknowledge receipt of IP packets and request retransmission of lost or corrupted packets. Furthermore, TCP allows the packets to be put back together on the receiving end in the same order they were sent.

TCP, however, carries a fair amount of overhead. Therefore, if the order of the data isn't particularly important and if the loss of individual packets won't completely corrupt the data stream, packets are sometimes sent without the guarantees that TCP provides using the UDP protocol. UDP is an unreliable protocol that does not guarantee that packets will arrive at their destination or that they will arrive in the same order they were sent. Although this would be a problem for uses such as file transfer, it is perfectly acceptable for applications where the loss of some data would go unnoticed by the end user. For example, losing a few bits from a video or audio signal won't cause much degradation; it would be a bigger problem if you had to wait for a protocol like TCP to request a retransmission of missing data. Furthermore, error-correcting codes can be built into UDP data streams at the application level to account for missing data.

A number of other protocols can run on top of IP. The most commonly requested is ICMP, the Internet Control Message Protocol, which uses raw IP datagrams to relay error messages between hosts. The best-known use of this protocol is in the ping program. Java does not support ICMP, nor does it allow the sending of raw IP datagrams (as opposed to TCP segments or UDP datagrams). The only protocols Java supports are TCP and UDP, and application layer protocols built on top of these. All other transport layer, internet layer, and lower layer protocols such as ICMP, IGMP, ARP, RARP, RSVP, and others can only be implemented in Java programs by linking to native code.

IP Addresses and Domain Names

As a Java programmer, you don't need to worry about the inner workings of IP, but you do need to know about addressing. Every computer on an IPv4 network is identified by a four-byte number. This is normally written in a *dotted quad* format like 199.1.32.90, where each of the four numbers is one unsigned byte ranging in value from 0 to 255. Every computer attached to an IPv4 network has a unique four-byte address. When data is transmitted across the network, the packet's header includes the address of the machine for which the packet is intended (the destination address) and the address of the machine that sent the packet (the source address). Routers along the way choose the best route on which to send the packet by inspecting the destination address. The source address is included so the recipient will know who to reply to.

There are a little more than four billion possible IP addresses, not even one for every person on the planet, much less for every computer. To make matters worse, the addresses aren't allocated very efficiently. In April 2011, Asia and Australia ran out. No more IPv4 addresses were available to be allocated to these regions; and they have since had to make do by recycling and reallocating from their existing supply. In September 2012, Europe ran out too. North America, Latin America, and Africa still have a few IP address blocks left to parcel out, but they're not going to last much longer.

A slow transition is under way to IPv6, which will use 16-byte addresses. This provides enough IP addresses to identify every person, every computer, and indeed every device on the planet. IPv6 addresses are customarily written in eight blocks of four hexadecimal digits separated by colons, such as *FEDC:BA98:7654:3210:FEDC:BA98:7654:3210*. Leading zeros do not need to be written. A double colon, at most one of which may appear in any address, indicates multiple zero blocks. For example, *FEDC: 0000:0000:0000:00DC:0000:7076:0010* could be written more compactly as *FEDC::DC: 0:7076:10*. In mixed networks of IPv6 and IPv4, the last four bytes of the IPv6 address are sometimes written as an IPv4 dotted quad address. For example, *FEDC:BA98:7654:3210:FEDC:BA98:7654:3210* could be written as *FEDC:BA98:7654:3210:FEDC:BA98:118.84.50.16*.

Although computers are very comfortable with numbers, human beings aren't very good at remembering them. Therefore, the Domain Name System (DNS) was developed to translate hostnames that humans can remember, such as "www.oreilly.com," into numeric Internet addresses such as 208.201.239.101. When Java programs access the network, they need to process both these numeric addresses and their corresponding hostnames. Methods for doing this are provided by the `java.net.InetAddress` class, which is discussed in Chapter 4.

Some computers, especially servers, have fixed addresses. Others, especially clients on local area networks and wireless connections, receive a different address every time they boot up, often provided by a DHCP server. Mostly you just need to remember that IP addresses may change over time, and not write any code that relies on a system having the same IP address. For instance, don't store the local IP address when saving application state. Instead, look it up fresh each time your program starts. It's also possible, although less likely, for an IP address to change while the program is running (e.g., if a DHCP lease expires), so you may want to check the current IP address every time you need it rather than caching it. Otherwise, the difference between a dynamically and manually assigned address is not significant to Java programs.

Several address blocks and patterns are special. All IPv4 addresses that begin with 10., 172.16. through 172.31. and 192.168. are unassigned. They can be used on internal networks, but no host using addresses in these blocks is allowed onto the global Internet. These *non-routable* addresses are useful for building private networks that can't be seen on the Internet. IPv4 addresses beginning with 127 (most commonly 127.0.0.1) always mean the *local loopback address*. That is, these addresses always point to the local computer, no matter which computer you're running on. The hostname for this address is often *localhost*. In IPv6, 0:0:0:0:0:0:0:1 (a.k.a. ::1) is the loopback address. The address 0.0.0.0 always refers to the originating host, but may only be used as a source address, not a destination. Similarly, any IPv4 address that begins with 0. (eight zero bits) is assumed to refer to a host on the same local network.

The IPv4 address that uses the same number for each of the four bytes (i.e., 255.255.255.255), is a broadcast address. Packets sent to this address are received by all nodes on the local network, though they are not routed beyond the local network. This is commonly used for discovery. For instance, when an ephemeral client such as a laptop boots up, it will send a particular message to 255.255.255.255 to find the local DHCP server. All nodes on the network receive the packet, but only the DHCP server responds. In particular, it sends the laptop information about the local network configuration, including the IP address that laptop should use for the remainder of its session and the address of a DNS server it can use to resolve hostnames.

Ports

Addresses would be all you needed if each computer did no more than one thing at a time. However, modern computers do many different things at once. Email needs to be separated from FTP requests, which need to be separated from web traffic. This is accomplished through *ports*. Each computer with an IP address has several thousand logical ports (65,535 per transport layer protocol, to be precise). These are purely abstractions in the computer's memory and do not represent anything physical, like a USB port. Each port is identified by a number between 1 and 65535. Each port can be allocated to a particular service.

For example, HTTP, the underlying protocol of the Web, commonly uses port 80. We say that a web server *listens* on port 80 for incoming connections. When data is sent to a web server on a particular machine at a particular IP address, it is also sent to a particular port (usually port 80) on that machine. The receiver checks each packet it sees for the port and sends the data to any program that is listening to that port. This is how different types of traffic are sorted out.

Port numbers between 1 and 1023 are reserved for well-known services like finger, FTP, HTTP, and IMAP. On Unix systems, including Linux and Mac OS X, only programs running as root can receive data from these ports, but all programs may send data to them. On Windows, any program may use these ports without special privileges. Table 1-1 shows the well-known ports for the protocols that are discussed in this book. These assignments are not absolutely guaranteed; in particular, web servers often run on ports other than 80, either because multiple servers need to run on the same machine or because the person who installed the server doesn't have the root privileges needed to run it on port 80. On Unix systems, a fairly complete listing of assigned ports is stored in the file */etc/services*.

Table 1-1. Well-known port assignments

Protocol	Port	Protocol	Purpose
echo	7	TCP/UDP	Echo is a test protocol used to verify that two machines are able to connect by having one echo back the other's input.
discard	9	TCP/UDP	Discard is a less useful test protocol in which all data received by the server is ignored.
daytime	13	TCP/UDP	Provides an ASCII representation of the current time on the server.
FTP data	20	TCP	FTP uses two well-known ports. This port is used to transfer files.

Protocol	Port	Protocol	Purpose
FTP	21	TCP	This port is used to send FTP commands like put and get.
SSH	22	TCP	Used for encrypted, remote logins.
Telnet	23	TCP	Used for interactive, remote command-line sessions.
smtp	25	TCP	The Simple Mail Transfer Protocol is used to send email between machines.
time	37	TCP/UDP	A time server returns the number of seconds that have elapsed on the server since midnight, January 1, 1900, as a four-byte, unsigned, big-endian integer.
whois	43	TCP	A simple directory service for Internet network administrators.
finger	79	TCP	A service that returns information about a user or users on the local system.
HTTP	80	TCP	The underlying protocol of the World Wide Web.
POP3	110	TCP	Post Office Protocol version 3 is a protocol for the transfer of accumulated email from the host to sporadically connected clients.
NNTP	119	TCP	Usenet news transfer; more formally known as the "Network News Transfer Protocol."
IMAP	143	TCP	Internet Message Access Protocol is a protocol for accessing mailboxes stored on a server.
dict	2628	TCP	A UTF-8 encoded dictionary service that provides definitions of words.

The Internet

The *Internet* is the world's largest IP-based network. It is an amorphous group of computers in many different countries on all seven continents (Antarctica included) that talk to one another using IP protocols. Each computer on the Internet has at least one IP address by which it can be identified. Many of them also have at least one name that maps to that IP address. The Internet is not owned by anyone, although pieces of it are. It is not governed by anyone, which is not to say that some governments don't try. It is simply a very large collection of computers that have agreed to talk to one another in a standard way.

The Internet is not the only IP-based network, but it is the largest one. Other IP networks are called *internets* with a little *i*: for example, a high-security internal network that is not connected to the global Internet. *Intranet* loosely describes corporate practices of putting lots of data on internal web servers that are not visible to users outside the local network.

Unless you're working in a high-security environment that's physically disconnected from the broader network, it's likely that the internet you'll be using is the Internet. To make sure that hosts on different networks on the Internet can communicate with each other, a few rules need to be followed that don't apply to purely internal internets. The most important rules deal with the assignment of addresses to different organizations, companies, and individuals. If everyone picked the Internet addresses they wanted at random, conflicts would arise almost immediately when different computers showed up on the Internet with the same address.

Internet Address Blocks

To avoid this problem, blocks of IPv4 addresses are assigned to Internet service providers (ISPs) by their regional Internet registry. When a company or an organization wants to set up an IP-based network connected to the Internet, their ISP assigns them a block of addresses. Each block has a fixed prefix. For instance if the prefix is 216.254.85, then the local network can use addresses from 216.254.85.0 to 216.254.85.255. Because this block fixes the first 24 bits, it's called a /24. A /23 specifies the first 23 bits, leaving 9 bits for 2^9 or 512 total local IP addresses. A /30 subnet (the smallest possible) specifies the first 30 bits of the IP addresses within the subnetwork, leaving 2 bits for 2^2 or 4 total local IP addresses. However, the lowest address in a block is used to identify the network itself, and the largest address in a block is a broadcast address for the network, so you have two fewer available addresses than you might first expect.

Network Address Translation

Because of the increasing scarcity of and demand for raw IP addresses, most networks today use Network Address Translation (NAT). In NAT-based networks most nodes only have local, non-routable addresses selected from either 10.x.x.x, 172.16.x.x to 172.31.x.x, or 192.168.x.x. The routers that connect the local networks to the ISP translate these local addresses to a much smaller set of routable addresses.

For instance, the dozen or so IP nodes in my apartment all share a single externally visible IP address. The computer on which I'm typing this has the IP address 192.168.1.5, but on your network that address may refer to a completely different host, if it exists at all. Nor could you reach my computer by sending data to 192.168.1.5. Instead, you'd have to send to 216.254.85.72 (and even then, the data would only get through if I had configured my NAT router to pass incoming connections on to 192.168.1.5).

The router watches my outgoing and incoming connections and adjusts the addresses in the IP packets. For an outgoing packet, it changes the source address to the router's external address (216.254.85.72 on my network). For an incoming packet, it changes the destination address to one of the local addresses, such as 192.168.1.12. Exactly how it keeps track of which connections come from and are aimed at which internal computers is not particularly important to a Java programmer. As long as your machines are configured properly, this process is mostly transparent. You just need to remember that the external and internal addresses may not be the same.

Eventually, IPv6 should make most of this obsolete. NAT will be pointless, though firewalls will still be useful. Subnets will still exist for routing, but they'll be much larger.

Firewalls

There are some naughty people on the Internet. To keep them out, it's often helpful to set up one point of access to a local network and check all traffic into or out of that access point. The hardware and software that sit between the Internet and the local network, checking all the data that comes in or out to make sure it's kosher, is called a *firewall*. The firewall is often part of the router that connects the local network to the broader Internet and may perform other tasks, such as network address translation. Then again, the firewall may be a separate machine. Modern operating systems like Mac OS X and Red Hat Linux often have built-in personal firewalls that monitor just the traffic sent to that one machine. Either way, the firewall is responsible for inspecting each packet that passes into or out of its network interface and accepting it or rejecting it according to a set of rules.

Filtering is usually based on network addresses and ports. For example, all traffic coming from the Class C network 193.28.25.x may be rejected because you had bad experiences with hackers from that network in the past. Outgoing SSH connections may be allowed, but incoming SSH connections may not. Incoming connections on port 80 (web) may be allowed, but only to the corporate web server. More intelligent firewalls look at the contents of the packets to determine whether to accept or reject them. The exact configuration of a firewall—which packets of data are and to pass through and which are not—depends on the security needs of an individual site. Java doesn't have much to do with firewalls—except insofar as they often get in your way.

Proxy Servers

Proxy servers are related to firewalls. If a firewall prevents hosts on a network from making direct connections to the outside world, a proxy server can act as a go-between. Thus, a machine that is prevented from connecting to the external network by a firewall would make a request for a web page from the local proxy server instead of requesting the web page directly from the remote web server. The proxy server would then request the page from the web server and forward the response back to the original requester. Proxies can also be used for FTP services and other connections. One of the security advantages of using a proxy server is that external hosts only find out about the proxy server. They do not learn the names and IP addresses of the internal machines, making it more difficult to hack into internal systems.

Whereas firewalls generally operate at the level of the transport or internet layer, proxy servers normally operate at the application layer. A proxy server has a detailed understanding of some application-level protocols, such as HTTP and FTP. (The notable exception are SOCKS proxy servers that operate at the transport layer, and can proxy for all TCP and UDP connections regardless of application layer protocol.) Packets that pass through the proxy server can be examined to ensure that they contain data appropriate for their type. For instance, FTP packets that seem to contain Telnet data can be rejected. Figure 1-4 shows how proxy servers fit into the layer model.

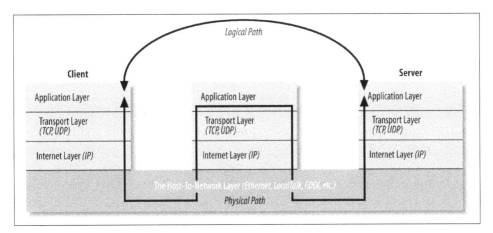

Figure 1-4. Layered connections through a proxy server

As long as all access to the Internet is forwarded through the proxy server, access can be tightly controlled. For instance, a company might choose to block access to *www.playboy.com* but allow access to *www.microsoft.com*. Some companies allow incoming FTP but disallow outgoing FTP so confidential data cannot be as easily smuggled out of the company. Other companies use proxy servers to track their employees' web usage so they can see who's using the Internet to get tech support and who's using it to check out the Playmate of the Month.

Proxy servers can also be used to implement local caching. When a file is requested from a web server, the proxy server first checks to see if the file is in its cache. If the file is in the cache, the proxy serves the file from the cache rather than from the Internet. If the file is not in the cache, the proxy server retrieves the file, forwards it to the requester, and stores it in the cache for the next time it is requested. This scheme can significantly reduce load on an Internet connection and greatly improve response time. America Online runs one of the largest farms of proxy servers in the world to speed the transfer of data to its users. If you look at a web server logfile, you'll probably find some hits from clients in the aol.com domain, but not as many as you'd expect given the more than three million AOL subscribers. That's because AOL proxy servers supply many pages out of their cache rather than re-requesting them for one another. Many other large ISPs do similarly.

The biggest problem with proxy servers is their inability to cope with all but a few protocols. Generally established protocols like HTTP, FTP, and SMTP are allowed to pass through, while newer protocols like BitTorrent are not. (Some network administrators consider this a feature.) In the rapidly changing world of the Internet, this is a significant disadvantage. It's a particular disadvantage for Java programmers because it limits the effectiveness of custom protocols. In Java, it's easy and often useful to create a new protocol that is optimized for your application. However, no proxy server will ever understand these one-of-a-kind protocols. Consequently, some developers have taken to tunneling their protocols through HTTP, most notably with SOAP. However, this has a significant negative impact on security. The firewall is normally there for a reason, not just to annoy Java programmers.

Applets that run in web browsers normally use the proxy server settings of the web browser itself, though these can be overridden in the Java Control Panel. Standalone Java applications can indicate the proxy server to use by setting the socksProxyHost and socksProxyPort properties (if you're using a SOCKS proxy server), or http.proxySet, http.proxyHost, http.proxyPort, https.proxySet, https.proxy Host, https.proxyPort, ftpProxySet, ftpProxyHost, ftpProxyPort, gopherProxy Set, gopherProxyHost, and gopherProxyPort system properties (if you're using protocol-specific proxies). You can set system properties from the command line using the -D flag, like this:

```
java -DsocksProxyHost=socks.cloud9.net  -DsocksProxyPort=1080 MyClass
```

The Client/Server Model

Most modern network programming is based on a client/server model. A client/server application typically stores large quantities of data on an expensive, high-powered server or cloud of servers while most of the program logic and the user interface is handled by client software running on relatively cheap personal computers. In most cases, a server primarily sends data while a client primarily receives it; but it is rare for one program to send or receive exclusively. A more reliable distinction is that a client initiates a conversation while a server waits for clients to start conversations with it. Figure 1-5 illustrates both possibilities. In some cases, the same program may be both a client and a server.

You are already familiar with many examples of client/server systems. In 2013, the most popular client/server system on the Internet is the Web. Web servers like Apache respond to requests from web clients like Firefox. Data is stored on the web server and is sent out to the clients that request it. Aside from the initial request for a page, almost all data is transferred from the server to the client, not from the client to the server. FTP is an older service that fits the client/server model. FTP uses different application protocols and different software, but is still split into FTP servers that send files and FTP clients that receive files. People often use FTP to upload files from the client to the server, so it's harder to say that the data transfer is primarily in one direction, but it is still true that an FTP client initiates the connection and the FTP server responds.

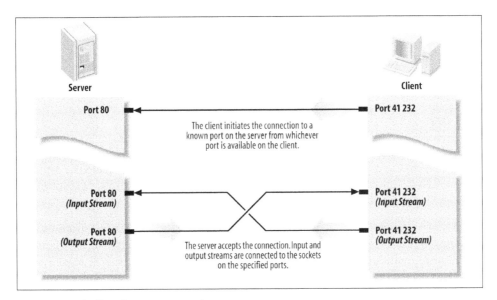

Figure 1-5. A client/server connection

Not all applications fit easily into a client/server model. For instance, in networked games, it seems likely that both players will send data back and forth roughly equally (at least in a fair game). These sorts of connections are called *peer-to-peer*. The telephone system is the classic example of a peer-to-peer network. Each phone can either call another phone or be called by another phone. You don't have to buy one phone to send calls and another to receive them.

Java does not have explicit peer-to-peer communication in its core networking API. However, applications can easily offer peer-to-peer communications in several ways, most commonly by acting as both a server and a client. Alternatively, the peers can communicate with each other through an intermediate server program that forwards data from one peer to the other peers. This neatly solves the discovery problem of how two peers find each other.

Internet Standards

This book discusses several application layer Internet protocols, most notably HTTP. However, this is not a book about those protocols. If you need detailed information about any protocol, the definitive source is the standards document for the protocol.

Although there are many standards organizations in the world, the two that produce most of the standards relevant to application layer network programming and protocols are the Internet Engineering Task Force (IETF) and the World Wide Web Consortium (W3C). The IETF is a relatively informal, democratic body open to participation by any interested party. Its standards are based on "rough consensus and running code" and tend to follow rather than lead implementations. IETF standards include TCP/IP, MIME, and SMTP. The W3C, by contrast, is a vendor organization, controlled by dues-paying member corporations, that explicitly excludes participation by individuals. For the most part, the W3C tries to define standards in advance of implementation. W3C standards include HTTP, HTML, and XML.

IETF RFCs

IETF standards and near-standards are published as Requests for Comments (RFCs). Despite the name, a published RFC is a finished work. It may be obsoleted or replaced by a new RFC, but it will not be changed. IETF working documents that are subject to revision and open for development are called "Internet drafts."

RFCs range from informational documents of general interest to detailed specifications of standard Internet protocols such as FTP. RFCs are available from many locations on the Internet, including *http://www.faqs.org/rfc/* and *http://www.ietf.org/rfc.html*. For the most part, RFCs, (particularly standards-oriented RFCs), are very technical, turgid, and nearly incomprehensible. Nonetheless, they are often the only complete and reliable source of information about a particular protocol.

Most proposals for an RFC begin when a person or group gets an idea and builds a prototype. The prototype is incredibly important. Before something can become an IETF standard, it must actually exist and work. This requirement ensures that IETF standards are at least feasible, unlike the standards promulgated by some other organizations.

Table 1-2 lists the RFCs that provide formal documentation for the protocols discussed in this book.

Table 1-2. Selected Internet RFCs

RFC	Title	Description
RFC 5000	Internet Official Protocol Standards	Describes the standardization process and the current status of the different Internet protocols. Periodically updated in new RFCs.
RFC 1122 RFC 1123	Host Requirements	Documents the protocols that must be supported by all Internet hosts at different layers (data link layer, IP layer, transport layer, and application layer).
RFC 791, RFC 919, RFC 922, RFC 950	Internet Protocol	The IP internet layer protocol.
RFC 768	User Datagram Protocol	An unreliable, connectionless transport layer protocol.
RFC 792	Internet Control Message Protocol (ICMP)	An internet layer protocol that uses raw IP datagrams but is not supported by Java. Its most familiar uses are *ping* and *traceroute*.
RFC 793	Transmission Control Protocol	A reliable, connection-oriented, streaming transport layer protocol.

RFC	Title	Description
RFC 2821	Simple Mail Transfer Protocol	The application layer protocol by which one host transfers email to another host. This standard doesn't say anything about email user interfaces; it covers the mechanism for passing email from one computer to another.
RFC 822	Format of Electronic Mail Messages	The basic syntax for ASCII text email messages. MIME is designed to extend this to support binary data while ensuring that the messages transferred still conform to this standard.
RFC 854, RFC 855	Telnet Protocol	An application layer remote login service for command-line environments based around an abstract network virtual terminal (NVT) and TCP.
RFC 862	Echo Protocol	An application layer protocol that echoes back all data it receives over both TCP and UDP; useful as a debugging tool.
RFC 863	Discard Protocol	An application layer protocol that receives packets of data over both TCP and UDP and sends no response to the client; useful as a debugging tool.
RFC 864	Character Generator Protocol	An application layer protocol that sends an indefinite sequence of ASCII characters to any client that connects over either TCP or UDP; also useful as a debugging tool.
RFC 865	Quote of the Day	An application layer protocol that returns a quotation to any user who connects over either TCP or UDP and then closes the connection.
RFC 867	Daytime Protocol	An application layer protocol that sends a human-readable ASCII string indicating the current date and time at the server to any client that connects over TCP or UDP. This contrasts with the various NTP and Time Server protocols, which do not return data that can be easily read by humans.
RFC 868	Time Protocol	An application layer protocol that sends the time in seconds since midnight, January 1, 1900, to a client connecting over TCP or UDP. The time is sent as a machine-readable, 32-bit unsigned integer. The standard is incomplete in that it does not specify how the integer is encoded in 32 bits, but in practice a big-endian integer is used.
RFC 959	File Transfer Protocol	An optionally authenticated, two-socket application layer protocol for file transfer that uses TCP.
RFC 977	Network News Transfer Protocol	The application layer protocol by which Usenet news is transferred from machine to machine over TCP; used by both news clients talking to news servers and news servers talking to each other.
RFC 1034, RFC 1035	Domain Name System	The collection of distributed software by which hostnames that human beings can remember, like www.oreilly.com, are translated into numbers that computers can understand, like 198.112.208.11. This RFC defines how domain name servers on different hosts communicate with each other using UDP.
RFC 1112	Host Extensions for IP Multicasting	The internet layer methods by which conforming systems can direct a single packet of data to multiple hosts. This is called multicasting. Java's support for multicasting is discussed in Chapter 13.
RFC 1288	Finger Protocol	An application layer protocol for requesting information about a user at a remote site. It can be a security risk.
RFC 1305	Network Time Protocol (Version 3)	A more precise application layer protocol for synchronizing clocks between systems that attempts to account for network latency.
RFC 1939	Post Office Protocol, Version 3	An application layer protocol used by sporadically connected email clients such as Eudora to retrieve mail from a server over TCP.

RFC	Title	Description
RFC 1945	Hypertext Transfer Protocol (HTTP 1.0)	Version 1.0 of the application layer protocol used by web browsers talking to web servers over TCP; developed by the W3C rather than the IETF.
RFC 2045, RFC 2046, RFC 2047	Multipurpose Internet Mail Extensions	A means of encoding binary data and non-ASCII text for transmission through Internet email and other ASCII-oriented protocols.
RFC 2141	Uniform Resource Names (URN) Syntax	Similar to URLs but intended to refer to actual resources in a persistent fashion rather than the transient location of those resources.
RFC 2616	Hypertext Transfer Protocol (HTTP 1.1)	Version 1.1 of the application layer protocol used by web browsers talking to web servers over TCP.
RFC 2373	IP Version 6 Addressing Architecture	The format and meaning of IPv6 addresses.
RFC 3501	Internet Message Access Protocol Version 4rev1	A protocol for remotely accessing a mailbox stored on a server including downloading messages, deleting messages, and moving messages into and out of different folders.
RFC 3986	Uniform Resource Identifiers (URI): Generic Syntax	Similar to URLs but cut a broader path. For instance, ISBN numbers may be URIs even if the book cannot be retrieved over the Internet.
RFC 3987	Internationalized Resource Identifiers (IRIs)	URIs that can contain non-ASCII characters.

The IETF has traditionally worked behind the scenes to codify and standardize existing practice. Although its activities are completely open to the public, it's been very low profile. There simply aren't that many people who get excited about network arcana like the Internet Gateway Message Protocol (IGMP). The participants in the process have mostly been engineers and computer scientists, including many from academia as well as the corporate world. Consequently, despite often vociferous debates about ideal implementations, most serious IETF efforts have produced reasonable standards.

Unfortunately, that can't be said of the IETF's efforts to produce web (as opposed to Internet) standards. In particular, the IETF's early effort to standardize HTML was a colossal failure. The refusal of Netscape and other key vendors to participate or even acknowledge the process was a crucial problem. That HTML was simple enough and high profile enough to attract the attention of assorted market droids and random flamers didn't help matters either. Thus, in October 1994, the World Wide Web Consortium was formed as a vendor-controlled body that might be able to avoid the pitfalls that plagued the IETF's efforts to standardize HTML and HTTP.

W3C Recommendations

Although the W3C standardization process is similar to the IETF process (a series of working drafts hashed out on mailing lists resulting in an eventual specification), the W3C is a fundamentally different organization. Whereas the IETF is open to participation by anyone, only corporations and other organizations may become members of the W3C. Individuals are specifically excluded, though they may become invited experts on particular working groups. However, the number of such individuals is quite small relative to the number of interested experts in the broader community. Membership in the W3C costs $50,000 a year ($5,000 a year for nonprofits) with a minimum 3-year commitment. Membership in the IETF costs $0 a year with no commitment beyond a willingness to participate. And although many people participate in developing W3C standards, each standard is ultimately approved or vetoed by one individual, W3C director Tim Berners-Lee. IETF standards are approved by a consensus of the people who worked on the standard. Clearly, the IETF is a much more democratic (some would say anarchic) and open organization than the W3C.

Despite the W3C's strong bias toward the corporate members that pay its bills, it has so far managed to do a better job of navigating the politically tricky waters of web standardization than the IETF. It has produced several HTML standards, as well as a variety of others such as HTTP, PICS, XML, CSS, MathML, and more. The W3C has had considerably less success in convincing vendors like Mozilla and Microsoft to fully and consistently implement its standards.

The W3C has five basic levels of standards:

Note
> A note is generally one of two things: either an unsolicited submission by a W3C member (similar to an IETF Internet draft) or random musings by W3C staff or related parties that do not actually describe a full proposal (similar to an IETF informational RFC). Notes will not necessarily lead to the formation of a working group or a W3C recommendation.

Working drafts
> A working draft is a reflection of the current thinking of some (not necessarily all) members of a working group. It should eventually lead to a proposed recommendation, but by the time it does so it may have changed substantially.

Candidate recommendation
> A candidate recommendation indicates that the working group has reached consensus on all major issues and is ready for third-party comment and implementations. If the implementations do not uncover any obstructions, the spec can be promoted to a proposed recommendation.

Proposed recommendation
> A proposed recommendation is mostly complete and unlikely to undergo more than minor editorial changes. The main purpose of a proposed recommendation is to work out bugs in the specification document rather than in the underlying technology being documented.

Recommendation

A recommendation is the highest level of W3C standard. However, the W3C is very careful not to actually call this a "standard" for fear of running afoul of antitrust statutes. The W3C describes a recommendation as a "work that represents consensus within W3C and has the Director's stamp of approval. W3C considers that the ideas or technology specified by a Recommendation are appropriate for widespread deployment and promote W3C's mission."

PR Standards

Companies seeking a little free press or perhaps a temporary boost to their stock price have sometimes abused both the W3C and IETF standards processes. The IETF will accept a submission from anyone, and the W3C will accept a submission from any W3C member. The IETF calls these submissions "Internet drafts" and publishes them for six months before deleting them. The W3C refers to such submissions as "acknowledged submissions" and publishes them indefinitely. However, neither organization actually promises to do more than acknowledge receipt of these documents. In particular, they do not promise to form a working group or begin the standardization process. Nonetheless, press releases invariably misrepresent the submission of such a document as a far more significant event than it actually is. PR reps can generally count on suckering at least a few clueless reporters who aren't up to speed on the intimate details of the standardization process. However, you should recognize these ploys for what they are.

CHAPTER 2

Streams

A large part of what network programs do is simple input and output: moving bytes from one system to another. Bytes are bytes; to a large extent, reading data a server sends you is not all that different from reading a file. Sending text to a client is not that different from writing a file. However, input and output (I/O) in Java is organized differently than it is in most other languages, such as Fortran, C, and C++. Consequently, I'll take a few pages to summarize Java's unique approach to I/O.

I/O in Java is built on *streams*. Input streams read data; output streams write data. Different stream classes, like `java.io.FileInputStream` and `sun.net.TelnetOutput Stream`, read and write particular sources of data. However, all output streams have the same basic methods to write data and all input streams use the same basic methods to read data. After a stream is created, you can often ignore the details of exactly what it is you're reading or writing.

Filter streams can be chained to either an input stream or an output stream. Filters can modify the data as it's read or written—for instance, by encrypting or compressing it— or they can simply provide additional methods for converting the data that's read or written into other formats. For instance, the `java.io.DataOutputStream` class provides a method that converts an `int` to four bytes and writes those bytes onto its underlying output stream.

Readers and writers can be chained to input and output streams to allow programs to read and write text (i.e., characters) rather than bytes. Used properly, readers and writers can handle a wide variety of character encodings, including multibyte character sets such as SJIS and UTF-8.

Streams are synchronous; that is, when a program (really a thread) asks a stream to read or write a piece of data, it waits for the data to be read or written before it does anything else. Java also offers nonblocking I/O using channels and buffers. Nonblocking I/O is a little more complicated, but can be much faster in some high-volume applications, such as web servers. Normally, the basic stream model is all you need and all you should use for clients. Because channels and buffers depend on streams, I'll start with streams and clients and later discuss nonblocking I/O for use with servers in Chapter 11.

Output Streams

Java's basic output class is `java.io.OutputStream`:

```
public abstract class OutputStream
```

This class provides the fundamental methods needed to write data. These are:

```
public abstract void write(int b) throws IOException
public void write(byte[] data) throws IOException
public void write(byte[] data, int offset, int length)
    throws IOException
public void flush() throws IOException
public void close() throws IOException
```

Subclasses of `OutputStream` use these methods to write data onto particular media. For instance, a `FileOutputStream` uses these methods to write data into a file. A `TelnetOutputStream` uses these methods to write data onto a network connection. A `ByteArrayOutputStream` uses these methods to write data into an expandable byte array. But whichever medium you're writing to, you mostly use only these same five methods. Sometimes you may not even know exactly what kind of stream you're writing onto. For instance, you won't find `TelnetOutputStream` in the Java class library documentation. It's deliberately hidden inside the sun packages. It's returned by various methods in various classes in `java.net`, like the `getOutputStream()` method of `java.net.Sock` et. However, these methods are declared to return only `OutputStream`, not the more specific subclass `TelnetOutputStream`. That's the power of polymorphism. If you know how to use the superclass, you know how to use all the subclasses, too.

`OutputStream`'s fundamental method is `write(int b)`. This method takes an integer from 0 to 255 as an argument and writes the corresponding byte to the output stream. This method is declared abstract because subclasses need to change it to handle their particular medium. For instance, a `ByteArrayOutputStream` can implement this method with pure Java code that copies the byte into its array. However, a `FileOutput` `Stream` will need to use native code that understands how to write data in files on the host platform.

Take note that although this method takes an `int` as an argument, it actually writes an unsigned byte. Java doesn't have an unsigned byte data type, so an `int` has to be used here instead. The only real difference between an unsigned byte and a signed byte is the interpretation. They're both made up of eight bits, and when you write an `int` onto a network connection using `write(int b)`, only eight bits are placed on the wire. If an `int` outside the range 0–255 is passed to `write(int b)`, the least significant byte of the number is written and the remaining three bytes are ignored. (This is the effect of casting an int to a byte.)

 On rare occasions, you may find a buggy third-party class that does something different when writing a value outside the range 0–255—for instance, throwing an IllegalArgumentException or always writing 255—so it's best to avoid writing ints outside the range 0–255 if possible.

For example, the character-generator protocol defines a server that sends out ASCII text. The most popular variation of this protocol sends 72-character lines containing printable ASCII characters. (The printable ASCII characters are those between 33 and 126 inclusive that exclude the various whitespace and control characters.) The first line contains characters 33 through 104, sorted. The second line contains characters 34 through 105. The third line contains characters 35 through 106. This continues through line 29, which contains characters 55 through 126. At that point, the characters wrap around so that line 30 contains characters 56 through 126 followed by character 33 again. Lines are terminated with a carriage return (ASCII 13) and a linefeed (ASCII 10). The output looks like this:

```
!"#$%&'()*+,-./0123456789:;<=>?@ABCDEFGHIJKLMNOPQRSTUVWXYZ[\]^_`abcdefgh
"#$%&'()*+,-./0123456789:;<=>?@ABCDEFGHIJKLMNOPQRSTUVWXYZ[\]^_`abcdefghi
#$%&'()*+,-./0123456789:;<=>?@ABCDEFGHIJKLMNOPQRSTUVWXYZ[\]^_`abcdefghij
$%&'()*+,-./0123456789:;<=>?@ABCDEFGHIJKLMNOPQRSTUVWXYZ[\]^_`abcdefghijk
%&'()*+,-./0123456789:;<=>?@ABCDEFGHIJKLMNOPQRSTUVWXYZ[\]^_`abcdefghijkl
&'()*+,-./0123456789:;<=>?@ABCDEFGHIJKLMNOPQRSTUVWXYZ[\]^_`abcdefghijklm
'()*+,-./0123456789:;<=>?@ABCDEFGHIJKLMNOPQRSTUVWXYZ[\]^_`abcdefghijklmn
```

Because ASCII is a 7-bit character set, each character is sent as a single byte. Consequently, this protocol is straightforward to implement using the basic write() methods, as the next code fragment demonstrates:

```
public static void generateCharacters(OutputStream out)
    throws IOException {

  int firstPrintableCharacter      = 33;
  int numberOfPrintableCharacters = 94;
  int numberOfCharactersPerLine    = 72;

  int start = firstPrintableCharacter;
  while (true) { /* infinite loop */
    for (int i = start; i < start + numberOfCharactersPerLine; i++) {
      out.write((
          (i - firstPrintableCharacter) % numberOfPrintableCharacters)
          + firstPrintableCharacter);
    }
    out.write('\r'); // carriage return
    out.write('\n'); // linefeed
```

```
      start = ((start + 1) - firstPrintableCharacter)
          % numberOfPrintableCharacters + firstPrintableCharacter;
    }
  }
```

An OutputStream is passed to the generateCharacters() method in the out argument. Bytes are written onto out one at a time. These bytes are given as integers in a rotating sequence from 33 to 126. Most of the arithmetic here is to make the loop rotate in that range. After each 72-character chunk is written, a carriage return and a linefeed are written onto the output stream. The next start character is calculated and the loop repeats. The entire method is declared to throw IOException. That's important because the character-generator server will terminate only when the client closes the connection. The Java code will see this as an IOException.

Writing a single byte at a time is often inefficient. For example, every TCP segment contains at least 40 bytes of overhead for routing and error correction. If each byte is sent by itself, you may be stuffing the network with 41 times more data than you think you are! Add overhead of the host-to-network layer protocol, and this can be even worse. Consequently, most TCP/IP implementations buffer data to some extent. That is, they accumulate bytes in memory and send them to their eventual destination only when a certain number have accumulated or a certain amount of time has passed. However, if you have more than one byte ready to go, it's not a bad idea to send them all at once. Using write(byte[] data) or write(byte[] data, int offset, int length) is normally much faster than writing all the components of the data array one at a time. For instance, here's an implementation of the generateCharacters() method that sends a line at a time by packing a complete line into a byte array:

```
public static void generateCharacters(OutputStream out)
    throws IOException {

  int firstPrintableCharacter = 33;
  int numberOfPrintableCharacters = 94;
  int numberOfCharactersPerLine = 72;
  int start = firstPrintableCharacter;
  byte[] line = new byte[numberOfCharactersPerLine + 2];
  // the +2 is for the carriage return and linefeed

  while (true) { /* infinite loop */
    for (int i = start; i < start + numberOfCharactersPerLine; i++) {
      line[i - start] = (byte) ((i - firstPrintableCharacter)
          % numberOfPrintableCharacters + firstPrintableCharacter);
    }
    line[72] = (byte) '\r'; // carriage return
    line[73] = (byte) '\n'; // line feed
    out.write(line);
    start = ((start + 1) - firstPrintableCharacter)
        % numberOfPrintableCharacters + firstPrintableCharacter;
```

```
    }
}
```

The algorithm for calculating which bytes to write when is the same as for the previous implementation. The crucial difference is that the bytes are packed into a byte array before being written onto the network. Also, notice that the int result of the calculation must be cast to a byte before being stored in the array. This wasn't necessary in the previous implementation because the single-byte write() method is declared to take an int as an argument.

Streams can also be buffered in software, directly in the Java code as well as in the network hardware. Typically, this is accomplished by chaining a BufferedOutput Stream or a BufferedWriter to the underlying stream, a technique we'll explore shortly. Consequently, if you are done writing data, it's important to flush the output stream. For example, suppose you've written a 300-byte request to an HTTP 1.1 server that uses HTTP Keep-Alive. You generally want to wait for a response before sending any more data. However, if the output stream has a 1,024-byte buffer, the stream may be waiting for more data to arrive before it sends the data out of its buffer. No more data will be written onto the stream until the server response arrives, but the response is never going to arrive because the request hasn't been sent yet! Figure 2-1 illustrates this catch-22. The flush() method breaks the deadlock by forcing the buffered stream to send its data even if the buffer isn't yet full.

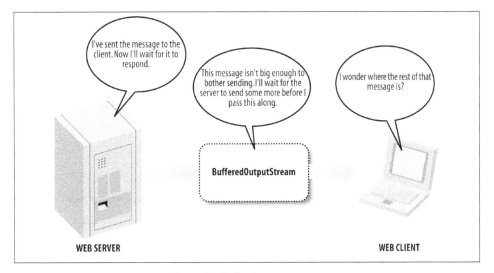

Figure 2-1. Data can get lost if you don't flush your streams

It's important to flush your streams whether you think you need to or not. Depending on how you got hold of a reference to the stream, you may or may not know whether it's buffered. (For instance, System.out is buffered whether you want it to be or not.) If flushing isn't necessary for a particular stream, it's a very low-cost operation. However, if it is necessary, it's very necessary. Failing to flush when you need to can lead to unpredictable, unrepeatable program hangs that are extremely hard to diagnose if you don't have a good idea of what the problem is in the first place. As a corollary to all this, you should flush all streams immediately before you close them. Otherwise, data left in the buffer when the stream is closed may get lost.

Finally, when you're done with a stream, close it by invoking its close() method. This releases any resources associated with the stream, such as file handles or ports. If the stream derives from a network connection, then closing the stream terminates the connection. Once an output stream has been closed, further writes to it throw IOExceptions. However, some kinds of streams may still allow you to do things with the object. For instance, a closed ByteArrayOutputStream can still be converted to an actual byte array and a closed DigestOutputStream can still return its digest.

Failure to close a stream in a long-running program can leak file handles, network ports, and other resources. Consequently, in Java 6 and earlier, it's wise to close the stream in a finally block. To get the right variable scope, you have to *declare* the stream variable outside the try block but *initialize* it inside the try block. Furthermore, to avoid NullPointerExceptions you need to check whether the stream variable is null before closing it. Finally, you usually want to ignore or at most log any exceptions that occur while closing the stream. For example:

```
OutputStream out = null;
try {
  out = new FileOutputStream("/tmp/data.txt");
  // work with the output stream...
} catch (IOException ex) {
  System.err.println(ex.getMessage());
} finally {
  if (out != null) {
    try {
      out.close();
    } catch (IOException ex) {
      // ignore
    }
  }
}
```

This technique is sometimes called the *dispose pattern*; and it's common for any object that needs to be cleaned up before it's garbage collected. You'll see it used not just for streams, but also for sockets, channels, JDBC connections and statements, and more.

Java 7 introduces the *try with resources* construct to make this cleanup neater. Instead of declaring the stream variable outside the try block, you declare it inside an argument list of the try block. For instance, the preceding fragment now becomes the much simpler:

```
try (OutputStream out = new FileOutputStream("/tmp/data.txt")) {
  // work with the output stream...
} catch (IOException ex) {
  System.err.println(ex.getMessage());
}
```

The finally clause is no longer needed. Java automatically invokes close() on any AutoCloseable objects declared inside the argument list of the try block.

 try with resources can be used with any object that implements the Closeable interface, which includes almost every object you need to dispose. So far, JavaMail Transport objects are the only exceptions I've encountered. Those still need to be disposed of explicitly.

Input Streams

Java's basic input class is java.io.InputStream:

```
public abstract class InputStream
```

This class provides the fundamental methods needed to read data as raw bytes. These are:

```
public abstract int read() throws IOException
public int read(byte[] input) throws IOException
public int read(byte[] input, int offset, int length) throws IOException
public long skip(long n) throws IOException
public int available() throws IOException
public void close() throws IOException
```

Concrete subclasses of InputStream use these methods to read data from particular media. For instance, a FileInputStream reads data from a file. A TelnetInputStream reads data from a network connection. A ByteArrayInputStream reads data from an array of bytes. But whichever source you're reading, you mostly use only these same six methods. Sometimes you don't know exactly what kind of stream you're reading from. For instance, TelnetInputStream is an undocumented class hidden inside the sun.net package. Instances of it are returned by various methods in the java.net package (e.g., the openStream() method of java.net.URL). However, these methods are declared to return only InputStream, not the more specific subclass TelnetInputStream. That's polymorphism at work once again. The instance of the subclass can be used transparently as an instance of its superclass. No specific knowledge of the subclass is required.

The basic method of InputStream is the noargs read() method. This method reads a single byte of data from the input stream's source and returns it as an int from 0 to 255. End of stream is signified by returning –1. The read() method waits and blocks execution of any code that follows it until a byte of data is available and ready to be read.

Input and output can be slow, so if your program is doing anything else of importance, try to put I/O in its own thread.

The read() method is declared abstract because subclasses need to change it to handle their particular medium. For instance, a ByteArrayInputStream can implement this method with pure Java code that copies the byte from its array. However, a TelnetInputStream needs to use a native library that understands how to read data from the network interface on the host platform.

The following code fragment reads 10 bytes from the InputStream in and stores them in the byte array input. However, if end of stream is detected, the loop is terminated early:

```
byte[] input = new byte[10];
for (int i = 0; i < input.length; i++) {
  int b = in.read();
  if (b == -1) break;
  input[i] = (byte) b;
}
```

Although read() only reads a byte, it returns an int. Thus, a cast is necessary before storing the result in the byte array. Of course, this produces a signed byte from –128 to 127 instead of the unsigned byte from 0 to 255 returned by the read() method. However, as long as you're clear about which one you're working with, this is not a major problem. You can convert a signed byte to an unsigned byte like this:

```
int i = b >= 0 ? b : 256 + b;
```

Reading a byte at a time is as inefficient as writing data one byte at a time. Consequently, there are two overloaded read() methods that fill a specified array with multiple bytes of data read from the stream read(byte[] input) and read(byte[] input, int offset, int length). The first method attempts to fill the specified array input. The second attempts to fill the specified subarray of input, starting at offset and continuing for length bytes.

Notice I said these methods *attempt* to fill the array, not that they necessarily succeed. An attempt may fail in several ways. For instance, it's not unheard of that while your program is reading data from a remote web server over DSL, a bug in a switch at a phone company central office will disconnect you and several hundred of your neighbors from the rest of the world. This would cause an IOException. More commonly, however, a read attempt won't completely fail but won't completely succeed either. Some of the requested bytes may be read, but not all of them. For example, you may try to read 1,024 bytes from a network connection, when only 512 have actually arrived from the server; the rest are still in transit. They'll arrive eventually, but they aren't available at this moment. To account for this, the multibyte read methods return the number of bytes actually read. For example, consider this code fragment:

```
byte[] input    = new byte[1024];
int bytesRead = in.read(input);
```

It attempts to read 1,024 bytes from the InputStream in into the array input. However, if only 512 bytes are available, that's all that will be read, and bytesRead will be set to 512. To guarantee that all the bytes you want are actually read, place the read in a loop that reads repeatedly until the array is filled. For example:

```
int bytesRead   = 0;
int bytesToRead = 1024;
byte[] input    = new byte[bytesToRead];
while (bytesRead < bytesToRead) {
  bytesRead += in.read(input, bytesRead, bytesToRead - bytesRead);
}
```

This technique is especially crucial for network streams. Chances are that if a file is available at all, all the bytes of a file are also available. However, because networks move much more slowly than CPUs, it is very easy for a program to empty a network buffer before all the data has arrived. In fact, if one of these two methods tries to read from a temporarily empty but open network buffer, it will generally return 0, indicating that no data is available but the stream is not yet closed. This is often preferable to the behavior of the single-byte read( ) method, which blocks the running thread in the same circumstances.

All three read( ) methods return –1 to signal the end of the stream. If the stream ends while there's still data that hasn't been read, the multibyte read( ) methods return the data until the buffer has been emptied. The next call to any of the read( ) methods will return –1. The –1 is never placed in the array. The array only contains actual data. The previous code fragment had a bug because it didn't consider the possibility that all 1,024 bytes might never arrive (as opposed to not being immediately available). Fixing that bug requires testing the return value of read( ) before adding it to bytesRead. For example:

```
int bytesRead = 0;
int bytesToRead = 1024;
byte[] input = new byte[bytesToRead];
while (bytesRead < bytesToRead) {
  int result = in.read(input, bytesRead, bytesToRead - bytesRead);
  if (result == -1) break; // end of stream
  bytesRead += result;
}
```

If you do not want to wait until all the bytes you need are immediately available, you can use the available( ) method to determine how many bytes can be read without blocking. This returns the minimum number of bytes you can read. You may in fact be able to read more, but you will be able to read at least as many bytes as available( ) suggests. For example:

```
int bytesAvailable = in.available();
byte[] input = new byte[bytesAvailable];
int bytesRead = in.read(input, 0, bytesAvailable);
// continue with rest of program immediately...
```

In this case, you can expect that bytesRead is exactly equal to bytesAvailable. You cannot, however, expect that bytesRead is greater than zero. It is possible that no bytes were available. On end of stream, available() returns 0. Generally, read(byte[] in put, int offset, int length) returns –1 on end of stream; but if length is 0, then it does not notice the end of stream and returns 0 instead.

On rare occasions, you may want to skip over data without reading it. The skip() method accomplishes this task. It's less useful on network connections than when reading from files. Network connections are sequential and normally quite slow, so it's not significantly more time consuming to read data than to skip over it. Files are random access so that skipping can be implemented simply by repositioning a file pointer rather than processing each byte to be skipped.

As with output streams, once your program has finished with an input stream, it should close it by invoking its close() method. This releases any resources associated with the stream, such as file handles or ports. Once an input stream has been closed, further reads from it throw IOExceptions. However, some kinds of streams may still allow you to do things with the object. For instance, you generally won't retrieve the message digest from a java.security.DigestInputStream until after the data has been read and the stream closed.

Marking and Resetting

The InputStream class also has three less commonly used methods that allow programs to back up and reread data they've already read. These are:

```
public void mark(int readAheadLimit)
public void reset() throws IOException
public boolean markSupported()
```

In order to reread data, mark the current position in the stream with the mark() method. At a later point, you can reset the stream to the marked position using the reset() method. Subsequent reads then return data starting from the marked position. However, you may not be able to reset as far back as you like. The number of bytes you can read from the mark and still reset is determined by the readAheadLimit argument to mark(). If you try to reset too far back, an IOException is thrown. Furthermore, there can be only one mark in a stream at any given time. Marking a second location erases the first mark.

Marking and resetting are usually implemented by storing every byte read from the marked position on in an internal buffer. However, not all input streams support this.

Before trying to use marking and resetting, check whether the markSupported() method returns true. If it does, the stream supports marking and resetting. Otherwise, mark() will do nothing and reset() will throw an IOException.

 In my opinion, this demonstrates very poor design. In practice, more streams *don't* support marking and resetting than *do*. Attaching functionality to an abstract superclass that is not available to many, probably most, subclasses is a very poor idea. It would be better to place these three methods in a separate interface that could be implemented by those classes that provided this functionality. The disadvantage of this approach is that you couldn't then invoke these methods on an arbitrary input stream of unknown type; but in practice, you can't do that anyway because not all streams support marking and resetting. Providing a method such as markSupported() to check for functionality at runtime is a more traditional, non-object-oriented solution to the problem. An object-oriented approach would embed this in the type system through interfaces and classes so that it could all be checked at compile time.

The only input stream classes in java.io that always support marking are BufferedInputStream and ByteArrayInputStream. However, other input streams such as TelnetInputStream may support marking if they're chained to a buffered input stream first.

Filter Streams

InputStream and OutputStream are fairly raw classes. They read and write bytes singly or in groups, but that's all. Deciding what those bytes mean—whether they're integers or IEEE 754 floating-point numbers or Unicode text—is completely up to the programmer and the code. However, there are certain extremely common data formats that can benefit from a solid implementation in the class library. For example, many integers passed as parts of network protocols are 32-bit big-endian integers. Much of the text sent over the Web is either 7-bit ASCII, 8-bit Latin-1, or multibyte UTF-8. Many files transferred by FTP are stored in the ZIP format. Java provides a number of filter classes you can attach to raw streams to translate the raw bytes to and from these and other formats.

The filters come in two versions: the filter streams, and the readers and writers. The filter streams still work primarily with raw data as bytes: for instance, by compressing the data or interpreting it as binary numbers. The readers and writers handle the special case of text in a variety of encodings such as UTF-8 and ISO 8859-1.

Filters are organized in a chain, as shown in Figure 2-2. Each link in the chain receives data from the previous filter or stream and passes the data along to the next link in the chain. In this example, a compressed, encrypted text file arrives from the local network interface, where native code presents it to the undocumented TelnetInputStream. A BufferedInputStream buffers the data to speed up the entire process. A CipherInput Stream decrypts the data. A GZIPInputStream decompresses the deciphered data. An InputStreamReader converts the decompressed data to Unicode text. Finally, the text is read into the application and processed.

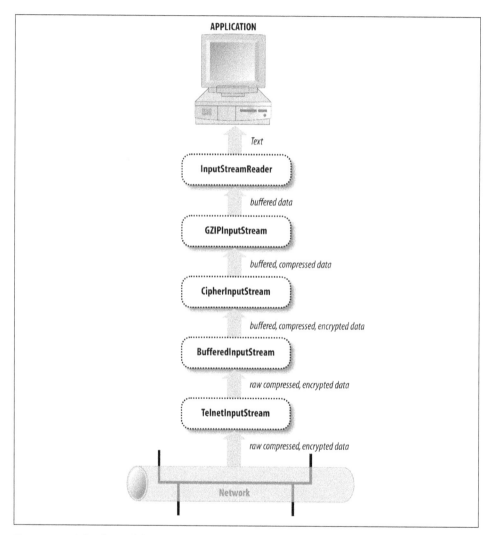

Figure 2-2. The flow of data through a chain of filters

Every filter output stream has the same write(), close(), and flush() methods as java.io.OutputStream. Every filter input stream has the same read(), close(), and available() methods as `java.io.InputStream`. In some cases, such as `BufferedInputStream` and `BufferedOutputStream`, these may be the only methods the filter has. The filtering is purely internal and does not expose any new public interface. However, in most cases, the filter stream adds public methods with additional purposes. Sometimes these are intended to be used in addition to the usual `read()` and `write()` methods, like the `unread()` method of `PushbackInputStream`. At other times, they almost completely replace the original interface. For example, it's relatively rare to use the `write()` method of `PrintStream` instead of one of its `print()` and `println()` methods.

Chaining Filters Together

Filters are connected to streams by their constructors. For example, the following code fragment buffers input from the file *data.txt*. First, a `FileInputStream` object `fin` is created by passing the name of the file as an argument to the `FileInputStream` constructor. Then, a `BufferedInputStream` object `bin` is created by passing `fin` as an argument to the `BufferedInputStream` constructor:

```
FileInputStream     fin = new FileInputStream("data.txt");
BufferedInputStream bin = new BufferedInputStream(fin);
```

From this point forward, it's possible to use the `read()` methods of both `fin` and `bin` to read data from the file *data.txt*. However, intermixing calls to different streams connected to the same source may violate several implicit contracts of the filter streams. Most of the time, you should only use the last filter in the chain to do the actual reading or writing. One way to write your code so that it's at least harder to introduce this sort of bug is to deliberately overwrite the reference to the underlying input stream. For example:

```
InputStream in = new FileInputStream("data.txt");
in = new BufferedInputStream(in);
```

After these two lines execute, there's no longer any way to access the underlying file input stream, so you can't accidentally read from it and corrupt the buffer. This example works because it's not necessary to distinguish between the methods of `InputStream` and those of `BufferedInputStream` given that `BufferedInputStream` is simply used polymorphically as an instance of `InputStream`. In cases where it is necessary to use the additional methods of the filter stream not declared in the superclass, you may be able to construct one stream directly inside another. For example:

```
DataOutputStream dout = new DataOutputStream(new BufferedOutputStream(
    new FileOutputStream("data.txt")));
```

Although these statements can get a little long, it's easy to split the statement across several lines, like this:

```
DataOutputStream dout = new DataOutputStream(
                    new BufferedOutputStream(
```

```
                    new FileOutputStream("data.txt")
                )
            );
```

Connection is permanent. Filters cannot be disconnected from a stream.

There are times when you may need to use the methods of multiple filters in a chain. For instance, if you're reading a Unicode text file, you may want to read the byte order mark in the first three bytes to determine whether the file is encoded as big-endian UCS-2, little-endian UCS-2, or UTF-8, and then select the matching Reader filter for the encoding. Or, if you're connecting to a web server, you may want to read the header the server sends to find the Content-encoding and then use that content encoding to pick the right Reader filter to read the body of the response. Or perhaps you want to send floating-point numbers across a network connection using a DataOutputStream and then retrieve a MessageDigest from the DigestOutputStream that the DataOut putStream is chained to. In all these cases, you need to save and use references to each of the underlying streams. However, under no circumstances should you ever read from or write to anything other than the last filter in the chain.

Buffered Streams

The BufferedOutputStream class stores written data in a buffer (a protected byte array field named buf) until the buffer is full or the stream is flushed. Then it writes the data onto the underlying output stream all at once. A single write of many bytes is almost always much faster than many small writes that add up to the same thing. This is especially true of network connections because each TCP segment or UDP packet carries a finite amount of overhead, generally about 40 bytes' worth. This means that sending 1 kilobyte of data 1 byte at a time actually requires sending 40 kilobytes over the wire, whereas sending it all at once only requires sending a little more than 1K of data. Most network cards and TCP implementations provide some level of buffering themselves, so the real numbers aren't quite this dramatic. Nonetheless, buffering network output is generally a huge performance win.

The BufferedInputStream class also has a protected byte array named buf that serves as a buffer. When one of the stream's read() methods is called, it first tries to get the requested data from the buffer. Only when the buffer runs out of data does the stream read from the underlying source. At this point, it reads as much data as it can from the source into the buffer, whether it needs all the data immediately or not. Data that isn't used immediately will be available for later invocations of read(). When reading files from a local disk, it's almost as fast to read several hundred bytes of data from the underlying stream as it is to read one byte of data. Therefore, buffering can substantially improve performance. The gain is less obvious on network connections where the bottleneck is often the speed at which the network can deliver data rather than the speed at which the network interface delivers data to the program or the speed at which the program runs. Nonetheless, buffering input rarely hurts and will become more important over time as network speeds increase.

`BufferedInputStream` has two constructors, as does `BufferedOutputStream`:

```
public BufferedInputStream(InputStream in)
public BufferedInputStream(InputStream in, int bufferSize)
public BufferedOutputStream(OutputStream out)
public BufferedOutputStream(OutputStream out, int bufferSize)
```

The first argument is the underlying stream from which unbuffered data will be read or to which buffered data will be written. The second argument, if present, specifies the number of bytes in the buffer. Otherwise, the buffer size is set to 2,048 bytes for an input stream and 512 bytes for an output stream. The ideal size for a buffer depends on what sort of stream you're buffering. For network connections, you want something a little larger than the typical packet size. However, this can be hard to predict and varies depending on local network connections and protocols. Faster, higher-bandwidth networks tend to use larger packets, although TCP segments are often no larger than a kilobyte.

`BufferedInputStream` does not declare any new methods of its own. It only overrides methods from `InputStream`. It does support marking and resetting. The two multibyte `read()` methods attempt to completely fill the specified array or subarray of data by reading from the underlying input stream as many times as necessary. They return only when the array or subarray has been completely filled, the end of stream is reached, or the underlying stream would block on further reads. Most input streams do not behave like this. They read from the underlying stream or data source only once before returning.

`BufferedOutputStream` also does not declare any new methods of its own. You invoke its methods exactly as you would in any output stream. The difference is that each write places data in the buffer rather than directly on the underlying output stream. Consequently, it is essential to flush the stream when you reach a point at which the data needs to be sent.

PrintStream

The `PrintStream` class is the first filter output stream most programmers encounter because `System.out` is a `PrintStream`. However, other output streams can also be chained to print streams, using these two constructors:

```
public PrintStream(OutputStream out)
public PrintStream(OutputStream out, boolean autoFlush)
```

By default, print streams should be explicitly flushed. However, if the `autoFlush` argument is `true`, the stream will be flushed every time a byte array or linefeed is written or a `println()` method is invoked.

As well as the usual `write()`, `flush()`, and `close()` methods, `PrintStream` has 9 over-loaded `print()` methods and 10 overloaded `println()` methods:

```
public void print(boolean b)
public void print(char c)
public void print(int i)
public void print(long l)
public void print(float f)
public void print(double d)
public void print(char[] text)
public void print(String s)
public void print(Object o)
public void println()
public void println(boolean b)
public void println(char c)
public void println(int i)
public void println(long l)
public void println(float f)
public void println(double d)
public void println(char[] text)
public void println(String s)
public void println(Object o)
```

Each `print()` method converts its argument to a string in a predictable fashion and writes the string onto the underlying output stream using the default encoding. The `println()` methods do the same thing, but they also append a platform-dependent line separator to the end of the line they write. This is a linefeed (\n) on Unix (including Mac OS X), a carriage return (\r) on Mac OS 9, and a carriage return/linefeed pair (\r \n) on Windows.

 `PrintStream` is evil and network programmers should avoid it like the plague!

The first problem is that the output from `println()` is platform dependent. Depending on what system runs your code, lines may sometimes be broken with a linefeed, a carriage return, or a carriage return/linefeed pair. This doesn't cause problems when writing to the console, but it's a disaster for writing network clients and servers that must follow a precise protocol. Most network protocols such as HTTP and Gnutella specify that lines should be terminated with a carriage return/linefeed pair. Using `println()` makes it easy to write a program that works on Windows but fails on Unix and the Mac. Although many servers and clients are liberal in what they accept and can handle incorrect line terminators, there are occasional exceptions.

The second problem is that `PrintStream` assumes the default encoding of the platform on which it's running. However, this encoding may not be what the server or client expects. For example, a web browser receiving XML files will expect them to be encoded in UTF-8 or UTF-16 unless the server tells it otherwise. However, a web server that uses `PrintStream` may well send the files encoded in CP1252 from a U.S.-localized Windows system or SJIS from a Japanese-localized system, whether the client expects or understands those encodings or not. `PrintStream` doesn't provide any mechanism for changing the default encoding. This problem can be patched over by using the related `Print Writer` class instead. But the problems continue.

The third problem is that `PrintStream` eats all exceptions. This makes `PrintStream` suitable for textbook programs such as HelloWorld, because simple console output can be taught without burdening students with first learning about exception handling and all that implies. However, network connections are much less reliable than the console. Connections routinely fail because of network congestion, phone company misfeasance, remote systems crashing, and many other reasons. Network programs must be prepared to deal with unexpected interruptions in the flow of data. The way to do this is by handling exceptions. However, `PrintStream` catches any exceptions thrown by the underlying output stream. Notice that the declaration of the standard five `Output Stream` methods in `PrintStream` does not have the usual `throws IOException` declaration:

```
public abstract void write(int b)
public void write(byte[] data)
public void write(byte[] data, int offset, int length)
public void flush()
public void close()
```

Instead, `PrintStream` relies on an outdated and inadequate error flag. If the underlying stream throws an exception, this internal error flag is set. The programmer is relied upon to check the value of the flag using the `checkError()` method:

```
public boolean checkError()
```

To do any error checking at all on a `PrintStream`, the code must explicitly check every call. Furthermore, once an error has occurred, there is no way to unset the flag so further errors can be detected. Nor is any additional information available about the error. In short, the error notification provided by `PrintStream` is wholly inadequate for unreliable network connections.

Data Streams

The `DataInputStream` and `DataOutputStream` classes provide methods for reading and writing Java's primitive data types and strings in a binary format. The binary formats used are primarily intended for exchanging data between two different Java programs through a network connection, a datafile, a pipe, or some other intermediary. What a data output stream writes, a data input stream can read. However, it happens that the formats are the same ones used for most Internet protocols that exchange binary numbers. For instance, the time protocol uses 32-bit big-endian integers, just like Java's `int` data type. The controlled-load network element service uses 32-bit IEEE 754 floating-point numbers, just like Java's `float` data type. (This is correlation rather than causation. Both Java and most network protocols were designed by Unix programmers, and consequently both tend to use the formats common to most Unix systems.) However, this isn't true for all network protocols, so check the details of any protocol you use. For instance, the Network Time Protocol (NTP) represents times as 64-bit unsigned fixed-point numbers with the integer part in the first 32 bits and the fraction part in the last 32 bits. This doesn't match any primitive data type in any common programming language, although it is straightforward to work with—at least as far as is necessary for NTP.

The `DataOutputStream` class offers these 11 methods for writing particular Java data types:

```
public final void writeBoolean(boolean b) throws IOException
public final void writeByte(int b) throws IOException
public final void writeShort(int s) throws IOException
public final void writeChar(int c) throws IOException
public final void writeInt(int i) throws IOException
public final void writeLong(long l) throws IOException
public final void writeFloat(float f) throws IOException
public final void writeDouble(double d) throws IOException
public final void writeChars(String s) throws IOException
public final void writeBytes(String s) throws IOException
public final void writeUTF(String s) throws IOException
```

All data is written in big-endian format. Integers are written in two's complement in the minimum number of bytes possible. Thus, a `byte` is written as one byte, a `short` as two bytes, an `int` as four bytes, and a `long` as eight bytes. Floats and doubles are written in IEEE 754 form in four and eight bytes, respectively. Booleans are written as a single byte with the value 0 for false and 1 for true. Chars are written as two unsigned bytes.

The last three methods are a little trickier. The `writeChars()` method simply iterates through the `String` argument, writing each character in turn as a two-byte, big-endian Unicode character (a UTF-16 code point, to be absolutely precise). The `writeBytes()` method iterates through the `String` argument but writes only the least significant byte of each character. Thus, information will be lost for any string with characters from outside the Latin-1 character set. This method may be useful on some network protocols that specify the ASCII encoding, but it should be avoided most of the time.

Neither `writeChars()` nor `writeBytes()` encodes the length of the string in the output stream. As a result, you can't really distinguish between raw characters and characters that make up part of a string. The `writeUTF()` method does include the length of the string. It encodes the string itself in a *variant* of the UTF-8 encoding of Unicode. Because this variant is subtly incompatible with most non-Java software, it should be used only for exchanging data with other Java programs that use a DataInputStream to read strings. For exchanging UTF-8 text with all other software, you should use an Input StreamReader with the appropriate encoding. (There wouldn't be any confusion if Sun had just called this method and its partner writeString() and readString() rather than writeUTF() and readUTF().)

Along with these methods for writing binary numbers and strings, DataOutput Stream of course has the usual write(), flush(), and close() methods any Output Stream class has.

DataInputStream is the complementary class to DataOutputStream. Every format that DataOutputStream writes, DataInputStream can read. In addition, DataInputStream has the usual read(), available(), skip(), and close() methods, as well as methods for reading complete arrays of bytes and lines of text.

There are 9 methods to read binary data that match the 11 methods in DataOutput Stream (there's no exact complement for writeBytes() or writeChars(); these are handled by reading the bytes and chars one at a time):

```
public final boolean readBoolean() throws IOException
public final byte readByte() throws IOException
public final char readChar() throws IOException
public final short readShort() throws IOException
public final int readInt() throws IOException
public final long readLong() throws IOException
public final float readFloat() throws IOException
public final double readDouble() throws IOException
public final String readUTF() throws IOException
```

In addition, DataInputStream provides two methods to read unsigned bytes and unsigned shorts and return the equivalent int. Java doesn't have either of these data types, but you may encounter them when reading binary data written by a C program:

```
public final int readUnsignedByte() throws IOException
public final int readUnsignedShort() throws IOException
```

DataInputStream has the usual two multibyte read() methods that read data into an array or subarray and return the number of bytes read. It also has two readFully() methods that repeatedly read data from the underlying input stream into an array until the requested number of bytes have been read. If enough data cannot be read, then an IOException is thrown. These methods are especially useful when you know in advance exactly how many bytes you have to read. This might be the case when you've read the Content-length field out of an HTTP header and thus know how many bytes of data there are:

```
public final int read(byte[] input) throws IOException
public final int read(byte[] input, int offset, int length)
    throws IOException
```

```
public final void readFully(byte[] input) throws IOException
public final void readFully(byte[] input, int offset, int length)
    throws IOException
```

Finally, DataInputStream provides the popular readLine() method that reads a line of text as delimited by a line terminator and returns a string:

```
public final String readLine() throws IOException
```

However, this method should not be used under any circumstances, both because it is deprecated and because it is buggy. It's deprecated because it doesn't properly convert non-ASCII characters to bytes in most circumstances. That task is now handled by the readLine() method of the BufferedReader class. However, that method and this one share the same insidious bug: they do not always recognize a single carriage return as ending a line. Rather, readLine() recognizes only a linefeed or a carriage return/linefeed pair. When a carriage return is detected in the stream, readLine() waits to see whether the next character is a linefeed before continuing. If it is a linefeed, the carriage return and the linefeed are thrown away and the line is returned as a String. If it isn't a linefeed, the carriage return is thrown away, the line is returned as a String, and the extra character that was read becomes part of the next line. However, if the carriage return is the last character in the stream, then readLine() hangs, waiting for the last character, which isn't forthcoming.

This problem isn't obvious when reading files because there will almost certainly be a next character: –1 for end of stream, if nothing else. However, on persistent network connections such as those used for FTP and late-model HTTP, a server or client may simply stop sending data after the last character and wait for a response without actually closing the connection. If you're lucky, the connection may eventually time out on one end or the other and you'll get an IOException, although this will probably take at least a couple of minutes, and cause you to lose the last line of data from the stream. If you're not lucky, the program will hang indefinitely.

Readers and Writers

Many programmers have a bad habit of writing code as if all text were ASCII or at least in the native encoding of the platform. Although some older, simpler network protocols, such as daytime, quote of the day, and chargen, do specify ASCII encoding for text, this is not true of HTTP and many other more modern protocols, that allow a wide variety of localized encodings, such as KOI8-R Cyrillic, Big-5 Chinese, and ISO 8859-9 for Turkish. Java's native character set is the UTF-16 encoding of Unicode. When the encoding is no longer ASCII, the assumption that bytes and chars are essentially the same things also breaks down. Consequently, Java provides an almost complete mirror of the input and output stream class hierarchy designed for working with characters instead of bytes.

In this mirror image hierarchy, two abstract superclasses define the basic API for reading and writing characters. The `java.io.Reader` class specifies the API by which characters are read. The `java.io.Writer` class specifies the API by which characters are written. Wherever input and output streams use bytes, readers and writers use Unicode characters. Concrete subclasses of `Reader` and `Writer` allow particular sources to be read and targets to be written. Filter readers and writers can be attached to other readers and writers to provide additional services or interfaces.

The most important concrete subclasses of `Reader` and `Writer` are the `InputStream Reader` and the `OutputStreamWriter` classes. An `InputStreamReader` contains an underlying input stream from which it reads raw bytes. It translates these bytes into Unicode characters according to a specified encoding. An `OutputStreamWriter` receives Unicode characters from a running program. It then translates those characters into bytes using a specified encoding and writes the bytes onto an underlying output stream.

In addition to these two classes, the `java.io` package provides several raw reader and writer classes that read characters without directly requiring an underlying input stream, including:

- `FileReader`
- `FileWriter`
- `StringReader`
- `StringWriter`
- `CharArrayReader`
- `CharArrayWriter`

The first two classes in this list work with files and the last four work inside Java, so they aren't of great use for network programming. However, aside from different constructors, these classes have pretty much the same public interface as all other reader and writer classes.

Writers

The `Writer` class mirrors the `java.io.OutputStream` class. It's abstract and has two protected constructors. Like `OutputStream`, the `Writer` class is never used directly; instead, it is used polymorphically, through one of its subclasses. It has five `write()` methods as well as a `flush()` and a `close()` method:

```
protected Writer()
protected Writer(Object lock)
public abstract void write(char[] text, int offset, int length)
    throws IOException
public void write(int c) throws IOException
```

```
public void write(char[] text) throws IOException
public void write(String s) throws IOException
public void write(String s, int offset, int length) throws IOException
public abstract void flush() throws IOException
public abstract void close() throws IOException
```

The `write(char[] text, int offset, int length)` method is the base method in terms of which the other four `write()` methods are implemented. A subclass must override at least this method as well as `flush()` and `close()`, although most override some of the other `write()` methods as well in order to provide more efficient implementations. For example, given a `Writer` object w, you can write the string "Network" like this:

```
char[] network = {'N', 'e', 't', 'w', 'o', 'r', 'k'};
w.write(network, 0, network.length);
```

The same task can be accomplished with these other methods, as well:

```
w.write(network);
for (int i = 0;  i < network.length;  i++) w.write(network[i]);
w.write("Network");
w.write("Network", 0, 7);
```

All of these examples are different ways of expressing the same thing. The one you choose to use in any given situation is mostly a matter of convenience and taste. However, how many and which bytes are written by these lines depends on the encoding w uses. If it's using big-endian UTF-16, it will write these 14 bytes (shown here in hexadecimal) in this order:

```
00 4E 00 65 00 74 00 77 00 6F 00 72 00 6B
```

On the other hand, if w uses little-endian UTF-16, this sequence of 14 bytes is written:

```
4E 00 65 00 74 00 77 00 6F 00 72 00 6B 00
```

If w uses Latin-1, UTF-8, or MacRoman, this sequence of seven bytes is written:

```
4E 65 74 77 6F 72 6B
```

Other encodings may write still different sequences of bytes. The exact output depends on the encoding.

Writers may be buffered, either directly by being chained to a `BufferedWriter` or indirectly because their underlying output stream is buffered. To force a write to be committed to the output medium, invoke the `flush()` method:

```
w.flush();
```

The `close()` method behaves similarly to the `close()` method of `OutputStream`. `close()` flushes the writer, then closes the underlying output stream and releases any resources associated with it:

```
public abstract void close() throws IOException
```

After a writer has been closed, further writes throw IOExceptions.

OutputStreamWriter

OutputStreamWriter is the most important concrete subclass of Writer. An Output StreamWriter receives characters from a Java program. It converts these into bytes according to a specified encoding and writes them onto an underlying output stream. Its constructor specifies the output stream to write to and the encoding to use:

```
public OutputStreamWriter(OutputStream out, String encoding)
    throws UnsupportedEncodingException
```

Valid encodings are listed in the documentation (*http://bit.ly/Sun-documentation*) for Sun's native2ascii tool included with the JDK. If no encoding is specified, the default encoding for the platform is used. In 2013, the default encoding is UTF-8 on the Mac and more often than not on Linux. However, on Linux it can vary if the local operating system is configured to use some other character set by default. On Windows, it varies depending on country and configuration, but in the United States it's Windows-1252, a.k.a CP1252 more often than not. Default character sets can cause unexpected problems at unexpected times. You're generally almost always better off explicitly specifying the character set rather than letting Java pick one for you. For example, this code fragment writes the first few words of Homer's Odyssey in the CP1253 Windows Greek encoding:

```
OutputStreamWriter w = new OutputStreamWriter(
    new FileOutputStream("OdysseyB.txt"), "Cp1253");
w.write("ἦμος δ᾽ ἠριγένεια φάνη ῥοδοδάκτυλος Ἠώς");
```

Other than the constructors, OutputStreamWriter has only the usual Writer methods (which are used exactly as they are for any Writer class) and one method to return the encoding of the object:

```
public String getEncoding()
```

Readers

The Reader class mirrors the java.io.InputStream class. It's abstract with two protected constructors. Like InputStream and Writer, the Reader class is never used directly, only through one of its subclasses. It has three read() methods, as well as skip(), close(), ready(), mark(), reset(), and markSupported() methods:

```
protected Reader()
protected Reader(Object lock)
public abstract int read(char[] text, int offset, int length)
    throws IOException
public int read() throws IOException
public int read(char[] text) throws IOException
public long skip(long n) throws IOException
public boolean ready()
```

```
public boolean markSupported()
public void mark(int readAheadLimit) throws IOException
public void reset() throws IOException
public abstract void close() throws IOException
```

The read(char[] text, int offset, int length) method is the fundamental method through which the other two read() methods are implemented. A subclass must override at least this method as well as close(), although most will override some of the other methods as well in order to provide more efficient implementations.

Most of these methods are easily understood by analogy with their InputStream counterparts. The read() method returns a single Unicode character as an int with a value from 0 to 65,535 or –1 on end of stream. (Technically it returns a UTF-16 code point, though almost always that's the same as a Unicode character.) The read(char[] text) method tries to fill the array text with characters and returns the actual number of characters read or –1 on end of stream. The read(char[] text, int offset, int length) method attempts to read length characters into the subarray of text beginning at offset and continuing for length characters. It also returns the actual number of characters read or –1 on end of stream. The skip(long n) method skips n characters. The mark() and reset() methods allow some readers to reset back to a marked position in the character sequence. The markSupported() method tells you whether the reader supports marking and resetting. The close() method closes the reader and any underlying input stream so that further attempts to read from it throw IOExceptions.

The exception to the rule of similarity is ready(), which has the same general purpose as available() but not quite the same semantics, even modulo the byte-to-char conversion. Whereas available() returns an int specifying a minimum number of bytes that may be read without blocking, ready() only returns a boolean indicating whether the reader may be read without blocking. The problem is that some character encodings, such as UTF-8, use different numbers of bytes for different characters. Thus, it's hard to tell how many characters are waiting in the network or filesystem buffer without actually reading them out of the buffer.

InputStreamReader is the most important concrete subclass of Reader. An Input StreamReader reads bytes from an underlying input stream such as a FileInput Stream or TelnetInputStream. It converts these into characters according to a specified encoding and returns them. The constructor specifies the input stream to read from and the encoding to use:

```
public InputStreamReader(InputStream in)
public InputStreamReader(InputStream in, String encoding)
    throws UnsupportedEncodingException
```

If no encoding is specified, the default encoding for the platform is used. If an unknown encoding is specified, an UnsupportedEncodingException is thrown.

For example, this method reads an input stream and converts it all to one Unicode string using the MacCyrillic encoding:

```
public static String getMacCyrillicString(InputStream in)
    throws IOException {

  InputStreamReader r = new InputStreamReader(in, "MacCyrillic");
  StringBuilder sb = new StringBuilder();
  int c;
  while ((c = r.read()) != -1) sb.append((char) c);
  return sb.toString();
}
```

Filter Readers and Writers

The InputStreamReader and OutputStreamWriter classes act as decorators on top of input and output streams that change the interface from a byte-oriented interface to a character-oriented interface. Once this is done, additional character-oriented filters can be layered on top of the reader or writer using the java.io.FilterReader and java.io.FilterWriter classes. As with filter streams, there are a variety of subclasses that perform specific filtering, including:

- BufferedReader
- BufferedWriter
- LineNumberReader
- PushbackReader
- PrintWriter

The BufferedReader and BufferedWriter classes are the character-based equivalents of the byte-oriented BufferedInputStream and BufferedOutputStream classes. Where BufferedInputStream and BufferedOutputStream use an internal array of bytes as a buffer, BufferedReader and BufferedWriter use an internal array of chars.

When a program reads from a BufferedReader, text is taken from the buffer rather than directly from the underlying input stream or other text source. When the buffer empties, it is filled again with as much text as possible, even if not all of it is immediately needed, making future reads much faster. When a program writes to a BufferedWriter, the text is placed in the buffer. The text is moved to the underlying output stream or other target only when the buffer fills up or when the writer is explicitly flushed, which can make writes much faster than would otherwise be the case.

BufferedReader and BufferedWriter have the usual methods associated with readers and writers, like read(), ready(), write(), and close(). They each have two constructors that chain the BufferedReader or BufferedWriter to an underlying reader or writer and set the size of the buffer. If the size is not set, the default size of 8,192 characters is used:

```
public BufferedReader(Reader in, int bufferSize)
public BufferedReader(Reader in)
public BufferedWriter(Writer out)
public BufferedWriter(Writer out, int bufferSize)
```

For example, the earlier `getMacCyrillicString()` example was less than efficient because it read characters one at a time. Because MacCyrillic is a 1-byte character set, it also read bytes one at a time. However, it's straightforward to make it run faster by chaining a `BufferedReader` to the `InputStreamReader`, like this:

```
public static String getMacCyrillicString(InputStream in)
    throws IOException {

  Reader r = new InputStreamReader(in, "MacCyrillic");
  r = new BufferedReader(r, 1024);
  StringBuilder sb = new StringBuilder();
  int c;
  while ((c = r.read()) != -1) sb.append((char) c);
  return sb.toString();
}
```

All that was needed to buffer this method was one additional line of code. None of the rest of the algorithm had to change, because the only `InputStreamReader` methods used were the `read()` and `close()` methods declared in the `Reader` superclass and shared by all `Reader` subclasses, including `BufferedReader`.

The `BufferedReader` class also has a `readLine()` method that reads a single line of text and returns it as a string:

```
public String readLine() throws IOException
```

This method replaces the deprecated `readLine()` method in `DataInputStream`, and it has mostly the same behavior as that method. The big difference is that by chaining a `BufferedReader` to an `InputStreamReader`, you can correctly read lines in character sets other than the default encoding for the platform.

The `BufferedWriter()` class adds one new method not included in its superclass, called `newLine()`, also geared toward writing lines:

```
public void newLine() throws IOException
```

This method inserts a platform-dependent line-separator string into the output. The `line.separator` system property determines exactly what the string is: probably a linefeed on Unix and Mac OS X, and a carriage return/linefeed pair on Windows. Because network protocols generally specify the required line terminator, you should not use this method for network programming. Instead, explicitly write the line terminator the protocol requires. More often than not, the required terminator is a carriage return/ linefeed pair.

PrintWriter

The PrintWriter class is a replacement for Java 1.0's PrintStream class that properly handles multibyte character sets and international text. Sun originally planned to deprecate PrintStream in favor of PrintWriter but backed off when it realized this step would invalidate too much existing code, especially code that depended on Sys tem.out. Nonetheless, new code should use PrintWriter instead of PrintStream.

Aside from the constructors, the PrintWriter class has an almost identical collection of methods to PrintStream. These include:

```
public PrintWriter(Writer out)
public PrintWriter(Writer out, boolean autoFlush)
public PrintWriter(OutputStream out)
public PrintWriter(OutputStream out, boolean autoFlush)
public void flush()
public void close()
public boolean checkError()
public void write(int c)
public void write(char[] text, int offset, int length)
public void write(char[] text)
public void write(String s, int offset, int length)
public void write(String s)
public void print(boolean b)
public void print(char c)
public void print(int i)
public void print(long l)
public void print(float f)
public void print(double d)
public void print(char[] text)
public void print(String s)
public void print(Object o)
public void println()
public void println(boolean b)
public void println(char c)
public void println(int i)
public void println(long l)
public void println(float f)
public void println(double d)
public void println(char[] text)
public void println(String s)
public void println(Object o)
```

Most of these methods behave the same for PrintWriter as they do for PrintStream. The exceptions are the four write() methods, which write characters rather than bytes; also, if the underlying writer properly handles character set conversion, so do all the methods of the PrintWriter. This is an improvement over the noninternationalizable

PrintStream class, but it's still not good enough for network programming. Unfortunately, PrintWriter still has the problems of platform dependency and minimal error reporting that plague PrintStream.

 This chapter has been a whirlwind tour of the java.io package, covering the bare minimum you need to know to write network programs. For a more detailed and comprehensive look with many more examples, check out my other book in this series, Java I/O (O'Reilly).

CHAPTER 3

Threads

Back in the good old days of the Net, circa the early 1990s, we didn't have the Web and HTTP and graphical browsers. Instead, we had Usenet news and FTP and command-line interfaces, and we liked it that way! But as good as the good old days were, there were some problems. For instance, when we were downloading kilobytes of free software from a popular FTP site over our 2,400 bps modems using Kermit, we would often encounter error messages like this one:

```
% ftp eunl.java.sun.com
Connected to eunl.javasoft.com.
220 softwarenl FTP server (wu-2.4.2-academ[BETA- 16]+opie-2.32(1) 981105)
    ready.
Name (eunl.java.sun.com:elharo): anonymous
530-
530-    Server is busy.  Please try again later or try one of our other
530-    ftp servers at ftp.java.sun.com.  Thank you.
530-
530 User anonymous access denied.
Login failed.
```

In fact, in the days when the Internet had only a few million users instead of a few billion, we were far more likely to come across an overloaded and congested site than we are today. The problem was that most FTP servers forked a new process for each connection (i.e., 100 simultaneous users meant 100 additional processes to handle). Because processes are fairly heavyweight items, too many could rapidly bring a server to its knees. The problem wasn't that the machines weren't powerful enough or the network fast enough; it was that the FTP servers were poorly implemented. Many more simultaneous users could be served if a new process wasn't needed for each connection.

Early web servers suffered from this problem as well, although the problem was masked a little by the transitory nature of HTTP connections. Because web pages and their embedded images tend to be small (at least compared to the software archives commonly retrieved by FTP) and because web browsers "hang up" the connection after each file is retrieved instead of staying connected for minutes or hours at a time, web users don't put nearly as much load on a server as FTP users do. However, web server performance still degrades as usage grows. The fundamental problem is that while it's easy to write code that handles each incoming connection and each new task as a separate process (at least on Unix), this solution doesn't scale. By the time a server is attempting to handle a thousand or more simultaneous connections, performance slows to a crawl.

There are at least two solutions to this problem. The first is to reuse processes rather than spawning new ones. When the server starts up, a fixed number of processes (say, 300) are spawned to handle requests. Incoming requests are placed in a queue. Each process removes one request from the queue, services the request, then returns to the queue to get the next request. There are still 300 separate processes running, but because all the overhead of building up and tearing down the processes is avoided, these 300 processes can now do the work of 1,000. These numbers are rough estimates. Your exact mileage may vary, especially if your server hasn't yet reached the volume where scalability issues come into play. Still, whatever mileage you get out of spawning new processes, you should be able to do much better by reusing old processes.

The second solution to this problem is to use lightweight threads instead of heavyweight processes to handle connections. Whereas each separate process has its own block of memory, threads are easier on resources because they share memory. Using threads instead of processes can buy you another factor of three in server performance. By combining this with a pool of reusable threads (as opposed to a pool of reusable processes), your server can run nine times faster, all on the same hardware and network connection! The impact of running many different threads on the server hardware is *relatively* minimal because they all run within one process. Most Java virtual machines keel over due to memory exhaustion somewhere between 4,000 and 20,000 simultaneous threads. However, by using a thread pool instead of spawning new threads for each connection, fewer than a hundred threads can handle thousands of short connections per minute.

Alternatives to Threading

If an application needs thousands of simultaneous long-lived connections (and that's a pretty rare application) it's time to start thinking about asynchronous I/O instead of threads. We'll take this up in Chapter 11. Selectors enable one thread to query a group of sockets to find out which ones are ready to be read from or written to, and then process the ready sockets sequentially. In this case, the I/O has to be designed around channels and buffers rather than streams.

Given the high performance of threads in modern virtual machines and operating systems, as well as the relative simplicity of building a thread-based server, a thread-based design is usually where you should start until you can prove you're hitting a wall. If you do hit a wall, you should seriously consider sharding the application across multiple

---

redundant servers rather than trying to eke out another factor of three increase on a single server.

Of course, sharding introduces design issues of its own, particularly around consistency, that aren't present in a single system. But it does offer you more scalability and redundancy than you'll ever get out of a single system, no matter how efficiently implemented.

Unfortunately, this increased performance doesn't come for free. There's a cost in program complexity. In particular, multithreaded servers (and other multithreaded programs) require developers to address concerns that aren't issues for single-threaded programs, particularly issues of safety and liveness. Because different threads share the same memory, it's entirely possible for one thread to stomp all over the variables and data structures used by another thread. This is similar to the way one program running on a nonmemory-protected operating system such as Windows 95 can crash the entire system. Consequently, different threads have to be extremely careful about which resources they use when. Generally, each thread must agree to use certain resources only when it's sure those resources can't change or that it has exclusive access to them. However, it's also possible for two threads to be too careful, each waiting for exclusive access to resources it will never get. This can lead to deadlock, in which two threads are each waiting for resources the other possesses. Neither thread can proceed without the resources that the other thread has reserved, but neither is willing to give up the resources it has already.

Running Threads

A *thread* with a little *t* is a separate, independent path of execution in the virtual machine. A Thread with a capital *T* is an instance of the `java.lang.Thread` class. There is a one-to-one relationship between threads executing in the virtual machine and Thread objects constructed by the virtual machine. Most of the time it's obvious from the context which one is meant if the difference is really important.

To start a new thread running in the virtual machine, you construct an instance of the Thread class and invoke its `start()` method, like this:

```
Thread t = new Thread();
t.start();
```

Of course, this thread isn't very interesting because it doesn't have anything to do. To give a thread something to do, you either subclass the Thread class and override its `run()` method, or implement the Runnable interface and pass the Runnable object to the Thread constructor. I generally prefer the second option because it separates the task that the thread performs from the thread itself more cleanly, but you will see both techniques used in this book and elsewhere. In both cases, the key is the `run()` method, which has this signature:

```
public void run()
```

You're going to put all the work the thread does in this one method. This method may invoke other methods; it may construct other objects; it may even spawn other threads. However, the thread starts here and it stops here. When the run() method completes, the thread dies. In essence, the run() method is to a thread what the main() method is to a traditional nonthreaded program. A single-threaded program exits when the main() method returns. A multithreaded program exits when both the main() method and the run() methods of all nondaemon threads return. (Daemon threads perform background tasks such as garbage collection and don't prevent the virtual machine from exiting.)

Subclassing Thread

Consider a program that calculates the Secure Hash Algorithm (SHA) digest for many files. To a large extent, this is an I/O-bound program (i.e., its speed is limited by the amount of time it takes to read the files from the disk). If you write it as a standard program that processes the files in series, the program is going to spend a lot of time waiting for the hard drive to return the data. This limit is even more characteristic of network programs: they execute faster than the network can supply input. Consequently, they spend a lot of time blocked. This is time that other threads could use, either to process other input sources or to do something that doesn't rely on slow input. (Not all threaded programs share this characteristic. Sometimes, even if none of the threads have a lot of spare time to allot to other threads, it's simply easier to design a program by breaking it into multiple threads that perform independent operations.)

Example 3-1 is a subclass of Thread whose run() method calculates a 256-bit SHA-2 message digest for a specified file. It does this by reading the file with a DigestInput Stream. This filter stream calculates a cryptographic hash function as it reads the file. When it's finished reading, the hash function is available from the digest() method.

Example 3-1. DigestThread

```java
import java.io.*;
import java.security.*;
import javax.xml.bind.*; // for DatatypeConverter; requires Java 6 or JAXB 1.0

public class DigestThread extends Thread {

  private String filename;

  public DigestThread(String filename) {
   this.filename = filename;
  }

  @Override
  public void run() {
```

```
  try {
    FileInputStream in = new FileInputStream(filename);
    MessageDigest sha = MessageDigest.getInstance("SHA-256");
    DigestInputStream din = new DigestInputStream(in, sha);
    while (din.read() != -1) ;
    din.close();
    byte[] digest = sha.digest();

    StringBuilder result = new StringBuilder(filename);
    result.append(": ");
    result.append(DatatypeConverter.printHexBinary(digest));
    System.out.println(result);
  } catch (IOException ex) {
    System.err.println(ex);
  } catch (NoSuchAlgorithmException ex) {
    System.err.println(ex);
  }
}

public static void main(String[] args) {
  for (String filename : args) {
    Thread t = new DigestThread(filename);
    t.start();
  }
}
}
```

The main() method reads filenames from the command line and starts a new DigestTh
read for each one. The work of the thread is actually performed in the run() method.
Here, a DigestInputStream reads the file. Then the resulting digest is printed on
System.out in hexadecimal encoding. Notice that the entire output from this thread is
first built in a local StringBuilder variable result. This is then printed on the console
with one method invocation. The more obvious path of printing the pieces one at a time
using System.out.print() is not taken. There's a reason for that, which we'll discuss
soon.

Because the signature of the run() method is fixed, you can't pass arguments to it or
return values from it. Consequently, you need different ways to pass information into
the thread and get information out of it. The simplest way to pass information in is to
pass arguments to the constructor, which sets fields in the Thread subclass, as done here.

Getting information out of a thread back into the original calling thread is trickier
because of the asynchronous nature of threads. Example 3-1 sidesteps that problem by
never passing any information back to the calling thread and simply printing the results
on System.out. Most of the time, however, you'll want to pass the information to other
parts of the program. You can store the result of the calculation in a field and provide
a getter method to return the value of that field. However, how do you know when the
calculation of that value is complete? What do you return if somebody calls the getter

method before the value has been calculated? This is quite tricky, and we'll discuss it more later in this chapter.

 If you subclass Thread, you should override run() *and nothing else!* The various other methods of the Thread class—for example, start(), interrupt(), join(), sleep(), and so on—all have very specific semantics and interactions with the virtual machine that are difficult to reproduce in your own code. You should override run() and provide additional constructors and other methods as necessary, but you should not replace any of the other standard Thread methods.

Implementing the Runnable Interface

One way to avoid overriding the standard Thread methods is not to subclass Thread. Instead, write the task you want the thread to perform as an instance of the Runnable interface. This interface declares the run() method, exactly the same as the Thread class:

```
public void run()
```

Other than this method, which any class implementing this interface must provide, you are completely free to create any other methods with any other names you choose, all without any possibility of unintentionally interfering with the behavior of the thread. This also allows you to place the thread's task in a subclass of some other class, such as Applet or HTTPServlet. To start a thread that performs the Runnable's task, pass the Runnable object to the Thread constructor. For example:

```
Thread t = new Thread(myRunnableObject);
t.start();
```

It's easy to recast most problems that subclass Thread into Runnable forms. Example 3-2 demonstrates this by rewriting Example 3-1 to use the Runnable interface rather than subclassing Thread. Aside from the name change, the only modifications that are necessary are changing extends Thread to implements Runnable and passing a DigestRunnable object to the Thread constructor in the main() method. The essential logic of the program is unchanged.

Example 3-2. DigestRunnable

```
import java.io.*;
import java.security.*;
import javax.xml.bind.*; // for DatatypeConverter; requires Java 6 or JAXB 1.0

public class DigestRunnable implements Runnable {

  private String filename;
```

```java
  public DigestRunnable(String filename) {
    this.filename = filename;
  }

  @Override
  public void run() {
    try {
      FileInputStream in = new FileInputStream(filename);
      MessageDigest sha = MessageDigest.getInstance("SHA-256");
      DigestInputStream din = new DigestInputStream(in, sha);
      while (din.read() != -1) ;
      din.close();
      byte[] digest = sha.digest();

      StringBuilder result = new StringBuilder(filename);
      result.append(": ");
      result.append(DatatypeConverter.printHexBinary(digest));
      System.out.println(result);
    } catch (IOException ex) {
      System.err.println(ex);
    } catch (NoSuchAlgorithmException ex) {
      System.err.println(ex);
    }
  }

  public static void main(String[] args) {
    for (String filename : args) {
      DigestRunnable dr = new DigestRunnable(filename);
      Thread t = new Thread(dr);
      t.start();
    }
  }
}
```

There's no strong reason to prefer implementing Runnable to extending Thread or vice versa in the general case. In a few special cases, such as Example 3-14 later in this chapter, it may be useful to invoke some instance methods of the Thread class from within the constructor for each Thread object. This requires using a subclass. In other specific cases, it may be necessary to place the run() method in a class that extends another class, such as HTTPServlet, in which case the Runnable interface is essential. Finally, some object-oriented purists argue that the task that a thread undertakes is not really a kind of Thread, and therefore should be placed in a separate class or interface such as Runnable rather than in a subclass of Thread. I half agree with them, although I don't think the argument is as strong as it's sometimes made out to be. Consequently, I'll mostly use the Runnable interface in this book, but you should feel free to do whatever seems most convenient.

Returning Information from a Thread

One of the hardest things for programmers accustomed to traditional, single-threaded procedural models to grasp when moving to a multithreaded environment is how to return information from a thread. Getting information out of a finished thread is one of the most commonly misunderstood aspects of multithreaded programming. The run() method and the start() method don't return any values. For example, suppose that instead of simply printing out the SHA-256 digest, as in Examples 3-1 and 3-2, the digest thread needs to return the digest to the main thread of execution. Most people's first reaction is to store the result in a field and provide a getter method, as shown in Examples 3-3 and 3-4. Example 3-3 is a Thread subclass that calculates a digest for a specified file. Example 3-4 is a simple command-line user interface that receives filenames and spawns threads to calculate digests for them.

Example 3-3. A thread that uses an accessor method to return the result

```java
import java.io.*;
import java.security.*;

public class ReturnDigest extends Thread {

  private String filename;
  private byte[] digest;

  public ReturnDigest(String filename) {
    this.filename = filename;
  }

  @Override
  public void run() {
    try {
      FileInputStream in = new FileInputStream(filename);
      MessageDigest sha = MessageDigest.getInstance("SHA-256");
      DigestInputStream din = new DigestInputStream(in, sha);
      while (din.read() != -1) ; // read entire file
      din.close();
      digest = sha.digest();
    } catch (IOException ex) {
      System.err.println(ex);
    } catch (NoSuchAlgorithmException ex) {
      System.err.println(ex);
    }
  }

  public byte[] getDigest() {
    return digest;
  }
}
```

Example 3-4. A main program that uses the accessor method to get the output of the thread

```
import javax.xml.bind.*; // for DatatypeConverter

public class ReturnDigestUserInterface {

  public static void main(String[] args) {
    for (String filename : args) {
      // Calculate the digest
      ReturnDigest dr = new ReturnDigest(filename);
      dr.start();

      // Now print the result
      StringBuilder result = new StringBuilder(filename);
      result.append(": ");
      byte[] digest = dr.getDigest();
      result.append(DatatypeConverter.printHexBinary(digest));
      System.out.println(result);
    }
  }
}
```

The ReturnDigest class stores the result of the calculation in the private field digest, which is accessed via getDigest(). The main() method in ReturnDigestUserInter face loops through a list of files from the command line. It starts a new ReturnDi gest thread for each file and then tries to retrieve the result using getDigest(). However, when you run this program, the result may not be what you expect:

```
D:\JAVA\JNP4\examples\03>java ReturnDigestUserInterface *.java
Exception in thread "main" java.lang.NullPointerException
    at javax.xml.bind.DatatypeConverterImpl.printHexBinary
    (DatatypeConverterImpl.java:358)
    at javax.xml.bind.DatatypeConverter.printHexBinary(DatatypeConverter.java:560)
    at ReturnDigestUserInterface.main(ReturnDigestUserInterface.java:15)
```

The problem is that the main program gets the digest and uses it before the thread has had a chance to initialize it. Although this flow of control would work in a single-threaded program in which dr.start() simply invoked the run() method in the same thread, that's not what happens here. The calculations that dr.start() kicks off may or may not finish before the main() method reaches the call to dr.getDigest(). If they haven't finished, dr.getDigest() returns null, and the first attempt to access digest throws a NullPointerException.

Race Conditions

One possibility is to move the call to dr.getDigest() later in the main() method, like this:

```
public static void main(String[] args) {

    ReturnDigest[] digests = new ReturnDigest[args.length];

    for (int i = 0; i < args.length; i++) {
      // Calculate the digest
      digests[i] = new ReturnDigest(args[i]);
      digests[i].start();
    }

    for (int i = 0; i < args.length; i++) {
      // Now print the result
      StringBuffer result = new StringBuffer(args[i]);
      result.append(": ");
      byte[] digest = digests[i].getDigest();
      result.append(DatatypeConverter.printHexBinary(digest));

      System.out.println(result);
    }
  }
}
```

If you're lucky, this will work and you'll get the expected output, like this:

```
D:\JAVA\JNP4\examples\03>java ReturnDigest2 *.java
AccumulatingError.java: 7B261F7D88467A1D30D66DD29EEEDE495EA16FCD3ADDB8B613BC2C5DC
BenchmarkScalb.java: AECE2AD497F11F672184E45F2885063C99B2FDD41A3FC7C7B5D4ECBFD2B0
CanonicalPathComparator.java: FE0AACF55D331BBF555528A876C919EAD826BC79B659C489D62
Catenary.java: B511A9A507B43C9CDAF626D5B3A8CCCD80149982196E66ED1BFFD5E55B11E226
...
```

However, let me emphasize that point about being *lucky*. You may not get this output. In fact, you may still get a NullPointerException. Whether this code works is completely dependent on whether every one of the ReturnDigest threads finishes before its getDigest() method is called. If the first for loop is too fast and the second for loop is entered before the threads spawned by the first loop start finishing, you're back where you started. Worse yet, the program may appear to hang with no output at all, not even a stack trace.

Whether you get the correct results, an exception, or a hung program depends on many factors, including how many threads the program spawns, the speed of the CPU and disk on the system where this is run, how many CPUs the system uses, and the algorithm the Java virtual machine uses to allot time to different threads. This is called a *race condition*. Getting the correct result depends on the relative speeds of different threads, and you can't control those! You need a better way to guarantee that the getDigest() method isn't called until the digest is ready.

Polling

The solution most novices adopt is to make the getter method return a flag value (or perhaps throw an exception) until the result field is set. Then the main thread periodically polls the getter method to see whether it's returning something other than the flag value. In this example, that would mean repeatedly testing whether the digest is null and using it only if it isn't. For example:

```
public static void main(String[] args) {

  ReturnDigest[] digests = new ReturnDigest[args.length];

  for (int i = 0; i < args.length; i++) {
    // Calculate the digest
    digests[i] = new ReturnDigest(args[i]);
    digests[i].start();
  }

  for (int i = 0; i < args.length; i++) {
    while (true) {
      // Now print the result
      byte[] digest = digests[i].getDigest();
      if (digest != null) {
        StringBuilder result = new StringBuilder(args[i]);
        result.append(": ");
        result.append(DatatypeConverter.printHexBinary(digest));
        System.out.println(result);
        break;
      }
    }
  }
}
```

This solution may work. If it works at all, it gives the correct answers in the correct order irrespective of how fast the individual threads run relative to each other. However, it's doing a lot more work than it needs to.

Worse yet, this solution is not guaranteed to work. On some virtual machines, the main thread takes all the time available and leaves no time for the actual worker threads. The main thread is so busy checking for job completion that there's no time left to actually complete the job! Clearly this isn't a good approach.

Callbacks

In fact, there's a much simpler, more efficient way to handle the problem. The infinite loop that repeatedly polls each ReturnDigest object to see whether it's finished can be eliminated. The trick is that rather than having the main program repeatedly ask each ReturnDigest thread whether it's finished (like a five-year-old repeatedly asking, "Are we there yet?" on a long car trip, and almost as annoying), you let the thread tell the main program when it's finished. It does this by invoking a method in the main class that started it. This is called a *callback* because the thread calls its creator back when it's done. This way, the main program can go to sleep while waiting for the threads to finish and not steal time from the running threads.

When the thread's run() method is nearly done, the last thing it does is invoke a known method in the main program with the result. Rather than the main program asking each thread for the answer, each thread tells the main program the answer. For instance, Example 3-5 shows a CallbackDigest class that is much the same as before. However, at the end of the run() method, it passes off the digest to the static CallbackDigestU serInterface.receiveDigest() method in the class that originally started the thread.

Example 3-5. CallbackDigest

```
import java.io.*;
import java.security.*;

public class CallbackDigest implements Runnable {

  private String filename;

  public CallbackDigest(String filename) {
   this.filename = filename;
  }

  @Override
  public void run() {
    try {
      FileInputStream in = new FileInputStream(filename);
      MessageDigest sha = MessageDigest.getInstance("SHA-256");
      DigestInputStream din = new DigestInputStream(in, sha);
      while (din.read() != -1) ; // read entire file
      din.close();
      byte[] digest = sha.digest();
      CallbackDigestUserInterface.receiveDigest(digest, filename);
    } catch (IOException ex) {
      System.err.println(ex);
    } catch (NoSuchAlgorithmException ex) {
      System.err.println(ex);
    }
  }
}
```

The CallbackDigestUserInterface class shown in Example 3-6 provides the main() method. However, unlike the main() methods in the other variations of this program, this one only starts the threads for the files named on the command line. It does not attempt to actually read, print out, or in any other way work with the results of the calculation. Those functions are handled by a separate method, receiveDigest(), which is not invoked by the main() method or by any method that can be reached by following the flow of control from the `main()` method. Instead, it is invoked by each thread separately. That is, `receiveDigest()` runs inside the digesting threads rather than inside the main thread of execution.

Example 3-6. CallbackDigestUserInterface

```
import javax.xml.bind.*; // for DatatypeConverter; requires Java 6 or JAXB 1.0

public class CallbackDigestUserInterface {

  public static void receiveDigest(byte[] digest, String name) {
    StringBuilder result = new StringBuilder(name);
    result.append(": ");
    result.append(DatatypeConverter.printHexBinary(digest));
    System.out.println(result);
  }

  public static void main(String[] args) {
    for (String filename : args) {
      // Calculate the digest
      CallbackDigest cb = new CallbackDigest(filename);
      Thread t = new Thread(cb);
      t.start();
    }
  }
}
```

Examples 3-5 and 3-6 use static methods for the callback so that `CallbackDigest` only needs to know the name of the method in `CallbackDigestUserInterface` to call. However, it's not much harder (and it's considerably more common) to call back to an instance method. In this case, the class making the callback must have a reference to the object it's calling back. Generally, this reference is provided as an argument to the thread's constructor. When the `run()` method is nearly done, the last thing it does is invoke the instance method on the callback object to pass along the result. For instance, Example 3-7 shows a `CallbackDigest` class that is much the same as before. However, it now has one additional field, an `InstanceCallbackDigestUserInterface` object called `callback`. At the end of the `run()` method, the `digest` is passed to `callback`'s `receiveDigest()` method. The `InstanceCallbackDigestUserInterface` object itself is set in the constructor.

Example 3-7. InstanceCallbackDigest

```
import java.io.*;
import java.security.*;

public class InstanceCallbackDigest implements Runnable {

  private String filename;
  private InstanceCallbackDigestUserInterface callback;
```

```
  public InstanceCallbackDigest(String filename,
   InstanceCallbackDigestUserInterface callback) {
    this.filename = filename;
    this.callback = callback;
  }

  @Override
  public void run() {
    try {
      FileInputStream in = new FileInputStream(filename);
      MessageDigest sha = MessageDigest.getInstance("SHA-256");
      DigestInputStream din = new DigestInputStream(in, sha);
      while (din.read() != -1) ;  // read entire file
      din.close();
      byte[] digest = sha.digest();
      callback.receiveDigest(digest);
    } catch (IOException | NoSuchAlgorithmException ex) {
      System.err.println(ex);
    }
  }
}
```

The `InstanceCallbackDigestUserInterface` class shown in Example 3-8 holds the
`main()` method as well as the `receiveDigest()` method used to handle an incoming
digest. Example 3-8 just prints out the digest, but a more expansive class could do other
things as well, such as storing the digest in a field, using it to start another thread, or
performing further calculations on it.

Example 3-8. InstanceCallbackDigestUserInterface

```
import javax.xml.bind.*; // for DatatypeConverter; requires Java 6 or JAXB 1.0

public class InstanceCallbackDigestUserInterface {

  private String filename;
  private byte[] digest;

  public InstanceCallbackDigestUserInterface(String filename) {
    this.filename = filename;
  }

  public void calculateDigest() {
    InstanceCallbackDigest cb = new InstanceCallbackDigest(filename, this);
    Thread t = new Thread(cb);
    t.start();
  }

  void receiveDigest(byte[] digest) {
    this.digest = digest;
    System.out.println(this);
  }
```

```
@Override
public String toString() {
  String result = filename + ": ";
  if (digest != null) {
    result += DatatypeConverter.printHexBinary(digest);
  } else {
    result += "digest not available";
  }
  return result;
}

public static void main(String[] args) {
  for (String filename : args) {
    // Calculate the digest
    InstanceCallbackDigestUserInterface d
        = new InstanceCallbackDigestUserInterface(filename);
    d.calculateDigest();
  }
}
}
```

Using instance methods instead of static methods for callbacks is a little more complicated but has a number of advantages. First, each instance of the main class (Instance CallbackDigestUserInterface, in this example) maps to exactly one file and can keep track of information about that file in a natural way without needing extra data structures. Furthermore, the instance can easily recalculate the digest for a particular file, if necessary. In practice, this scheme proves a lot more flexible. However, there is one caveat. Notice the addition of the calculateDigest() method to start the thread. You might logically think that this belongs in a constructor. However, starting threads in a constructor is dangerous, especially threads that will call back to the originating object. There's a race condition here that may allow the new thread to call back before the constructor is finished and the object is fully initialized. It's unlikely in this case, because starting the new thread is the last thing this constructor does. Nonetheless, it's at least theoretically possible. Therefore, it's good form to avoid launching threads from constructors.

The first advantage of the callback scheme over the polling scheme is that it doesn't waste so many CPU cycles. However, a much more important advantage is that callbacks are more flexible and can handle more complicated situations involving many more threads, objects, and classes. For instance, if more than one object is interested in the result of the thread's calculation, the thread can keep a list of objects to call back. Particular objects can register their interest by invoking a method in the Thread or Runna ble class to add themselves to the list. If instances of more than one class are interested in the result, a new interface can be defined that all these classes implement. The interface would declare the callback methods.

If you're experiencing déjà vu right now, that's probably because you have seen this scheme before. This is *exactly* how events are handled in Swing, the AWT, and JavaBeans. The AWT runs in a separate thread from the rest of the program. Components and beans inform you of events by calling back to methods declared in particular interfaces, such as `ActionListener` and `PropertyChangeListener`. Your listener objects register their interests in events fired by particular components using methods in the `Compo nent` class, such as `addActionListener()` and `addPropertyChangeListener()`. Inside the component, the registered listeners are stored in a linked list built out of `java.awt.AWTEventMulticaster` objects. More generally this is known as the *Observer* design pattern.

Futures, Callables, and Executors

Java 5 introduced a new approach to multithreaded programming that makes it somewhat easier to handle callbacks by hiding the details. Instead of directly creating a thread, you create an `ExecutorService` that will create threads for you as needed. You submit `Callable` jobs to the `ExecutorService` and for each one you get back a `Future`. At a later point, you can ask the `Future` for the result of the job. If the result is ready, you get it immediately. If it's not ready, the polling thread blocks until it is ready. The advantage is that you can spawn off many different threads, then get the answers you need in the order you need them.

For example, suppose you need to find the maximum value in a large array of numbers. Implemented naively, this takes O(n) time where n is the number of elements in the array. However, you can go faster than that if you split the work into multiple threads, each running on a separate core. For purposes of illustration, let's assume two threads are desired.

The `Callable` interface defines a single `call()` method that can generically return any type. Example 3-9 is a `Callable` that finds the maximum value in a subsection of an array in the most obvious way possible.

Example 3-9. FindMaxTask

```
import java.util.concurrent.Callable;

class FindMaxTask implements Callable<Integer> {

  private int[] data;
  private int start;
  private int end;

  FindMaxTask(int[] data, int start, int end) {
    this.data = data;
    this.start = start;
    this.end = end;
  }
```

```
  public Integer call() {
    int max = Integer.MIN_VALUE;
    for (int i = start; i < end; i++) {
      if (data[i] > max) max = data[i];
    }
    return max;
  }
}
```

Although you could invoke the call() method directly, that is not its purpose. Instead, you submit Callable objects to an Executor that spins up a thread for each one. (There are other strategies an Executor could use—for instance, it could use a single thread to invoke the callables in order—but one thread per callable is a good strategy for this problem.) Example 3-10 demonstrates.

Example 3-10. MultithreadedMaxFinder

```
import java.util.concurrent.*;

public class MultithreadedMaxFinder {

  public static int max(int[] data) throws InterruptedException, ExecutionException {

    if (data.length == 1) {
      return data[0];
    } else if (data.length == 0) {
      throw new IllegalArgumentException();
    }

    // split the job into 2 pieces
    FindMaxTask task1 = new FindMaxTask(data, 0, data.length/2);
    FindMaxTask task2 = new FindMaxTask(data, data.length/2, data.length);

    // spawn 2 threads
    ExecutorService service = Executors.newFixedThreadPool(2);

    Future<Integer> future1 = service.submit(task1);
    Future<Integer> future2 = service.submit(task2);

    return Math.max(future1.get(), future2.get());
  }
}
```

Each subarray is searched at the same time, so on suitable hardware and a large input this program can run almost twice as fast. Nonetheless, the code is almost as simple and straightforward as finding the maximum in the first half of the array and then finding the maximum in the second half of the array, without ever worrying about threads or asynchronicity. However, there's one key difference. In the last statement of Example 3-10, when future1.get() is called, the method blocks and waits for the first

FindMaxTask to finish. Only when this has happened does it call future2.get(). It's possible that the second thread has already finished, in which case the value is immediately returned; but if not, execution waits for that thread to finish too. Once both threads have finished, their results are compared and the maximum is returned.

Futures are a very convenient means of launching multiple threads to work on different pieces of a problem, and then waiting for them all to finish before proceeding. Executors and executor services let you assign jobs to different threads with different strategies. This example used just two threads once each, but it's possible to use many more threads, and to reuse threads for multiple tasks. Executors hide a lot of the nitty-gritty details of asynchronicity as long as you can divide your job up into reasonably independent parts.

Synchronization

My shelves are overflowing with books, including many duplicate books, out-of-date books, and books I haven't looked at for 10 years and probably never will again. Over the years, these books have cost me tens of thousands of dollars, maybe more, to acquire. By contrast, two blocks down the street from my apartment, you'll find the Central Brooklyn Public Library. Its shelves are also overflowing with books, and over its 100 years, it's spent millions on its collection. But the difference is that its books are shared among all the residents of Brooklyn, and consequently the books have very high turnover. Most books in the collection are used several times a year. Although the public library spends a lot more money buying and storing books than I do, the cost per page read is much lower at the library than for my personal shelves. That's the advantage of a shared resource.

Of course, there are disadvantages to shared resources, too. If I need a book from the library, I have to walk over there. I have to find the book I'm looking for on the shelves. I have to stand in line to check the book out, or else I have to use it right there in the library rather than bringing it home with me. Sometimes somebody else has checked the book out, and I have to fill out a form requesting that the book be saved for me when it's returned. And I can't write notes in the margins, highlight paragraphs, or tear pages out to paste on my bulletin board. (Well, I can, but if I do, it significantly reduces the usefulness of the book for future borrowers, and if the library catches me, I may lose my borrowing privileges.) There's a significant time and convenience penalty associated with borrowing a book from the library rather than purchasing my own copy, but it does save me money and storage space.

A thread is like a borrower at a library; the thread borrows from a central pool of resources. Threads make programs more efficient by sharing memory, file handles, sockets, and other resources. As long as two threads don't want to use the same resource at the same time, a multithreaded program is much more efficient than the multiprocess alternative, in which each process has to keep its own copy of every resource. The downside of a multithreaded program is that if two threads want the same resource at the same time, one of them will have to wait for the other to finish. If one of them doesn't wait, the resource may get corrupted. Let's look at a specific example. Consider the run() method of Examples 3-1 and 3-2. As previously mentioned, the method builds the result as a String, and then prints the String on the console using one call to Sys tem.out.println(). The output looks like this:

```
Triangle.java: B4C7AF1BAE952655A96517476BF9DAC97C4AF02411E40DD386FECB58D94CC769
InterfaceLister.java: 267D0EFE73896CD550DC202935D20E87CA71536CB176AF78F915935A6
Squares.java: DA2E27EA139785535122A2420D3DB472A807841D05F6C268A43695B9FDFE1B11
UlpPrinter.java: C8009AB1578BF7E730BD2C3EADA54B772576E265011DF22D171D60A1881AFF51
```

Four threads run in parallel to produce this output. Each writes one line to the console. The order in which the lines are written is unpredictable because thread scheduling is unpredictable, but each line is written as a unified whole. Suppose, however, you used this variation of the run() method, which, rather than storing intermediate parts of the result in the String variable result, simply prints them on the console as they become available:

```java
@Override
public void run() {
  try {
    FileInputStream in = new FileInputStream(filename);
    MessageDigest sha = MessageDigest.getInstance("SHA-256");
    DigestInputStream din = new DigestInputStream(in, sha);
    while (din.read() != -1) ; // read entire file
    din.close();
    byte[] digest = sha.digest();
    System.out.print(input + ": ");
    System.out.print(DatatypeConverter.printHexBinary(digest));
    System.out.println();
  } catch (IOException ex) {
    System.err.println(ex);
  } catch (NoSuchAlgorithmException ex) {
    System.err.println(ex);
  }
}
```

When you run the program on the same input, the output looks something like this:

```
Triangle.java: B4C7AF1BAE952655A96517476BF9DAC97C4AF02411E40DD386FECB58D94CC769
InterfaceLister.java: Squares.java: UlpPrinter.java:
C8009AB1578BF7E730BD2C3EADA54B772576E265011DF22D171D60A1881AFF51
267D0EFE73896CD550DC202935D20E87CA71536CB176AF78F915935A6E81B034
DA2E27EA139785535122A2420D3DB472A807841D05F6C268A43695B9FDFE1B11
```

The digests of the different files are all mixed up! There's no telling which number belongs to which digest. Clearly, this is a problem.

The reason this mix-up occurs is that System.out is shared between the four different threads. When one thread starts writing to the console through several System.out.print() statements, it may not finish all its writes before another thread breaks in and starts writing its output. The exact order in which one thread preempts the other threads is indeterminate. You'll probably see slightly different output every time you run this program.

You need a way to assign exclusive access to a shared resource to one thread for a specific series of statements. In this example, that shared resource is System.out, and the statements that need exclusive access are:

```
System.out.print(input + ": ");
System.out.print(DatatypeConverter.printHexBinary(digest));
System.out.println();
```

Synchronized Blocks

To indicate that these five lines of code should be executed together, wrap them in a synchronized block that synchronizes on the System.out object, like this:

```
synchronized (System.out) {
  System.out.print(input + ": ");
  System.out.print(DatatypeConverter.printHexBinary(digest));
  System.out.println();
}
```

Once one thread starts printing out the values, all other threads will have to stop and wait for it to finish before they can print out their values. Synchronization forces all code that synchronizes on the same object to run in series, never in parallel. For instance, if some other code in a different class and different thread also happened to synchronize on System.out, it too would not be able to run in parallel with this block. However, other code that synchronizes on a different object or doesn't synchronize at all can still run in parallel with this code. It can do so even if it also uses System.out. Java provides no means to stop all other threads from using a shared resource. It can only prevent other threads that synchronize on the same object from using the shared resource.

 In fact, the PrintStream class internally synchronizes most methods on the PrintStream object (System.out, in this example). In other words, every other thread that calls System.out.println() will be synchronized on System.out and will have to wait for this code to finish. PrintStream is unique in this respect. Most other Output Stream subclasses do not synchronize themselves.

Synchronization must be considered any time multiple threads share resources. These threads may be instances of the same Thread subclass or use the same Runnable class, or they may be instances of completely different classes. The key is the resources they share, not what classes they are. Synchronization becomes an issue only when two threads both possess references to the same object. In the previous example, the problem was that several threads had access to the same `PrintStream` object, `System.out`. In this case, it was a static class variable that led to the conflict. However, instance variables can also have problems.

For example, suppose your web server keeps a logfile. The logfile may be represented by a class like the one shown in Example 3-11. This class itself doesn't use multiple threads. However, if the web server uses multiple threads to handle incoming connections, then each of those threads will need access to the same logfile and consequently to the same `LogFile` object.

Example 3-11. LogFile

```
import java.io.*;
import java.util.*;

public class LogFile {

  private Writer out;

  public LogFile(File f) throws IOException {
    FileWriter fw = new FileWriter(f);
    this.out = new BufferedWriter(fw);
  }

  public void writeEntry(String message) throws IOException {
    Date d = new Date();
    out.write(d.toString());
    out.write('\t');
    out.write(message);
    out.write("\r\n");
  }

  public void close() throws IOException {
    out.flush();
    out.close();
  }
}
```

In this class, the `writeEntry()` method finds the current date and time, then writes into the underlying file using four separate invocations of `out.write()`. A problem occurs if two or more threads each have a reference to the same `LogFile` object and one of those threads interrupts another in the process of writing the data. One thread may write the date and a tab, then the next thread might write three complete entries; then, the first thread could write the message, a carriage return, and a linefeed. The solution, once again, is synchronization. However, here there are two good choices for which object to synchronize on. The first choice is to synchronize on the `Writer` object out. For example:

```
public void writeEntry(String message) throws IOException {
  synchronized (out) {
    Date d = new Date();
    out.write(d.toString());
    out.write('\t');
    out.write(message);
    out.write("\r\n");
  }
}
```

This works because all the threads that use this LogFile object also use the same out object that's part of that LogFile. It doesn't matter that out is private. Although it is used by the other threads and objects, it's referenced only within the LogFile class. Furthermore, although you're synchronizing here on the out object, it's the writeEntry() method that needs to be protected from interruption. The Writer classes all have their own internal synchronization, which protects one thread from interfering with a write() method in another thread. (This is not true of input and output streams, with the exception of PrintStream. It is possible for a write to an output stream to be interrupted by another thread.) Each Writer class has a lock field that specifies the object on which writes to that writer synchronize.

The second possibility is to synchronize on the LogFile object itself. This is simple enough to arrange with the this keyword. For example:

```
public void writeEntry(String message) throws IOException {
  synchronized (this) {
    Date d = new Date();
    out.write(d.toString());
    out.write('\t');
    out.write(message);
    out.write("\r\n");
  }
}
```

Synchronized Methods

Because synchronizing the entire method body on the object itself is such a common thing to do, Java provides a shortcut. You can synchronize an entire method on the current object (the this reference) by adding the synchronized modifier to the method declaration. For example:

```
public synchronized void writeEntry(String message) throws IOException {
  Date d = new Date();
  out.write(d.toString());
  out.write('\t');
  out.write(message);
  out.write("\r\n");
}
```

Simply adding the synchronized modifier to all methods is not a catchall solution for synchronization problems. For one thing, it exacts a severe performance penalty in many VMs (though more recent VMs have improved greatly in this respect), potentially slowing down your code by a factor of three or more. Second, it dramatically increases the chances of deadlock. Third, and most importantly, it's not always the object itself you need to protect from simultaneous modification or access, and synchronizing on the instance of the method's class may not protect the object you really need to protect. For instance, in this example, what you're really trying to prevent is two threads simultaneously writing onto out. If some other class had a reference to out completely unrelated to the LogFile, this attempt would fail. However, in this example, synchronizing on the LogFile object is sufficient because out is a private instance variable. Because you never expose a reference to this object, there's no way for any other object to invoke its methods except through the LogFile class. Therefore, synchronizing on the Log File object has the same effect as synchronizing on out.

Alternatives to Synchronization

Synchronization is not always the best solution to the problem of inconsistent behavior caused by thread scheduling. There are a number of techniques that avoid the need for synchronization entirely. The first is to use local variables instead of fields wherever possible. Local variables do not have synchronization problems. Every time a method is entered, the virtual machine creates a completely new set of local variables for the method. These variables are invisible from outside the method and are destroyed when the method exits. As a result, it's impossible for one local variable to be shared by two different threads. Every thread has its own separate set of local variables.

Method arguments of primitive types are also safe from modification in separate threads because Java passes arguments by value rather than by reference. A corollary of this is that pure functions such as Math.sqrt() that take zero or more primitive data type arguments, perform some calculation, and return a value without ever interacting with the fields of any class are inherently thread safe. These methods often either are or should be declared static.

Method arguments of object types are a little trickier because the actual argument passed by value is a reference to the object. Suppose, for example, you pass a reference to an array into a sort() method. While the method is sorting the array, there's nothing to stop some other thread that also has a reference to the array from changing the values in the array.

String arguments are safe because they're *immutable* (i.e., once a String object has been created, it cannot be changed by any thread). An immutable object never changes state. The values of its fields are set once when the constructor runs and never altered thereafter. StringBuilder arguments are not safe because they're not immutable; they can be changed after they're created.

A constructor normally does not have to worry about issues of thread safety. Until the constructor returns, no thread has a reference to the object, so it's impossible for two threads to have a reference to the object. (The most likely issue is if a constructor depends on another object in another thread that may change while the constructor runs, but that's uncommon. There's also a potential problem if a constructor somehow passes a reference to the object it's creating into a different thread, but this is also uncommon.)

You can take advantage of immutability in your own classes. It's usually the easiest way to make a class thread safe, often much easier than determining exactly which methods or code blocks to synchronize. To make an object immutable, simply declare all its fields private and final and don't write any methods that can change them. A lot of classes in the core Java library are immutable (e.g., `java.lang.String`, `java.lang.Integer`, `java.lang.Double`, and many more). This makes these classes less useful for some purposes, but it does make them a lot more thread safe.

A third technique is to use a thread-unsafe class but only as a private field of a class that is thread safe. As long as the containing class accesses the unsafe class only in a thread-safe fashion and as long as it never lets a reference to the private field leak out into another object, the class is safe. An example of this technique might be a web server that uses an unsynchronized `LogFile` class but gives each separate thread its own separate log so no resources are shared between the individual threads.

In some cases, you can use a designedly thread-safe but mutable class from the `java.util.concurrent.atomic` package. In particular, rather than using an `int`, you can use an `AtomicInteger`. Rather than using a `long`, you can use an `AtomicLong`. Rather than using a `boolean`, you can use an `AtomicBoolean`. Rather than using an `int[]`, you can use an `AtomicIntegerArray`. Rather than a reference variable, you can store an object inside an `AtomicReference`, though note well that this doesn't make the object itself thread safe, just the getting and setting of the reference variable. These classes may be faster than synchronized access to their respective primitive types if they can take advantage of fast machine-level thread-safe instructions on modern CPUs.

For collections such as maps and lists, you can wrap them in a thread-safe version using the methods of `java.util.Collections`. For instance, if you have a set `foo`, you can get a thread-safe view of this set with `Collections.synchronizedSet(foo)`. If you have a list `foo`, you'd use `Collections.synchronizedList(foo)` instead. For a map, call `Collections.synchronizedMap(foo)`, and so forth. In order for this to work, you must use only the view returned by `Collections.synchronizedSet/List/Map`. If at any point you access the original, underlying data structure, neither the original nor the synchronized view will be thread safe.

In all cases, realize that it's just a single method invocation that is atomic. If you need to perform two operations on the atomic value in succession without possible interruption, you'll still need to synchronize. Thus, for instance, even if a list is synchronized via

`Collections.synchronizedList()`, you'll still need to synchronize on it if you want to iterate through the list because that involves many consecutive atomic operations. Although each method call is safely atomic, the sequence of operations is not without explicit synchronization.

Deadlock

Synchronization can lead to another possible problem: *deadlock*. Deadlock occurs when two threads need exclusive access to the same set of resources and each thread holds the lock on a different subset of those resources. If neither thread is willing to give up the resources it has, both threads come to an indefinite halt. This isn't quite a hang in the classical sense because the program is still active and behaving normally from the perspective of the OS, but to a user the difference is insignificant.

To return to the library example, deadlock is what occurs when Jack and Jill are each writing a term paper on Thomas Jefferson and they both need the two books *Thomas Jefferson and Sally Hemings: An American Controversy* and *Sally Hemings and Thomas Jefferson: History, Memory, and Civic Culture*. If Jill has checked out the first book and Jack has checked out the second, and neither is willing to give up the book they have, neither can finish the paper. Eventually, the deadline expires and they both get an F. That's the problem of deadlock.

Worse yet, deadlock can be a sporadic, hard-to-detect bug. Deadlock usually depends on unpredictable issues of timing. Most of the time, either Jack or Jill will get to the library first and check out both books. In this case, the one who gets the books first writes a paper and returns the books; then the other one gets the books and writes his or her paper. Only rarely will they arrive at the same time and each get one of the two books. Ninety-nine times out of 100 or 999 times out of 1,000, a program will run to completion perfectly normally. Only rarely will it hang for no apparent reason. Of course, if a multithreaded server is handling hundreds of requests per second, even a problem that occurs only once every million requests can hang the server in short order.

The most important technique for preventing deadlock is to avoid unnecessary synchronization. If there's an alternative approach for ensuring thread safety, such as making objects immutable or keeping a local copy of an object, use it. Synchronization should be a last resort for ensuring thread safety. If you do need to synchronize, keep the synchronized blocks small and try not to synchronize on more than one object at a time. This can be tricky, though, because many of the methods from the Java class library that your code may invoke synchronize on objects you aren't aware of. Consequently, you may in fact be synchronizing on many more objects than you expect.

The best you can do in the general case is carefully consider whether deadlock is likely to be a problem and design your code around it. If multiple objects need the same set of shared resources to operate, make sure they request them in the same order. For instance, if class A and class B need exclusive access to object X and object Y, make sure that both classes request X first and Y second. If neither requests Y unless it already possesses X, deadlock is not a problem.

Thread Scheduling

When multiple threads are running at the same time (more properly, when multiple threads are available to be run at the same time), you have to consider issues of thread scheduling. You need to make sure that all important threads get at least some time to run and that the more important threads get more time. Furthermore, you want to ensure that the threads execute in a reasonable order. If your web server has 10 queued requests, each of which requires 5 seconds to process, you don't want to process them in series. If you do, the first request will finish in 5 seconds but the second will take 10, the third 15, and so on until the last request, which will have to wait almost a minute to be serviced. By that point, the user has likely gone to another page. By running threads in parallel, you might be able to process all 10 requests in only 10 seconds total. The reason this strategy works is that there's a lot of dead time in servicing a typical web request, time in which the thread is simply waiting for the network to catch up with the CPU—time the VM's thread scheduler can put to good use by other threads. However, CPU-bound threads (as opposed to the I/O-bound threads more common in network programs) may never reach a point where they have to wait for more input. It is possible for such a thread to starve all other threads by taking all the available CPU resources. With a little thought, you can avoid this problem. In fact, starvation is a considerably easier problem to avoid than either mis-synchronization or deadlock.

Priorities

Not all threads are created equal. Each thread has a priority, specified as an integer from 0 to 10. When multiple threads are ready to run, the VM will generally run only the highest-priority thread, although that's not a hard-and-fast rule. In Java, 10 is the highest priority and 0 is the lowest. The default priority is 5, and this is the priority that your threads will have unless you deliberately set them otherwise.

 This is the exact opposite of the normal Unix way of prioritizing processes, in which the higher the priority number of a process, the less CPU time the process gets.

These three priorities (1, 5, and 10) are often specified as the three named constants Thread.MIN_PRIORITY, Thread.NORM_PRIORITY, and Thread.MAX_PRIORITY:

```
public static final int MIN_PRIORITY  = 1;
public static final int NORM_PRIORITY = 5;
public static final int MAX_PRIORITY  = 10;
```

 Not all operating systems support 11 different priorities. For in-stance, Windows only has 7. On Windows, priorities 1 and 2, 3 and 4, 6 and 7, and 8 and 9 are treated equally (e.g., a priority 9 thread will not necessarily preempt a priority 8 thread).

Sometimes you want to give one thread more time than another. Threads that interact with the user should get very high priorities so that perceived responsiveness will be very quick. On the other hand, threads that calculate in the background should get low priorities. Tasks that will complete quickly should have high priorities. Tasks that take a long time should have low priorities so that they won't get in the way of other tasks. You can change the priority of the thread using the setPriority() method:

```
public final void setPriority(int newPriority)
```

Attempting to exceed the maximum priority or set a nonpositive priority throws an IllegalArgumentException.

For instance, in Example 3-11, you might want to give higher priorities to the threads that do the calculating than the main program that spawns the threads. This is easily achieved by changing the calculateDigest() method to set the priority of each spawned thread to 8:

```
public void calculateDigest() {
  ListCallbackDigest cb = new ListCallbackDigest(filename);
  cb.addDigestListener(this);
  Thread t = new Thread(cb);
  t.setPriority(8);
  t.start();
}
```

In general, though, try to avoid using too high a priority for threads, because you run the risk of starving other, lower-priority threads.

Preemption

Every virtual machine has a thread scheduler that determines which thread to run at any given time. There are two main kinds of thread scheduling: *preemptive* and *coop-erative*. A preemptive thread scheduler determines when a thread has had its fair share of CPU time, pauses that thread, and then hands off control of the CPU to a different thread. A cooperative thread scheduler waits for the running thread to pause itself before handing off control of the CPU to a different thread. A virtual machine that uses co-operative thread scheduling is much more susceptible to thread starvation than a virtual machine that uses preemptive thread scheduling, because one high-priority, uncooperative thread can hog an entire CPU.

All Java virtual machines are guaranteed to use preemptive thread scheduling between priorities. That is, if a lower-priority thread is running when a higher-priority thread becomes ready to run, the virtual machine will sooner or later (and probably sooner) pause the lower-priority thread to allow the higher-priority thread to run. The higher-priority thread *preempts* the lower-priority thread.

The situation when multiple threads of the same priority are ready to run is trickier. A preemptive thread scheduler will occasionally pause one of the threads to allow the next one in line to get some CPU time. However, a cooperative thread scheduler will not. It will wait for the running thread to explicitly give up control or come to a stopping point. If the running thread never gives up control and never comes to a stopping point and if no higher-priority threads preempt the running thread, all other threads will starve. This is a bad thing. It's important to make sure all your threads periodically pause themselves so that other threads have an opportunity to run.

 A starvation problem can be hard to spot if you're developing on a VM that uses preemptive thread scheduling. Just because the problem doesn't arise on your machine doesn't mean it won't arise on your customers' machines if their VMs use cooperative thread scheduling. Most current VMs use preemptive thread scheduling, but some older VMs are cooperatively scheduled, and you may also encounter cooperative scheduling in special-purpose Java VMs such as for embedded environments.

There are 10 ways a thread can pause in favor of other threads or indicate that it is ready to pause. These are:

- It can block on I/O.
- It can block on a synchronized object.
- It can yield.
- It can go to sleep.
- It can join another thread.
- It can wait on an object.
- It can finish.
- It can be preempted by a higher-priority thread.
- It can be suspended.
- It can stop.

Inspect every `run()` method you write to make sure that one of these conditions will occur with reasonable frequency. The last two possibilities are deprecated because they have the potential to leave objects in inconsistent states, so let's look at the other eight ways a thread can be a cooperative citizen of the virtual machine.

Blocking

Blocking occurs any time a thread has to stop and wait for a resource it doesn't have. The most common way a thread in a network program will voluntarily give up control of the CPU is by blocking on I/O. Because CPUs are much faster than networks and disks, a network program will often block while waiting for data to arrive from the network or be sent out to the network. Even though it may block for only a few milliseconds, this is enough time for other threads to do significant work.

Threads can also block when they enter a synchronized method or block. If the thread does not already possess the lock for the object being synchronized on and some other thread does possess that lock, the thread will pause until the lock is released. If the lock is never released, the thread is permanently stopped.

Neither blocking on I/O nor blocking on a lock will release any locks the thread already possesses. For I/O blocks, this is not such a big deal, because eventually the I/O will either unblock and the thread will continue or an `IOException` will be thrown and the thread will then exit the synchronized block or method and release its locks. However, a thread blocking on a lock that it doesn't possess will never give up its own locks. If one thread is waiting for a lock that a second thread owns and the second thread is waiting for a lock that the first thread owns, deadlock results.

Yielding

The second way for a thread to give up control is to explicitly yield. A thread does this by invoking the static `Thread.yield()` method. This signals to the virtual machine that it can run another thread if one is ready to run. Some virtual machines, particularly on real-time operating systems, may ignore this hint.

Before yielding, a thread should make sure that it or its associated `Runnable` object is in a consistent state that can be used by other objects. Yielding does not release any locks the thread holds. Therefore, ideally, a thread should not be synchronized on anything when it yields. If the only other threads waiting to run when a thread yields are blocked because they need the synchronized resources that the yielding thread possesses, then the other threads won't be able to run. Instead, control will return to the only thread that can run, the one that just yielded, which pretty much defeats the purpose of yielding.

Making a thread yield is quite simple in practice. If the thread's `run()` method simply consists of an infinite loop, just put a call to `Thread.yield()` at the end of the loop. For example:

```
public void run() {
  while (true) {
    // Do the thread's work...
    Thread.yield();
  }
}
```

This gives other threads of the same priority the opportunity to run.

If each iteration of the loop takes a significant amount of time, you may want to inter-sperse more calls to `Thread.yield()` in the rest of the code. This precaution should have minimal effect in the event that yielding isn't necessary.

Sleeping

Sleeping is a more powerful form of yielding. Whereas yielding indicates only that a thread is willing to pause and let other equal-priority threads have a turn, a thread that goes to sleep will pause whether any other thread is ready to run or not. This gives an opportunity to run not only to other threads of the same priority, but also to threads of lower priorities. However, a thread that goes to sleep does hold onto all the locks it's grabbed. Consequently, other threads that need the same locks will be blocked even if the CPU is available. Therefore, try to avoid sleeping threads inside a synchronized method or block.

A thread goes to sleep by invoking one of two overloaded static `Thread.sleep()` meth-ods. The first takes the number of milliseconds to sleep as an argument. The second takes both the number of milliseconds and the number of nanoseconds:

```
public static void sleep(long milliseconds) throws InterruptedException
public static void sleep(long milliseconds, int nanoseconds)
    throws InterruptedException
```

Although most modern computer clocks have at least close-to-millisecond accuracy, nanosecond accuracy is rarer. There's no guarantee that you can actually time the sleep to within a nanosecond or even within a millisecond on any particular virtual machine. If the local hardware can't support that level of accuracy, the sleep time is simply rounded to the nearest value that can be measured. For example, this `run()` method attempts to load a certain page every five minutes and, if it fails, emails the webmaster to alert him of the problem:

```
public void run() {
  while (true) {
    if (!getPage("http://www.ibiblio.org/")) {
      mailError("webmaster@ibiblio.org");
    }
    try {
      Thread.sleep(300000); // 300,000 milliseconds == 5 minutes
    } catch (InterruptedException ex) {
      break;
    }
  }
```

```
    }
  }
```

The thread is not guaranteed to sleep as long as it wants to. On occasion, the thread may not wake up until some time after its requested wake-up call, simply because the VM is busy doing other things. It is also possible that some other thread will do something to wake up the sleeping thread before its time. Generally, this is accomplished by invoking the sleeping thread's `interrupt()` method.

```
    public void interrupt()
```

This is one of those cases where the distinction between the thread and the Thread object is important. Just because the thread is sleeping doesn't mean that other threads that are awake can't work with the corresponding Thread object through its methods and fields. In particular, another thread can invoke the sleeping Thread object's `interrupt()` method, which the sleeping thread experiences as an `InterruptedException`. From that point forward, the thread is awake and executes as normal, at least until it goes to sleep again. In the previous example, an `InterruptedException` is used to terminate a thread that would otherwise run forever. When the `InterruptedException` is thrown, the infinite loop is broken, the `run()` method finishes, and the thread dies. The user-interface thread can invoke this thread's `interrupt()` method when the user selects Exit from a menu or otherwise indicates that he wants the program to quit.

 If a thread is blocked on an I/O operation such as a read or write, the effect of interrupting the thread is highly platform dependent. More often than not, it is a noop. That is, the thread continues to be blocked. On Solaris, the `read()` or `write()` method may throw an `InterruptedIOException`, a subclass of `IOException` instead. However, this is unlikely to happen on other platforms, and may not work with all stream classes on Solaris. If your program architecture requires interruptible I/O, you should seriously consider using the nonblocking I/O discussed in Chapter 11 rather than streams. Unlike streams, buffers and channels are explicitly designed to support interruption while blocked on a read or write.

Joining threads

It's not uncommon for one thread to need the result of another thread. For example, a web browser loading an HTML page in one thread might spawn a separate thread to retrieve every image embedded in the page. If the IMG elements don't have HEIGHT and WIDTH attributes, the main thread might have to wait for all the images to load before it can finish by displaying the page. Java provides three `join()` methods to allow one thread to wait for another thread to finish before continuing. These are:

```
    public final void join() throws InterruptedException
    public final void join(long milliseconds) throws InterruptedException
```

```
public final void join(long milliseconds, int nanoseconds)
    throws InterruptedException
```

The first variant waits indefinitely for the *joined* thread to finish. The second two variants wait for the specified amount of time, after which they continue even if the joined thread has not finished. As with the `sleep()` method, nanosecond accuracy is not guaranteed.

The joining thread (i.e., the one that invokes the `join()` method) waits for the joined thread (i.e, the one whose `join()` method is invoked) to finish. For instance, consider this code fragment. You want to find the minimum, maximum, and median of a random array of doubles. It's quicker to do this with a sorted array. You spawn a new thread to sort the array, then join to that thread to await its results. Only when it's done do you read out the desired values.

```
double[] array = new double[10000];                                 // 1
for (int i = 0; i < array.length; i++) {                            // 2
  array[i] = Math.random();                                         // 3
}                                                                   // 4
SortThread t = new SortThread(array);                               // 5
t.start();                                                          // 6
try {                                                               // 7
  t.join();                                                         // 8
  System.out.println("Minimum: " + array[0]);                       // 9
  System.out.println("Median: " + array[array.length/2]);          // 10
  System.out.println("Maximum: " + array[array.length-1]);         // 11
} catch (InterruptedException ex) {                                 // 12
}                                                                   // 13
```

First lines 1 through 4 execute, filling the array with random numbers. Then line 5 creates a new `SortThread`. Line 6 starts the thread that will sort the array. Before you can find the minimum, median, and maximum of the array, you need to wait for the sorting thread to finish. Therefore, line 8 joins the current thread to the sorting thread. At this point, the thread executing these lines of code stops in its tracks. It waits for the sorting thread to finish running. The minimum, median, and maximum are not retrieved in lines 9 through 10 until the sorting thread has finished running and died. Notice that at no point is there a reference to the thread that pauses. It's not the `Thread` object on which the `join()` method is invoked; it's not passed as an argument to that method. It exists implicitly only as the current thread. If this is within the normal flow of control of the `main()` method of the program, there may not be any `Thread` variable anywhere that points to this thread.

A thread that's joined to another thread can be interrupted just like a sleeping thread if some other thread invokes its `interrupt()` method. The thread experiences this invocation as an `InterruptedException`. From that point forward, it executes as normal, starting from the `catch` block that caught the exception. In the preceding example, if the thread is interrupted, it skips over the calculation of the minimum, median, and maximum because they won't be available if the sorting thread was interrupted before it could finish.

You can use join() to fix up Example 3-4. Its problem was that the main() method tended to outpace the threads whose results the main() method was using. It's straightforward to fix this by joining to each thread before trying to use its result. Example 3-12 demonstrates.

Example 3-12. Avoid a race condition by joining to the thread that has a result you need

```
import javax.xml.bind.DatatypeConverter;

public class JoinDigestUserInterface {

  public static void main(String[] args) {

    ReturnDigest[] digestThreads = new ReturnDigest[args.length];

    for (int i = 0; i < args.length; i++) {
      // Calculate the digest
      digestThreads[i] = new ReturnDigest(args[i]);
      digestThreads[i].start();
    }

    for (int i = 0; i < args.length; i++) {
      try {
        digestThreads[i].join();
        // Now print the result
        StringBuffer result = new StringBuffer(args[i]);
        result.append(": ");
        byte[] digest = digestThreads[i].getDigest();
        result.append(DatatypeConverter.printHexBinary(digest));
        System.out.println(result);
      } catch (InterruptedException ex) {
        System.err.println("Thread Interrupted before completion");
      }
    }
  }
}
```

Because Example 3-12 joins to threads in the same order as the threads are started, this fix also has the side effect of printing the output in the same order as the arguments used to construct the threads, rather than in the order the threads finish. This modification doesn't make the program any slower, but it may occasionally be an issue if you want to get the output of a thread as soon as it's done, without waiting for other unrelated threads to finish first.

Joining is perhaps not as important as it was prior to Java 5. In particular, many designs that used to require join() can now more easily be implemented using an Executor and a Future instead.

Waiting on an object

A thread can *wait* on an object it has locked. While waiting, it releases the lock on the object and pauses until it is notified by some other thread. Another thread changes the object in some way, notifies the thread waiting on that object, and then continues. This differs from joining in that neither the waiting nor the notifying thread has to finish before the other thread can continue. Waiting pauses execution until an object or resource reaches a certain state. Joining pauses execution until a thread finishes.

Waiting on an object is one of the lesser-known ways a thread can pause. That's because it doesn't involve any methods in the Thread class. Instead, to wait on a particular object, the thread that wants to pause must first obtain the lock on the object using synchronized and then invoke one of the object's three overloaded wait() methods:

```
public final void wait() throws InterruptedException
public final void wait(long milliseconds) throws InterruptedException
public final void wait(long milliseconds, int nanoseconds)
    throws InterruptedException
```

These methods are not in the Thread class; rather, they are in the java.lang.Object class. Consequently, they can be invoked on any object of any class. When one of these methods is invoked, the thread that invoked it releases the lock on the object it's waiting on (though not any locks it possesses on other objects) and goes to sleep. It remains asleep until one of three things happens:

- The timeout expires.
- The thread is interrupted.
- The object is notified.

The *timeout* is the same as for the sleep() and join() methods; that is, the thread wakes up after the specified amount of time has passed (within the limits of the local hardware clock accuracy). When the timeout expires, execution of the thread resumes with the statement immediately following the invocation of wait(). However, if the thread can't immediately regain the lock on the object it was waiting on, it may still be blocked for some time.

Interruption works the same way as sleep() and join(): some other thread invokes the thread's interrupt() method. This causes an InterruptedException, and execution resumes in the catch block that catches the exception. The thread regains the lock on the object it was waiting on before the exception is thrown, however, so the thread may still be blocked for some time after the interrupt() method is invoked.

The third possibility, *notification*, is new. Notification occurs when some other thread invokes the notify() or notifyAll() method on the object on which the thread is waiting. Both of these methods are in the java.lang.Object class:

```
public final void notify()
public final void notifyAll()
```

These must be invoked on the object the thread was waiting on, not generally on the Thread itself. Before notifying an object, a thread must first obtain the lock on the object using a synchronized method or block. The notify() method selects one thread more or less at random from the list of threads waiting on the object and wakes it up. The notifyAll() method wakes up every thread waiting on the given object.

Once a waiting thread is notified, it attempts to regain the lock of the object it was waiting on. If it succeeds, execution resumes with the statement immediately following the invocation of wait(). If it fails, it blocks on the object until its lock becomes available; then execution resumes with the statement immediately following the invocation of wait().

For example, suppose one thread is reading a JAR archive from a network connection. The first entry in the archive is the manifest file. Another thread might be interested in the contents of the manifest file even before the rest of the archive is available. The interested thread could create a custom ManifestFile object, pass a reference to this object to the thread that would read the JAR archive, and wait on it. The thread reading the archive would first fill the ManifestFile with entries from the stream, then notify the ManifestFile, then continue reading the rest of the JAR archive. When the reader thread notified the ManifestFile, the original thread would wake up and do whatever it planned to do with the now fully prepared ManifestFile object. The first thread works something like this:

```
ManifestFile m = new ManifestFile();
JarThread    t = new JarThread(m, in);
synchronized (m) {
  t.start();
  try {
    m.wait();
    // work with the manifest file...
  } catch (InterruptedException ex) {
    // handle exception...
  }
}
```

The JarThread class works like this:

```
ManifestFile theManifest;
InputStream in;
```

```
public JarThread(Manifest m, InputStream in) {
  theManifest = m;
  this.in= in;
}

@Override
public void run() {
  synchronized (theManifest) {
    // read the manifest from the stream in...
    theManifest.notify();
  }
  // read the rest of the stream...
}
```

Waiting and notification are more commonly used when multiple threads want to wait on the same object. For example, one thread may be reading a web server logfile in which each line contains one entry to be processed. Each line is placed in a `java.util.List` as it's read. Several threads wait on the `List` to process entries as they're added. Every time an entry is added, the waiting threads are notified using the `notifyAll()` method. If more than one thread is waiting on an object, `notifyAll()` is preferred, because there's no way to select which thread to notify. When all threads waiting on one object are notified, all will wake up and try to get the lock on the object. However, only one can succeed immediately. That one continues; the rest are blocked until the first one releases the lock. If several threads are all waiting on the same object, a significant amount of time may pass before the last one gets its turn at the lock on the object and continues. It's entirely possible that the object on which the thread was waiting will once again have been placed in an unacceptable state during this time. Thus, you'll generally put the call to `wait()` in a loop that checks the current state of the object. Do not assume that just because the thread was notified, the object is now in the correct state. Check it explicitly if you can't guarantee that once the object reaches a correct state it will never again reach an incorrect state. For example, this is how the client threads waiting on the logfile entries might look:

```
private List<String> entries;

public void processEntry() {

  synchronized (entries) { // must synchronize on the object we wait on
    while (entries.isEmpty()) {
      try {
        entries.wait();
        // We stopped waiting because entries.size() became non-zero
        // However we don't know that it's still non-zero so we
        // pass through the loop again to test its state now.
      } catch (InterruptedException ex) {
        // If interrupted, the last entry has been processed so
        return;
      }
```

```
      }
      String entry = entries.remove(entries.size()-1);
      // process this entry...
    }
  }
```

The code reading the logfile and adding entries to the list might look something like this:

```
public void readLogFile() {
  while (true) {
    String entry = log.getNextEntry();
    if (entry == null) {
      // There are no more entries to add to the list so
      // we interrupt all threads that are still waiting.
      // Otherwise, they'll wait forever.
      for (Thread thread : threads) thread.interrupt();
      break;
    }
    synchronized (entries) {
      entries.add(0, entry);
      entries.notifyAll();
    }
  }
}
```

Finish

The final way a thread can give up control of the CPU in an orderly fashion is by *finishing*. When the run() method returns, the thread dies and other threads can take over. In network applications, this tends to occur with threads that wrap a single blocking operation, such as downloading a file from a server, so that the rest of the application won't be blocked.

Otherwise, if your run() method is so simple that it always finishes quickly enough without blocking, there's a very real question of whether you should spawn a thread at all. There's a nontrivial amount of overhead for the virtual machine in setting up and tearing down threads. If a thread is finishing in a small fraction of a second anyway, chances are it would finish even faster if you used a simple method call rather than a separate thread.

Thread Pools and Executors

Adding multiple threads to a program dramatically improves performance, especially for I/O-bound programs such as most network programs. However, threads are not without overhead of their own. Starting a thread and cleaning up after a thread that has died takes a noticeable amount of work from the virtual machine, especially if a program spawns hundreds of threads—not an unusual occurrence for even a low- to medium-volume network server. Even if the threads finish quickly, this can overload the garbage collector or other parts of the VM and hurt performance, just like allocating thousands of any other kind of object every minute. Even more importantly, switching between running threads carries overhead. If the threads are blocking naturally—for instance, by waiting for data from the network—there's no real penalty to this; but if the threads are CPU-bound, then the total task may finish more quickly if you can avoid a lot of switching between threads. Finally, and most importantly, although threads help make more efficient use of a computer's limited CPU resources, there is still only a finite amount of resources to go around. Once you've spawned enough threads to use all the computer's available idle time, spawning more threads just wastes MIPS and memory on thread management.

The `Executors` class in `java.util.concurrent` makes it quite easy to set up thread pools. You simply submit each task as a `Runnable` object to the pool. You get back a `Future` object you can use to check on the progress of the task.

Let's look at an example. Suppose you want to gzip every file in the current directory using a `java.util.zip.GZIPOutputStream`. This is a filter stream that compresses all the data it writes.

On the one hand, this is an I/O-heavy operation because all the files have to be read and written. On the other hand, data compression is a very CPU-intensive operation, so you don't want too many threads running at once. This is a good opportunity to use a thread pool. Each client thread will compress files while the main program will determine which files to compress. In this example, the main program is likely to significantly outpace the compressing threads because all it has to do is list the files in a directory. Therefore, it's not out of the question to fill the pool first, then start the threads that compress the files in the pool. However, to make this example as general as possible, you'll allow the main program to run in parallel with the zipping threads.

Example 3-13 shows the `GZipRunnable` class. It has a single field that identifies the file to compress. The `run()` method compresses this file and returns.

Example 3-13. The GZipRunnable class

```
import java.io.*;
import java.util.zip.*;

public class GZipRunnable implements Runnable {

  private final File input;

  public GZipRunnable(File input) {
    this.input = input;
  }

  @Override
  public void run() {
```

```
    // don't compress an already compressed file
    if (!input.getName().endsWith(".gz")) {
      File output = new File(input.getParent(), input.getName() + ".gz");
      if (!output.exists()) { // Don't overwrite an existing file
        try ( // with resources; requires Java 7
          InputStream in = new BufferedInputStream(new FileInputStream(input));
        OutputStream out = new BufferedOutputStream(
          new GZIPOutputStream(
            new FileOutputStream(output)));
        ) {
            int b;
            while ((b = in.read()) != -1) out.write(b);
            out.flush();
        } catch (IOException ex) {
          System.err.println(ex);
        }
      }
    }
  }
}
```

Notice the use of Java 7's try-with-resources statement in GZipRunnable. Both the input and output stream are declared at the beginning of the try block and automatically closed at the end of the try block.

Also notice the buffering of both input and output. This is very important for performance in I/O-limited applications, and especially important in network programs. At worst, buffering has no impact on performance, while at best it can give you an order of magnitude speedup or more.

Example 3-14 is the main program. It constructs the pool with a fixed thread count of four, and iterates through all the files and directories listed on the command line. Each of those files and files in those directories is used to construct a GZipRunnable. This runnable is submitted to the pool for eventual processing by one of the four threads.

Example 3-14. The GZipThread user interface class

```
import java.io.*;
import java.util.concurrent.*;

public class GZipAllFiles {

  public final static int THREAD_COUNT = 4;

  public static void main(String[] args) {

    ExecutorService pool = Executors.newFixedThreadPool(THREAD_COUNT);

    for (String filename : args) {
      File f = new File(filename);
      if (f.exists()) {
```

```
        if (f.isDirectory()) {
          File[] files = f.listFiles();
          for (int i = 0; i < files.length; i++) {
            if (!files[i].isDirectory()) { // don't recurse directories
              Runnable task = new GZipRunnable(files[i]);
              pool.submit(task);
            }
          }
        } else {
          Runnable task = new GZipRunnable(f);
          pool.submit(task);
        }
      }
    }

    pool.shutdown();
  }
}
```

Once you have added all the files to the pool, you call pool.shutdown(). Chances are this happens while there's still work to be done. This method does not abort pending jobs. It simply notifies the pool that no further tasks will be added to its internal queue and that it should shut down once it has finished all pending work.

Shutting down like this is mostly atypical of the heavily threaded network programs you'll write because it does have such a definite ending point: the point at which all files are processed. Most network servers continue indefinitely until shut down through an administration interface. In those cases, you may want to invoke shutdownNow() instead to abort currently processing tasks and skip any pending tasks.

CHAPTER 4

Internet Addresses

Devices connected to the Internet are called *nodes*. Nodes that are computers are called *hosts*. Each node or host is identified by at least one unique number called an Internet address or an IP address. Most current IP addresses are 4-byte-long IPv4 addresses. However, a small but growing number of IP addresses are 16-byte-long IPv6 addresses. (4 and 6 refer to the version of the Internet Protocol, not the number of the bytes in the address.) Both IPv4 and IPv6 addresses are ordered sequences of bytes, like an array. They aren't numbers, and they aren't ordered in any predictable or useful sense.

An IPv4 address is normally written as four unsigned bytes, each ranging from 0 to 255, with the most significant byte first. Bytes are separated by periods for the convenience of human eyes. For example, the address for *login.ibiblio.org* is 152.19.134.132. This is called the *dotted quad* format.

An IPv6 address is normally written as eight blocks of four hexadecimal digits separated by colons. For example, at the time of this writing, the address of *www.hamiltonweather.tk* is *2400:cb00:2048:0001:0000:0000:6ca2:c665*. Leading zeros do not need to be written. Therefore, the address of *www.hamiltonweather.tk* can be written as *2400:cb00:2048:1:0:0:6ca2:c665*. A double colon, at most one of which may appear in any address, indicates multiple zero blocks. For example, the address *2001:4860:4860:0000:0000:0000:0000:8888* can be written more compactly as *2001:4860:4860::8888*. In mixed networks of IPv6 and IPv4, the last four bytes of the IPv6 address are sometimes written as an IPv4 dotted quad address. For example, *FEDC:BA98:7654:3210:FEDC:BA98:7654:3210* could instead be written as *FEDC:BA98:7654:3210:FEDC:BA98:118.84.50.16*.

IP addresses are great for computers, but they are a problem for humans, who have a hard time remembering long numbers. In the 1950s, G. A. Miller discovered that most people could remember about seven digits per number; some can remember as many as nine, while others remember as few as five. For more information on this, see "The Magical Number Seven, Plus or Minus Two: Some Limits on Our Capacity for Processing Information," in the *Psychological Review*, Vol. 63, pp. 81–97. This is why phone numbers are broken into three- and four-digit pieces with three-digit area codes. Obviously, an IP address, which can have as many as 12 decimal digits, is beyond the capacity of most humans to remember. I can remember about two IP addresses, and then only if I use both daily and the second is on the same subnet as the first.

To avoid the need to carry around Rolodexes full of IP addresses, the Internet's designers invented the Domain Name System (DNS). DNS associates hostnames that humans can remember (such as *login.ibiblio.org*) with IP addresses that computers can remember (such as *152.19.134.132*). Servers usually have at least one hostname. Clients often have a hostname, but often don't, especially if their IP address is dynamically assigned at startup.

 Colloquially, people often use "Internet address" to mean a hostname (or even an email address, or full URL). In a book about network programming, it is crucial to be precise about addresses and hostnames. In this book, an address is always a numeric IP address, never a human-readable hostname.

Some machines have multiple names. For instance, *www.beand.com* and *xom.nu* are really the same Linux box. The name *www.beand.com* really refers to a website rather than a particular machine. In the past, when this website moved from one machine to another, the name was reassigned to the new machine so it always pointed to the site's current server. This way, URLs around the Web don't need to be updated just because the site has moved to a new host. Some common names like *www* and *news* are often aliases for the machines providing those services. For example, *news.speakeasy.net* is an alias for my ISP's news server. Because the server may change over time, the alias can move with the service.

On occasion, one name maps to multiple IP addresses. It is then the responsibility of the DNS server to randomly choose machines to respond to each request. This feature is most frequently used for very high-traffic websites, where it splits the load across multiple systems. For instance, *www.oreilly.com* is actually two machines, one at 208.201.239.100 and one at 208.201.239.101.

Every computer connected to the Internet should have access to a machine called a *domain name server*, generally a Unix box running special DNS software that knows the mappings between different hostnames and IP addresses. Most domain name servers only know the addresses of the hosts on their local network, plus the addresses of a few domain name servers at other sites. If a client asks for the address of a machine outside the local domain, the local domain name server asks a domain name server at the remote location and relays the answer to the requester.

Most of the time, you can use hostnames and let DNS handle the translation to IP addresses. As long as you can connect to a domain name server, you don't need to worry about the details of how names and addresses are passed between your machine, the local domain name server, and the rest of the Internet. However, you will need access to at least one domain name server to use the examples in this chapter and most of the rest of this book. These programs will not work on a standalone computer. Your machine must be connected to the Internet.

The InetAddress Class

The `java.net.InetAddress` class is Java's high-level representation of an IP address, both IPv4 and IPv6. It is used by most of the other networking classes, including `Socket`, `ServerSocket`, `URL`, `DatagramSocket`, `DatagramPacket`, and more. Usually, it includes both a hostname and an IP address.

Creating New InetAddress Objects

There are no public constructors in the `InetAddress` class. Instead, `InetAddress` has static factory methods that connect to a DNS server to resolve a hostname. The most common is `InetAddress.getByName()`. For example, this is how you look up *www.oreilly.com*:

```
InetAddress address = InetAddress.getByName("www.oreilly.com");
```

This method does not merely set a private `String` field in the `InetAddress` class. It actually makes a connection to the local DNS server to look up the name and the numeric address. (If you've looked up this host previously, the information may be cached locally, in which case a network connection is not required.) If the DNS server can't find the address, this method throws an `UnknownHostException`, a subclass of `IOException`.

Example 4-1 shows a complete program that creates an `InetAddress` object for *www.oreilly.com* including all the necessary imports and exception handling.

Example 4-1. A program that prints the address of www.oreilly.com

```
import java.net.*;

public class OReillyByName {

  public static void main (String[] args) {
    try {
      InetAddress address = InetAddress.getByName("www.oreilly.com");
      System.out.println(address);
    } catch (UnknownHostException ex) {
      System.out.println("Could not find www.oreilly.com");
    }
```

```
    }
}
```

Here's the result:

```
% java OReillyByName
www.oreilly.com/208.201.239.36
```

You can also do a reverse lookup by IP address. For example, if you want the hostname for the address 208.201.239.100, pass the dotted quad address to `InetAddress.getByName()`:

```
InetAddress address = InetAddress.getByName("208.201.239.100");
System.out.println(address.getHostName());
```

If the address you look up does not have a hostname, `getHostName()` simply returns the dotted quad address you supplied.

I mentioned earlier that *www.oreilly.com* actually has two addresses. Which one `getHostName()` returns is indeterminate. If, for some reason, you need all the addresses of a host, call `getAllByName()` instead, which returns an array:

```
try {
  InetAddress[] addresses = InetAddress.getAllByName("www.oreilly.com");
  for (InetAddress address : addresses) {
    System.out.println(address);
  }
} catch (UnknownHostException ex) {
  System.out.println("Could not find www.oreilly.com");
}
```

Finally, the `getLocalHost()` method returns an `InetAddress` object for the host on which your code is running:

```
InetAddress me = InetAddress.getLocalHost();
```

This method tries to connect to DNS to get a real hostname and IP address such as "elharo.laptop.corp.com" and "192.1.254.68"; but if that fails it may return the *loopback* address instead. This is the hostname "localhost" and the dotted quad address "127.0.0.1".

Example 4-2 prints the address of the machine it's run on.

Example 4-2. Find the address of the local machine

```
import java.net.*;

public class MyAddress {

  public static void main (String[] args) {
    try {
      InetAddress address = InetAddress.getLocalHost();
      System.out.println(address);
```

```
    } catch (UnknownHostException ex) {
      System.out.println("Could not find this computer's address.");
    }
  }
}
```

Here's the output; I ran the program on *titan.oit.unc.edu*:

```
% java MyAddress
titan.oit.unc.edu/152.2.22.14
```

Whether you see a fully qualified name like *titan.oit.unc.edu* or a partial name like *titan* depends on what the local DNS server returns for hosts in the local domain. If you're not connected to the Internet, and the system does not have a fixed IP address or domain name, you'll probably see *localhost* as the domain name and 127.0.0.1 as the IP address.

If you know a numeric address, you can create an InetAddress object from that address without talking to DNS using InetAddress.getByAddress(). This method can create addresses for hosts that do not exist or cannot be resolved:

```
public static InetAddress getByAddress(byte[] addr) throws UnknownHostException
public static InetAddress getByAddress(String hostname, byte[] addr)
    throws UnknownHostException
```

The first InetAddress.getByAddress() factory method creates an InetAddress object with an IP address and no hostname. The second InetAddress.getByAddress() method creates an InetAddress object with an IP address and a hostname. For example, this code fragment makes an InetAddress for 107.23.216.196:

```
byte[] address = {107, 23, (byte) 216, (byte) 196};
InetAddress lessWrong = InetAddress.getByAddress(address);
InetAddress lessWrongWithname = InetAddress.getByAddress(
    "lesswrong.com", address);
```

Note that it had to cast the two large values to bytes.

Unlike the other factory methods, these two methods make no guarantees that such a host exists or that the hostname is correctly mapped to the IP address. They throw an UnknownHostException only if a byte array of an illegal size (neither 4 nor 16 bytes long) is passed as the address argument. This could be useful if a domain name server is not available or might have inaccurate information. For example, none of the computers, printers, or routers in my basement area network are registered with any DNS server. Because I can never remember which addresses I've assigned to which systems, I wrote a simple program that attempts to connect to all 254 possible local addresses in turn to see which ones are active. (This only took me about 10 times as long as writing down all the addresses on a piece of paper.)

Caching

Because DNS lookups can be relatively expensive (on the order of several seconds for a request that has to go through several intermediate servers, or one that's trying to resolve an unreachable host) the InetAddress class caches the results of lookups. Once it has the address of a given host, it won't look it up again, even if you create a new InetAddress object for the same host. As long as IP addresses don't change while your program is running, this is not a problem.

Negative results (host not found errors) are slightly more problematic. It's not uncommon for an initial attempt to resolve a host to fail, but the immediately following one to succeed. The first attempt timed out while the information was still in transit from the remote DNS server. Then the address arrived at the local server and was immediately available for the next request. For this reason, Java only caches unsuccessful DNS queries for 10 seconds.

These times can be controlled by the system properties networkaddress.cache.ttl and networkaddress.cache.negative.ttl. The first of those, networkad dress.cache.ttl, specifies the number of seconds a successful DNS lookup will remain in Java's cache. networkaddress.cache.negative.ttl is the number of seconds an unsuccessful lookup will be cached. Attempting to look up the same host again within these limits will only return the same value. Negative 1 is interpreted as "never expire."

Besides local caching inside the InetAddress class, the local host, the local domain name server, and other DNS servers elsewhere on the Internet also cache the results of various queries. Java provides no way to control this. As a result, it may take several hours for the information about an IP address change to propagate across the Internet. In the meantime, your program may encounter various exceptions, including UnknownHos tException, NoRouteToHostException, and ConnectException, depending on the changes made to the DNS.

Lookups by IP address

When you call getByName() with an IP address string as an argument, it creates an InetAddress object for the requested IP address without checking with DNS. This means it's possible to create InetAddress objects for hosts that don't really exist and that you can't connect to. The hostname of an InetAddress object created from a string containing an IP address is initially set to that string. A DNS lookup for the actual hostname is only performed when the hostname is requested, either explicitly via a getHostName() or implicitly by toString(). That's how *www.oreilly.com* was determined from the dotted quad address 208.201.239.37. If, at the time the hostname is requested and a DNS lookup is finally performed, the host with the specified IP address can't be found, the hostname remains the original dotted quad string. However, no UnknownHostException is thrown.

Hostnames are much more stable than IP addresses. Some services have lived at the same hostname for years, but have switched IP addresses several times. If you have a choice between using a hostname such as *www.oreilly.com* or an IP address such as 208.201.239.37, always choose the hostname. Use an IP address only when a hostname is not available.

Security issues

Creating a new `InetAddress` object from a hostname is considered a potentially insecure operation because it requires a DNS lookup. An untrusted applet under the control of the default security manager will only be allowed to get the IP address of the host it came from (its *codebase*) and possibly the local host. Untrusted code is not allowed to create an `InetAddress` object from any other hostname. This is true whether the code uses the `InetAddress.getByName()` method, the `InetAddress.getAllByName()` method, the `InetAddress.getLocalHost()` method, or something else. Untrusted code can construct an `InetAddress` object from the string form of the IP address, though it will not perform DNS lookups for such addresses.

Untrusted code is not allowed to perform arbitrary DNS lookups for third-party hosts because of the prohibition against making network connections to hosts other than the codebase. Arbitrary DNS lookups would open a covert channel by which a program could talk to third-party hosts. For instance, suppose an applet downloaded from *www.bigisp.com* wants to send the message "macfaq.dialup.cloud9.net is vulnerable" to *crackersinc.com*. All it has to do is request DNS information for *macfaq.dial-up.cloud9.net.is.vulnerable.crackersinc.com*. To resolve that hostname, the applet would contact the local DNS server. The local DNS server would contact the DNS server at *crackersinc.com*. Even though these hosts don't exist, the cracker can inspect the DNS error log for *crackersinc.com* to retrieve the message. This scheme could be considerably more sophisticated with compression, error correction, encryption, custom DNS servers that email the messages to a fourth site, and more, but this version is good enough for a proof of concept. Arbitrary DNS lookups are prohibited because arbitrary DNS lookups leak information.

Untrusted code is allowed to call `InetAddress.getLocalHost()`. However, in such an environment, `getLocalHost()` always returns a hostname of *localhost/127.0.0.1*. The reason for prohibiting the applet from finding out the true hostname and address is that the computer on which the applet is running may be deliberately hidden behind a firewall. In this case, an applet should not be a channel for information the web server doesn't already have.

Like all security checks, prohibitions against DNS resolutions can be relaxed for trusted code. The specific `SecurityManager` method used to test whether a host can be resolved is `checkConnect()`:

```
public void checkConnect(String hostname, int port)
```

When the `port` argument is –1, this method checks whether DNS may be invoked to resolve the specified host. (If the `port` argument is greater than –1, this method checks whether a connection to the named host on the specified port is allowed.) The `host` argument may be either a hostname such as *www.oreilly.com*, a dotted quad IP address such as *208.201.239.37*, or a hexadecimal IPv6 address such as *FEDC::DC:0:7076:10*.

Getter Methods

The `InetAddress` class contains four getter methods that return the hostname as a string and the IP address as both a string and a byte array:

```
public String getHostName()
public String getCanonicalHostName()
public byte[] getAddress()
public String getHostAddress()
```

There are no corresponding `setHostName()` and `setAddress()` methods, which means that packages outside of `java.net` can't change an `InetAddress` object's fields behind its back. This makes `InetAddress` immutable and thus thread safe.

The `getHostName()` method returns a `String` that contains the name of the host with the IP address represented by this `InetAddress` object. If the machine in question doesn't have a hostname or if the security manager prevents the name from being determined, a dotted quad format of the numeric IP address is returned. For example:

```
InetAddress machine = InetAddress.getLocalHost();
String localhost = machine.getHostName();
```

The `getCanonicalHostName()` method is similar, but it's a bit more aggressive about contacting DNS. `getHostName()` will only call DNS if it doesn't think it already knows the hostname. `getCanonicalHostName()` calls DNS if it can, and may replace the existing cached hostname. For example:

```
InetAddress machine = InetAddress.getLocalHost();
String localhost = machine.getCanonicalHostName();
```

The `getCanonicalHostName()` method is particularly useful when you're starting with a dotted quad IP address rather than the hostname. Example 4-3 converts the dotted quad address *208.201.239.37* into a hostname by using `InetAddress.getByName()` and then applying `getCanonicalHostName()` on the resulting object.

Example 4-3. Given the address, find the hostname

```
import java.net.*;

public class ReverseTest {

  public static void main (String[] args) throws UnknownHostException {
    InetAddress ia = InetAddress.getByName("208.201.239.100");
```

```
    System.out.println(ia.getCanonicalHostName());
  }
}
```

Here's the result:

```
% java ReverseTest
oreilly.com
```

The getHostAddress() method returns a string containing the dotted quad format of the IP address. Example 4-4 uses this method to print the IP address of the local machine in the customary format.

Example 4-4. Find the IP address of the local machine

```
import java.net.*;

public class MyAddress {

  public static void main(String[] args) {
    try {
      InetAddress me = InetAddress.getLocalHost();
      String dottedQuad = me.getHostAddress();
      System.out.println("My address is " + dottedQuad);
    } catch (UnknownHostException ex) {
      System.out.println("I'm sorry. I don't know my own address.");
    }
  }
}
```

Here's the result:

```
% java MyAddress
My address is 152.2.22.14.
```

Of course, the exact output depends on where the program is run.

If you want to know the IP address of a machine (and you rarely do), then use the getAddress() method, which returns an IP address as an array of bytes in network byte order. The most significant byte (i.e., the first byte in the address's dotted quad form) is the first byte in the array, or element zero. To be ready for IPv6 addresses, try not to assume anything about the length of this array. If you need to know the length of the array, use the array's length field:

```
InetAddress me = InetAddress.getLocalHost();
byte[] address = me.getAddress();
```

The bytes returned are unsigned, which poses a problem. Unlike C, Java doesn't have an unsigned byte primitive data type. Bytes with values higher than 127 are treated as negative numbers. Therefore, if you want to do anything with the bytes returned by getAddress(), you need to promote the bytes to ints and make appropriate adjustments. Here's one way to do it:

```
int unsignedByte = signedByte < 0 ? signedByte + 256 : signedByte;
```

Here, signedByte may be either positive or negative. The conditional operator ? tests whether signedByte is negative. If it is, 256 is added to signedByte to make it positive. Otherwise, it's left alone. signedByte is automatically promoted to an int before the addition is performed, so wraparound is not a problem.

One reason to look at the raw bytes of an IP address is to determine the type of the address. Test the number of bytes in the array returned by getAddress() to determine whether you're dealing with an IPv4 or IPv6 address. Example 4-5 demonstrates.

Example 4-5. Determining whether an IP address is v4 or v6

```java
import java.net.*;

public class AddressTests {

  public static int getVersion(InetAddress ia) {
    byte[] address = ia.getAddress();
    if (address.length == 4) return 4;
    else if (address.length == 16) return 6;
    else return -1;
  }
}
```

Address Types

Some IP addresses and some patterns of addresses have special meanings. For instance, I've already mentioned that 127.0.0.1 is the local loopback address. IPv4 addresses in the range 224.0.0.0 to 239.255.255.255 are multicast addresses that send to several sub-scribed hosts at once. Java includes 10 methods for testing whether an InetAddress object meets any of these criteria:

```java
public boolean isAnyLocalAddress()
public boolean isLoopbackAddress()
public boolean isLinkLocalAddress()
public boolean isSiteLocalAddress()
public boolean isMulticastAddress()
public boolean isMCGlobal()
public boolean isMCNodeLocal()
public boolean isMCLinkLocal()
public boolean isMCSiteLocal()
public boolean isMCOrgLocal()
```

The isAnyLocalAddress() method returns true if the address is a *wildcard address*, false otherwise. A wildcard address matches any address of the local system. This is important if the system has multiple network interfaces, as might be the case on a system with multiple Ethernet cards or an Ethernet card and an 802.11 WiFi interface. In IPv4, the wildcard address is 0.0.0.0. In IPv6, this address is 0:0:0:0:0:0:0:0 (a.k.a. ::).

The `isLoopbackAddress()` method returns true if the address is the loopback address, false otherwise. The loopback address connects to the same computer directly in the IP layer without using any physical hardware. Thus, connecting to the loopback address enables tests to bypass potentially buggy or nonexistent Ethernet, PPP, and other drivers, helping to isolate problems. Connecting to the loopback address is not the same as connecting to the system's normal IP address from the same system. In IPv4, this address is 127.0.0.1. In IPv6, this address is 0:0:0:0:0:0:0:1 (a.k.a. ::1).

The `isLinkLocalAddress()` method returns true if the address is an IPv6 link-local address, false otherwise. This is an address used to help IPv6 networks self-configure, much like DHCP on IPv4 networks but without necessarily using a server. Routers do not forward packets addressed to a link-local address beyond the local subnet. All link-local addresses begin with the eight bytes FE80:0000:0000:0000. The next eight bytes are filled with a local address, often copied from the Ethernet MAC address assigned by the Ethernet card manufacturer.

The `isSiteLocalAddress()` method returns true if the address is an IPv6 site-local address, false otherwise. Site-local addresses are similar to link-local addresses except that they may be forwarded by routers within a site or campus but should not be forwarded beyond that site. Site-local addresses begin with the eight bytes FEC0:0000:0000:0000. The next eight bytes are filled with a local address, often copied from the Ethernet MAC address assigned by the Ethernet card manufacturer.

The `isMulticastAddress()` method returns true if the address is a multicast address, false otherwise. Multicasting broadcasts content to all subscribed computers rather than to one particular computer. In IPv4, multicast addresses all fall in the range 224.0.0.0 to 239.255.255.255. In IPv6, they all begin with byte FF. Multicasting will be discussed in Chapter 13.

The `isMCGlobal()` method returns true if the address is a global multicast address, false otherwise. A global multicast address may have subscribers around the world. All multicast addresses begin with FF. In IPv6, global multicast addresses begin with FF0E or FF1E depending on whether the multicast address is a well known permanently assigned address or a transient address. In IPv4, all multicast addresses have global scope, at least as far as this method is concerned. As you'll see in Chapter 13, IPv4 uses time-to-live (TTL) values to control scope rather than addressing.

The `isMCOrgLocal()` method returns true if the address is an organization-wide multicast address, false otherwise. An organization-wide multicast address may have subscribers within all the sites of a company or organization, but not outside that organization. Organization multicast addresses begin with FF08 or FF18, depending on whether the multicast address is a well known permanently assigned address or a transient address.

The isMCSiteLocal() method returns true if the address is a site-wide multicast address, false otherwise. Packets addressed to a site-wide address will only be transmitted within their local site. Site-wide multicast addresses begin with FF05 or FF15, depending on whether the multicast address is a well known permanently assigned address or a transient address.

The isMCLinkLocal() method returns true if the address is a subnet-wide multicast address, false otherwise. Packets addressed to a link-local address will only be transmitted within their own subnet. Link-local multicast addresses begin with FF02 or FF12, depending on whether the multicast address is a well known permanently assigned address or a transient address.

The isMCNodeLocal() method returns true if the address is an interface-local multicast address, false otherwise. Packets addressed to an interface-local address are not sent beyond the network interface from which they originate, not even to a different network interface on the same node. This is primarily useful for network debugging and testing. Interface-local multicast addresses begin with the two bytes FF01 or FF11, depending on whether the multicast address is a well known permanently assigned address or a transient address.

 The method name is out of sync with current terminology. Earlier drafts of the IPv6 protocol called this type of address "node-local," hence the name "isMCNodeLocal." The IPNG working group actually changed the name before this method was added to the JDK, but Sun didn't get the memo in time.

Example 4-6 is a simple program to test the nature of an address entered from the command line using these 10 methods.

Example 4-6. Testing the characteristics of an IP address

```java
import java.net.*;

public class IPCharacteristics {

  public static void main(String[] args) {

    try {
      InetAddress address = InetAddress.getByName(args[0]);

      if (address.isAnyLocalAddress()) {
        System.out.println(address + " is a wildcard address.");
      }
      if (address.isLoopbackAddress()) {
        System.out.println(address + " is loopback address.");
      }
```

```
    if (address.isLinkLocalAddress()) {
      System.out.println(address + " is a link-local address.");
    } else if (address.isSiteLocalAddress()) {
      System.out.println(address + " is a site-local address.");
    } else {
      System.out.println(address + " is a global address.");
    }

    if (address.isMulticastAddress()) {
      if (address.isMCGlobal()) {
        System.out.println(address + " is a global multicast address.");
      } else if (address.isMCOrgLocal()) {
        System.out.println(address
          + " is an organization wide multicast address.");
      } else if (address.isMCSiteLocal()) {
        System.out.println(address + " is a site wide multicast
                            address.");
      } else if (address.isMCLinkLocal()) {
        System.out.println(address + " is a subnet wide multicast
                            address.");
      } else if (address.isMCNodeLocal()) {
        System.out.println(address
          + " is an interface-local multicast address.");
      } else {
        System.out.println(address + " is an unknown multicast
                            address type.");
      }
    } else {
      System.out.println(address + " is a unicast address.");
    }
  } catch (UnknownHostException ex) {
    System.err.println("Could not resolve " + args[0]);
  }
 }
}
```

Here's the output from an IPv4 and IPv6 address:

```
$ java  IPCharacteristics 127.0.0.1
/127.0.0.1 is loopback address.
/127.0.0.1 is a global address.
/127.0.0.1 is a unicast address.
$ java  IPCharacteristics 192.168.254.32
/192.168.254.32 is a site-local address.
/192.168.254.32 is a unicast address.
$ java  IPCharacteristics www.oreilly.com
www.oreilly.com/208.201.239.37 is a global address.
www.oreilly.com/208.201.239.37 is a unicast address.
$ java  IPCharacteristics 224.0.2.1
/224.0.2.1 is a global address.
/224.0.2.1 is a global multicast address.
$ java  IPCharacteristics FF01:0:0:0:0:0:0:1
/ff01:0:0:0:0:0:0:1 is a global address.
```

```
/ff01:0:0:0:0:0:0:1 is an interface-local multicast address.
$ java  IPCharacteristics FF05:0:0:0:0:0:0:101
/ff05:0:0:0:0:0:0:101 is a global address.
/ff05:0:0:0:0:0:0:101 is a site wide multicast address.
$ java  IPCharacteristics 0::1
/0:0:0:0:0:0:0:1 is loopback address.
/0:0:0:0:0:0:0:1 is a global address.
/0:0:0:0:0:0:0:1 is a unicast address.
```

Testing Reachability

The InetAddress class has two isReachable() methods that test whether a particular node is reachable from the current host (i.e., whether a network connection can be made). Connections can be blocked for many reasons, including firewalls, proxy servers, misbehaving routers, and broken cables, or simply because the remote host is not turned on when you try to connect.

```
public boolean isReachable(int timeout) throws IOException
public boolean isReachable(NetworkInterface interface, int ttl, int timeout)
    throws IOException
```

These methods attempt to use traceroute (more specifically, ICMP echo requests) to find out if the specified address is reachable. If the host responds within timeout milliseconds, the methods return true; otherwise, they return false. An IOException will be thrown if there's a network error. The second variant also lets you specify the local network interface the connection is made from and the "time-to-live" (the maximum number of network hops the connection will attempt before being discarded).

Object Methods

Like every other class, java.net.InetAddress inherits from java.lang.Object. Thus, it has access to all the methods of that class. It overrides three methods to provide more specialized behavior:

```
public boolean equals(Object o)
public int hashCode()
public String toString()
```

An object is equal to an InetAddress object only if it is itself an instance of the InetAddress class and it has the same IP address. It does not need to have the same hostname. Thus, an InetAddress object for *www.ibiblio.org* is equal to an InetAddress object for *www.cafeaulait.org* because both names refer to the same IP address. Example 4-7 creates InetAddress objects for *www.ibiblio.org* and *helios.ibiblio.org* and then tells you whether they're the same machine.

Example 4-7. Are www.ibiblio.org and helios.ibiblio.org the same?

```java
import java.net.*;

public class IBiblioAliases {

  public static void main (String args[]) {
    try {
      InetAddress ibiblio = InetAddress.getByName("www.ibiblio.org");
      InetAddress helios = InetAddress.getByName("helios.ibiblio.org");
      if (ibiblio.equals(helios)) {
        System.out.println
            ("www.ibiblio.org is the same as helios.ibiblio.org");
      } else {
        System.out.println
            ("www.ibiblio.org is not the same as helios.ibiblio.org");
      }
    } catch (UnknownHostException ex) {
      System.out.println("Host lookup failed.");
    }
  }
}
```

When you run this program, you discover:

```
% java IBiblioAliases
www.ibiblio.org is the same as helios.ibiblio.org
```

The hashCode() method is consistent with the equals() method. The int that hash Code() returns is calculated solely from the IP address. It does not take the hostname into account. If two InetAddress objects have the same address, then they have the same hash code, even if their hostnames are different.

Like all good classes, java.net.InetAddress has a toString() method that returns a short text representation of the object. Example 4-1 and Example 4-2 implicitly called this method when passing InetAddress objects to System.out.println(). As you saw, the string produced by toString() has the form:

```
hostname/dotted quad address
```

Not all InetAddress objects have hostnames. If one doesn't, the dotted quad address is substituted in Java 1.3 and earlier. In Java 1.4 and later, the hostname is set to the empty string.

Inet4Address and Inet6Address

Java uses two classes, Inet4Address and Inet6Address, in order to distinguish IPv4 addresses from IPv6 addresses:

```
public final class Inet4Address extends InetAddress
public final class Inet6Address extends InetAddress
```

Most of the time, you really shouldn't be concerned with whether an address is an IPv4 or IPv6 address. In the application layer where Java programs reside, you simply don't need to know this (and even if you do need to know, it's quicker to check the size of the byte array returned by `getAddress()` than to use `instanceof` to test which subclass you have). `Inet4Address` overrides several of the methods in `InetAddress` but doesn't change their behavior in any public way. `Inet6Address` is similar, but it does add one new method not present in the superclass, `isIPv4CompatibleAddress()`:

```
public boolean isIPv4CompatibleAddress()
```

This method returns true if and only if the address is essentially an IPv4 address stuffed into an IPv6 container—which means only the last four bytes are nonzero. That is, the address has the form *0:0:0:0:0:0:xxxx*. If this is the case, you can pull off the last four bytes from the array returned by `getBytes()` and use this data to create an `Inet4Address` instead. However, you rarely need to do this.

The NetworkInterface Class

The `NetworkInterface` class represents a local IP address. This can either be a physical interface such as an additional Ethernet card (common on firewalls and routers) or it can be a virtual interface bound to the same physical hardware as the machine's other IP addresses. The `NetworkInterface` class provides methods to enumerate all the local addresses, regardless of interface, and to create `InetAddress` objects from them. These `InetAddress` objects can then be used to create sockets, server sockets, and so forth.

Factory Methods

Because `NetworkInterface` objects represent physical hardware and virtual addresses, they cannot be constructed arbitrarily. As with the `InetAddress` class, there are static factory methods that return the `NetworkInterface` object associated with a particular network interface. You can ask for a `NetworkInterface` by IP address, by name, or by enumeration.

public static NetworkInterface getByName(String name) throws SocketException

The `getByName()` method returns a `NetworkInterface` object representing the network interface with the particular name. If there's no interface with that name, it returns null. If the underlying network stack encounters a problem while locating the relevant network interface, a `SocketException` is thrown, but this isn't too likely to happen.

The format of the names is platform dependent. On a typical Unix system, the Ethernet interface names have the form eth0, eth1, and so forth. The local loopback address is probably named something like "lo". On Windows, the names are strings like "CE31" and "ELX100" that are derived from the name of the vendor and model of hardware on that particular network interface. For example, this code fragment attempts to find the primary Ethernet interface on a Unix system:

```
try {
  NetworkInterface ni = NetworkInterface.getByName("eth0");
  if (ni == null) {
    System.err.println("No such interface:  eth0");
  }
} catch (SocketException ex) {
  System.err.println("Could not list sockets.");
}
```

public static NetworkInterface getByInetAddress(InetAddress address) throws SocketException

The getByInetAddress() method returns a NetworkInterface object representing the network interface bound to the specified IP address. If no network interface is bound to that IP address on the local host, it returns null. If anything goes wrong, it throws a SocketException. For example, this code fragment finds the network interface for the local loopback address:

```
try {
  InetAddress local = InetAddress.getByName("127.0.0.1");
  NetworkInterface ni = NetworkInterface.getByInetAddress(local);
  if (ni == null) {
    System.err.println("That's weird. No local loopback address.");
  }
} catch (SocketException ex) {
  System.err.println("Could not list network interfaces." );
} catch (UnknownHostException ex) {
  System.err.println("That's weird. Could not lookup 127.0.0.1.");
}
```

public static Enumeration getNetworkInterfaces() throws SocketException

The getNetworkInterfaces() method returns a java.util.Enumeration listing all the network interfaces on the local host. Example 4-8 is a simple program to list all network interfaces on the local host:

Example 4-8. A program that lists all the network interfaces

```
import java.net.*;
import java.util.*;

public class InterfaceLister {

  public static void main(String[] args) throws SocketException {
    Enumeration<NetworkInterface> interfaces = NetworkInterface.
    getNetworkInterfaces();
    while (interfaces.hasMoreElements()) {
```

```
        NetworkInterface ni = interfaces.nextElement();
        System.out.println(ni);
    }
  }
}
```

Here's the result of running this on the IBiblio login server:

```
% java InterfaceLister
name:eth1 (eth1) index: 3 addresses:
/192.168.210.122;

name:eth0 (eth0) index: 2 addresses:
/152.2.210.122;

name:lo (lo) index: 1 addresses:
/127.0.0.1;
```

You can see that this host has two separate Ethernet cards plus the local loopback address. The Ethernet card with index 2 has the IP address 152.2.210.122. The Ethernet card with index 3 has the IP address 192.168.210.122. The loopback interface has address 127.0.0.1, as always.

Getter Methods

Once you have a NetworkInterface object, you can inquire about its IP address and name. This is pretty much the only thing you can do with these objects.

public Enumeration getInetAddresses()

A single network interface may be bound to more than one IP address. This situation isn't common these days, but it does happen. The getInetAddresses() method returns a java.util.Enumeration containing an InetAddress object for each IP address the interface is bound to. For example, this code fragment lists all the IP addresses for the eth0 interface:

```
NetworkInterface eth0 = NetworkInterrface.getByName("eth0");
Enumeration addresses = eth0.getInetAddresses();
while (addresses.hasMoreElements()) {
    System.out.println(addresses.nextElement());
}
```

public String getName()

The getName() method returns the name of a particular NetworkInterface object, such as eth0 or lo.

public String getDisplayName()

The getDisplayName() method allegedly returns a more human-friendly name for the particular NetworkInterface—something like "Ethernet Card 0." However, in my tests on Unix, it always returned the same string as getName(). On Windows, you may see slightly friendlier names such as "Local Area Connection" or "Local Area Connection 2."

Some Useful Programs

You now know everything there is to know about the java.net.InetAddress class. The tools in this class alone let you write some genuinely useful programs. Here you'll look at two examples: one that queries your domain name server interactively and another that can improve the performance of your web server by processing logfiles offline.

SpamCheck

A number of services monitor spammers, and inform clients whether a host attempting to connect to them is a known spammer or not. These *real-time blackhole lists* need to respond to queries extremely quickly, and process a very high load. Thousands, maybe millions, of hosts query them repeatedly to find out whether an IP address attempting a connection is or is not a known spammer.

The nature of the problem requires that the response be fast, and ideally it should be cacheable. Furthermore, the load should be distributed across many servers, ideally ones located around the world. Although this could conceivably be done using a web server, SOAP, UDP, a custom protocol, or some other mechanism, this service is in fact cleverly implemented using DNS and DNS alone.

To find out if a certain IP address is a known spammer, reverse the bytes of the address, add the domain of the blackhole service, and look it up. If the address is found, it's a spammer. If it isn't, it's not. For instance, if you want to ask *sbl.spamhaus.org* if 207.87.34.17 is a spammer, you would look up the hostname *17.34.87.207.sbl.spamhaus.org*. (Note that despite the numeric component, this is a hostname ASCII string, not a dotted quad IP address.)

If the DNS query succeeds (and, more specifically, if it returns the address 127.0.0.2), then the host is known to be a spammer. If the lookup fails—that is, it throws an UnknownHostException—it isn't. Example 4-9 implements this check.

Example 4-9. SpamCheck

```
import java.net.*;

public class SpamCheck {

  public static final String BLACKHOLE = "sbl.spamhaus.org";
```

```
public static void main(String[] args) throws UnknownHostException {
    for (String arg: args) {
        if (isSpammer(arg)) {
            System.out.println(arg + " is a known spammer.");
        } else {
            System.out.println(arg + " appears legitimate.");
        }
    }
}

private static boolean isSpammer(String arg) {
    try {
        InetAddress address = InetAddress.getByName(arg);
        byte[] quad = address.getAddress();
        String query = BLACKHOLE;
        for (byte octet : quad) {
            int unsignedByte = octet < 0 ? octet + 256 : octet;
            query = unsignedByte + "." + query;
        }
        InetAddress.getByName(query);
        return true;
    } catch (UnknownHostException e) {
        return false;
    }
}
}
```

Here's some sample output:

```
$ java SpamCheck 207.34.56.23 125.12.32.4 130.130.130.130
207.34.56.23 appears legitimate.
125.12.32.4 appears legitimate.
130.130.130.130 appears legitimate.
```

If you use this technique, be careful to stay on top of changes to blackhole list policies and addresses. For obvious reasons, blackhole servers are frequent targets of DDOS and other attacks, so you want to be careful that if the blackhole server changes its address or simply stops responding to any queries, you don't begin blocking all traffic.

Further note that different blackhole lists can follow slightly different protocols. For example, a few lists return *127.0.0.1* for spamming IPs instead of *127.0.0.2*.

Processing Web Server Logfiles

Web server logs track the hosts that access a website. By default, the log reports the IP addresses of the sites that connect to the server. However, you can often get more information from the names of those sites than from their IP addresses. Most web servers have an option to store hostnames instead of IP addresses, but this can hurt performance because the server needs to make a DNS request for each hit. It is much more efficient to log the IP addresses and convert them to hostnames at a later time, when the server isn't busy or even on another machine completely. Example 4-10 is a program called Weblog that reads a web server logfile and prints each line with IP addresses converted to hostnames.

Most web servers have standardized on the common logfile format. A typical line in the common logfile format looks like this:

```
205.160.186.76 unknown - [17/Jun/2013:22:53:58 -0500]
                        "GET /bgs/greenbg.gif HTTP 1.0" 200 50
```

This line indicates that a web browser at IP address 205.160.186.76 requested the file */bgs/greenbg.gif* from this web server at 11:53 P.M (and 58 seconds) on June 17, 2013. The file was found (response code 200) and 50 bytes of data were successfully transferred to the browser.

The first field is the IP address or, if DNS resolution is turned on, the hostname from which the connection was made. This is followed by a space. Therefore, for our purposes, parsing the logfile is easy: everything before the first space is the IP address, and everything after it does not need to be changed.

The dotted quad format IP address is converted into a hostname using the usual methods of java.net.InetAddress. Example 4-10 shows the code.

Example 4-10. Process web server logfiles

```java
import java.io.*;
import java.net.*;

public class Weblog {

  public static void main(String[] args) {
    try (FileInputStream fin =  new FileInputStream(args[0]);
      Reader in = new InputStreamReader(fin);
      BufferedReader bin = new BufferedReader(in);) {

      for (String entry = bin.readLine();
        entry != null;
        entry = bin.readLine()) {
        // separate out the IP address
        int index = entry.indexOf(' ');
        String ip = entry.substring(0, index);
        String theRest = entry.substring(index);

        // Ask DNS for the hostname and print it out
        try {
          InetAddress address = InetAddress.getByName(ip);
          System.out.println(address.getHostName() + theRest);
        } catch (UnknownHostException ex) {
          System.err.println(entry);
        }
```

```
      }
    } catch (IOException ex) {
      System.out.println("Exception: " + ex);
    }
  }
}
```

The name of the file to be processed is passed to `Weblog` as the first argument on the command line. A `FileInputStream` `fin` is opened from this file and an `InputStream Reader` is chained to `fin`. This `InputStreamReader` is buffered by chaining it to an instance of the `BufferedReader` class. The file is processed line by line in a `for` loop.

Each pass through the loop places one line in the `String` variable `entry`. `entry` is then split into two substrings: `ip`, which contains everything before the first space, and `theRest`, which is everything from the first space to the end of the string. The position of the first space is determined by `entry.indexOf(" ")`. The substring `ip` is converted to an `InetAddress` object using `getByName()`. `getHostName()` then looks up the hostname. Finally, the hostname and everything else on the line (`theRest`) are printed on `System.out`. Output can be sent to a new file through the standard means for redirecting output.

`Weblog` is more efficient than you might expect. Most web browsers generate multiple logfile entries per page served, because there's an entry in the log not just for the page itself but for each graphic on the page. And many visitors request multiple pages while visiting a site. DNS lookups are expensive and it simply doesn't make sense to look up each site every time it appears in the logfile. The `InetAddress` class caches requested addresses. If the same address is requested again, it can be retrieved from the cache much more quickly than from DNS.

Nonetheless, this program could certainly be faster. In my initial tests, it took more than a second per log entry. (Exact numbers depend on the speed of your network connection, the speed of the local and remote DNS servers, and network congestion when the program is run.) The program spends a huge amount of time sitting and waiting for DNS requests to return. Of course, this is exactly the problem multithreading is designed to solve. One main thread can read the logfile and pass off individual entries to other threads for processing.

A thread pool is absolutely necessary here. Over the space of a few days, even low-volume web servers can generate a logfile with hundreds of thousands of lines. Trying to process such a logfile by spawning a new thread for each entry would rapidly bring even the strongest virtual machine to its knees, especially because the main thread can read logfile entries much faster than individual threads can resolve domain names and die. Consequently, reusing threads is essential. The number of threads is stored in a tunable parameter, `numberOfThreads`, so that it can be adjusted to fit the VM and network stack. (Launching too many simultaneous DNS requests can also cause problems.)

This program is now divided into two classes. The first class, LookupTask, shown in Example 4-11, is a Callable that parses a logfile entry, looks up a single address, and replaces that address with the corresponding hostname. This doesn't seem like a lot of work and CPU-wise, it isn't. However, because it involves a network connection, and possibly a hierarchical series of network connections between many different DNS servers, it has a lot of downtime that can be put to better use by other threads.

Example 4-11. LookupTask

```java
import java.net.*;
import java.util.concurrent.Callable;

public class LookupTask implements Callable<String> {

  private String line;

  public LookupTask(String line) {
    this.line = line;
  }

  @Override
  public String call() {
    try {
      // separate out the IP address
      int index = line.indexOf(' ');
      String address = line.substring(0, index);
      String theRest = line.substring(index);
      String hostname = InetAddress.getByName(address).getHostName();
      return hostname + " " + theRest;
    } catch (Exception ex) {
      return line;
    }
  }
}
```

The second class, PooledWeblog, shown in Example 4-12, contains the main() method that reads the file and creates one LookupTask per line. Each task is submitted to an executor that can run multiple (though not all) tasks in parallel and in sequence.

The Future that is returned from the submit() method is stored in a queue, along with the original line (in case something goes wrong in the asynchronous thread). A loop reads values out of the queue and prints them. This maintains the original order of the logfile.

Example 4-12. PooledWebLog

```java
import java.io.*;
import java.util.*;
import java.util.concurrent.*;

// Requires Java 7 for try-with-resources and multi-catch
```

```java
public class PooledWeblog {

  private final static int NUM_THREADS = 4;

  public static void main(String[] args) throws IOException {
    ExecutorService executor = Executors.newFixedThreadPool(NUM_THREADS);
    Queue<LogEntry> results = new LinkedList<LogEntry>();

    try (BufferedReader in = new BufferedReader(
      new InputStreamReader(new FileInputStream(args[0]), "UTF-8"));) {
      for (String entry = in.readLine(); entry != null; entry = in.readLine()) {
        LookupTask task = new LookupTask(entry);
        Future<String> future = executor.submit(task);
        LogEntry result = new LogEntry(entry, future);
        results.add(result);
      }
    }

    // Start printing the results. This blocks each time a result isn't ready.
    for (LogEntry result : results) {
      try {
        System.out.println(result.future.get());
      } catch (InterruptedException | ExecutionException ex) {
        System.out.println(result.original);
      }
    }

    executor.shutdown();
  }

  private static class LogEntry {
    String original;
    Future<String> future;

    LogEntry(String original, Future<String> future) {
      this.original = original;
      this.future = future;
    }
  }
}
```

Using threads like this lets the same logfiles be processed in parallel—a huge time savings. In my unscientific tests, the threaded version is 10 to 50 times faster than the sequential version. The tech editor ran the same test on a different system and only saw a factor of four improvement, but either way it's still a significant gain.

There's still one downside to this design. Although the queue of Callable tasks is much more efficient than spawning a thread for each logfile entry, logfiles can be huge and this program can still burn a lot of memory. To avoid this, you could put the output into a separate thread that shared the queue with the input thread. Because early entries could be processed and output while the input was still being parsed, the queue would not grow so large. This does, however, introduce another problem. You'd need a separate signal to tell you when the output was complete because an empty queue is no longer sufficient to prove the job is complete. The easiest way is simply to count the number of input lines and make sure it matches up to the number of output lines.

CHAPTER 5

URLs and URIs

In the last chapter, you learned how to address hosts on the Internet via host names and IP addresses. In this chapter, we increase the granularity by addressing resources, any number of which may reside on any given host.

HTML is a *hypertext* markup language because it includes a way to specify links to other documents identified by URLs. A URL unambiguously identifies the location of a resource on the Internet. A URL is the most common type of URI, or Uniform Resource Identifier. A URI can identify a resource by its network location, as in a URL, or by its name, number, or other characteristics.

The URL class is the simplest way for a Java program to locate and retrieve data from the network. You do not need to worry about the details of the protocol being used, or how to communicate with the server; you simply tell Java the URL and it gets the data for you.

URIs

A Uniform Resource Identifier (URI) is a string of characters in a particular syntax that identifies a resource. The resource identified may be a file on a server; but it may also be an email address, a news message, a book, a person's name, an Internet host, the current stock price of Oracle, or something else.

A resource is a thing that is identified by a URI. A URI is a string that identifies a resource. Yes, it is exactly that circular. Don't spend too much time worrying about what a resource is or isn't, because you'll never see one anyway. All you ever receive from a server is a *representation* of a resource which comes in the form of bytes. However a single resource may have different representations. For instance, *https://www.un.org/en/documents/udhr/* identifies the Universal Declaration of Human Rights; but there are *representations* of the declaration in plain text, XML, PDF, and other formats. There are also representations of this resource in English, French, Arabic, and many other languages.

Some of these representations may themselves be resources. For instance, *https://www.un.org/en/documents/udhr/* identifies specifically the English version of the Universal Declaration of Human Rights.

 One of the key principles of good web architecture is to be profligate with URIs. If anyone might want to address something or refer to something, give it a URI (and in practice a URL). Just because a resource is a part of another resource, or a collection of other resources, or a state of another resource at a particular time, doesn't mean it can't have its own URI. For instance, in an email service, every user, every message received, every message sent, every filtered view of the inbox, every contact, every filter rule, and every single page a user might ever look at should have a unique URI.

Although architecturally URIs are opaque strings, in practice it's useful to design them with human-readable substructure. For instance, *http://mail.example.com/* might be a particular mail server, *http://mail.example.com/johndoe* might be John Doe's mail box on that server, and *http://mail.example.com/johndoe?messageID=162977.1361.JavaMail.nobody%40meetup.com* might be a particular message in that mailbox.

The syntax of a URI is composed of a scheme and a scheme-specific part, separated by a colon, like this:

    scheme: scheme-specific-part

The syntax of the scheme-specific part depends on the scheme being used. Current schemes include:

data
    Base64-encoded data included directly in a link; see RFC 2397

file
    A file on a local disk

ftp
    An FTP server

http
    A World Wide Web server using the Hypertext Transfer Protocol

mailto
    An email address

magnet
    A resource available for download via peer-to-peer networks such as BitTorrent

telnet

    A connection to a Telnet-based service

urn

    A Uniform Resource Name

In addition, Java makes heavy use of nonstandard custom schemes such as *rmi*, *jar*, *jndi*, and *doc* for various purposes.

There is no specific syntax that applies to the scheme-specific parts of all URIs. However, many have a hierarchical form, like this:

```
//authority/path?query
```

The *authority* part of the URI names the authority responsible for resolving the rest of the URI. For instance, the URI *http://www.ietf.org/rfc/rfc3986.txt* has the scheme *http*, the authority *www.ietf.org*, and the path */rfc/rfc3986.txt* (initial slash included). This means the server at www.ietf.org is responsible for mapping the path */rfc/rfc3986.txt* to a resource. This URI does not have a query part. The URI *http://www.powells.com/cgi-bin/biblio?inkey=62-1565928709-0* has the scheme *http*, the authority *www.powells.com*, the path */cgi-bin/biblio*, and the query `inkey=62-1565928709-0`. The URI *urn:isbn:156592870* has the scheme *urn* but doesn't follow the hierarchical *//authority/ path?query* form for scheme-specific parts.

Although most current examples of URIs use an Internet host as an authority, future schemes may not. However, if the authority is an Internet host, optional usernames and ports may also be provided to make the authority more specific. For example, the URI *ftp://mp3:mp3@ci43198-a.ashvil1.nc.home.com:33/VanHalen-Jump.mp3* has the authority *mp3:mp3@ci43198-a.ashvil1.nc.home.com:33*. This authority has the username *mp3*, the password *mp3*, the host *ci43198-a.ashvil1.nc.home.com*, and the port *33*. It has the scheme *ftp* and the path */VanHalen-Jump.mp3*. (In most cases, including the password in the URI is a big security hole unless, as here, you really do want everyone in the universe to know the password.)

The path is a string that the authority can use to determine which resource is identified. Different authorities may interpret the same path to refer to different resources. For instance, the path */index.html* means one thing when the authority is *www.landover-baptist.org* and something very different when the authority is *www.churchofsatan.com*. The path may be hierarchical, in which case the individual parts are separated by forward slashes, and the . and .. operators are used to navigate the hierarchy. These are derived from the pathname syntax on the Unix operating systems where the Web and URLs were invented. They conveniently map to a filesystem stored on a Unix web server. However, there is no guarantee that the components of any particular path actually correspond to files or directories on any particular filesystem. For example, in the URI   *http://www.amazon.com/exec/obidos/ISBN%3D1565924851/cafeaulaitA/ 002-3777605-3043449*, all the pieces of the hierarchy are just used to pull information out of a database that's never stored in a filesystem. *ISBN%3D1565924851* selects the particular book from the database by its ISBN number, *cafeaulaitA* specifies who gets the referral fee if a purchase is made from this link, and *002-3777605-3043449* is a session key used to track the visitor's path through the site.

Some URIs aren't at all hierarchical, at least in the filesystem sense. For example, *snews:// secnews.netscape.com/netscape.devs-java* has a path of */netscape.devs-java*. Although there's some hierarchy to the newsgroup names indicated by the period between *netscape* and *devs-java*, it's not encoded as part of the URI.

The scheme part is composed of lowercase letters, digits, and the plus sign, period, and hyphen. The other three parts of a typical URI (authority, path, and query) should each be composed of the ASCII alphanumeric characters (i.e., the letters A–Z, a–z, and the digits 0–9). In addition, the punctuation characters - _ . ! and ~ may also be used. Delimiters such as / ? & and = may be used for their predefined purposes. All other characters, including non-ASCII alphanumerics such as á and ζ as well as delimiters not being used as delimiters should be escaped by a percent sign (%) followed by the hexadecimal codes for the character as encoded in UTF-8. For instance, in UTF-8, á is the two bytes 0xC3 0xA1 so it would be encoded as %c3%a1. The Chinese character 木 is Unicode code point 0x6728. In UTF-8, this is encoded as the three bytes E6, 9C, and A8. Thus, in a URI it would be encoded as %E6%9C%A8.

If you don't hexadecimally encode non-ASCII characters like this, but just include them directly, then instead of a URI you have an IRI (an Internationalized Resource Identifier). IRIs are easier to type and much easier to read, but a lot of software and protocols expect and support only ASCII URIs.

Punctuation characters such as / and @ must also be encoded with percent escapes if they are used in any role other than what's specified for them in the scheme-specific part of a particular URL. For example, the forward slashes in the URI *http://www.cafeaulait.org/books/javaio2/* do not need to be encoded as *%2F* because they serve to delimit the hierarchy as specified for the *http* URI scheme. However, if a filename includes a / character—for instance, if the last directory were named *Java I/O* instead of *javaio2* to more closely match the name of the book—the URI would have to be written as *http:// www.cafeaulait.org/books/Java%20I%2FO/*. This is not as far-fetched as it might sound to Unix or Windows users. Mac filenames frequently include a forward slash. Filenames on many platforms often contain characters that need to be encoded, including @, $, +, =, and many more. And of course URLs are, more often than not, not derived from filenames at all.

URLs

A URL is a URI that, as well as identifying a resource, provides a specific network location for the resource that a client can use to retrieve a representation of that resource. By contrast, a generic URI may tell you what a resource is, but not actually tell you where or how to get that resource. In the physical world, it's the difference between the title "Harry Potter and The Deathly Hallows" and the library location "Room 312, Row 28, Shelf 7". In Java, it's the difference between the `java.net.URI` class that only identifies resources and the `java.net.URL` class that can both identify and retrieve resources.

The network location in a URL usually includes the protocol used to access a server (e.g., FTP, HTTP), the hostname or IP address of the server, and the path to the resource on that server. A typical URL looks like *http://www.ibiblio.org/javafaq/javatutorial.html*. This specifies that there is a file called *javatutorial.html* in a directory called *javafaq* on the server *www.ibiblio.org*, and that this file can be accessed via the HTTP protocol.

The syntax of a URL is:

```
protocol://userInfo@host:port/path?query#fragment
```

Here the protocol is another word for what was called the scheme of the URI. (*Scheme* is the word used in the URI RFC. *Protocol* is the word used in the Java documentation.) In a URL, the protocol part can be *file*, *ftp*, *http*, *https*, *magnet*, *telnet*, or various other strings (though not *urn*).

The *host* part of a URL is the name of the server that provides the resource you want. It can be a hostname such as *www.oreilly.com* or *utopia.poly.edu* or an IP address, such as 204.148.40.9 or 128.238.3.21.

The *userInfo* is optional login information for the server. If present, it contains a username and, rarely, a password.

The *port* number is also optional. It's not necessary if the service is running on its default port (port 80 for HTTP servers).

Together, the userInfo, host, and port constitute the *authority*.

The *path* points to a particular resource on the specified server. It often looks like a filesystem path such as */forum/index.php*. However, it may or may not actually map to a filesystem on the server. If it does map to a filesystem, the path is relative to the document root of the server, not necessarily to the root of the filesystem on the server. As a rule, servers that are open to the public do not show their entire filesystem to clients. Rather, they show only the contents of a specified directory. This directory is called the document root, and all paths and filenames are relative to it. Thus, on a Unix server, all files that are available to the public might be in */var/public/html*, but to somebody connecting from a remote machine, this directory looks like the root of the filesystem.

The *query* string provides additional arguments for the server. It's commonly used only in *http* URLs, where it contains form data for input to programs running on the server.

Finally, the *fragment* references a particular part of the remote resource. If the remote resource is HTML, the fragment identifier names an anchor in the HTML document.

If the remote resource is XML, the fragment identifier is an XPointer. Some sources refer to the fragment part of the URL as a "section". Java rather unaccountably refers to the fragment identifier as a "Ref". Fragment identifier targets are created in an HTML document with an *id* attribute, like this:

```
<h3 id="xtocid1902914">Comments</h3>
```

This tag identifies a particular point in a document. To refer to this point, a URL includes not only the document's filename but the fragment identifier separated from the rest of the URL by a #:

```
http://www.cafeaulait.org/javafaq.html#xtocid1902914
```

 Technically, a string that contains a fragment identifier is a *URL reference*, not a URL. Java, however, does not distinguish between URLs and URL references.

Relative URLs

A URL tells a web browser a lot about a document: the protocol used to retrieve the document, the host where the document lives, and the path to the document on that host. Most of this information is likely to be the same for other URLs that are referenced in the document. Therefore, rather than requiring each URL to be specified in its entirety, a URL may inherit the protocol, hostname, and path of its parent document (i.e., the document in which it appears). URLs that aren't complete but inherit pieces from their parent are called *relative* URLs. In contrast, a completely specified URL is called an *absolute URL*. In a relative URL, any pieces that are missing are assumed to be the same as the corresponding pieces from the URL of the document in which the URL is found. For example, suppose that while browsing *http://www.ibiblio.org/javafaq/javatutorial.html* you click on this hyperlink:

```
<a href="javafaq.html">
```

The browser cuts *javatutorial.html* off the end of *http://www.ibiblio.org/javafaq/javatutorial.html* to get *http://www.ibiblio.org/javafaq/*. Then it attaches *javafaq.html* onto the end of *http://www.ibiblio.org/javafaq/* to get *http://www.ibiblio.org/javafaq/javafaq.html*. Finally, it loads that document.

If the relative link begins with a /, then it is relative to the document root instead of relative to the current file. Thus, if you click on the following link while browsing *http://www.ibiblio.org/javafaq/javatutorial.html*:

```
<a href="/projects/ipv6/">
```

the browser would throw away */javafaq/javatutorial.html* and attach */projects/ipv6/* to the end of *http://www.ibiblio.org* to get *http://www.ibiblio.org/projects/ipv6/*.

Relative URLs have a number of advantages. First—and least important—they save a little typing. More importantly, relative URLs allow a single document tree to be served by multiple protocols: for instance, both HTTP and FTP. HTTP might be used for direct surfing, while FTP could be used for mirroring the site. Most importantly of all, relative URLs allow entire trees of documents to be moved or copied from one site to another without breaking all the internal links.

The URL Class

The `java.net.URL` class is an abstraction of a Uniform Resource Locator such as *http://www.lolcats.com/* or *ftp://ftp.redhat.com/pub/*. It extends `java.lang.Object`, and it is a final class that cannot be subclassed. Rather than relying on inheritance to configure instances for different kinds of URLs, it uses the strategy design pattern. Protocol handlers are the strategies, and the `URL` class itself forms the context through which the different strategies are selected.

Although storing a URL as a string would be trivial, it is helpful to think of URLs as objects with fields that include the scheme (a.k.a. the protocol), hostname, port, path, query string, and fragment identifier (a.k.a. the ref), each of which may be set independently. Indeed, this is almost exactly how the `java.net.URL` class is organized, though the details vary a little between different versions of Java.

URLs are immutable. After a `URL` object has been constructed, its fields do not change. This has the side effect of making them thread safe.

Creating New URLs

Unlike the `InetAddress` objects in Chapter 4, you can construct instances of `java.net.URL`. The constructors differ in the information they require:

```
public URL(String url) throws MalformedURLException
public URL(String protocol, String hostname, String file)
    throws MalformedURLException
public URL(String protocol, String host, int port, String file)
    throws MalformedURLException
public URL(URL base, String relative) throws MalformedURLException
```

Which constructor you use depends on the information you have and the form it's in. All these constructors throw a `MalformedURLException` if you try to create a URL for an unsupported protocol or if the URL is syntactically incorrect.

Exactly which protocols are supported is implementation dependent. The only protocols that have been available in all virtual machines are http and file, and the latter is notoriously flaky. Today, Java also supports the https, jar, and ftp protocols. Some virtual machines support mailto and gopher as well as some custom protocols like doc, netdoc, systemresource, and verbatim used internally by Java.

If the protocol you need isn't supported by a particular VM, you may be able to install a *protocol handler* for that scheme to enable the URL class to speak that protocol. In practice, this is way more trouble than it's worth. You're better off using a library that exposes a custom API just for that protocol.

Other than verifying that it recognizes the URL scheme, Java does not check the correctness of the URLs it constructs. The programmer is responsible for making sure that URLs created are valid. For instance, Java does not check that the hostname in an HTTP URL does not contain spaces or that the query string is x-www-form-URL-encoded. It does not check that a mailto URL actually contains an email address. You can create URLs for hosts that don't exist and for hosts that do exist but that you won't be allowed to connect to.

Constructing a URL from a string

The simplest URL constructor just takes an absolute URL in string form as its single argument:

```
public URL(String url) throws MalformedURLException
```

Like all constructors, this may only be called after the new operator, and like all URL constructors, it can throw a MalformedURLException. The following code constructs a URL object from a String, catching the exception that might be thrown:

```
try {
  URL u = new URL("http://www.audubon.org/");
} catch (MalformedURLException ex)  {
  System.err.println(ex);
}
```

Example 5-1 is a simple program for determining which protocols a virtual machine supports. It attempts to construct a URL object for each of 15 protocols (8 standard protocols, 3 custom protocols for various Java APIs, and 4 undocumented protocols used internally by Java). If the constructor succeeds, you know the protocol is supported. Otherwise, a MalformedURLException is thrown and you know the protocol is not supported.

Example 5-1. Which protocols does a virtual machine support?

```
import java.net.*;

public class ProtocolTester {

  public static void main(String[] args) {

    // hypertext transfer protocol
    testProtocol("http://www.adc.org");
```

```java
    // secure http
    testProtocol("https://www.amazon.com/exec/obidos/order2/");

    // file transfer protocol
    testProtocol("ftp://ibiblio.org/pub/languages/java/javafaq/");

    // Simple Mail Transfer Protocol
    testProtocol("mailto:elharo@ibiblio.org");

    // telnet
    testProtocol("telnet://dibner.poly.edu/");

    // local file access
    testProtocol("file:///etc/passwd");

    // gopher
    testProtocol("gopher://gopher.anc.org.za/");

    // Lightweight Directory Access Protocol
    testProtocol(
        "ldap://ldap.itd.umich.edu/o=University%20of%20Michigan,c=US?postalAddress");

    // JAR
    testProtocol(
        "jar:http://cafeaulait.org/books/javaio/ioexamples/javaio.jar!"
        + "/com/macfaq/io/StreamCopier.class");

    // NFS, Network File System
    testProtocol("nfs://utopia.poly.edu/usr/tmp/");

    // a custom protocol for JDBC
    testProtocol("jdbc:mysql://luna.ibiblio.org:3306/NEWS");

    // rmi, a custom protocol for remote method invocation
    testProtocol("rmi://ibiblio.org/RenderEngine");

    // custom protocols for HotJava
    testProtocol("doc:/UsersGuide/release.html");
    testProtocol("netdoc:/UsersGuide/release.html");
    testProtocol("systemresource://www.adc.org/+/index.html");
    testProtocol("verbatim:http://www.adc.org/");
  }

  private static void testProtocol(String url) {
    try {
      URL u = new URL(url);
      System.out.println(u.getProtocol() + " is supported");
    } catch (MalformedURLException ex) {
      String protocol = url.substring(0, url.indexOf(':'));
      System.out.println(protocol + " is not supported");
    }
```

```
    }
}
```

The results of this program depend on which virtual machine runs it. Here are the results from Java 7 on Mac OS X:

```
http is supported
https is supported
ftp is supported
mailto is supported
telnet is not supported
file is supported
gopher is not supported
ldap is not supported
jar is supported
nfs is not supported
jdbc is not supported
rmi is not supported
doc is not supported
netdoc is supported
systemresource is not supported
verbatim is not supported
```

The nonsupport of RMI and JDBC is actually a little deceptive; in fact, the JDK does support these protocols. However, that support is through various parts of the `java.rmi` and `java.sql` packages, respectively. These protocols are not accessible through the URL class like the other supported protocols (although I have no idea why Sun chose to wrap up RMI and JDBC parameters in URL clothing if it wasn't intending to interface with these via Java's quite sophisticated mechanism for handling URLs).

Other Java 7 virtual machines will show similar results. VMs that are not derived from the Oracle codebase may vary somewhat in which protocols they support. For example, Android's Dalvik VM only supports the required http, https, file, ftp, and jar protocols.

Constructing a URL from its component parts

You can also build a URL by specifying the protocol, the hostname, and the file:

```
public URL(String protocol, String hostname, String file)
    throws MalformedURLException
```

This constructor sets the port to -1 so the default port for the protocol will be used. The `file` argument should begin with a slash and include a path, a filename, and optionally a fragment identifier. Forgetting the initial slash is a common mistake, and one that is not easy to spot. Like all URL constructors, it can throw a `MalformedURLException`. For example:

```
try {
  URL u = new URL("http", "www.eff.org", "/blueribbon.html#intro");
} catch (MalformedURLException ex)  {
```

```
    throw new RuntimeException("shouldn't happen; all VMs recognize http");
}
```

This creates a URL object that points to *http://www.eff.org/blueribbon.html#intro*, using the default port for the HTTP protocol (port 80). The file specification includes a reference to a named anchor. The code catches the exception that would be thrown if the virtual machine did not support the HTTP protocol. However, this shouldn't happen in practice.

For the rare occasions when the default port isn't correct, the next constructor lets you specify the port explicitly as an `int`. The other arguments are the same. For example, this code fragment creates a URL object that points to *http://fourier.dur.ac.uk:8000/~dma3mjh/jsci/*, specifying port 8000 explicitly:

```
try {
  URL u = new URL("http", "fourier.dur.ac.uk", 8000, "/~dma3mjh/jsci/");
} catch (MalformedURLException ex)  {
  throw new RuntimeException("shouldn't happen; all VMs recognize http");
}
```

Constructing relative URLs

This constructor builds an absolute URL from a relative URL and a base URL:

```
public URL(URL base, String relative) throws MalformedURLException
```

For instance, you may be parsing an HTML document at *http://www.ibiblio.org/javafaq/index.html* and encounter a link to a file called *mailinglists.html* with no further qualifying information. In this case, you use the URL to the document that contains the link to provide the missing information. The constructor computes the new URL as *http://www.ibiblio.org/javafaq/mailinglists.html*. For example:

```
try {
  URL u1 = new URL("http://www.ibiblio.org/javafaq/index.html");
  URL u2 = new URL (u1, "mailinglists.html");
} catch (MalformedURLException ex) {
  System.err.println(ex);
}
```

The filename is removed from the path of u1 and the new filename *mailinglists.html* is appended to make u2. This constructor is particularly useful when you want to loop through a list of files that are all in the same directory. You can create a URL for the first file and then use this initial URL to create URL objects for the other files by substituting their filenames.

Other sources of URL objects

Besides the constructors discussed here, a number of other methods in the Java class library return URL objects. In applets, getDocumentBase() returns the URL of the page that contains the applet and getCodeBase() returns the URL of the applet *.class* file.

The java.io.File class has a toURL() method that returns a *file* URL matching the given file. The exact format of the URL returned by this method is platform dependent. For example, on Windows it may return something like *file:/D:/JAVA/JNP4/05/ ToURLTest.java*. On Linux and other Unixes, you're likely to see *file:/home/elharo/ books/JNP4/05/ToURLTest.java*. In practice, *file* URLs are heavily platform and program dependent. Java file URLs often cannot be interchanged with the URLs used by web browsers and other programs, or even with Java programs running on different platforms.

Class loaders are used not only to load classes but also to load resources such as images and audio files. The static ClassLoader.getSystemResource(String name) method returns a URL from which a single resource can be read. The ClassLoader.getSystem Resources(String name) method returns an Enumeration containing a list of URLs from which the named resource can be read. And finally, the instance method getRe source(String name) searches the path used by the referenced class loader for a URL to the named resource. The URLs returned by these methods may be file URLs, HTTP URLs, or some other scheme. The full path of the resource is a package qualified Java name with slashes instead of periods such as */com/macfaq/sounds/swale.au* or *com/ macfaq/images/headshot.jpg*. The Java virtual machine will attempt to find the requested resource in the classpath, potentially inside a JAR archive.

There are a few other methods that return URL objects here and there throughout the class library, but most are simple getter methods that return a URL you probably already know because you used it to construct the object in the first place; for instance, the getPage() method of javax.swing.JEditorPane and the getURL() method of java.net.URLConnection.

Retrieving Data from a URL

Naked URLs aren't very exciting. What's interesting is the data contained in the documents they point to. The URL class has several methods that retrieve data from a URL:

```
public InputStream openStream() throws IOException
public URLConnection openConnection() throws IOException
public URLConnection openConnection(Proxy proxy) throws IOException
public Object getContent() throws IOException
public Object getContent(Class[] classes) throws IOException
```

The most basic and most commonly used of these methods is openStream(), which returns an InputStream from which you can read the data. If you need more control over the download process, call openConnection() instead, which gives you a URLCon nection which you can configure, and then get an InputStream from it. We'll take this up in Chapter 7. Finally, you can ask the URL for its content with getContent() which may give you a more complete object such as String or an Image. Then again, it may just give you an InputStream anyway.

public final InputStream openStream() throws IOException

The openStream() method connects to the resource referenced by the URL, performs any necessary handshaking between the client and the server, and returns an Input Stream from which data can be read. The data you get from this InputStream is the raw (i.e., uninterpreted) content the URL references: ASCII if you're reading an ASCII text file, raw HTML if you're reading an HTML file, binary image data if you're reading an image file, and so forth. It does not include any of the HTTP headers or any other protocol-related information. You can read from this InputStream as you would read from any other InputStream. For example:

```
try {
  URL u = new URL("http://www.lolcats.com");
  InputStream in = u.openStream();
  int c;
  while ((c = in.read()) != -1) System.out.write(c);
  in.close();
} catch (IOException ex) {
  System.err.println(ex);
}
```

The preceding code fragment catches an IOException, which also catches the Malfor medURLException that the URL constructor can throw, since MalformedURLException subclasses IOException.

As with most network streams, reliably closing the stream takes a bit of effort. In Java 6 and earlier, we use the dispose pattern: declare the stream variable outside the try block, set it to null, and then close it in the finally block if it's not null. For example:

```
InputStream in = null
try {
  URL u = new URL("http://www.lolcats.com");
  in = u.openStream();
  int c;
  while ((c = in.read()) != -1) System.out.write(c);
} catch (IOException ex) {
  System.err.println(ex);
} finally {
  try {
    if (in != null) {
      in.close();
    }
  } catch (IOException ex) {
```

```
      // ignore
    }
  }
```

Java 7 makes this somewhat cleaner by using a nested try-with-resources statement:

```
try {
  URL u = new URL("http://www.lolcats.com");
  try (InputStream in = u.openStream()) {
    int c;
    while ((c = in.read()) != -1) System.out.write(c);
  }
} catch (IOException ex) {
  System.err.println(ex);
}
```

Example 5-2 reads a URL from the command line, opens an InputStream from that URL, chains the resulting InputStream to an InputStreamReader using the default encoding, and then uses InputStreamReader's read() method to read successive characters from the file, each of which is printed on System.out. That is, it prints the raw data located at the URL if the URL references an HTML file; the program's output is raw HTML.

Example 5-2. Download a web page

```
import java.io.*;
import java.net.*;

public class SourceViewer {

  public static void main (String[] args) {

    if (args.length > 0) {
      InputStream in = null;
      try {
        // Open the URL for reading
        URL u = new URL(args[0]);
        in = u.openStream();
        // buffer the input to increase performance
        in = new BufferedInputStream(in);
        // chain the InputStream to a Reader
        Reader r = new InputStreamReader(in);
        int c;
        while ((c = r.read()) != -1) {
          System.out.print((char) c);
        }
      } catch (MalformedURLException ex) {
        System.err.println(args[0] + " is not a parseable URL");
      } catch (IOException ex) {
        System.err.println(ex);
      } finally {
        if (in != null) {
```

```
      try {
        in.close();
      } catch (IOException e) {
        // ignore
      }
    }
  }
}
```

And here are the first few lines of output when `SourceViewer` downloads *http://www.oreilly.com*:

```
<!DOCTYPE HTML PUBLIC "-//W3C//DTD HTML 4.01 Transitional//EN">
<html xmlns="http://www.w3.org/1999/xhtml" lang="en-US" xml:lang="en-US">
<head>
<title>oreilly.com -- Welcome to O'Reilly Media, Inc. -- computer books,
software conferences, online publishing</title>
<meta name="keywords" content="O'Reilly, oreilly, computer books, technical
books, UNIX, unix, Perl, Java, Linux, Internet, Web, C, C++, Windows, Windows
NT, Security, Sys Admin, System Administration, Oracle, PL/SQL, online books,
books online, computer book online, e-books, ebooks, Perl Conference, Open Source
Conference, Java Conference, open source, free software, XML, Mac OS X, .Net, dot
net, C#, PHP, CGI, VB, VB Script, Java Script, javascript, Windows 2000, XP,
```

There are quite a few more lines in that web page; if you want to see them, you can fire up your web browser.

The shakiest part of this program is that it blithely assumes that the URL points to text, which is not necessarily true. It could well be pointing to a GIF or JPEG image, an MP3 sound file, or something else entirely. Even if does resolve to text, the document encoding may not be the same as the default encoding of the client system. The remote host and local client may not have the same default character set. As a general rule, for pages that use a character set radically different from ASCII, the HTML will include a META tag in the header specifying the character set in use. For instance, this META tag specifies the Big-5 encoding for Chinese:

```
<meta http-equiv="Content-Type" content="text/html; charset=big5">
```

An XML document will likely have an XML declaration instead:

```
<?xml version="1.0" encoding="Big5"?>
```

In practice, there's no easy way to get at this information other than by parsing the file and looking for a header like this one, and even that approach is limited. Many HTML files handcoded in Latin alphabets don't have such a META tag. Since Windows, Mac, and most Unixes have somewhat different interpretations of the characters from 128 to 255, the extended characters in these documents do not translate correctly on platforms other than the one on which they were created.

And as if this isn't confusing enough, the HTTP header that precedes the actual document is likely to have its own encoding information, which may completely contradict what the document itself says. You can't read this header using the URL class, but you can with the URLConnection object returned by the openConnection() method. Encoding detection and declaration is one of the thornier parts of the architecture of the Web.

public URLConnection openConnection() throws IOException

The openConnection() method opens a socket to the specified URL and returns a URLConnection object. A URLConnection represents an open connection to a network resource. If the call fails, openConnection() throws an IOException. For example:

```
try {
  URL u = new URL("https://news.ycombinator.com/");
  try {
    URLConnection uc = u.openConnection();
    InputStream in = uc.getInputStream();
    // read from the connection...
  } catch (IOException ex) {
    System.err.println(ex);
  }
} catch (MalformedURLException ex) {
  System.err.println(ex);
}
```

You should use this method when you want to communicate directly with the server. The URLConnection gives you access to everything sent by the server: in addition to the document itself in its raw form (e.g., HTML, plain text, binary image data), you can access all the metadata specified by the protocol. For example, if the scheme is HTTP or HTTPS, the URLConnection lets you access the HTTP headers as well as the raw HTML. The URLConnection class also lets you write data to as well as read from a URL —for instance, in order to send email to a mailto URL or post form data. The URLConnection class will be the primary subject of Chapter 7.

An overloaded variant of this method specifies the proxy server to pass the connection through:

```
public URLConnection openConnection(Proxy proxy) throws IOException
```

This overrides any proxy server set with the usual socksProxyHost, socksProxyPort, http.proxyHost, http.proxyPort, http.nonProxyHosts, and similar system properties. If the protocol handler does not support proxies, the argument is ignored and the connection is made directly if possible.

public final Object getContent() throws IOException

The getContent() method is the third way to download data referenced by a URL. The getContent() method retrieves the data referenced by the URL and tries to make it into some type of object. If the URL refers to some kind of text such as an ASCII or HTML file, the object returned is usually some sort of InputStream. If the URL refers to an image such as a GIF or a JPEG file, getContent() usually returns a java.awt.Image Producer. What unifies these two disparate classes is that they are not the thing itself but a means by which a program can construct the thing:

```
URL u = new URL("http://mesola.obspm.fr/");
Object o = u.getContent();
// cast the Object to the appropriate type
// work with the Object...
```

getContent() operates by looking at the Content-type field in the header of the data it gets from the server. If the server does not use MIME headers or sends an unfamiliar Content-type, getContent() returns some sort of InputStream with which the data can be read. An IOException is thrown if the object can't be retrieved. Example 5-3 demonstrates this.

Example 5-3. Download an object

```
import java.io.*;
import java.net.*;

public class ContentGetter {

  public static void main (String[] args) {

    if  (args.length > 0) {
      // Open the URL for reading
      try {
        URL u = new URL(args[0]);
        Object o = u.getContent();
        System.out.println("I got a " + o.getClass().getName());
      } catch (MalformedURLException ex) {
        System.err.println(args[0] + " is not a parseable URL");
      } catch (IOException ex) {
        System.err.println(ex);
      }
    }
  }
}
```

Here's the result of trying to get the content of *http://www.oreilly.com*:

```
% java ContentGetter http://www.oreilly.com/ I got a
sun.net.www.protocol.http.HttpURLConnection$HttpInputStream
```

The exact class may vary from one version of Java to the next (in earlier versions, it's been `java.io.PushbackInputStream` or `sun.net.www.http.KeepAliveStream`) but it should be some form of `InputStream`.

Here's what you get when you try to load a header image from that page:

```
% java ContentGetter http://www.oreilly.com/graphics_new/animation.gif
I got a sun.awt.image.URLImageSource
```

Here's what happens when you try to load a Java applet using `getContent()`:

```
% java ContentGetter http://www.cafeaulait.org/RelativeURLTest.class
I got a sun.net.www.protocol.http.HttpURLConnection$HttpInputStream
```

Here's what happens when you try to load an audio file using `getContent()`:

```
% java ContentGetter http://www.cafeaulait.org/course/week9/spacemusic.au
I got a sun.applet.AppletAudioClip
```

The last result is the most unusual because it is as close as the Java core API gets to a class that represents a sound file. It's not just an interface through which you can load the sound data.

This example demonstrates the biggest problems with using `getContent()`: it's hard to predict what kind of object you'll get. You could get some kind of `InputStream` or an `ImageProducer` or perhaps an `AudioClip`; it's easy to check using the `instanceof` operator. This information should be enough to let you read a text file or display an image.

public final Object getContent(Class[] classes) throws IOException

A URL's content handler may provide different views of a resource. This overloaded variant of the `getContent()` method lets you choose which class you'd like the content to be returned as. The method attempts to return the URL's content in the first available format. For instance, if you prefer an HTML file to be returned as a `String`, but your second choice is a `Reader` and your third choice is an `InputStream`, write:

```
URL u = new URL("http://www.nwu.org");
Class<?>[] types = new Class[3];
types[0] = String.class;
types[1] = Reader.class;
types[2] = InputStream.class;
Object o = u.getContent(types);
```

If the content handler knows how to return a string representation of the resource, then it returns a `String`. If it doesn't know how to return a string representation of the resource, then it returns a `Reader`. And if it doesn't know how to present the resource as a reader, then it returns an `InputStream`. You have to test for the type of the returned object using `instanceof`. For example:

```
if (o instanceof String) {
    System.out.println(o);
```

```
  } else if (o instanceof Reader) {
    int c;
    Reader r = (Reader) o;
    while ((c = r.read()) != -1) System.out.print((char) c);
    r.close();
  } else if (o instanceof InputStream) {
    int c;
    InputStream in = (InputStream) o;
    while ((c = in.read()) != -1) System.out.write(c);
    in.close();
  } else {
    System.out.println("Error: unexpected type " + o.getClass());
  }
```

Splitting a URL into Pieces

URLs are composed of five pieces:

- The scheme, also known as the protocol
- The authority
- The path
- The fragment identifier, also known as the section or ref
- The query string

For example, in the URL *http://www.ibiblio.org/javafaq/books/jnp/index.html? isbn=1565922069#toc*, the scheme is *http*, the authority is *www.ibiblio.org*, the path is */ javafaq/books/jnp/index.html*, the fragment identifier is *toc*, and the query string is *isbn=1565922069*. However, not all URLs have all these pieces. For instance, the URL *http://www.faqs.org/rfcs/rfc3986.html* has a scheme, an authority, and a path, but no fragment identifier or query string.

The authority may further be divided into the user info, the host, and the port. For example, in the URL *http://admin@www.blackstar.com:8080/*, the authority is *ad min@www.blackstar.com:8080*. This has the user info *admin*, the host *www.black-star.com*, and the port *8080*.

Read-only access to these parts of a URL is provided by nine public methods: get File(), getHost(), getPort(), getProtocol(), getRef(), getQuery(), getPath(), getUserInfo(), and getAuthority().

public String getProtocol()

The getProtocol() method returns a String containing the scheme of the URL (e.g., "http", "https", or "file"). For example, this code fragment prints *https*:

```
URL u = new URL("https://xkcd.com/727/");
System.out.println(u.getProtocol());
```

public String getHost()

The getHost() method returns a String containing the hostname of the URL. For example, this code fragment prints *xkcd.com*:

```
URL u = new URL("https://xkcd.com/727/");
System.out.println(u.getHost());
```

public int getPort()

The getPort() method returns the port number specified in the URL as an int. If no port was specified in the URL, getPort() returns -1 to signify that the URL does not specify the port explicitly, and will use the default port for the protocol. For example, if the URL is *http://www.userfriendly.org/*, getPort() returns -1; if the URL is *http://www.userfriendly.org:80/*, getPort() returns 80. The following code prints -1 for the port number because it isn't specified in the URL:

```
URL u = new URL("http://www.ncsa.illinois.edu/AboutUs/");
System.out.println("The port part of " + u + " is " + u.getPort());
```

public int getDefaultPort()

The getDefaultPort() method returns the default port used for this URL's protocol when none is specified in the URL. If no default port is defined for the protocol, then getDefaultPort() returns -1. For example, if the URL is *http://www.userfriendly.org/*, getDefaultPort() returns 80; if the URL is *ftp://ftp.userfriendly.org:8000/*, getDefault Port() returns 21.

public String getFile()

The getFile() method returns a String that contains the path portion of a URL; remember that Java does not break a URL into separate path and file parts. Everything from the first slash (/) after the hostname until the character preceding the # sign that begins a fragment identifier is considered to be part of the file. For example:

```
URL page = this.getDocumentBase();
System.out.println("This page's path is " + page.getFile());
```

If the URL does not have a file part, Java sets the file to the empty string.

public String getPath()

The getPath() method is a near synonym for getFile(); that is, it returns a String containing the path and file portion of a URL. However, unlike getFile(), it does not include the query string in the String it returns, just the path.

Note that the getPath() method does not return only the directory path and getFile() does not return only the filename, as you might expect. Both getPath() and getFile() return the full path and filename. The only difference is that getFile() also returns the query string and getPath() does not.

public String getRef()

The getRef() method returns the fragment identifier part of the URL. If the URL doesn't have a fragment identifier, the method returns null. In the following code, getRef() returns the string xtocid1902914:

```
URL u = new URL(
    "http://www.ibiblio.org/javafaq/javafaq.html#xtocid1902914");
System.out.println("The fragment ID of " + u + " is " + u.getRef());
```

public String getQuery()

The getQuery() method returns the query string of the URL. If the URL doesn't have a query string, the method returns null. In the following code, getQuery() returns the string category=Piano:

```
URL u = new URL(
    "http://www.ibiblio.org/nywc/compositions.phtml?category=Piano");
System.out.println("The query string of " + u + " is " + u.getQuery());
```

public String getUserInfo()

Some URLs include usernames and occasionally even password information. This information comes after the scheme and before the host; an @ symbol delimits it. For instance, in the URL *http://elharo@java.oreilly.com/*, the user info is *elharo*. Some URLs also include passwords in the user info. For instance, in the URL *ftp://mp3:secret@ftp.example.com/c%3a/stuff/mp3/*, the user info is *mp3:secret*. However, most of the time, including a password in a URL is a security risk. If the URL doesn't have any user info, getUserInfo() returns null.

Mailto URLs may not behave like you expect. In a URL like *mailto:elharo@ibiblio.org*, "elharo@ibiblio.org" is the path, not the user info and the host. That's because the URL specifies the remote recipient of the message rather than the username and host that's sending the message.

public String getAuthority()

Between the scheme and the path of a URL, you'll find the authority. This part of the URI indicates the authority that resolves the resource. In the most general case, the authority includes the user info, the host, and the port. For example, in the URL *ftp://mp3:mp3@138.247.121.61:21000/c%3a/*, the authority is *mp3:mp3@138.247.121.61:21000*, the user info is *mp3:mp3*, the host is *138.247.121.61*, and the port is *21000*. However, not all URLs have all parts. For instance, in the URL *http://conferences.oreilly.com/java/speakers/*, the authority is simply the hostname *conferences.oreilly.com*. The `getAuthority()` method returns the authority as it exists in the URL, with or without the user info and port.

Example 5-4 uses these methods to split URLs entered on the command line into their component parts.

Example 5-4. The parts of a URL

```java
import java.net.*;

public class URLSplitter {

  public static void main(String args[]) {

    for (int i = 0; i < args.length; i++) {
      try {
        URL u = new URL(args[i]);
        System.out.println("The URL is " + u);
        System.out.println("The scheme is " + u.getProtocol());
        System.out.println("The user info is " + u.getUserInfo());

        String host = u.getHost();
        if (host != null) {
          int atSign = host.indexOf('@');
          if (atSign != -1) host = host.substring(atSign+1);
          System.out.println("The host is " + host);
        } else {
          System.out.println("The host is null.");
        }

        System.out.println("The port is " + u.getPort());
        System.out.println("The path is " + u.getPath());
        System.out.println("The ref is " + u.getRef());
        System.out.println("The query string is " + u.getQuery());
      } catch (MalformedURLException ex) {
        System.err.println(args[i] + " is not a URL I understand.");
      }
      System.out.println();
    }
  }
}
```

Here's the result of running this against several of the URL examples in this chapter:

```
% java URLSplitter    \
ftp://mp3:mp3@138.247.121.61:21000/c%3a/                    \
http://www.oreilly.com                                      \
http://www.ibiblio.org/nywc/compositions.phtml?category=Piano \
http://admin@www.blackstar.com:8080/                        \
```

```
The URL is ftp://mp3:mp3@138.247.121.61:21000/c%3a/
The scheme is ftp
The user info is mp3:mp3
The host is 138.247.121.61
The port is 21000
The path is /c%3a/
The ref is null
The query string is null

The URL is http://www.oreilly.com
The scheme is http
The user info is null
The host is www.oreilly.com
The port is -1
The path is
The ref is null
The query string is null

The URL is http://www.ibiblio.org/nywc/compositions.phtml?category=Piano
The scheme is http
The user info is null
The host is www.ibiblio.org
The port is -1
The path is /nywc/compositions.phtml
The ref is null
The query string is category=Piano

The URL is http://admin@www.blackstar.com:8080/
The scheme is http
The user info is admin
The host is www.blackstar.com
The port is 8080
The path is /
The ref is null
The query string is null
```

Equality and Comparison

The URL class contains the usual equals() and hashCode() methods. These behave almost as you'd expect. Two URLs are considered equal if and only if both URLs point to the same resource on the same host, port, and path, with the same fragment identifier and query string. However there is one surprise here. The equals() method actually tries to resolve the host with DNS so that, for example, it can tell that *http://www.ibiblio.org/* and *http://ibiblio.org/* are the same.

This means that `equals()` on a URL is potentially *a blocking I/O operation!* For this reason, you should avoid storing URLs in data structure that depend on `equals()` such as `java.util.HashMap`. Prefer `java.net.URI` for this, and convert back and forth from URIs to URLs when necessary.

On the other hand, `equals()` does not go so far as to actually compare the resources identified by two URLs. For example, *http://www.oreilly.com/* is not equal to *http://www.oreilly.com/index.html*; and *http://www.oreilly.com:80* is not equal to *http://www.oreilly.com/*.

Example 5-5 creates URL objects for *http://www.ibiblio.org/* and *http://ibiblio.org/* and tells you if they're the same using the `equals()` method.

Example 5-5. Are http://www.ibiblio.org and http://ibiblio.org the same?

```
import java.net.*;

public class URLEquality {

  public static void main (String[] args) {
    try {
      URL www = new URL ("http://www.ibiblio.org/");
      URL ibiblio = new URL("http://ibiblio.org/");
      if (ibiblio.equals(www)) {
        System.out.println(ibiblio + " is the same as " + www);
      } else {
        System.out.println(ibiblio + " is not the same as " + www);
      }
    } catch (MalformedURLException ex) {
      System.err.println(ex);
    }
  }
}
```

When you run this program, you discover:

```
% java URLEquality
http://www.ibiblio.org/ is the same as http://ibiblio.org/
```

URL does not implement `Comparable`.

The URL class also has a `sameFile()` method that checks whether two URLs point to the same resource:

```
public boolean sameFile(URL other)
```

The comparison is essentially the same as with `equals()`, DNS queries included, except that `sameFile()` does not consider the fragment identifier. This `sameFile()` returns true when comparing *http://www.oreilly.com/index.html#p1* and *http://www.oreil-ly.com/index.html#q2* while `equals()` would return false.

Here's a fragment of code that uses `sameFile()` to compare two URLs:

```
URL u1 = new URL("http://www.ncsa.uiuc.edu/HTMLPrimer.html#GS");
URL u2 = new URL("http://www.ncsa.uiuc.edu/HTMLPrimer.html#HD");
if (u1.sameFile(u2)) {
  System.out.println(u1 + " is the same file as \n" + u2);
} else {
  System.out.println(u1 + " is not the same file as \n" + u2);
}
```

The output is:

```
http://www.ncsa.uiuc.edu/HTMLPrimer.html#GS is the same file as
http://www.ncsa.uiuc.edu/HTMLPrimer.html#HD
```

Conversion

URL has three methods that convert an instance to another form: `toString()`, `toExternalForm()`, and `toURI()`.

Like all good classes, `java.net.URL` has a `toString()` method. The `String` produced by `toString()` is always an absolute URL, such as *http://www.cafeaulait.org/javatutorial.html*. It's uncommon to call `toString()` explicitly. Print statements call to `String()` implicitly. Outside of print statements, it's more proper to use `toExternal Form()` instead:

```
public String toExternalForm()
```

The `toExternalForm()` method converts a URL object to a string that can be used in an HTML link or a web browser's Open URL dialog.

The `toExternalForm()` method returns a human-readable `String` representing the URL. It is identical to the `toString()` method. In fact, all the `toString()` method does is return `toExternalForm()`.

Finally, the `toURI()` method converts a URL object to an equivalent URI object:

```
public URI toURI() throws URISyntaxException
```

We'll take up the URI class shortly. In the meantime, the main thing you need to know is that the URI class provides much more accurate, specification-conformant behavior than the URL class. For operations like absolutization and encoding, you should prefer the URI class where you have the option. You should also prefer the URI class if you need to store URLs in a hashtable or other data structure, since its `equals()` method is not blocking. The URL class should be used primarily when you want to download content from a server.

The URI Class

A URI is a generalization of a URL that includes not only Uniform Resource Locators but also Uniform Resource Names (URNs). Most URIs used in practice are URLs, but most specifications and standards such as XML are defined in terms of URIs. In Java, URIs are represented by the `java.net.URI` class. This class differs from the `java.net.URL` class in three important ways:

- The `URI` class is purely about identification of resources and parsing of URIs. It provides no methods to retrieve a representation of the resource identified by its URI.

- The `URI` class is more conformant to the relevant specifications than the `URL` class.

- A URI object can represent a relative URI. The `URL` class absolutizes all URIs before storing them.

In brief, a `URL` object is a representation of an application layer protocol for network retrieval, whereas a `URI` object is purely for string parsing and manipulation. The `URI` class has no network retrieval capabilities. The `URL` class has some string parsing methods, such as `getFile()` and `getRef()`, but many of these are broken and don't always behave exactly as the relevant specifications say they should. Normally, you should use the `URL` class when you want to download the content at a URL and the `URI` class when you want to use the URL for identification rather than retrieval, for instance, to represent an XML namespace. When you need to do both, you may convert from a URI to a URL with the `toURL()` method, and from a URL to a URI using the `toURI()` method.

Constructing a URI

URIs are built from strings. You can either pass the entire URI to the constructor in a single string, or the individual pieces:

```
public URI(String uri) throws URISyntaxException
public URI(String scheme, String schemeSpecificPart, String fragment)
    throws URISyntaxException
public URI(String scheme, String host, String path, String fragment)
    throws URISyntaxException
public URI(String scheme, String authority, String path, String query,
    String fragment) throws URISyntaxException
public URI(String scheme, String userInfo, String host, int port,
    String path, String query, String fragment) throws URISyntaxException
```

Unlike the `URL` class, the `URI` class does not depend on an underlying protocol handler. As long as the URI is syntactically correct, Java does not need to understand its protocol in order to create a representative URI object. Thus, unlike the `URL` class, the `URI` class can be used for new and experimental URI schemes.

The first constructor creates a new URI object from any convenient string. For example:

```
URI voice = new URI("tel:+1-800-9988-9938");
URI web   = new URI("http://www.xml.com/pub/a/2003/09/17/stax.html#id=_hbc");
URI book  = new URI("urn:isbn:1-565-92870-9");
```

If the string argument does not follow URI syntax rules—for example, if the URI begins with a colon—this constructor throws a URISyntaxException. This is a checked exception, so either catch it or declare that the method where the constructor is invoked can throw it. However, one syntax rule is not checked. In contradiction to the URI specification, the characters used in the URI are not limited to ASCII. They can include other Unicode characters, such as ø and é. Syntactically, there are very few restrictions on URIs, especially once the need to encode non-ASCII characters is removed and relative URIs are allowed. Almost any string can be interpreted as a URI.

The second constructor that takes a scheme specific part is mostly used for nonhierarchical URIs. The scheme is the URI's protocol, such as http, urn, tel, and so forth. It must be composed exclusively of ASCII letters and digits and the three punctuation characters +, -, and .. It must begin with a letter. Passing null for this argument omits the scheme, thus creating a relative URI. For example:

```
URI absolute = new URI("http", "//www.ibiblio.org" , null);
URI relative = new URI(null, "/javafaq/index.shtml", "today");
```

The scheme-specific part depends on the syntax of the URI scheme; it's one thing for an http URL, another for a mailto URL, and something else again for a tel URI. Because the URI class encodes illegal characters with percent escapes, there's effectively no syntax error you can make in this part.

Finally, the third argument contains the fragment identifier, if any. Again, characters that are forbidden in a fragment identifier are escaped automatically. Passing null for this argument simply omits the fragment identifier.

The third constructor is used for hierarchical URIs such as http and ftp URLs. The host and path together (separated by a /) form the scheme-specific part for this URI. For example:

```
URI today= new URI("http", "www.ibiblio.org", "/javafaq/index.html", "today");
```

This produces the URI *http://www.ibiblio.org/javafaq/index.html#today*.

If the constructor cannot form a legal hierarchical URI from the supplied pieces—for instance, if there is a scheme so the URI has to be absolute but the path doesn't start with /—then it throws a URISyntaxException.

The fourth constructor is basically the same as the third, with the addition of a query string. For example:

```
URI today = new URI("http", "www.ibiblio.org", "/javafaq/index.html",
    "referrer=cnet&date=2014-02-23", "today");
```

As usual, any unescapable syntax errors cause a URISyntaxException to be thrown and null can be passed to omit any of the arguments.

The fifth constructor is the master hierarchical URI constructor that the previous two invoke. It divides the authority into separate user info, host, and port parts, each of which has its own syntax rules. For example:

```
URI styles = new URI("ftp", "anonymous:elharo@ibiblio.org",
    "ftp.oreilly.com", 21, "/pub/stylesheet", null, null);
```

However, the resulting URI still has to follow all the usual rules for URIs; and again null can be passed for any argument to omit it from the result.

If you're sure your URIs are legal and do not violate any of the rules, you can use the static factory URI.create() method instead. Unlike the constructors, it does not throw a URISyntaxException. For example, this invocation creates a URI for anonymous FTP access using an email address as password:

```
URI styles = URI.create(
    "ftp://anonymous:elharo%40ibiblio.org@ftp.oreilly.com:21/pub/stylesheet");
```

If the URI does prove to be malformed, then an IllegalArgumentException is thrown by this method. This is a runtime exception, so you don't have to explicitly declare it or catch it.

The Parts of the URI

A URI reference has up to three parts: a scheme, a scheme-specific part, and a fragment identifier. The general format is:

> scheme:scheme-specific-part:fragment

If the scheme is omitted, the URI reference is relative. If the fragment identifier is omitted, the URI reference is a pure URI. The URI class has getter methods that return these three parts of each URI object. The getRawFoo() methods return the encoded forms of the parts of the URI, while the equivalent getFoo() methods first decode any percent-escaped characters and then return the decoded part:

```
public String getScheme()
public String getSchemeSpecificPart()
public String getRawSchemeSpecificPart()
public String getFragment()
public String getRawFragment()
```

 There's no getRawScheme() method because the URI specification requires that all scheme names be composed exclusively of URI-legal ASCII characters and does not allow percent escapes in scheme names.

These methods all return null if the particular URI object does not have the relevant component: for example, a relative URI without a scheme or an http URI without a fragment identifier.

A URI that has a scheme is an *absolute* URI. A URI without a scheme is *relative*. The `isAbsolute()` method returns true if the URI is absolute, false if it's relative:

```
public boolean isAbsolute()
```

The details of the scheme-specific part vary depending on the type of the scheme. For example, in a *tel* URL, the scheme-specific part has the syntax of a telephone number. However, in many useful URIs, including the very common *file* and *http* URLs, the scheme-specific part has a particular hierarchical format divided into an authority, a path, and a query string. The authority is further divided into user info, host, and port. The `isOpaque()` method returns false if the URI is hierarchical, true if it's not hierarchical—that is, if it's opaque:

```
public boolean isOpaque()
```

If the URI is opaque, all you can get is the scheme, scheme-specific part, and fragment identifier. However, if the URI is hierarchical, there are getter methods for all the different parts of a hierarchical URI:

```
public String getAuthority()
public String getFragment()
public String getHost()
public String getPath()
public String getPort()
public String getQuery()
public String getUserInfo()
```

These methods all return the decoded parts; in other words, percent escapes, such as %3C, are changed into the characters they represent, such as <. If you want the raw, encoded parts of the URI, there are five parallel `getRaw_Foo_()` methods:

```
public String getRawAuthority()
public String getRawFragment()
public String getRawPath()
public String getRawQuery()
public String getRawUserInfo()
```

Remember the URI class differs from the URI specification in that non-ASCII characters such as é and ü are never percent escaped in the first place, and thus will still be present in the strings returned by the `getRawFoo()` methods unless the strings originally used to construct the URI object were encoded.

There are no `getRawPort()` and `getRawHost()` methods because these components are always guaranteed to be made up of ASCII characters.

In the event that the specific URI does not contain this information—for instance, the URI *http://www.example.com* has no user info, path, port, or query string—the relevant methods return null. `getPort()` is the single exception. Since it's declared to return an `int`, it can't return `null`. Instead, it returns -1 to indicate an omitted port.

For various technical reasons that don't have a lot of practical impact, Java can't always initially detect syntax errors in the authority component. The immediate symptom of this failing is normally an inability to return the individual parts of the authority, port, host, and user info. In this event, you can call `parseServerAuthority()` to force the authority to be reparsed:

```
public URI parseServerAuthority() throws URISyntaxException
```

The original `URI` does not change (`URI` objects are immutable), but the `URI` returned will have separate authority parts for user info, host, and port. If the authority cannot be parsed, a `URISyntaxException` is thrown.

Example 5-6 uses these methods to split URIs entered on the command line into their component parts. It's similar to Example 5-4 but works with any syntactically correct URI, not just the ones Java has a protocol handler for.

Example 5-6. The parts of a URI

```java
import java.net.*;

public class URISplitter {

  public static void main(String args[]) {

    for (int i = 0; i < args.length; i++) {
      try {
        URI u = new URI(args[i]);
        System.out.println("The URI is " + u);
        if (u.isOpaque()) {
          System.out.println("This is an opaque URI.");
          System.out.println("The scheme is " + u.getScheme());
          System.out.println("The scheme specific part is "
              + u.getSchemeSpecificPart());
          System.out.println("The fragment ID is " + u.getFragment());
        } else {
          System.out.println("This is a hierarchical URI.");
          System.out.println("The scheme is " + u.getScheme());
          try {
```

```
          u = u.parseServerAuthority();
          System.out.println("The host is " + u.getHost());
          System.out.println("The user info is " + u.getUserInfo());
          System.out.println("The port is " + u.getPort());
        } catch (URISyntaxException ex) {
          // Must be a registry based authority
          System.out.println("The authority is " + u.getAuthority());
        }
        System.out.println("The path is " + u.getPath());
        System.out.println("The query string is " + u.getQuery());
        System.out.println("The fragment ID is " + u.getFragment());
      }
    } catch (URISyntaxException ex) {
      System.err.println(args[i] + " does not seem to be a URI.");
    }
    System.out.println();
  }
 }
}
```

Here's the result of running this against three of the URI examples in this section:

```
% java URISplitter tel:+1-800-9988-9938 \
  http://www.xml.com/pub/a/2003/09/17/stax.html#id=_hbc \
  urn:isbn:1-565-92870-9
The URI is tel:+1-800-9988-9938
This is an opaque URI.
The scheme is tel
The scheme specific part is +1-800-9988-9938
The fragment ID is null

The URI is http://www.xml.com/pub/a/2003/09/17/stax.html#id=_hbc
This is a hierarchical URI.
The scheme is http
The host is www.xml.com
The user info is null
The port is -1
The path is /pub/a/2003/09/17/stax.html
The query string is null
The fragment ID is id=_hbc

The URI is urn:isbn:1-565-92870-9
This is an opaque URI.
The scheme is urn
The scheme specific part is isbn:1-565-92870-9
The fragment ID is null
```

Resolving Relative URIs

The URI class has three methods for converting back and forth between relative and absolute URIs:

```
public URI resolve(URI uri)
public URI resolve(String uri)
public URI relativize(URI uri)
```

The `resolve()` methods compare the `uri` argument to this URI and use it to construct a new `URI` object that wraps an absolute URI. For example, consider these three lines of code:

```
URI absolute = new URI("http://www.example.com/");
URI relative = new URI("images/logo.png");
URI resolved = absolute.resolve(relative);
```

After they've executed, `resolved` contains the absolute URI *http://www.example.com/ images/logo.png*.

If the invoking `URI` does not contain an absolute URI itself, the `resolve()` method resolves as much of the URI as it can and returns a new relative URI object as a result. For example, take these two statements:

```
URI top = new URI("javafaq/books/");
URI resolved = top.resolve("jnp3/examples/07/index.html");
```

After they've executed, `resolved` now contains the relative URI *javafaq/books/jnp3/ examples/07/index.html* with no scheme or authority.

It's also possible to reverse this procedure; that is, to go from an absolute URI to a relative one. The `relativize()` method creates a new `URI` object from the `uri` argument that is relative to the invoking `URI`. The argument is not changed. For example:

```
URI absolute = new URI("http://www.example.com/images/logo.png");
URI top = new URI("http://www.example.com/");
URI relative = top.relativize(absolute);
```

The `URI` object `relative` now contains the relative URI *images/logo.png*.

Equality and Comparison

URIs are tested for equality pretty much as you'd expect. It's not quite direct string comparison. Equal URIs must both either be hierarchical or opaque. The scheme and authority parts are compared without considering case. That is, *http* and *HTTP* are the same scheme, and *www.example.com* is the same authority as *www.EXAMPLE.com*. The rest of the URI is case sensitive, except for hexadecimal digits used to escape illegal characters. Escapes are *not* decoded before comparing. *http://www.example.com/A* and *http://www.example.com/%41* are unequal URIs.

The `hashCode()` method is consistent with equals. Equal URIs do have the same hash code and unequal URIs are fairly unlikely to share the same hash code.

URI implements `Comparable`, and thus URIs can be ordered. The ordering is based on string comparison of the individual parts, in this sequence:

1. If the schemes are different, the schemes are compared, without considering case.

2. Otherwise, if the schemes are the same, a hierarchical URI is considered to be less than an opaque URI with the same scheme.

3. If both URIs are opaque URIs, they're ordered according to their scheme-specific parts.

4. If both the scheme and the opaque scheme-specific parts are equal, the URIs are compared by their fragments.

5. If both URIs are hierarchical, they're ordered according to their authority components, which are themselves ordered according to user info, host, and port, in that order. Hosts are case insensitive.

6. If the schemes and the authorities are equal, the path is used to distinguish them.

7. If the paths are also equal, the query strings are compared.

8. If the query strings are equal, the fragments are compared.

URIs are not comparable to any type except themselves. Comparing a URI to anything except another URI causes a ClassCastException.

String Representations

Two methods convert URI objects to strings, toString() and toASCIIString():

```
public String toString()
public String toASCIIString()
```

The toString() method returns an *unencoded* string form of the URI (i.e., characters like é and \ are not percent escaped). Therefore, the result of calling this method is not guaranteed to be a syntactically correct URI, though it is in fact a syntactically correct IRI. This form is sometimes useful for display to human beings, but usually not for retrieval.

The toASCIIString() method returns an *encoded* string form of the URI. Characters like é and \ are always percent escaped whether or not they were originally escaped. This is the string form of the URI you should use most of the time. Even if the form returned by toString() is more legible for humans, they may still copy and paste it into areas that are not expecting an illegal URI. toASCIIString() always returns a syntactically correct URI.

x-www-form-urlencoded

One of the challenges faced by the designers of the Web was dealing with the differences between operating systems. These differences can cause problems with URLs: for example, some operating systems allow spaces in filenames; some don't. Most operating systems won't complain about a # sign in a filename; but in a URL, a # sign indicates that the filename has ended, and a fragment identifier follows. Other special characters, nonalphanumeric characters, and so on, all of which may have a special meaning inside a URL or on another operating system, present similar problems. Furthermore, Unicode was not yet ubiquitous when the Web was invented, so not all systems could handle characters such as é and 本. To solve these problems, characters used in URLs must come from a fixed subset of ASCII, specifically:

- The capital letters A–Z
- The lowercase letters a–z
- The digits 0–9
- The punctuation characters - _ . ! ~ * ' (and ,)

The characters : / & ? @ # ; $ + = and % may also be used, but only for their specified purposes. If these characters occur as part of a path or query string, they and all other characters should be encoded.

The encoding is very simple. Any characters that are not ASCII numerals, letters, or the punctuation marks specified earlier are converted into bytes and each byte is written as a percent sign followed by two hexadecimal digits. Spaces are a special case because they're so common. Besides being encoded as %20, they can be encoded as a plus sign (+). The plus sign itself is encoded as %2B. The / # = & and ? characters should be encoded when they are used as part of a name, and not as a separator between parts of the URL.

The URL class does not encode or decode automatically. You can construct URL objects that use illegal ASCII and non-ASCII characters and/or percent escapes. Such characters and escapes are not automatically encoded or decoded when output by methods such as getPath() and toExternalForm(). You are responsible for making sure all such characters are properly encoded in the strings used to construct a URL object.

Luckily, Java provides URLEncoder and URLDecoder classes to cipher strings in this format.

URLEncoder

To URL encode a string, pass the string and the character set name to the URLEncoder.encode() method. For example:

```
String encoded = URLEncoder.encode("This*string*has*asterisks", "UTF-8");
```

URLEncoder.encode() returns a copy of the input string with a few changes. Any non-alphanumeric characters are converted into % sequences (except the space, underscore, hyphen, period, and asterisk characters). It also encodes all non-ASCII characters. The space is converted into a plus sign. This method is a little overaggressive; it also converts tildes, single quotes, exclamation points, and parentheses to percent escapes, even though they don't absolutely have to be. However, this change isn't forbidden by the URL specification, so web browsers deal reasonably with these excessively encoded URLs.

Although this method allows you to specify the character set, the only such character set you should ever pick is UTF-8. UTF-8 is compatible with the IRI specification, the URI class, modern web browsers, and more additional software than any other encoding you could choose.

Example 5-7 is a program that uses URLEncoder.encode() to print various encoded strings.

Example 5-7. x-www-form-urlencoded strings

```
import java.io.*;
import java.net.*;

public class EncoderTest {

  public static void main(String[] args) {

    try {
      System.out.println(URLEncoder.encode("This string has spaces",
                                      "UTF-8"));
      System.out.println(URLEncoder.encode("This*string*has*asterisks",
                                      "UTF-8"));
      System.out.println(URLEncoder.encode("This%string%has%percent%signs",
                                      "UTF-8"));
      System.out.println(URLEncoder.encode("This+string+has+pluses",
                                      "UTF-8"));
      System.out.println(URLEncoder.encode("This/string/has/slashes",
                                      "UTF-8"));
      System.out.println(URLEncoder.encode("This\"string\"has\"quote\"marks",
                                      "UTF-8"));
      System.out.println(URLEncoder.encode("This:string:has:colons",
                                      "UTF-8"));
      System.out.println(URLEncoder.encode("This~string~has~tildes",
                                      "UTF-8"));
      System.out.println(URLEncoder.encode("This(string)has(parentheses)",
                                      "UTF-8"));
      System.out.println(URLEncoder.encode("This.string.has.periods",
                                      "UTF-8"));
      System.out.println(URLEncoder.encode("This=string=has=equals=signs",
                                      "UTF-8"));
      System.out.println(URLEncoder.encode("This&string&has&ampersands",
                                      "UTF-8"));
      System.out.println(URLEncoder.encode("Thiséstringéhasé
                                      non-ASCII characters", "UTF-8"));
    } catch (UnsupportedEncodingException ex) {
      throw new RuntimeException("Broken VM does not support UTF-8");
```

```
        }
      }
    }
}
```

Here is the output (note that the code needs to be saved in something other than ASCII, and the encoding chosen should be passed as an argument to the compiler to account for the non-ASCII characters in the source code):

```
% javac -encoding UTF8 EncoderTest
% java EncoderTest
This+string+has+spaces
This*string*has*asterisks
This%25string%25has%25percent%25signs
This%2Bstring%2Bhas%2Bpluses
This%2Fstring%2Fhas%2Fslashes
This%22string%22has%22quote%22marks
This%3Astring%3Ahas%3Acolons
This%7Estring%7Ehas%7Etildes
This%28string%29has%28parentheses%29
This.string.has.periods
This%3Dstring%3Dhas%3Dequals%3Dsigns
This%26string%26has%26ampersands
This%C3%A9string%C3%A9has%C3%A9non-ASCII+characters
```

Notice in particular that this method encodes the forward slash, the ampersand, the equals sign, and the colon. It does not attempt to determine how these characters are being used in a URL. Consequently, you have to encode URLs piece by piece rather than encoding an entire URL in one method call. This is an important point, because the most common use of URLEncoder is preparing query strings for communicating with server-side programs that use GET. For example, suppose you want to encode this URL for a Google search:

```
https://www.google.com/search?hl=en&as_q=Java&as_epq=I/O
```

This code fragment encodes it:

```
String query = URLEncoder.encode(
    "https://www.google.com/search?hl=en&as_q=Java&as_epq=I/O", "UTF-8");
System.out.println(query);
```

Unfortunately, the output is:

```
https%3A%2F%2Fwww.google.com%2Fsearch%3Fhl%3Den%26as_q%3DJava%26as_epq%3DI%2FO
```

The problem is that URLEncoder.encode() encodes blindly. It can't distinguish between special characters used as part of the URL or query string, like / and =, and characters that need to be encoded. Consequently, URLs need to be encoded a piece at a time like this:

```
String url = "https://www.google.com/search?";
url += URLEncoder.encode("hl", "UTF-8");
url += "=";
```

```
url += URLEncoder.encode("en", "UTF-8");
url += "&";
url += URLEncoder.encode("as_q", "UTF-8");
url += "=";
url += URLEncoder.encode("Java", "UTF-8");
url += "&";
url += URLEncoder.encode("as_epq", "UTF-8");
url += "=";
url += URLEncoder.encode("I/O", "UTF-8");

System.out.println(url);
```

The output of this is what you actually want:

```
https://www.google.com/search?hl=en&as_q=Java&as_epq=I%2FO
```

In this case, you could have skipped encoding several of the constant strings such as "Java" because you know from inspection that they don't contain any characters that need to be encoded. However, in general, these values will be variables, not constants; and you'll need to encode each piece to be safe.

Example 5-8 is a `QueryString` class that uses `URLEncoder` to encode successive name and value pairs in a Java object, which will be used for sending data to server-side programs. To add name-value pairs, call the `add()` method, which takes two strings as arguments and encodes them. The `getQuery()` method returns the accumulated list of encoded name-value pairs.

Example 5-8. The QueryString class

```java
import java.io.UnsupportedEncodingException;
import java.net.URLEncoder;

public class QueryString {

  private StringBuilder query = new StringBuilder();

  public QueryString() {
  }

  public synchronized void add(String name, String value) {
    query.append('&');
    encode(name, value);
  }

  private synchronized void encode(String name, String value) {
    try {
      query.append(URLEncoder.encode(name, "UTF-8"));
      query.append('=');
      query.append(URLEncoder.encode(value, "UTF-8"));
    } catch (UnsupportedEncodingException ex) {
      throw new RuntimeException("Broken VM does not support UTF-8");
    }
```

```
  }

  public synchronized String getQuery() {
    return query.toString();
  }

  @Override
  public String toString() {
    return getQuery();
  }
}
```

Using this class, we can now encode the previous example:

```
QueryString qs = new QueryString();
qs.add("hl", "en");
qs.add("as_q", "Java");
qs.add("as_epq", "I/O");
String url = "http://www.google.com/search?" + qs;
System.out.println(url);
```

URLDecoder

The corresponding URLDecoder class has a static decode() method that decodes strings encoded in x-www-form-url-encoded format. That is, it converts all plus signs to spaces and all percent escapes to their corresponding character:

```
public static String decode(String s, String encoding)
    throws UnsupportedEncodingException
```

If you have any doubt about which encoding to use, pick UTF-8. It's more likely to be correct than anything else.

An IllegalArgumentException should be thrown if the string contains a percent sign that isn't followed by two hexadecimal digits or decodes into an illegal sequence.

Since URLDecoder does not touch non-escaped characters, you can pass an entire URL to it rather than splitting it into pieces first. For example:

```
String input = "https://www.google.com/" +
    "search?hl=en&as_q=Java&as_epq=I%2FO";
String output = URLDecoder.decode(input, "UTF-8");
System.out.println(output);
```

Proxies

Many systems access the Web and sometimes other non-HTTP parts of the Internet through *proxy servers*. A proxy server receives a request for a remote server from a local client. The proxy server makes the request to the remote server and forwards the result back to the local client. Sometimes this is done for security reasons, such as to prevent remote hosts from learning private details about the local network configuration. Other times it's done to prevent users from accessing forbidden sites by filtering outgoing requests and limiting which sites can be viewed. For instance, an elementary school might want to block access to *http://www.playboy.com*. And still other times it's done purely for performance, to allow multiple users to retrieve the same popular documents from a local cache rather than making repeated downloads from the remote server.

Java programs based on the URL class can work through most common proxy servers and protocols. Indeed, this is one reason you might want to choose to use the URL class rather than rolling your own HTTP or other client on top of raw sockets.

System Properties

For basic operations, all you have to do is set a few system properties to point to the addresses of your local proxy servers. If you are using a pure HTTP proxy, set http.proxyHost to the domain name or the IP address of your proxy server and http.proxyPort to the port of the proxy server (the default is 80). There are several ways to do this, including calling System.setProperty() from within your Java code or using the -D options when launching the program. This example sets the proxy server to 192.168.254.254 and the port to 9000:

```
% java -Dhttp.proxyHost=192.168.254.254  -Dhttp.proxyPort=9000
com.domain.Program
```

If the proxy requires a username and password, you'll need to install an Authentica tor, as we'll discuss shortly in "Accessing Password-Protected Sites" on page 163.

If you want to exclude a host from being proxied and connect directly instead, set the http.nonProxyHosts system property to its hostname or IP address. To exclude multiple hosts, separate their names by vertical bars. For example, this code fragment proxies everything except *java.oreilly.com* and *xml.oreilly.com*:

```
System.setProperty("http.proxyHost", "192.168.254.254");
System.setProperty("http.proxyPort", "9000");
System.setProperty("http.nonProxyHosts", "java.oreilly.com|xml.oreilly.com");
```

You can also use an asterisk as a wildcard to indicate that all the hosts within a particular domain or subdomain should not be proxied. For example, to proxy everything except hosts in the *oreilly.com* domain:

```
% java -Dhttp.proxyHost=192.168.254.254  -Dhttp.nonProxyHosts=*.oreilly.com
com.domain.Program
```

If you are using an FTP proxy server, set the ftp.proxyHost, ftp.proxyPort, and ftp.nonProxyHosts properties in the same way.

Java does not support any other application layer proxies, but if you're using a transport layer SOCKS proxy for all TCP connections, you can identify it with the socksProxy

Host and socksProxyPort system properties. Java does not provide an option for non-proxying with SOCKS. It's an all-or-nothing decision.

The Proxy Class

The Proxy class allows more fine-grained control of proxy servers from within a Java program. Specifically, it allows you to choose different proxy servers for different remote hosts. The proxies themselves are represented by instances of the java.net.Proxy class. There are still only three kinds of proxies, HTTP, SOCKS, and direct connections (no proxy at all), represented by three constants in the Proxy.Type enum:

- Proxy.Type.DIRECT
- Proxy.Type.HTTP
- Proxy.Type.SOCKS

Besides its type, the other important piece of information about a proxy is its address and port, given as a SocketAddress object. For example, this code fragment creates a Proxy object representing an HTTP proxy server on port 80 of *proxy.example.com*:

```
SocketAddress address = new InetSocketAddress("proxy.example.com", 80);
Proxy proxy = new Proxy(Proxy.Type.HTTP, address);
```

Although there are only three kinds of proxy objects, there can be many proxies of the same type for different proxy servers on different hosts.

The ProxySelector Class

Each running virtual machine has a single java.net.ProxySelector object it uses to locate the proxy server for different connections. The default ProxySelector merely inspects the various system properties and the URL's protocol to decide how to connect to different hosts. However, you can install your own subclass of ProxySelector in place of the default selector and use it to choose different proxies based on protocol, host, path, time of day, or other criteria.

The key to this class is the abstract select() method:

```
public abstract List<Proxy> select(URI uri)
```

Java passes this method a URI object (not a URL object) representing the host to which a connection is needed. For a connection made with the URL class, this object typically has the form *http://www.example.com/* or *ftp://ftp.example.com/pub/files/*, for example. For a pure TCP connection made with the Socket class, this URI will have the form *socket://host:port:*, for instance, *socket://www.example.com:80*. The ProxySelector object then chooses the right proxies for this type of object and returns them in a List<Proxy>.

The second abstract method in this class you must implement is `connectFailed()`:

```
public void connectFailed(URI uri, SocketAddress address, IOException ex)
```

This is a callback method used to warn a program that the proxy server isn't actually making the connection. Example 5-9 demonstrates with a `ProxySelector` that attempts to use the proxy server at *proxy.example.com* for all HTTP connections unless the proxy server has previously failed to resolve a connection to a particular URL. In that case, it suggests a direct connection instead.

Example 5-9. A ProxySelector that remembers what it can connect to

```java
import java.io.*;
import java.net.*;
import java.util.*;

public class LocalProxySelector extends ProxySelector {

  private List<URI> failed = new ArrayList<URI>();

  public List<Proxy> select(URI uri) {

    List<Proxy> result = new ArrayList<Proxy>();
    if (failed.contains(uri)
        || !"http".equalsIgnoreCase(uri.getScheme())) {
      result.add(Proxy.NO_PROXY);
    } else {
      SocketAddress proxyAddress
          = new InetSocketAddress( "proxy.example.com", 8000);
      Proxy proxy = new Proxy(Proxy.Type.HTTP, proxyAddress);
      result.add(proxy);
    }

    return result;
  }

  public void connectFailed(URI uri, SocketAddress address, IOException ex) {
    failed.add(uri);
  }
}
```

As I said, each virtual machine has exactly one `ProxySelector`. To change the `Proxy Selector`, pass the new selector to the static `ProxySelector.setDefault()` method, like so:

```
ProxySelector selector = new LocalProxySelector():
ProxySelector.setDefault(selector);
```

From this point forward, all connections opened by that virtual machine will ask the `ProxySelector` for the right proxy to use. You normally shouldn't use this in code running in a shared environment. For instance, you wouldn't change the `ProxySelector` in a servlet because that would change the `ProxySelector` for all servlets running in the same container.

Communicating with Server-Side Programs Through GET

The URL class makes it easy for Java applets and applications to communicate with server-side programs such as CGIs, servlets, PHP pages, and others that use the GET method. (Server-side programs that use the POST method require the `URLConnection` class and are discussed in Chapter 7.) All you need to know is what combination of names and values the program expects to receive. Then you can construct a URL with a query string that provides the requisite names and values. All names and values must be x-www-form-url-encoded—as by the `URLEncoder.encode()` method, discussed earlier in this chapter.

There are a number of ways to determine the exact syntax for a query string that talks to a particular program. If you've written the server-side program yourself, you already know the name-value pairs it expects. If you've installed a third-party program on your own server, the documentation for that program should tell you what it expects. If you're talking to a documented external network API such as the eBay Shopping API (*http://go.developer.ebay.com/developers/ebay/products/shopping-api*), then the service usually provides fairly detailed documentation to tell you exactly what data to send for which purposes.

Many programs are designed to process form input. If this is the case, it's straightforward to figure out what input the program expects. The method the form uses should be the value of the METHOD attribute of the FORM element. This value should be either GET, in which case you use the process described here, or POST, in which case you use the process described in Chapter 7. The part of the URL that precedes the query string is given by the value of the ACTION attribute of the FORM element. Note that this may be a relative URL, in which case you'll need to determine the corresponding absolute URL. Finally, the names in the name-value pairs are simply the values of the NAME attributes of the INPUT elements. The values of the pairs are whatever the user types into the form.

For example, consider this HTML form for the local search engine on my Cafe con Leche site. You can see that it uses the GET method. The program that processes the form is accessed via the URL *http://www.google.com/search*. It has four separate name-value pairs, three of which have default values:

```
<form name="search" action="http://www.google.com/search" method="get">
  <input name="q" />
  <input type="hidden" value="cafeconleche.org" name="domains" />
  <input type="hidden" name="sitesearch" value="cafeconleche.org" />
  <input type="hidden" name="sitesearch2" value="cafeconleche.org" />
  <br />
  <input type="image" height="22" width="55"
```

```
        src="images/search_blue.gif" alt="search" border="0"
        name="search-image" />
  </form>
```

The type of the INPUT field doesn't matter. For instance, it doesn't matter if it's a set of checkboxes, a pop-up list, or a text field. Only the name of each INPUT field and the value you give it is significant. The submit input tells the web browser when to send the data but does not give the server any extra information. Sometimes you find hidden INPUT fields that must have particular required default values. This form has three hidden INPUT fields. There are many different form tags in HTML that produce pop-up menus, radio buttons, and more. However, although these input widgets appear different to the user, the format of data they send to the server is the same. Each form element provides a name and an encoded string value.

In some cases, the program you're talking to may not be able to handle arbitrary text strings for values of particular inputs. However, since the form is meant to be read and filled in by human beings, it should provide sufficient clues to figure out what input is expected; for instance, that a particular field is supposed to be a two-letter state abbreviation or a phone number. Sometimes the inputs may not have such obvious names. There may not even be a form, just links to follow. In this case, you have to do some experimenting, first copying some existing values and then tweaking them to see what values are and aren't accepted. You don't need to do this in a Java program. You can simply edit the URL in the address or location bar of your web browser window.

 The likelihood that other hackers may experiment with your own server-side programs in such a fashion is a good reason to make them extremely robust against unexpected input.

Regardless of how you determine the set of name-value pairs the server expects, communicating with it once you know them is simple. All you have to do is create a query string that includes the necessary name-value pairs, then form a URL that includes that query string. Send the query string to the server and read its response using the same methods you use to connect to a server and retrieve a static HTML page. There's no special protocol to follow once the URL is constructed. (There is a special protocol to follow for the POST method, however, which is why discussion of that method will have to wait until Chapter 7.)

To demonstrate this procedure, let's write a very simple command-line program to look up topics in the Open Directory (*http://dmoz.org/*). This site is shown in Figure 5-1 and it has the advantage of being really simple.

Figure 5-1. The user interface for the Open Directory

The Open Directory interface is a simple form with one input field named `search`; input typed in this field is sent to a program at *http://search.dmoz.org/cgi-bin/search*, which does the actual search. The HTML for the form looks like this:

```
<form class="center mb1em" action="search" method="GET">
  <input style="*vertical-align:middle;" size="45" name="q" value="" class="qN">
  <input style="*vertical-align:middle; *padding-top:1px;" value="Search"
      class="btn" type="submit">
  <a href="search?type=advanced"><span class="advN">advanced</span></a>
</form>
```

There are only two input fields in this form: the Submit button and a text field named *q*. Thus, to submit a search request to the Open Directory, you just need to append *q=searchTerm* to *http://www.dmoz.org/search*. For example, to search for "java", you would open a connection to the URL *http://www.dmoz.org/search/?q=java* and read the resulting input stream. Example 5-10 does exactly this.

Example 5-10. Do an Open Directory search

```java
import java.io.*;
import java.net.*;

public class DMoz {

  public static void main(String[] args) {

    String target = "";
    for (int i = 0; i < args.length; i++) {
      target += args[i] + " ";
    }
    target = target.trim();

    QueryString query = new QueryString();
    query.add("q", target);
    try {
      URL u = new URL("http://www.dmoz.org/search/?" + query);
      try (InputStream in = new BufferedInputStream(u.openStream())) {
        InputStreamReader theHTML = new InputStreamReader(in);
        int c;
        while ((c = theHTML.read()) != -1) {
          System.out.print((char) c);
        }
      }
    } catch (MalformedURLException ex) {
      System.err.println(ex);
    } catch (IOException ex) {
      System.err.println(ex);
    }
  }
}
```

Of course, a lot more effort could be expended on parsing and displaying the results. But notice how simple the code was to talk to this server. Aside from the funky-looking URL and the slightly greater likelihood that some pieces of it need to be x-www-form-url-encoded, talking to a server-side program that uses GET is no harder than retrieving any other HTML page.

Accessing Password-Protected Sites

Many popular sites require a username and password for access. Some sites, such as the W3C member pages, implement this through HTTP authentication. Others, such as the *New York Times* website, implement it through cookies and HTML forms. Java's URL class can access sites that use HTTP authentication, although you'll of course need to tell it which username and password to use.

Supporting sites that use nonstandard, cookie-based authentication is more challenging, not least because this varies a lot from one site to another. Implementing cookie authentication is hard short of implementing a complete web browser with full HTML forms and cookie support; we'll discuss Java's cookie support in Chapter 7. Accessing sites protected by standard HTTP authentication is much easier.

The Authenticator Class

The java.net package includes an Authenticator class you can use to provide a username and password for sites that protect themselves using HTTP authentication:

```
public abstract class Authenticator extends Object
```

Since Authenticator is an abstract class, you must subclass it. Different subclasses may retrieve the information in different ways. For example, a character mode program might just ask the user to type the username and password on System.in. A GUI program would likely put up a dialog box like the one shown in Figure 5-2. An automated robot might read the username out of an encrypted file.

Figure 5-2. An authentication dialog

To make the URL class use the subclass, install it as the default authenticator by passing it to the static Authenticator.setDefault() method:

```
public static void setDefault(Authenticator a)
```

For example, if you've written an Authenticator subclass named DialogAuthenticator, you'd install it like this:

```
Authenticator.setDefault(new DialogAuthenticator());
```

You only need to do this once. From this point forward, when the URL class needs a username and password, it will ask the DialogAuthenticator using the static Authenticator.requestPasswordAuthentication() method:

```
public static PasswordAuthentication requestPasswordAuthentication(
    InetAddress address, int port, String protocol, String prompt, String scheme)
    throws SecurityException
```

The `address` argument is the host for which authentication is required. The `port` argument is the port on that host, and the `protocol` argument is the application layer protocol by which the site is being accessed. The HTTP server provides the `prompt`. It's typically the name of the realm for which authentication is required. (Some large web servers such as *www.ibiblio.org* have multiple realms, each of which requires different usernames and passwords.) The `scheme` is the authentication scheme being used. (Here the word *scheme* is not being used as a synonym for *protocol*. Rather, it is an HTTP authentication scheme, typically basic.)

Untrusted applets are not allowed to ask the user for a name and password. Trusted applets can do so, but only if they possess the `requestPasswordAuthentication Net Permission`. Otherwise, `Authenticator.requestPasswordAuthentication()` throws a `SecurityException`.

The `Authenticator` subclass must override the `getPasswordAuthentication()` method. Inside this method, you collect the username and password from the user or some other source and return it as an instance of the `java.net.PasswordAuthentication` class:

```
protected PasswordAuthentication getPasswordAuthentication()
```

If you don't want to authenticate this request, return `null`, and Java will tell the server it doesn't know how to authenticate the connection. If you submit an incorrect username or password, Java will call `getPasswordAuthentication()` again to give you another chance to provide the right data. You normally have five tries to get the username and password correct; after that, `openStream()` throws a `ProtocolException`.

Usernames and passwords are cached within the same virtual machine session. Once you set the correct password for a realm, you shouldn't be asked for it again unless you've explicitly deleted the password by zeroing out the `char` array that contains it.

You can get more details about the request by invoking any of these methods inherited from the `Authenticator` superclass:

```
protected final InetAddress getRequestingSite()
protected final int         getRequestingPort()
protected final String      getRequestingProtocol()
protected final String      getRequestingPrompt()
protected final String      getRequestingScheme()
protected final String      getRequestingHost()
protected final String      getRequestingURL()
protected Authenticator.RequestorType getRequestorType()
```

These methods either return the information as given in the last call to `requestPass wordAuthentication()` or return `null` if that information is not available. (If the port isn't available, `getRequestingPort()` returns -1.)

The getRequestingURL() method returns the complete URL for which authentication has been requested—an important detail if a site uses different names and passwords for different files. The getRequestorType() method returns one of the two named constants (i.e., Authenticator.RequestorType.PROXY or Authenticator.Requestor Type.SERVER) to indicate whether the server or the proxy server is requesting the authentication.

The PasswordAuthentication Class

PasswordAuthentication is a very simple final class that supports two read-only properties: username and password. The username is a String. The password is a char array so that the password can be erased when it's no longer needed. A String would have to wait to be garbage collected before it could be erased, and even then it might still exist somewhere in memory on the local system, possibly even on disk if the block of memory that contained it had been swapped out to virtual memory at one point. Both username and password are set in the constructor:

```
public PasswordAuthentication(String userName, char[] password)
```

Each is accessed via a getter method:

```
public String getUserName()
public char[] getPassword()
```

The JPasswordField Class

One useful tool for asking users for their passwords in a more or less secure fashion is the JPasswordField component from Swing:

```
public class JPasswordField extends JTextField
```

This lightweight component behaves almost exactly like a text field. However, anything the user types into it is echoed as an asterisk. This way, the password is safe from anyone looking over the user's shoulder at what's being typed on the screen.

JPasswordField also stores the passwords as a char array so that when you're done with the password you can overwrite it with zeros. It provides the getPassword() method to return this:

```
public char[] getPassword()
```

Otherwise, you mostly use the methods it inherits from the JTextField superclass. Example 5-11 demonstrates a Swing-based Authenticator subclass that brings up a dialog to ask the user for his username and password. Most of this code handles the GUI. A JPasswordField collects the password and a simple JTextField retrieves the username. Flip back to Figure 5-2 to see the rather simple dialog box this produces.

Example 5-11. A GUI authenticator

```java
import java.awt.*;
import java.awt.event.*;
import java.net.*;
import javax.swing.*;

public class DialogAuthenticator extends Authenticator {

  private JDialog passwordDialog;
  private JTextField usernameField = new JTextField(20);
  private JPasswordField passwordField = new JPasswordField(20);
  private JButton okButton = new JButton("OK");
  private JButton cancelButton = new JButton("Cancel");
  private JLabel mainLabel
      = new JLabel("Please enter username and password: ");

  public DialogAuthenticator() {
    this("", new JFrame());
  }

  public DialogAuthenticator(String username) {
    this(username, new JFrame());
  }

  public DialogAuthenticator(JFrame parent) {
    this("", parent);
  }

  public DialogAuthenticator(String username, JFrame parent) {
    this.passwordDialog = new JDialog(parent, true);
    Container pane = passwordDialog.getContentPane();
    pane.setLayout(new GridLayout(4, 1));

    JLabel userLabel = new JLabel("Username: ");
    JLabel passwordLabel = new JLabel("Password: ");
    pane.add(mainLabel);
    JPanel p2 = new JPanel();
    p2.add(userLabel);
    p2.add(usernameField);
    usernameField.setText(username);
    pane.add(p2);
    JPanel p3 = new JPanel();
    p3.add(passwordLabel);
    p3.add(passwordField);
    pane.add(p3);
    JPanel p4 = new JPanel();
    p4.add(okButton);
    p4.add(cancelButton);
    pane.add(p4);
    passwordDialog.pack();

    ActionListener al = new OKResponse();
```

```java
    okButton.addActionListener(al);
    usernameField.addActionListener(al);
    passwordField.addActionListener(al);
    cancelButton.addActionListener(new CancelResponse());
  }

  private void show() {
    String prompt = this.getRequestingPrompt();
    if (prompt == null) {
      String site     = this.getRequestingSite().getHostName();
      String protocol = this.getRequestingProtocol();
      int    port     = this.getRequestingPort();
      if (site != null & protocol != null) {
        prompt = protocol + "://" + site;
        if (port > 0) prompt += ":" + port;
      } else {
        prompt = "";
      }
    }

    mainLabel.setText("Please enter username and password for "
        + prompt + ": ");
    passwordDialog.pack();
    passwordDialog.setVisible(true);
  }

  PasswordAuthentication response = null;

  class OKResponse implements ActionListener {
    @Override
    public void actionPerformed(ActionEvent e) {
      passwordDialog.setVisible(false);
      // The password is returned as an array of
      // chars for security reasons.
      char[] password = passwordField.getPassword();
      String username = usernameField.getText();
      // Erase the password in case this is used again.
      passwordField.setText("");
      response = new PasswordAuthentication(username, password);
    }
  }

  class CancelResponse implements ActionListener {
    @Override
    public void actionPerformed(ActionEvent e) {
      passwordDialog.setVisible(false);
      // Erase the password in case this is used again.
      passwordField.setText("");
      response = null;
    }
  }
}
```

```
  public PasswordAuthentication getPasswordAuthentication() {
    this.show();
    return this.response;
  }
}
```

Example 5-12 is a revised SourceViewer program that asks the user for a name and password using the DialogAuthenticator class.

Example 5-12. A program to download password-protected web pages

```
import java.io.*;
import java.net.*;

public class SecureSourceViewer {

  public static void main (String args[]) {

    Authenticator.setDefault(new DialogAuthenticator());

    for (int i = 0; i < args.length; i++) {
      try {
        // Open the URL for reading
        URL u = new URL(args[i]);
        try (InputStream in = new BufferedInputStream(u.openStream())) {
          // chain the InputStream to a Reader
          Reader r = new InputStreamReader(in);
          int c;
          while ((c = r.read()) != -1) {
            System.out.print((char) c);
          }
        }
      } catch (MalformedURLException ex) {
        System.err.println(args[0] + " is not a parseable URL");
      } catch (IOException ex) {
        System.err.println(ex);
      }

      // print a blank line to separate pages
      System.out.println();
    }

    // Since we used the AWT, we have to explicitly exit.
    System.exit(0);
  }
}
```

CHAPTER 6

HTTP

The Hypertext Transfer Protocol (HTTP) is a standard that defines how a web client talks to a server and how data is transferred from the server back to the client. Although HTTP is usually thought of as a means of transferring HTML files and the pictures embedded in them, HTTP is data format agnostic. It can be used to transfer TIFF pictures, Microsoft Word documents, Windows *.exe* files, or anything else that can be represented in bytes. To write programs that use HTTP, you'll need to understand HTTP at a deeper level than the average web page designer. This chapter goes behind the scenes to show you what actually happens when you type *http://www.google.com* into the browser's address bar and press Return.

The Protocol

HTTP is the standard protocol for communication between web browsers and web servers. HTTP specifies how a client and server establish a connection, how the client requests data from the server, how the server responds to that request, and finally, how the connection is closed. HTTP connections use the TCP/IP protocol for data transfer. For each request from client to server, there is a sequence of four steps:

1. The client opens a TCP connection to the server on port 80, by default; other ports may be specified in the URL.

2. The client sends a message to the server requesting the resource at a specified path. The request includes a header, and optionally (depending on the nature of the request) a blank line followed by data for the request.

3. The server sends a response to the client. The response begins with a response code, followed by a header full of metadata, a blank line, and the requested document or an error message.

4. The server closes the connection.

This is the basic HTTP 1.0 procedure. In HTTP 1.1 and later, multiple requests and responses can be sent in series over a single TCP connection. That is, steps 2 and 3 can repeat multiple times in between steps 1 and 4. Furthermore, in HTTP 1.1, requests and responses can be sent in multiple chunks. This is more scalable.

Each request and response has the same basic form: a header line, an HTTP header containing metadata, a blank line, and then a message body. A typical client request looks something like this:

```
GET /index.html HTTP/1.1
User-Agent: Mozilla/5.0 (Macintosh; Intel Mac OS X 10.8; rv:20.0)
 Gecko/20100101 Firefox/20.0
Host: en.wikipedia.org
Connection: keep-alive
Accept-Language: en-US,en;q=0.5
Accept-Encoding: gzip, deflate
Accept: text/html,application/xhtml+xml,application/xml;q=0.9,*/*;q=0.8
```

GET requests like this one do not contain a message body, so the request ends with a blank line.

The first line is called the *request line*, and includes a method, a path to a resource, and the version of HTTP. The method specifies the operation being requested. The GET method asks the server to return a representation of a resource. */index.html* is the path to the resource requested from the server. HTTP/1.1 is the version of the protocol that the client understands.

Although the request line is all that is required, a client request usually includes other information as well in a header. Each line takes the following form:

```
Keyword: Value
```

Keywords are not case sensitive. Values sometimes are and sometimes aren't. Both keywords and values should be ASCII only. If a value is too long, you can add a space or tab to the beginning of the next line and continue it.

Lines in the header are terminated by a carriage-return linefeed pair.

The first keyword in this example is User-Agent, which lets the server know what browser is being used and allows it to send files optimized for the particular browser type. The following line says that the request comes from version 2.4 of the Lynx browser:

```
User-Agent: Lynx/2.4 libwww/2.1.4
```

All but the oldest first-generation browsers also include a Host field specifying the server's name, which allows web servers to distinguish between different named hosts served from the same IP address:

```
Host: www.cafeaulait.org
```

The last keyword in this example is `Accept`, which tells the server the types of data the client can handle (though servers often ignore this). For example, the following line says that the client can handle four MIME media types, corresponding to HTML documents, plain text, and JPEG and GIF images:

```
Accept: text/html, text/plain, image/gif, image/jpeg
```

`MIME` types arc classified at two levels: a type and a subtype. The type shows very generally what kind of data is contained: is it a picture, text, or movie? The subtype identifies the specific type of data: GIF image, JPEG image, TIFF image. For example, HTML's content type is `text/html`; the type is `text`, and the subtype is `html`. The content type for a JPEG image is `image/jpeg`; the type is `image`, and the subtype is `jpeg`. Eight top-level types have been defined:

- text/* for human-readable words
- image/* for pictures
- model/* for 3D models such as VRML files
- audio/* for sound
- video/* for moving pictures, possibly including sound
- application/* for binary data
- message/* for protocol-specific envelopes such as email messages and HTTP responses
- multipart/* for containers of multiple documents and resources

Each of these has many different subtypes.

The most current list of registered MIME types is available from *http://www.iana.org/assignments/media-types/*. In addition, nonstandard custom types and subtypes can be freely defined as long as they begin with *x-*. For example, Flash files are commonly assigned the type *application/x-shockwave-flash*.

Finally, the request is terminated with a blank line—that is, two carriage return/linefeed pairs, `\r\n\r\n`.

Once the server sees that blank line, it begins sending its response to the client over the same connection. The response begins with a status line, followed by a header describing the response using the same "name: value" syntax as the request header, a blank line, and the requested resource. A typical successful response looks something like this:

```
HTTP/1.1 200 OK
Date: Sun, 21 Apr 2013 15:12:46 GMT
Server: Apache
Connection: close
Content-Type: text/html; charset=ISO-8859-1
Content-length: 115
```

```
<html>
<head>
<title>
A Sample HTML file
</title>
</head>
<body>
The rest of the document goes here
</body>
</html>
```

The first line indicates the protocol the server is using (HTTP/1.1), followed by a response code. 200 OK is the most common response code, indicating that the request was successful. The other header lines identify the date the request was made in the server's time frame, the server software (Apache), a promise that the server will close the connection when it's finished sending, the MIME media type, and the length of the document delivered (not counting this header)—in this case, 107 bytes.

Table 6-1 lists the standard and experimental response codes you're most likely to encounter, minus a few used by WebDAV.

Table 6-1. The HTTP 1.1 response codes

Code and message	Meaning	HttpURLConnection constant
1XX	Informational.	
100 Continue	The server is prepared to accept the request body and the client should send it; allows clients to ask whether the server will accept a request before they send a large amount of data as part of the request.	N/A
101 Switching Protocols	The server accepts the client's request in the Upgrade header field to change the application protocol (e.g., from HTTP to WebSockets.)	N/A
2XX Successful	Request succeeded.	
200 OK	The most common response code. If the request method was GET or POST, the requested data is contained in the response along with the usual headers. If the request method was HEAD, only the header information is included.	HTTP_OK
201 Created	The server has created a resource at the URL specified in the body of the response. The client should now attempt to load that URL. This code is only sent in response to POST requests.	HTTP_CREATED
202 Accepted	This rather uncommon response indicates that a request (generally from POST) is being processed, but the processing is not yet complete, so no response can be returned. However, the server should return an HTML page that explains the situation to the user and provide an estimate of when the request is likely to be completed, and, ideally, a link to a status monitor of some kind.	HTTP_ACCEPTED
203 Non-authoritative Information	The resource representation was returned from a caching proxy or other local source and is not guaranteed to be up to date.	HTTP_NOT_AUTHORITA TIVE

Code and message	Meaning	HttpURLConnection constant
204 No Content	The server has successfully processed the request but has no information to send back to the client. This is normally the result of a poorly written form-processing program on the server that accepts data but does not return a response to the user.	HTTP_NO_CONTENT
205 Reset Content	The server has successfully processed the request but has no information to send back to the client. Furthermore, the client should clear the form to which the request is sent.	HTTP_RESET
206 Partial Content	The server has returned the part of the resource the client requested using the byte range extension to HTTP, rather than the whole document.	HTTP_PARTIAL
226 IM Used	Response is delta encoded.	N/A
3XX Redirection	Relocation and redirection.	
300 Multiple Choices	The server is providing a list of different representations (e.g., PostScript and PDF) for the requested document.	HTTP_MULT_CHOICE
301 Moved Permanently	The resource has moved to a new URL. The client should automatically load the resource at this URL and update any bookmarks that point to the old URL.	HTTP_MOVED_PERM
302 Moved Temporarily	The resource is at a new URL temporarily, but its location will change again in the foreseeable future; therefore, bookmarks should not be updated. Sometimes used by proxies that require the user to log in locally before accessing the Web.	HTTP_MOVED_TEMP
303 See Other	Generally used in response to a POST form request, this code indicates that the user should retrieve a resource from a different URL using GET.	HTTP_SEE_OTHER
304 Not Modified	The If-Modified-Since header indicates that the client wants the document only if it has been recently updated. This status code is returned if the document has not been updated. In this case, the client should load the document from its cache.	HTTP_NOT_MODIFIED
305 Use Proxy	The Location header field contains the address of a proxy that will serve the response.	HTTP_USE_PROXY
307 Temporary Redirect	Similar to 302 but without allowing the HTTP method to change.	N/A
308 Permanent Redirect	Similar to 301 but without allowing the HTTP method to change.	N/A
4XX	Client error.	
400 Bad Request	The client request to the server used improper syntax. This is rather unusual in normal web browsing but more common when debugging custom clients.	HTTP_BAD_REQUEST
401 Unauthorized	Authorization, generally a username and password, is required to access this page. Either a username and password have not yet been presented or the username and password are invalid.	HTTP_UNAUTHORIZED

Code and message	Meaning	HttpURLConnection constant
402 Payment Required	Not used today, but may be used in the future to indicate that some sort of payment is required to access the resource.	`HTTP_PAYMENT_RE QUIRED`
403 Forbidden	The server understood the request, but is deliberately refusing to process it. Authorization will not help. This is sometimes used when a client has exceeded its quota.	`HTTP_FORBIDDEN`
404 Not Found	This most common error response indicates that the server cannot find the requested resource. It may indicate a bad link, a document that has moved with no forwarding address, a mistyped URL, or something similar.	`HTTP_NOT_FOUND`
405 Method Not Allowed	The request method is not allowed for the specified resource; for instance, you tried to PUT a file on a web server that doesn't support PUT or tried to POST to a URI that only allows GET.	`HTTP_BAD_METHOD`
406 Not Acceptable	The requested resource cannot be provided in a format the client is willing to accept, as indicated by the Accept field of the request HTTP header.	`HTTP_NOT_ACCEPTABLE`
407 Proxy Authentication Required	An intermediate proxy server requires authentication from the client, probably in the form of a username and password, before it will retrieve the requested resource.	`HTTP_PROXY_AUTH`
408 Request Timeout	The client took too long to send the request, perhaps because of network congestion.	`HTTP_CLIENT_TIMEOUT`
409 Conflict	A temporary conflict prevents the request from being fulfilled; for instance, two clients are trying to PUT the same file at the same time.	`HTTP_CONFLICT`
410 Gone	Like a 404, but makes a stronger assertion about the existence of the resource. The resource has been deliberately deleted (not moved) and will not be restored. Links to it should be removed.	`HTTP_GONE`
411 Length Required	The client must but did not send a Content-length field in the client request HTTP header.	`HTTP_LENGTH_REQUIRED`
412 Precondition Failed	A condition for the request that the client specified in the request HTTP header is not satisfied.	`HTTP_PRECON_FAILED`
413 Request Entity Too Large	The body of the client request is larger than the server is able to process at this time.	`HTTP_ENTI TY_TOO_LARGE`
414 Request-URI Too Long	The URI of the request is too long. This is important to prevent certain buffer overflow attacks.	`HTTP_REQ_TOO_LONG`
415 Unsupported Media Type	The server does not understand or accept the MIME content type of the request body.	`HTTP_UNSUPPOR TED_TYPE`
416 Requested range Not Satisfiable	The server cannot send the byte range the client requested.	N/A
417 Expectation Failed	The server cannot meet the client's expectation given in an Expect-request header field.	N/A
418 I'm a teapot	Attempting to brew coffee with a teapot.	N/A
420 Enhance Your Calm	The server is rate limiting the request. Nonstandard; used only by Twitter.	N/A

Code and message	Meaning	HttpURLConnection constant
422 Unprocessable Entity	The content type of the request body is recognized, and the body is syntactically correct, but nonetheless the server can't process it.	N/A
424 Failed Dependency	Request failed as a result of the failure of a previous request.	N/A
426 Upgrade Required	Client is using a too old or insecure a version of the HTTP protocol.	N/A
428 Precondition Required	Request must supply an If-Match header.	N/A
429 Too Many Requests	The client is being rate limited and should slow down.	N/A
431 Request Header Fields Too Large	Either the header as a whole is too large, or one particular header field is too large.	N/A
451 Unavailable For Legal Reasons	Experimental; the server is prohibited by law from servicing the request.	N/A
5XX	Server error.	
500 Internal Server Error	An unexpected condition occurred that the server does not know how to handle.	HTTP_SERVER_ERROR HTTP_INTERNAL_ERROR
501 Not Implemented	The server does not have a feature that is needed to fulfill this request. A server that cannot handle PUT requests might send this response to a client that tried to PUT form data to it.	HTTP_NOT_IMPLEMENTED
502 Bad Gateway	This code is applicable only to servers that act as proxies or gateways. It indicates that the proxy received an invalid response from a server it was connecting to in an effort to fulfill the request.	HTTP_BAD_GATEWAY
503 Service Unavailable	The server is temporarily unable to handle the request, perhaps due to overloading or maintenance.	HTTP_UNAVAILABLE
504 Gateway Timeout	The proxy server did not receive a response from the upstream server within a reasonable amount of time, so it can't send the desired response to the client.	HTTP_GATEWAY_TIMEOUT
505 HTTP Version Not Supported	The server does not support the version of HTTP the client is using (e.g., the as-yet-nonexistent HTTP 2.0).	HTTP_VERSION
507 Insufficient Storage	Server does not have enough space to store the supplied request entity; typically used for POST or PUT.	
511 Network Authentication Required	The client needs to authenticate to gain network access (e.g., on a hotel wireless network).	N/A

Regardless of version, a response code from 100 to 199 always indicates an informational response, 200 to 299 always indicates success, 300 to 399 always indicates redirection, 400 to 499 always indicates a client error, and 500 to 599 indicates a server error.

Keep-Alive

HTTP 1.0 opens a new connection for each request. In practice, the time taken to open and close all the connections in a typical web session can outweigh the time taken to transmit the data, especially for sessions with many small documents. This is even more problematic for encrypted HTTPS connections using SSL or TLS, because the handshake to set up a secure socket is substantially more work than setting up a regular socket.

In HTTP 1.1 and later, the server doesn't have to close the socket after it sends its response. It can leave it open and wait for a new request from the client on the same socket. Multiple requests and responses can be sent in series over a single TCP connection. However, the lockstep pattern of a client request followed by a server response remains the same.

A client indicates that it's willing to reuse a socket by including a *Connection* field in the HTTP request header with the value *Keep-Alive*:

```
Connection: Keep-Alive
```

The URL class transparently supports HTTP Keep-Alive unless explicitly turned off. That is, it will reuse a socket if you connect to the same server again before the server has closed the connection. You can control Java's use of HTTP Keep-Alive with several system properties:

- Set `http.keepAlive` to "true or false" to enable/disable HTTP Keep-Alive. (It is enabled by default.)

- Set `http.maxConnections` to the number of sockets you're willing to hold open at one time. The default is 5.

- Set `http.keepAlive.remainingData` to true to let Java clean up after abandoned connections (Java 6 or later). It is false by default.

- Set `sun.net.http.errorstream.enableBuffering` to true to attempt to buffer the relatively short error streams from 400- and 500-level responses, so the connection can be freed up for reuse sooner. It is false by default.

- Set `sun.net.http.errorstream.bufferSize` to the number of bytes to use for buffering error streams. The default is 4,096 bytes.

- Set `sun.net.http.errorstream.timeout` to the number of milliseconds before timing out a read from the error stream. It is 300 milliseconds by default.

The defaults are reasonable, except that you probably do want to set `sun.net.http.errorstream.enableBuffering` to true unless you want to read the error streams from failed requests.

HTTP 2.0, which is mostly based on the SPDY protocol invented at Google, further optimizes HTTP transfers through header compression, pipelining requests and responses, and asynchronous connection multiplexing. However, these optimizations are usually performed in a translation layer that shields application programmers from the details, so the code you write will still mostly follow the preceding steps 1–4. Java does not yet support HTTP 2.0; but when the capability is added, your programs shouldn't need to change to take advantage of it, as long as you access HTTP servers via the URL and URLConnection classes.

HTTP Methods

Communication with an HTTP server follows a request-response pattern: one stateless request followed by one stateless response. Each HTTP request has two or three parts:

- A start line containing the HTTP method and a path to the resource on which the method should be executed
- A header of name-value fields that provide meta-information such as authentication credentials and preferred formats to be used in the request
- A request body containing a representation of a resource (POST and PUT only)

There are four main HTTP methods, four verbs if you will, that identify the operations that can be performed:

- GET
- POST
- PUT
- DELETE

If that seems like too few, especially compared to the infinite number of object-oriented methods you may be accustomed to designing programs around, that's because HTTP puts most of the emphasis on the nouns: the resources identified by URIs. The uniform interface provided by these four methods is sufficient for nearly all practical purposes.

These four methods are not arbitrary. They have specific semantics that applications should adhere to. The GET method retrieves a representation of a resource. GET is side-effect free, and can be repeated without concern if it fails. Furthermore, its output is often cached, though that can be controlled with the right headers, as you'll see shortly. In a properly architected system, GET requests can be bookmarked and prefetched without concern. For example, one should not allow a file to be deleted merely by following a link because a browser may GET all links on a page before the user asks it to.

By contrast, a well-behaved browser or web spider will not POST to a link without explicit user action.

The PUT method uploads a representation of a resource to the server at a known URL. It is not side-effect free, but it is *idempotent*. That is, it can be repeated without concern if it fails. Putting the same document in the same place on the same server twice in a row leaves the server in the same state as only putting it once.

The DELETE method removes a resource from a specified URL. It, too, is not side-effect free, but is idempotent. If you aren't sure whether a delete request succeeded—for instance, because the socket disconnected after you sent the request but before you received a response—just send the request again. Deleting the same resource twice is not a mistake.

The POST method is the most general method. It too uploads a representation of a resource to a server at a known URL, but it does not specify what the server is to do with the newly supplied resource. For instance, the server does not necessarily have to make that resource available at the target URL, but may instead move it to a different URL. Or the server might use the data to update the state of one or more completely different resources. POST should be used for unsafe operations that should not be repeated, such as making a purchase.

Because GET requests include all necessary information in the URL, they can be book-marked, linked to, spidered, and so forth. POST, PUT, and DELETE requests cannot be. This is deliberate. GET is intended for noncommittal actions, like browsing a static web page. The other methods, especially POST, are intended for actions that commit to something. For example, adding an item to a shopping cart should send a GET, because this action doesn't commit; the user can still abandon the cart. However, placing the order should send a POST because that action makes a commitment. This is why browsers ask you if you're sure when you go back to a page that uses POST (as shown in Figure 6-1). Reposting data may buy two copies of a book and charge your credit card twice.

Figure 6-1. Repost confirmation

In practice, POST is vastly overused on the Web today. Any safe operation that does not commit the user to anything should use GET rather than POST. Only operations that commit the user should use POST.

One sometimes mistaken reason for preferring POST over GET is when forms require large amounts of input. There's an outdated misconception that browsers can only work with query strings of a few hundred bytes. Although this was true in the mid-1990s, today all major browsers are good up to URL lengths of at least 2,000 characters. If you have more form data to submit than that, you may indeed need to support POST; but safe operations should still prefer GET for nonbrowser clients. This is less common than you might think, though. You usually only exceed those limits if you're uploading data to the server to create a new resource, rather than merely locating an existing resource on the server; and in these cases POST or PUT is usually the right answer anyway.

In addition to these four main HTTP methods, a few others are used in special circumstances. The most common such method is HEAD, which acts like a GET except it only returns the header for the resource, not the actual data. This is commonly used to check the modification date of a file, to see whether a copy stored in the local cache is still valid.

The other two that Java supports are OPTIONS, which lets the client ask the server what it can do with a specified resource; and TRACE, which echoes back the client request for debugging purposes, especially when proxy servers are misbehaving. Different servers recognize other nonstandard methods including COPY and MOVE, but Java does not send these.

The URL class described in the previous chapter uses GET to communicate with HTTP servers. The URLConnection class (coming up in the Chapter 7) can use all four of these methods.

The Request Body

The GET method retrieves a representation of a resource identified by a URL. The exact location of the resource you want to GET from a server is specified by the various parts of the path and query string. How different paths and query strings map to different resources is determined by the server. The URL class doesn't really care about that. As long as it knows the URL, it can download from it.

POST and PUT are more complex. In these cases, the client supplies the representation of the resource, in addition to the path and the query string. The representation of the resource is sent in the body of the request, after the header. That is, it sends these four items in order:

1. A starter line including the method, path and query string, and HTTP version

---

2. An HTTP header

3. A blank line (two successive carriage return/linefeed pairs)

4. The body

For example, this POST request sends form data to a server:

```
POST /cgi-bin/register.pl HTTP 1.0
Date: Sun, 27 Apr 2013 12:32:36
Host: www.cafeaulait.org
Content-type: application/x-www-form-urlencoded
Content-length: 54

username=Elliotte+Harold&email=elharo%40ibiblio.org
```

In this example, the body contains an *application/x-www-form-urlencoded* data, but that's just one possibility. In general, the body can contain arbitrary bytes. However, the HTTP header should include two fields that specify the nature of the body:

- A Content-length field that specifies how many bytes are in the body (54 in the preceding example)

- A Content-type field that specifies the MIME media type of the bytes (*application/x-www-form-urlencoded* in the preceeding example).

The *application/x-www-form-urlencoded* MIME type used in the preceding example is common because it's how web browsers encode most form submissions. Thus it's used by a lot of server-side programs that talk to browsers. However, it's hardly the only possible type you can send in the body. For example, a camera uploading a picture to a photo sharing site can send image/jpeg. A text editor might send text/html. It's all just bytes in the end. For example, here's a PUT request that uploads an Atom document:

```
PUT /blog/software-development/the-power-of-pomodoros/ HTTP/1.1
Host: elharo.com
User-Agent: AtomMaker/1.0
Authorization: Basic ZGFmZnk6c2VjZXJldA==
Content-Type: application/atom+xml;type=entry
Content-Length: 322

<?xml version="1.0"?>
<entry xmlns="http://www.w3.org/2005/Atom">
 <title>The Power of Pomodoros</title>
 <id>urn:uuid:101a41a6-722b-4d9b-8afb-ccfb01d77499</id>
 <updated>2013-02-22T19:40:52Z</updated>
 <author><name>Elliotte Harold</name></author>
 <content>I hadn't paid much attention to Pomodoro...</content>
</entry>
```

Cookies

Many websites use small strings of text known as *cookies* to store persistent client-side state between connections. Cookies are passed from server to client and back again in the HTTP headers of requests and responses. Cookies can be used by a server to indicate session IDs, shopping cart contents, login credentials, user preferences, and more. For instance, a cookie set by an online bookstore might have the value ISBN=0802099912&price=$34.95 to specify a book that I've put in my shopping cart. However, more likely, the value is a meaningless string such as ATVPDKIKX0DER, which identifies a particular record in a database of some kind where the real information is kept. Usually the cookie values do not contain the data but merely point to it on the server.

Cookies are limited to nonwhitespace ASCII text, and may not contain commas or semicolons.

To set a cookie in a browser, the server includes a Set-Cookie header line in the HTTP header. For example, this HTTP header sets the cookie "cart" to the value "ATVPD-KIKX0DER":

```
HTTP/1.1 200 OK
Content-type: text/html
Set-Cookie: cart=ATVPDKIKX0DER
```

If a browser makes a second request to the same server, it will send the cookie back in a Cookie line in the HTTP request header like so:

```
GET /index.html HTTP/1.1
Host: www.example.org
Cookie: cart=ATVPDKIKX0DER
Accept: text/html
```

As long as the server doesn't reuse cookies, this enables it to track individual users and sessions across multiple, otherwise stateless, HTTP connections.

Servers can set more than one cookie. For example, a request I just made to Amazon fed my browser five cookies:

```
Set-Cookie:skin=noskin
Set-Cookie:ubid-main=176-5578236-9590213
Set-Cookie:session-token=Zg6afPNqbaMv2WmYFOv57zCU1O6Ktr
Set-Cookie:session-id-time=2082787201l
Set-Cookie:session-id=187-4969589-3049309
```

In addition to a simple name=value pair, cookies can have several attributes that control their scope including expiration date, path, domain, port, version, and security options.

For example, by default, a cookie applies to the server it came from. If a cookie is originally set by *www.foo.example.com*, the browser will only send the cookie back to *www.foo.example.com*. However, a site can also indicate that a cookie applies within an entire subdomain, not just at the original server. For example, this request sets a user cookie for the entire *foo.example.com* domain:

```
Set-Cookie: user=elharo;Domain=.foo.example.com
```

The browser will echo this cookie back not just to *www.foo.example.com*, but also to *lothar.foo.example.com*, *eliza.foo.example.com*, *enoch.foo.example.com*, and any other host somewhere in the *foo.example.com* domain. However, a server can only set cookies for domains it immediately belongs to. *www.foo.example.com* cannot set a cookie for *www.oreilly.com*, *example.com*, or *.com*, no matter how it sets the domain.

 Websites work around this restriction by embedding an image or other content hosted on one domain in a page hosted at a second domain. The cookies set by the embedded content, not the page itself, are called *third-party cookies*. Many users block all third-party cookies, and some web browsers are starting to block them by default for privacy reasons.

Cookies are also scoped by path, so they're returned for some directories on the server, but not all. The default scope is the original URL and any subdirectories. For instance, if a cookie is set for the URL *http://www.cafeconleche.org/XOM/*, the cookie also applies in *http://www.cafeconleche.org/XOM/apidocs/*, but not in *http://www.cafeconleche.org/slides/* or *http://www.cafeconleche.org/*. However, the default scope can be changed using a Path attribute in the cookie. For example, this next response sends the browser a cookie with the name "user" and the value "elharo" that applies only within the server's */restricted* subtree, not on the rest of the site:

```
Set-Cookie: user=elharo; Path=/restricted
```

When requesting a document in the subtree */restricted* from the same server, the client echoes that cookie back. However, it does not use the cookie in other directories on the site.

A cookie can include both a domain and a path. For instance, this cookie applies in the */restricted* path on any servers within the *example.com* domain:

```
Set-Cookie: user=elharo;Path=/restricted;Domain=.example.com
```

The order of the different cookie attributes doesn't matter, as long as they're all separated by semicolons and the cookie's own name and value come first. However, this isn't true when the client is sending the cookie back to the server. In this case, the path must precede the domain, like so:

```
Cookie: user=elharo; Path=/restricted;Domain=.foo.example.com
```

A cookie can be set to expire at a certain point in time by setting the expires attribute to a date in the form Wdy, DD-Mon-YYYY HH:MM:SS GMT. Weekday and month are given as three-letter abbreviations. The rest are numeric, padded with initial zeros if necessary. In the pattern language used by `java.text.SimpleDateFormat`, this is `E, dd-MMM-yyyy H:m:s z`. For instance, this cookie expires at 3:23 P.M. on December 21, 2015:

```
Set-Cookie: user=elharo; expires=Wed, 21-Dec-2015 15:23:00 GMT
```

The browser should remove this cookie from its cache after that date has passed.

The `Max-Age` attribute that sets the cookie to expire after a certain number of seconds have passed instead of at a specific moment. For instance, this cookie expires one hour (3,600 seconds) after it's first set:

```
Set-Cookie: user="elharo"; Max-Age=3600
```

The browser should delete this cookie after this amount of time has elapsed.

Because cookies can contain sensitive information such as passwords and session keys, some cookie transactions should be secure. Most of the time this means using HTTPS instead of HTTP; but whatever it means, each cookie can have a secure attribute with no value, like so:

```
Set-Cookie: key=etrogl7*;Domain=.foo.example.com; secure
```

Browsers are supposed to refuse to send such cookies over insecure channels.

For additional security against cookie-stealing attacks like XSRF, cookies can set the `HttpOnly` attribute. This tells the browser to only return the cookie via HTTP and HTTPS and specifically *not* by JavaScript:

```
Set-Cookie: key=etrogl7*;Domain=.foo.example.com; secure; httponly
```

That's how cookies work behind the scenes. Here's a complete set of cookies sent by Amazon:

```
Set-Cookie: skin=noskin; path=/; domain=.amazon.com;
 expires=Fri, 03-May-2013 21:46:43 GMT
Set-Cookie: ubid-main=176-5578236-9590213; path=/;
 domain=.amazon.com; expires=Tue, 01-Jan-2036 08:00:01 GMT
Set-Cookie: session-token=Zg6afPNqbaMv2WmYFOv57zCU1O6KtrMMdskcmllbZ
 cY4q6t0PrMywqO82PR6AgtfIJhtBABhomNUW2dITwuLfOZuhXILp7Toya+
 AvWaYJxpfY1lj4ci4cnJxiuUZTev1WV31p5bcwzRM1Cmn3QOCezNNqenhzZD8TZUnOL/9Ya;
 path=/; domain=.amazon.com; expires=Thu, 28-Apr-2033 21:46:43 GMT
Set-Cookie: session-id-time=2082787201l; path=/; domain=.amazon.com;
 expires=Tue, 01-Jan-2036 08:00:01 GMT
Set-Cookie: session-id=187-4969589-3049309; path=/; domain=.amazon.com;
 expires=Tue, 01-Jan-2036 08:00:01 GMT
```

Amazon wants my browser to send these cookie with the request for any page in the *amazon.com* domain, for the next 30–33 years. Of course, browsers are free to ignore all these requests, and users can delete or block cookies at any time.

CookieManager

Java 5 includes an abstract `java.net.CookieHandler` class that defines an API for storing and retrieving cookies. However, it does not include an implementation of that abstract class, so it requires a lot of grunt work. Java 6 fleshes this out by adding a concrete `java.net.CookieManager` subclass of `CookieHandler` that you can use. However, it is not turned on by default. Before Java will store and return cookies, you need to enable it:

```
CookieManager manager = new CookieManager();
CookieHandler.setDefault(manager);
```

If all you want is to receive cookies from sites and send them back to those sites, you're done. That's all there is to it. After installing a `CookieManager` with those two lines of code, Java will store any cookies sent by HTTP servers you connect to with the URL class, and will send the stored cookies back to those same servers in subsequent requests.

However, you may wish to be a bit more careful about whose cookies you accept. You can do this by specifying a `CookiePolicy`. Three policies are predefined:

- `CookiePolicy.ACCEPT_ALL` All cookies allowed
- `CookiePolicy.ACCEPT_NONE` No cookies allowed
- `CookiePolicy.ACCEPT_ORIGINAL_SERVER` Only first party cookies allowed

For example, this code fragment tells Java to block third-party cookies but accept first-party cookies:

```
CookieManager manager = new CookieManager();
manager.setCookiePolicy(CookiePolicy.ACCEPT_ORIGINAL_SERVER);
CookieHandler.setDefault(manager);
```

That is, it will only accept cookies for the server that you're talking to, not for any server on the Internet.

If you want more fine-grained control, for instance to allow cookies from some known domains but not others, you can implement the `CookiePolicy` interface yourself and override the `shouldAccept()` method:

```
public boolean shouldAccept(URI uri, HttpCookie cookie)
```

Example 6-1 shows a simple `CookiePolicy` that blocks cookies from *.gov* domains, but allows others.

Example 6-1. A cookie policy that blocks all .gov cookies but allows others

```
import java.net.*;

public class NoGovernmentCookies implements CookiePolicy {
```

```
  @Override
  public boolean shouldAccept(URI uri, HttpCookie cookie) {
    if (uri.getAuthority().toLowerCase().endsWith(".gov")
        || cookie.getDomain().toLowerCase().endsWith(".gov")) {
      return false;
    }
    return true;
  }
}
```

CookieStore

It is sometimes necessary to put and get cookies locally. For instance, when an application quits, it can save the cookie store to disk and load those cookies again when it next starts up. You can retrieve the store in which the CookieManager saves its cookies with the getCookieStore() method:

```
CookieStore store = manager.getCookieStore();
```

The CookieStore class allows you to add, remove, and list cookies so you can control the cookies that are sent outside the normal flow of HTTP requests and responses:

```
public void add(URI uri, HttpCookie cookie)
public List<HttpCookie> get(URI uri)
public List<HttpCookie> getCookies()
public List<URI> getURIs()
public boolean remove(URI uri, HttpCookie cookie)
public boolean removeAll()
```

Each cookie in the store is encapsulated in an HttpCookie object that provides methods for inspecting the attributes of the cookie summarized in Example 6-2.

Example 6-2. The HTTPCookie class

```
package java.net;

public class HttpCookie implements Cloneable {
  public HttpCookie(String name, String value)

  public boolean hasExpired()
  public void setComment(String comment)
  public String getComment()
  public void setCommentURL(String url)
  public String getCommentURL()
  public void setDiscard(boolean discard)
  public boolean getDiscard()
  public void setPortlist(String ports)
  public String getPortlist()
  public void setDomain(String domain)
  public String getDomain()
  public void setMaxAge(long expiry)
  public long getMaxAge()
```

```
   public void setPath(String path)
   public String getPath()
   public void setSecure(boolean flag)
   public boolean getSecure()
   public String getName()
   public void setValue(String value)
   public String getValue()
   public int getVersion()
   public void setVersion(int v)

   public static boolean domainMatches(String domain, String host)
   public static List<HttpCookie> parse(String header)

   public String toString()
   public boolean equals(Object obj)
   public int hashCode()
   public Object clone()
}
```

Several of these attributes are not actually used any more. In particular comment, comment URL, discard, and version are only used by the now obsolete Cookie 2 specification that never caught on.

CHAPTER 7

URLConnections

URLConnection is an abstract class that represents an active connection to a resource specified by a URL. The URLConnection class has two different but related purposes. First, it provides more control over the interaction with a server (especially an HTTP server) than the URL class. A URLConnection can inspect the header sent by the server and respond accordingly. It can set the header fields used in the client request. Finally, a URLConnection can send data back to a web server with POST, PUT, and other HTTP request methods. We will explore all of these techniques in this chapter.

Second, the URLConnection class is part of Java's *protocol handler* mechanism, which also includes the URLStreamHandler class. The idea behind protocol handlers is simple: they separate the details of processing a protocol from processing particular data types, providing user interfaces, and doing the other work that a monolithic web browser performs. The base java.net.URLConnection class is abstract; to implement a specific protocol, you write a subclass. These subclasses can be loaded at runtime by applications. For example, if the browser runs across a URL with a strange scheme, such as *compress*, rather than throwing up its hands and issuing an error message, it can download a protocol handler for this unknown protocol and use it to communicate with the server.

Only abstract URLConnection classes are present in the java.net package. The concrete subclasses are hidden inside the sun.net package hierarchy. Many of the methods and fields as well as the single constructor in the URLConnection class are *protected*. In other words, they can only be accessed by instances of the URLConnection class or its subclasses. It is rare to instantiate URLConnection objects directly in your source code; instead, the runtime environment creates these objects as needed, depending on the protocol in use. The class (which is unknown at compile time) is then instantiated using the forName() and newInstance() methods of the java.lang.Class class.

URLConnection does not have the best-designed API in the Java class library. One of several problems is that the URLConnection class is too closely tied to the HTTP protocol. For instance, it assumes that each file transferred is preceded by a MIME header or something very much like one. However, most classic protocols such as FTP and SMTP don't use MIME headers.

Opening URLConnections

A program that uses the URLConnection class directly follows this basic sequence of steps:

1. Construct a URL object.

2. Invoke the URL object's openConnection( ) method to retrieve a URLConnection object for that URL.

3. Configure the URLConnection.

4. Read the header fields.

5. Get an input stream and read data.

6. Get an output stream and write data.

7. Close the connection.

You don't always perform all these steps. For instance, if the default setup for a particular kind of URL is acceptable, you can skip step 3. If you only want the data from the server and don't care about any metainformation, or if the protocol doesn't provide any metainformation, you can skip step 4. If you only want to receive data from the server but not send data to the server, you'll skip step 6. Depending on the protocol, steps 5 and 6 may be reversed or interlaced.

The single constructor for the URLConnection class is protected:

```
protected URLConnection(URL url)
```

Consequently, unless you're subclassing URLConnection to handle a new kind of URL (i.e., writing a protocol handler), you create one of these objects by invoking the open Connection( ) method of the URL class. For example:

```
try {
  URL u = new URL("http://www.overcomingbias.com/");
  URLConnection uc = u.openConnection();
  // read from the URL...
} catch (MalformedURLException ex) {
  System.err.println(ex);
} catch (IOException ex) {
```

```
    System.err.println(ex);
  }
```

The URLConnection class is declared abstract. However, all but one of its methods are implemented. You may find it convenient or necessary to override other methods in the class; but the single method that subclasses must implement is connect(), which makes a connection to a server and thus depends on the type of service (HTTP, FTP, and so on). For example, a sun.net.www.protocol.file.FileURLConnection's connect() method converts the URL to a filename in the appropriate directory, creates MIME information for the file, and then opens a buffered FileInputStream to the file. The connect() method of sun.net.www.protocol.http.HttpURLConnection creates a sun.net.www.http.HttpClient object, which is responsible for connecting to the server:

```
    public abstract void connect() throws IOException
```

When a URLConnection is first constructed, it is unconnected; that is, the local and remote host cannot send and receive data. There is no socket connecting the two hosts. The connect() method establishes a connection—normally using TCP sockets but possibly through some other mechanism—between the local and remote host so they can send and receive data. However, getInputStream(), getContent(), getHeader Field(), and other methods that require an open connection will call connect() if the connection isn't yet open. Therefore, you rarely need to call connect() directly.

Reading Data from a Server

The following is the minimal set of steps needed to retrieve data from a URL using a URLConnection object:

1. Construct a URL object.
2. Invoke the URL object's openConnection() method to retrieve a URLConnection object for that URL.
3. Invoke the URLConnection's getInputStream() method.
4. Read from the input stream using the usual stream API.

The getInputStream() method returns a generic InputStream that lets you read and parse the data that the server sends. Example 7-1 uses the getInputStream() method to download a web page.

Example 7-1. Download a web page with a URLConnection

```
import java.io.*;
import java.net.*;

public class SourceViewer2 {
```

```
public static void main (String[] args) {
  if  (args.length > 0) {
    try {
      // Open the URLConnection for reading
      URL u = new URL(args[0]);
      URLConnection uc = u.openConnection();
      try (InputStream raw = uc.getInputStream()) { // autoclose
        InputStream buffer = new BufferedInputStream(raw);
        // chain the InputStream to a Reader
        Reader reader = new InputStreamReader(buffer);
        int c;
        while ((c = reader.read()) != -1) {
          System.out.print((char) c);
        }
      }
    } catch (MalformedURLException ex) {
      System.err.println(args[0] + " is not a parseable URL");
    } catch (IOException ex) {
      System.err.println(ex);
    }
  }
}
```

It is no accident that this program is almost the same as Example 5-2. The open
Stream() method of the URL class just returns an InputStream from its own URLCon
nection object. The output is identical as well, so I won't repeat it here.

The differences between URL and URLConnection aren't apparent with just a simple input
stream as in this example. The biggest differences between the two classes are:

- URLConnection provides access to the HTTP header.
- URLConnection can configure the request parameters sent to the server.
- URLConnection can write data to the server as well as read data from the server.

Reading the Header

HTTP servers provide a substantial amount of information in the header that precedes
each response. For example, here's a typical HTTP header returned by an Apache web
server:

```
HTTP/1.1 301 Moved Permanently
Date: Sun, 21 Apr 2013 15:12:46 GMT
Server: Apache
Location: http://www.ibiblio.org/
Content-Length: 296
```

```
Connection: close
Content-Type: text/html; charset=iso-8859-1
```

There's a lot of information there. In general, an HTTP header may include the content type of the requested document, the length of the document in bytes, the character set in which the content is encoded, the date and time, the date the content expires, and the date the content was last modified. However, the information depends on the server; some servers send all this information for each request, others send some information, and a few don't send anything. The methods of this section allow you to query a URL Connection to find out what metadata the server has provided.

Aside from HTTP, very few protocols use MIME headers (and technically speaking, even the HTTP header isn't actually a MIME header; it just looks a lot like one). When writing your own subclass of URLConnection, it is often necessary to override these methods so that they return sensible values. The most important piece of information you may be lacking is the content type. URLConnection provides some utility methods that guess the data's content type based on its filename or the first few bytes of the data itself.

Retrieving Specific Header Fields

The first six methods request specific, particularly common fields from the header. These are:

- Content-type
- Content-length
- Content-encoding
- Date
- Last-modified
- Expires

public String getContentType()

The getContentType() method returns the MIME media type of the response body. It relies on the web server to send a valid content type. It throws no exceptions and returns null if the content type isn't available. text/html will be the most common content type you'll encounter when connecting to web servers. Other commonly used types include text/plain, image/gif, application/xml, and image/jpeg.

If the content type is some form of text, this header may also contain a character set part identifying the document's character encoding. For example:

```
Content-type: text/html; charset=UTF-8
```

Or:

```
Content-Type: application/xml; charset=iso-2022-jp
```

In this case, getContentType() returns the full value of the Content-type field, including the character encoding. You can use this to improve on Example 7-1 by using the encoding specified in the HTTP header to decode the document, or ISO-8859-1 (the HTTP default) if no such encoding is specified. If a nontext type is encountered, an exception is thrown. Example 7-2 demonstrates.

Example 7-2. Download a web page with the correct character set

```
import java.io.*;
import java.net.*;

public class EncodingAwareSourceViewer {

  public static void main (String[] args) {
    for (int i = 0; i < args.length; i++) {
      try {
        // set default encoding
        String encoding = "ISO-8859-1";
        URL u = new URL(args[i]);
        URLConnection uc = u.openConnection();
        String contentType = uc.getContentType();
        int encodingStart = contentType.indexOf("charset=");
        if (encodingStart != -1) {
            encoding = contentType.substring(encodingStart + 8);
        }
        InputStream in = new BufferedInputStream(uc.getInputStream());
        Reader r = new InputStreamReader(in, encoding);
        int c;
        while ((c = r.read()) != -1) {
          System.out.print((char) c);
        }
        r.close();
      } catch (MalformedURLException ex) {
        System.err.println(args[0] + " is not a parseable URL");
      } catch (UnsupportedEncodingException ex) {
        System.err.println(
            "Server sent an encoding Java does not support: " + ex.getMessage());
      } catch (IOException ex) {
        System.err.println(ex);
      }
    }
  }
}
```

public int getContentLength()

The getContentLength() method tells you how many bytes there are in the content. If there is no Content-length header, getContentLength() returns –1. The method throws no exceptions. It is used when you need to know exactly how many bytes to read or when you need to create a buffer large enough to hold the data in advance.

As networks get faster and files get bigger, it is actually possible to find resources whose size exceeds the maximum int value (about 2.1 billion bytes). In this case, getConten tLength() returns –1. Java 7 adds a getContentLengthLong() method that works just like getContentLength() except that it returns a long instead of an int and thus can handle much larger resources:

```
public long getContentLengthLong // Java 7
```

Chapter 5 showed how to use the openStream() method of the URL class to download text files from an HTTP server. Although in theory you should be able to use the same method to download a binary file, such as a GIF image or a *.class* byte code file, in practice this procedure presents a problem. HTTP servers don't always close the connection exactly where the data is finished; therefore, you don't know when to stop reading. To download a binary file, it is more reliable to use a URLConnection's getConten tLength() method to find the file's length, then read exactly the number of bytes indicated. Example 7-3 is a program that uses this technique to save a binary file on a disk.

Example 7-3. Downloading a binary file from a website and saving it to disk

```
import java.io.*;
import java.net.*;

public class BinarySaver {

  public static void main (String[] args) {
    for (int i = 0; i < args.length; i++) {
      try {
        URL root = new URL(args[i]);
        saveBinaryFile(root);
      } catch (MalformedURLException ex) {
        System.err.println(args[i] + " is not URL I understand.");
      } catch (IOException ex) {
        System.err.println(ex);
      }
    }
  }

  public static void saveBinaryFile(URL u) throws IOException {
    URLConnection uc = u.openConnection();
    String contentType = uc.getContentType();
    int contentLength = uc.getContentLength();
    if (contentType.startsWith("text/") || contentLength == -1 ) {
      throw new IOException("This is not a binary file.");
    }

    try (InputStream raw = uc.getInputStream()) {
      InputStream in  = new BufferedInputStream(raw);
```

```
    byte[] data = new byte[contentLength];
    int offset = 0;
    while (offset < contentLength) {
       int bytesRead = in.read(data, offset, data.length - offset);
       if (bytesRead == -1) break;
       offset += bytesRead;
    }

    if (offset != contentLength) {
      throw new IOException("Only read " + offset
          + " bytes; Expected " + contentLength + " bytes");
    }
    String filename = u.getFile();
    filename = filename.substring(filename.lastIndexOf('/') + 1);
    try (FileOutputStream fout = new FileOutputStream(filename)) {
      fout.write(data);
      fout.flush();
    }
   }
  }
}
```

As usual, the main() method loops over the URLs entered on the command line, passing each URL to the saveBinaryFile() method. saveBinaryFile() opens a URLConnec tion uc to the URL. It puts the type into the variable contentType and the content length into the variable contentLength. Next, an if statement checks whether the content type is text or the Content-length field is missing or invalid (contentLength == -1). If either of these is true, an IOException is thrown. If these checks are both false, you have a binary file of known length: that's what you want.

Now that you have a genuine binary file on your hands, you prepare to read it into an array of bytes called data. data is initialized to the number of bytes required to hold the binary object, contentLength. Ideally, you would like to fill data with a single call to read() but you probably won't get all the bytes at once, so the read is placed in a loop. The number of bytes read up to this point is accumulated into the offset variable, which also keeps track of the location in the data array at which to start placing the data retrieved by the next call to read(). The loop continues until offset equals or exceeds contentLength; that is, the array has been filled with the expected number of bytes. You also break out of the while loop if read() returns –1, indicating an unexpected end of stream. The offset variable now contains the total number of bytes read, which should be equal to the content length. If they are not equal, an error has occurred, so saveBi naryFile() throws an IOException. This is the general procedure for reading binary files from HTTP connections.

Now you're ready to save the data in a file. saveBinaryFile() gets the filename from the URL using the getFile() method and strips any path information by calling file name.substring(theFile.lastIndexOf(/) + 1). A new FileOutputStream fout is opened into this file and the data is written in one large burst with `fout.write(b)`. `AutoCloseable` is used to clean up throughout.

public String getContentEncoding()

The `getContentEncoding()` method returns a `String` that tells you how the content is encoded. If the content is sent unencoded (as is commonly the case with HTTP servers), this method returns `null`. It throws no exceptions. The most commonly used content encoding on the Web is probably x-gzip, which can be straightforwardly decoded using a `java.util.zip.GZipInputStream`.

The content encoding is not the same as the character encoding. The character encoding is determined by the Content-type header or information internal to the document, and specifies how characters are encoded in bytes. Content encoding specifies how the bytes are encoded in other bytes.

public long getDate()

The `getDate()` method returns a `long` that tells you when the document was sent, in milliseconds since midnight, Greenwich Mean Time (GMT), January 1, 1970. You can convert it to a `java.util.Date`. For example:

```
Date documentSent = new Date(uc.getDate());
```

This is the time the document was sent as seen from the server; it may not agree with the time on your local machine. If the HTTP header does not include a Date field, `getDate()` returns 0.

public long getExpiration()

Some documents have server-based expiration dates that indicate when the document should be deleted from the cache and reloaded from the server. `getExpiration()` is very similar to `getDate()`, differing only in how the return value is interpreted. It returns a `long` indicating the number of milliseconds after 12:00 A.M., GMT, January 1, 1970, at which the document expires. If the HTTP header does not include an Expiration field, `getExpiration()` returns 0, which means that the document does not expire and can remain in the cache indefinitely.

public long getLastModified()

The final date method, `getLastModified()`, returns the date on which the document was last modified. Again, the date is given as the number of milliseconds since midnight, GMT, January 1, 1970. If the HTTP header does not include a Last-modified field (and many don't), this method returns 0.

Example 7-4 reads URLs from the command line and uses these six methods to print their content type, content length, content encoding, date of last modification, expiration date, and current date.

Example 7-4. Return the header

```java
import java.io.*;
import java.net.*;
import java.util.*;

public class HeaderViewer {

  public static void main(String[] args) {
    for (int i = 0; i < args.length; i++) {
      try {
        URL u = new URL(args[0]);
        URLConnection uc = u.openConnection();
        System.out.println("Content-type: " + uc.getContentType());
        if (uc.getContentEncoding() != null) {
          System.out.println("Content-encoding: "
              + uc.getContentEncoding());
        }
        if (uc.getDate() != 0) {
          System.out.println("Date: " + new Date(uc.getDate()));
        }
        if (uc.getLastModified() != 0) {
          System.out.println("Last modified: "
              + new Date(uc.getLastModified()));
        }
        if (uc.getExpiration() != 0) {
          System.out.println("Expiration date: "
              + new Date(uc.getExpiration()));
        }
        if (uc.getContentLength() != -1) {
          System.out.println("Content-length: " + uc.getContentLength());
        }
      } catch (MalformedURLException ex) {
        System.err.println(args[i] + " is not a URL I understand");
      } catch (IOException ex) {
        System.err.println(ex);
      }
      System.out.println();
    }
  }
}
```

Here's the result when used to look at *http://www.oreilly.com*:

```
% java HeaderViewer http://www.oreilly.com
Content-type: text/html; charset=utf-8
Date: Fri May 31 18:08:09 EDT 2013
Last modified: Fri May 31 17:04:14 EDT 2013
```

```
Expiration date: Fri May 31 22:08:09 EDT 2013
Content-length: 83273
```

The content type of the file at *http://www.oreilly.com* is text/html. No content encoding was used. The file was sent on Friday, May 31, 2013 at 6:08 P.M., Eastern Daylight Time. It was last modified on the same day at 5:04 P.M. and it expires four hours in the future.

There was no Content-length header. Many servers don't bother to provide a Content-length header for text files. However, a Content-length header should always be sent for a binary file. Here's the HTTP header you get when you request the GIF image *http://oreilly.com/favicon.ico*. Now the server sends a Content-length header with a value of 2294:

```
% java HeaderViewer http://oreilly.com/favicon.ico
Content-type: image/x-icon
Date: Fri May 31 18:16:01 EDT 2013
Last modified: Wed Mar 26 19:14:36 EST 2003
Expiration date: Fri Jun 07 18:16:01 EDT 2013
Content-length: 2294
```

Retrieving Arbitrary Header Fields

The last six methods requested specific fields from the header, but there's no theoretical limit to the number of header fields a message can contain. The next five methods inspect arbitrary fields in a header. Indeed, the methods of the preceding section are just thin wrappers over the methods discussed here; you can use these methods to get header fields that Java's designers did not plan for. If the requested header is found, it is returned. Otherwise, the method returns null.

public String getHeaderField(String name)

The getHeaderField() method returns the value of a named header field. The name of the header is not case sensitive and does not include a closing colon. For example, to get the value of the Content-type and Content-encoding header fields of a URLConnection object uc, you could write:

```
String contentType = uc.getHeaderField("content-type");
String contentEncoding = uc.getHeaderField("content-encoding"));
```

To get the Date, Content-length, or Expires headers, you'd do the same:

```
String data = uc.getHeaderField("date");
String expires = uc.getHeaderField("expires");
String contentLength = uc.getHeaderField("Content-length");
```

These methods all return String, not int or long as the getContentLength(), getExpirationDate(), getLastModified(), and getDate() methods that the preceding section did. If you're interested in a numeric value, convert the String to a long or an int.

Do not assume the value returned by getHeaderField() is valid. You must check to make sure it is nonnull.

public String getHeaderFieldKey(int n)

This method returns the key (i.e., the field name) of the nth header field (e.g., Content-length or Server). The request method is header zero and has a null key. The first header is one. For example, in order to get the sixth key of the header of the URLConnection uc, you would write:

```
String header6 = uc.getHeaderFieldKey(6);
```

public String getHeaderField(int n)

This method returns the value of the nth header field. In HTTP, the starter line containing the request method and path is header field zero and the first actual header is one. Example 7-5 uses this method in conjunction with getHeaderFieldKey() to print the entire HTTP header.

Example 7-5. Print the entire HTTP header

```
import java.io.*;
import java.net.*;

public class AllHeaders {

  public static void main(String[] args) {
    for (int i = 0; i < args.length; i++) {
      try {
        URL u = new URL(args[i]);
        URLConnection uc = u.openConnection();
        for (int j = 1; ; j++) {
          String header = uc.getHeaderField(j);
          if (header == null) break;
          System.out.println(uc.getHeaderFieldKey(j) + ": " + header);
        }
      } catch (MalformedURLException ex) {
        System.err.println(args[i] + " is not a URL I understand.");
      } catch (IOException ex) {
        System.err.println(ex);
      }
      System.out.println();
    }
  }
}
```

For example, here's the output when this program is run against *http://www.oreilly.com*:

```
% java AllHeaders http://www.oreilly.com
Date: Sat, 04 May 2013 11:28:26 GMT
Server: Apache
```

```
Last-Modified: Sat, 04 May 2013 07:35:04 GMT
Accept-Ranges: bytes
Content-Length: 80366
Content-Type: text/html; charset=utf-8
Cache-Control: max-age=14400
Expires: Sat, 04 May 2013 15:28:26 GMT
Vary: Accept-Encoding
Keep-Alive: timeout=3, max=100
Connection: Keep-Alive
```

Besides the headers with named getter methods, this server also provides Server, Accept-Ranges, Cache-control, Vary, Keep-Alive, and Connection headers. Other servers may have different sets of headers.

public long getHeaderFieldDate(String name, long default)

This method first retrieves the header field specified by the name argument and tries to convert the string to a long that specifies the milliseconds since midnight, January 1, 1970, GMT. getHeaderFieldDate() can be used to retrieve a header field that represents a date (e.g., the Expires, Date, or Last-modified headers). To convert the string to an integer, getHeaderFieldDate() uses the parseDate() method of java.util.Date. The parseDate() method does a decent job of understanding and converting most common date formats, but it can be stumped—for instance, if you ask for a header field that contains something other than a date. If parseDate() doesn't understand the date or if getHeaderFieldDate() is unable to find the requested header field, getHeaderField Date() returns the default argument. For example:

```
Date expires = new Date(uc.getHeaderFieldDate("expires", 0));
long lastModified = uc.getHeaderFieldDate("last-modified", 0);
Date now = new Date(uc.getHeaderFieldDate("date", 0));
```

You can use the methods of the java.util.Date class to convert the long to a String.

public int getHeaderFieldInt(String name, int default)

This method retrieves the value of the header field name and tries to convert it to an int. If it fails, either because it can't find the requested header field or because that field does not contain a recognizable integer, getHeaderFieldInt() returns the default argument. This method is often used to retrieve the Content-length field. For example, to get the content length from a URLConnection uc, you would write:

```
int contentLength = uc.getHeaderFieldInt("content-length", -1);
```

In this code fragment, getHeaderFieldInt() returns –1 if the Content-length header isn't present.

Caches

Web browsers have been caching pages and images for years. If a logo is repeated on every page of a site, the browser normally loads it from the remote server only once, stores it in its cache, and reloads it from the cache whenever it's needed rather than requesting it from the remote server every time the logo is encountered. Several HTTP headers, including Expires and Cache-control, can control caching.

By default, the assumption is that a page accessed with GET over HTTP can and should be cached. A page accessed with HTTPS or POST usually shouldn't be. However, HTTP headers can adjust this:

- An Expires header (primarily for HTTP 1.0) indicates that it's OK to cache this representation until the specified time.
- The Cache-control header (HTTP 1.1) offers fine-grained cache policies:
  - max-age=[*seconds*]: Number of seconds from now before the cached entry should expire
  - s-maxage=[*seconds*]: Number of seconds from now before the cached entry should expire from a shared cache. Private caches can store the entry for longer.
  - public: OK to cache an authenticated response. Otherwise authenticated responses are not cached.
  - private: Only single user caches should store the response; shared caches should not.
  - no-cache: Not quite what it sounds like. The entry may still be cached, but the client should reverify the state of the resource with an ETag or Last-modified header on each access.
  - no-store: Do not cache the entry no matter what.

  Cache-control overrides Expires if both are present. A server can send multiple Cache-control headers in a single header as long as they don't conflict.
- The Last-modified header is the date when the resource was last changed. A client can use a HEAD request to check this and only come back for a full GET if its local cached copy is older than the Last-modified date.
- The ETag header (HTTP 1.1) is a unique identifier for the resource that changes when the resource does. A client can use a HEAD request to check this and only come back for a full GET if its local cached copy has a different ETag.

For example, this HTTP response says that the resource may be cached for 604,800 seconds (HTTP 1.1) or one week later (HTTP 1.0). It also says it was last modified on April 20 and has an ETag, so if the local cache already has a copy more recent than that, there's no need to load the whole document now:

```
HTTP/1.1 200 OK
Date: Sun, 21 Apr 2013 15:12:46 GMT
Server: Apache
Connection: close
Content-Type: text/html; charset=ISO-8859-1
Cache-control: max-age=604800
Expires: Sun, 28 Apr 2013 15:12:46 GMT
Last-modified: Sat, 20 Apr 2013 09:55:04 GMT
ETag: "67099097696afcf1b67e"
```

Example 7-6 is a simple Java class for parsing and querying Cache-control headers.

Example 7-6. How to inspect a Cache-control header

```java
import java.util.Date;
import java.util.Locale;


public class CacheControl {

  private Date maxAge = null;
  private Date sMaxAge = null;
  private boolean mustRevalidate = false;
  private boolean noCache = false;
  private boolean noStore = false;
  private boolean proxyRevalidate = false;
  private boolean publicCache = false;
  private boolean privateCache = false;

  public CacheControl(String s) {
    if (s == null || !s.contains(":")) {
      return; // default policy
    }

    String value = s.split(":")[1].trim();
    String[] components = value.split(",");

    Date now = new Date();
    for (String component : components) {
      try {
        component = component.trim().toLowerCase(Locale.US);
        if (component.startsWith("max-age=")) {
          int secondsInTheFuture = Integer.parseInt(component.substring(8));
          maxAge = new Date(now.getTime() + 1000 * secondsInTheFuture);
        } else if (component.startsWith("s-maxage=")) {
          int secondsInTheFuture = Integer.parseInt(component.substring(8));
          sMaxAge = new Date(now.getTime() + 1000 * secondsInTheFuture);
        } else if (component.equals("must-revalidate")) {
          mustRevalidate = true;
        } else if (component.equals("proxy-revalidate")) {
          proxyRevalidate = true;
        } else if (component.equals("no-cache")) {
          noCache = true;
```

```
        } else if (component.equals("public")) {
          publicCache = true;
        } else if (component.equals("private")) {
          privateCache = true;
        }
      } catch (RuntimeException ex) {
        continue;
      }
    }
  }
}

public Date getMaxAge() {
  return maxAge;
}

public Date getSharedMaxAge() {
  return sMaxAge;
}

public boolean mustRevalidate() {
  return mustRevalidate;
}

public boolean proxyRevalidate() {
  return proxyRevalidate;
}

public boolean noStore() {
  return noStore;
}

public boolean noCache() {
  return noCache;
}

public boolean publicCache() {
  return publicCache;
}

public boolean privateCache() {
  return privateCache;
}
}
```

A client can take advantage of this information:

- If a representation of the resource is available in the local cache, and its expiry date has not arrived, just use it. Don't even bother talking to the server.

- If a representation of the resource is available in the local cache, but the expiry date has arrived, check the server with HEAD to see if the resource has changed before performing a full GET.

Web Cache for Java

By default, Java does not cache anything. To install a system-wide cache of the URL class will use, you need the following:

- A concrete subclass of ResponseCache
- A concrete subclass of CacheRequest
- A concrete subclass of CacheResponse

You install your subclass of ResponseCache that works with your subclass of CacheRequest and CacheResponse by passing it to the static method ResponseCache.setDefault(). This installs your cache object as the system default. A Java virtual machine can only support a single shared cache.

Once a cache is installed whenever the system tries to load a new URL, it will first look for it in the cache. If the cache returns the desired content, the URLConnection won't need to connect to the remote server. However, if the requested data is not in the cache, the protocol handler will download it. After it's done so, it will put its response into the cache so the content is more quickly available the next time that URL is loaded.

Two abstract methods in the ResponseCache class store and retrieve data from the system's single cache:

```
public abstract CacheResponse get(URI uri, String requestMethod,
    Map<String, List<String>> requestHeaders) throws IOException
public abstract CacheRequest put(URI uri, URLConnection connection)
    throws IOException
```

The put() method returns a CacheRequest object that wraps an OutputStream into which the URL will write cacheable data it reads. CacheRequest is an abstract class with two methods, as shown in Example 7-7.

Example 7-7. The CacheRequest class

```
package java.net;

public abstract class CacheRequest {
  public abstract OutputStream getBody() throws IOException;
  public abstract void abort();
}
```

The getOutputStream() method in the subclass should return an OutputStream that points into the cache's data store for the URI passed to the put() method at the same time. For instance, if you're storing the data in a file, you'd return a FileOutput Stream connected to that file. The protocol handler will copy the data it reads onto this OutputStream. If a problem arises while copying (e.g., the server unexpectedly closes the connection), the protocol handler calls the abort() method. This method should then remove any data from the cache that has been stored for this request.

Example 7-8 demonstrates a basic CacheRequest subclass that passes back a ByteArrayOutputStream. Later, the data can be retrieved using the getData() method, a custom method in this subclass just retrieving the data Java wrote onto the Output Stream this class supplied. An obvious alternative strategy would be to store results in files and use a FileOutputStream instead.

Example 7-8. A concrete CacheRequest subclass

```
import java.io.*;
import java.net.*;

public class SimpleCacheRequest extends CacheRequest {

  private ByteArrayOutputStream out = new ByteArrayOutputStream();

  @Override
  public OutputStream getBody() throws IOException {
    return out;
  }

  @Override
  public void abort() {
    out.reset();
  }

  public byte[] getData() {
    if (out.size() == 0) return null;
    else return out.toByteArray();
  }
}
```

The get() method in ResponseCache retrieves the data and headers from the cache and returns them wrapped in a CacheResponse object. It returns null if the desired URI is not in the cache, in which case the protocol handler loads the URI from the remote server as normal. Again, this is an abstract class that you have to implement in a subclass. Example 7-9 summarizes this class. It has two methods: one to return the data of the request and one to return the headers. When caching the original response, you need to store both. The headers should be returned in an unmodifiable map with keys that are the HTTP header field names and values that are lists of values for each named HTTP header.

Example 7-9. The CacheResponse class

```java
public abstract class CacheResponse {
  public abstract Map<String, List<String>> getHeaders() throws IOException;
  public abstract InputStream getBody() throws IOException;
}
```

Example 7-10 shows a simple `CacheResponse` subclass that is tied to a `SimpleCacheRe` quest and a `CacheControl`. In this example, shared references pass data from the request class to the response class. If you were storing responses in files, you'd just need to share the filenames instead. Along with the `SimpleCacheRequest` object from which it will read the data, you must also pass the original `URLConnection` object into the constructor. This is used to read the HTTP header so it can be stored for later retrieval. The object also keeps track of the expiration date and cache-control (if any) provided by the server for the cached representation of the resource.

Example 7-10. A concrete CacheResponse subclass

```java
import java.io.*;
import java.net.*;
import java.util.*;

public class SimpleCacheResponse extends CacheResponse {

  private final Map<String, List<String>> headers;
  private final SimpleCacheRequest request;
  private final Date expires;
  private final CacheControl control;

  public SimpleCacheResponse(
      SimpleCacheRequest request, URLConnection uc, CacheControl control)
      throws IOException {

    this.request = request;
    this.control = control;
    this.expires = new Date(uc.getExpiration());
    this.headers = Collections.unmodifiableMap(uc.getHeaderFields());
  }

  @Override
  public InputStream getBody() {
    return new ByteArrayInputStream(request.getData());
  }

  @Override
  public Map<String, List<String>> getHeaders()
      throws IOException {
      return headers;
  }
```

```
  public CacheControl getControl() {
    return control;
  }

  public boolean isExpired() {
    Date now = new Date();
    if (control.getMaxAge().before(now)) return true;
    else if (expires != null && control.getMaxAge() != null) {
      return expires.before(now);
    } else {
      return false;
    }
  }
}
```

Finally, you need a simple `ResponseCache` subclass that stores and retrieves the cached values as requested while paying attention to the original Cache-control header. Example 7-11 demonstrates such a simple class that stores a finite number of responses in memory in one big thread-safe `HashMap`. This class is suitable for a single-user, private cache (because it ignores the private and public attributes of Cache-control).

Example 7-11. An in-memory ResponseCache

```
import java.io.*;
import java.net.*;
import java.util.*;
import java.util.concurrent.*;

public class MemoryCache extends ResponseCache {

  private final Map<URI, SimpleCacheResponse> responses
      = new ConcurrentHashMap<URI, SimpleCacheResponse>();
  private final int maxEntries;

  public MemoryCache() {
    this(100);
  }

  public MemoryCache(int maxEntries) {
    this.maxEntries = maxEntries;
  }

  @Override
  public CacheRequest put(URI uri, URLConnection conn)
      throws IOException {

    if (responses.size() >= maxEntries) return null;

    CacheControl control = new CacheControl(conn.getHeaderField("Cache-Control"));
    if (control.noStore()) {
      return null;
    } else if (!conn.getHeaderField(0).startsWith("GET ")) {
```

```
    // only cache GET
    return null;
  }

  SimpleCacheRequest request = new SimpleCacheRequest();
  SimpleCacheResponse response = new SimpleCacheResponse(request, conn, control);

  responses.put(uri, response);
  return request;
}

@Override
public CacheResponse get(URI uri, String requestMethod,
    Map<String, List<String>> requestHeaders)
    throws IOException {

  if ("GET".equals(requestMethod)) {
    SimpleCacheResponse response = responses.get(uri);
    // check expiration date
    if (response != null && response.isExpired()) {
      responses.remove(response);
      response = null;
    }
    return response;
  } else {
    return null;
  }
}
}
```

Java only allows one URL cache at a time. To install or change the cache, use the static `ResponseCache.setDefault()` and `ResponseCache.getDefault()` methods:

```
public static ResponseCache getDefault()
public static void setDefault(ResponseCache responseCache)
```

These set the single cache used by all programs running within the same Java virtual machine. For example, this one line of code installs Example 7-11 in an application:

```
ResponseCache.setDefault(new MemoryCache());
```

Once a `ResponseCache` like Example 7-11 is installed, HTTP `URLConnections` always use it.

Each retrieved resource stays in the `HashMap` until it expires. This example waits for an expired document to be requested again before it deletes it from the cache. A more sophisticated implementation could use a low-priority thread to scan for expired documents and remove them to make way for others. Instead of or in addition to this, an implementation might cache the representations in a queue and remove the oldest documents or those closest to their expiration date as necessary to make room for new ones. An even more sophisticated implementation could track how often each document in the store was accessed and expunge only the oldest and least-used documents.

I've already mentioned that you could implement a cache on top of the filesystem instead of on top of the Java Collections API. You could also store the cache in a database, and you could do a lot of less-common things as well. For instance, you could redirect requests for certain URLs to a local server rather than a remote server halfway around the world, in essence using a local web server as the cache. Or a `ResponseCache` could load a fixed set of files at launch time and then only serve those out of memory. This might be useful for a server that processes many different SOAP requests, all of which adhere to a few common schemas that can be stored in the cache. The abstract `ResponseCache` class is flexible enough to support all of these and other usage patterns.

Configuring the Connection

The `URLConnection` class has seven protected instance fields that define exactly how the client makes the request to the server. These are:

```
protected URL      url;
protected boolean doInput = true;
protected boolean doOutput = false;
protected boolean allowUserInteraction = defaultAllowUserInteraction;
protected boolean useCaches = defaultUseCaches;
protected long     ifModifiedSince = 0;
protected boolean connected = false;
```

For instance, if `doOutput` is `true`, you'll be able to write data to the server over this `URLConnection` as well as read data from it. If `useCaches` is `false`, the connection bypasses any local caching and downloads the file from the server afresh.

Because these fields are all protected, their values are accessed and modified via obviously named setter and getter methods:

```
public URL      getURL()
public void     setDoInput(boolean doInput)
public boolean getDoInput()
public void     setDoOutput(boolean doOutput)
public boolean getDoOutput()
public void     setAllowUserInteraction(boolean allowUserInteraction)
public boolean getAllowUserInteraction()
public void     setUseCaches(boolean useCaches)
public boolean getUseCaches()
public void     setIfModifiedSince(long ifModifiedSince)
public long     getIfModifiedSince()
```

You can modify these fields only before the `URLConnection` is connected (before you try to read content or headers from the connection). Most of the methods that set fields throw an `IllegalStateException` if they are called while the connection is open. In general, you can set the properties of a URLConnection object only before the connection is opened.

There are also some getter and setter methods that define the default behavior for all instances of URLConnection. These are:

```
public boolean         getDefaultUseCaches()
public void            setDefaultUseCaches(boolean defaultUseCaches)
public static void     setDefaultAllowUserInteraction(
    boolean defaultAllowUserInteraction)
public static boolean  getDefaultAllowUserInteraction()
public static FileNameMap getFileNameMap()
public static void     setFileNameMap(FileNameMap map)
```

Unlike the instance methods, these methods can be invoked at any time. The new defaults will apply only to URLConnection objects constructed after the new default values are set.

protected URL url

The url field specifies the URL that this URLConnection connects to. The constructor sets it when the URLConnection is created and it should not change thereafter. You can retrieve the value by calling the getURL() method. Example 7-12 opens a URLConnection to *http://www.oreilly.com/*, gets the URL of that connection, and prints it.

Example 7-12. Print the URL of a URLConnection to http://www.oreilly.com/

```java
import java.io.*;
import java.net.*;

public class URLPrinter {

  public static void main(String[] args) {
    try {
      URL u = new URL("http://www.oreilly.com/");
      URLConnection uc = u.openConnection();
      System.out.println(uc.getURL());
    } catch (IOException ex) {
      System.err.println(ex);
    }
  }
}
```

Here's the result, which should be no great surprise. The URL that is printed is the one used to create the URLConnection.

```
% java URLPrinter
http://www.oreilly.com/
```

protected boolean connected

The boolean field connected is true if the connection is open and false if it's closed. Because the connection has not yet been opened when a new URLConnection object is created, its initial value is false. This variable can be accessed only by instances of java.net.URLConnection and its subclasses.

There are no methods that directly read or change the value of connected. However, any method that causes the URLConnection to connect should set this variable to true, including connect(), getInputStream(), and getOutputStream(). Any method that causes the URLConnection to disconnect should set this field to false. There are no such methods in java.net.URLConnection, but some of its subclasses, such as java.net.HttpURLConnection, have disconnect() methods.

If you subclass URLConnection to write a protocol handler, you are responsible for setting connected to true when you are connected and resetting it to false when the connection closes. Many methods in java.net.URLConnection read this variable to determine what they can do. If it's set incorrectly, your program will have severe bugs that are not easy to diagnose.

protected boolean allowUserInteraction

Some URLConnections need to interact with a user. For example, a web browser may need to ask for a username and password. However, many applications cannot assume that a user is present to interact with it. For instance, a search engine robot is probably running in the background without any user to provide a username and password. As its name suggests, the allowUserInteraction field specifies whether user interaction is allowed. It is false by default.

This variable is protected, but the public getAllowUserInteraction() method can read its value and the public setAllowUserInteraction() method can change it:

```
public void    setAllowUserInteraction(boolean allowUserInteraction)
public boolean getAllowUserInteraction()
```

The value true indicates that user interaction is allowed; false indicates that there is no user interaction. The value may be read at any time but may be set only before the URLConnection is connected. Calling setAllowUserInteraction() when the URLConnection is connected throws an IllegalStateException.

For example, this code fragment opens a connection that could ask the user for authentication if it's required:

```
URL u = new URL("http://www.example.com/passwordProtectedPage.html");
URLConnection uc = u.openConnection();
uc.setAllowUserInteraction(true);
InputStream in = uc.getInputStream();
```

Java does not include a default GUI for asking the user for a username and password. If the request is made from an applet, the browser's usual authentication dialog can be relied on. In a standalone application, you first need to install an `Authenticator`, as discussed in "Accessing Password-Protected Sites" on page 163.

Figure 7-1 shows the dialog box that pops up when you try to access a password-protected page. If you cancel this dialog, you'll get a 401 Authorization Required error and whatever text the server sends to unauthorized users. However, if you refuse to send authorization at all—which you can do by clicking OK, then answering No when asked if you want to retry authorization—then `getInputStream()` will throw a `ProtocolEx ception`.

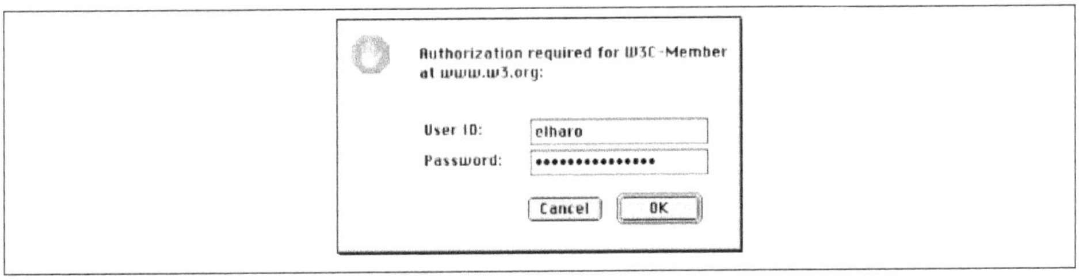

Figure 7-1. An authentication dialog

The static methods `getDefaultAllowUserInteraction()` and `setDefaultAllowUser Interaction()` determine the default behavior for `URLConnection` objects that have not set `allowUserInteraction` explicitly. Because the `allowUserInteraction` field is `static` (i.e., a class variable instead of an instance variable), setting it changes the default behavior for all instances of the `URLConnection` class that are created after `setDefaul tAllowUserInteraction()` is called.

For instance, the following code fragment checks to see whether user interaction is allowed by default with `getDefaultAllowUserInteraction()`. If user interaction is not allowed by default, the code uses `setDefaultAllowUserInteraction()` to make allowing user interaction the default behavior:

```
if (!URLConnection.getDefaultAllowUserInteraction()) {
  URLConnection.setDefaultAllowUserInteraction(true);
}
```

protected boolean doInput

A `URLConnection` can be used for reading from a server, writing to a server, or both. The protected boolean field `doInput` is `true` if the `URLConnection` can be used for reading, `false` if it cannot be. The default is `true`. To access this protected variable, use the public `getDoInput()` and `setDoInput()` methods:

```
public void    setDoInput(boolean doInput)
public boolean getDoInput()
```

For example:

```
try {
  URL u = new URL("http://www.oreilly.com");
  URLConnection uc = u.openConnection();
  if (!uc.getDoInput()) {
    uc.setDoInput(true);
  }
  // read from the connection...
} catch (IOException ex) {
  System.err.println(ex);
}
```

protected boolean doOutput

Programs can use a URLConnection to send output back to the server. For example, a program that needs to send data to the server using the POST method could do so by getting an output stream from a URLConnection. The protected boolean field doOutput is true if the URLConnection can be used for writing, false if it cannot be; it is false by default. To access this protected variable, use the getDoOutput() and setDoOutput() methods:

```
public void    setDoOutput(boolean dooutput)
public boolean getDoOutput()
```

For example:

```
try {
  URL u = new URL("http://www.oreilly.com");
  URLConnection uc = u.openConnection();
  if (!uc.getDoOutput()) {
    uc.setDoOutput(true);
  }
  // write to the connection...
} catch (IOException ex) {
  System.err.println(ex);
}
```

When you set doOutput to true for an *http* URL, the request method is changed from GET to POST. We'll explore this in more detail later in "Writing Data to a Server" on page 220.

protected boolean ifModifiedSince

Many clients, especially web browsers and proxies, keep caches of previously retrieved documents. If the user asks for the same document again, it can be retrieved from the cache. However, it may have changed on the server since it was last retrieved. The only way to tell is to ask the server. Clients can include an If-Modified-Since in the client request HTTP header. This header includes a date and time. If the document has changed since that time, the server should send it. Otherwise, it should not. Typically, this time is the last time the client fetched the document. For example, this client request says the document should be returned only if it has changed since 7:22:07 A.M., October 31, 2014, Greenwich Mean Time:

```
GET / HTTP/1.1
Host: login.ibiblio.org:56452
Accept: text/html, image/gif, image/jpeg, *; q=.2, */*; q=.2
Connection: close
If-Modified-Since: Fri, 31 Oct 2014 19:22:07 GMT
```

If the document has changed since that time, the server will send it as usual. Otherwise, it replies with a 304 Not Modified message, like this:

```
HTTP/1.0 304 Not Modified
Server: WN/1.15.1
Date: Sun, 02 Nov 2014 16:26:16 GMT
Last-modified: Fri, 29 Oct 2004 23:40:06 GMT
```

The client then loads the document from its cache. Not all web servers respect the If-Modified-Since field. Some will send the document whether it's changed or not.

The `ifModifiedSince` field in the `URLConnection` class specifies the date (in milliseconds since midnight, Greenwich Mean Time, January 1, 1970), which will be placed in the If-Modified-Since header field. Because `ifModifiedSince` is `protected`, programs should call the `getIfModifiedSince()` and `setIfModifiedSince()` methods to read or modify it:

```
public long getIfModifiedSince()
public void setIfModifiedSince(long ifModifiedSince)
```

Example 7-13 prints the default value of `ifModifiedSince`, sets its value to 24 hours ago, and prints the new value. It then downloads and displays the document—but only if it's been modified in the last 24 hours.

Example 7-13. Set ifModifiedSince to 24 hours prior to now

```
import java.io.*;
import java.net.*;
import java.util.*;

public class Last24 {

  public static void main (String[] args) {

    // Initialize a Date object with the current date and time
    Date today = new Date();
    long millisecondsPerDay = 24 * 60 * 60 * 1000;
```

```
for (int i = 0; i < args.length; i++) {
  try {
    URL u = new URL(args[i]);
    URLConnection uc = u.openConnection();
    System.out.println("Original if modified since: "
        + new Date(uc.getIfModifiedSince()));
    uc.setIfModifiedSince((new Date(today.getTime()
        - millisecondsPerDay)).getTime());
    System.out.println("Will retrieve file if it's modified since "
        + new Date(uc.getIfModifiedSince()));
    try (InputStream in = new BufferedInputStream(uc.getInputStream())) {
      Reader r = new InputStreamReader(in);
      int c;
      while ((c = r.read()) != -1) {
        System.out.print((char) c);
      }
      System.out.println();
    }
  } catch (IOException ex) {
    System.err.println(ex);
  }
}
}
}
```

Here's the result. First, you see the default value: midnight, January 1, 1970, GMT, converted to Pacific Standard Time. Next, you see the new time, which you set to 24 hours prior to the current time:

```
% java Last24 http://www.elharo.com
Original if modified since: Wed Dec 31 19:00:00 EST 1969
Will retrieve file if it's modified since Sat Jun 01 11:11:27 EDT 2013
```

Because this document hasn't changed in the last 24 hours, it is not reprinted.

protected boolean useCaches

Some clients, notably web browsers, can retrieve a document from a local cache, rather than retrieving it from a server. Applets may have access to the browser's cache. Standalone applications can use the java.net.ResponseCache class. The useCaches variable determines whether a cache will be used if it's available. The default value is true, meaning that the cache will be used; false means the cache won't be used.Because useCaches is protected, programs access it using the getUseCaches() and setUseCaches() methods:

```
public void    setUseCaches(boolean useCaches)
public boolean getUseCaches()
```

This code fragment disables caching to ensure that the most recent version of the document is retrieved by setting useCaches to false:

```
try {
  URL u = new URL("http://www.sourcebot.com/");
  URLConnection uc = u.openConnection();
  uc.setUseCaches(false);
  // read the document...
} catch (IOException ex) {
  System.err.println(ex);
}
```

Two methods define the initial value of the useCaches field, getDefaultUseCaches() and setDefaultUseCaches():

```
public void    setDefaultUseCaches(boolean useCaches)
public boolean getDefaultUseCaches()
```

Although nonstatic, these methods do set and get a static field that determines the default behavior for all instances of the URLConnection class created after the change. The next code fragment disables caching by default; after this code runs, URLConnections that want caching must enable it explicitly using setUseCaches(true):

```
if (uc.getDefaultUseCaches()) {
  uc.setDefaultUseCaches(false);
}
```

Timeouts

Four methods query and modify the timeout values for connections; that is, how long the underlying socket will wait for a response from the remote end before throwing a SocketTimeoutException. These are:

```
public void setConnectTimeout(int timeout)
public int  getConnectTimeout()
public void setReadTimeout(int timeout)
public int  getReadTimeout()
```

The setConnectTimeout()/getConnectTimeout() methods control how long the socket waits for the initial connection. The setReadTimeout()/getReadTimeout() methods control how long the input stream waits for data to arrive. All four methods measure timeouts in milliseconds. All four interpret zero as meaning never time out. Both setter methods throw an IllegalArgumentException if the timeout is negative.

For example, this code fragment requests a 30-second connect timeout and a 45-second read timeout:

```
URL u = new URL("http://www.example.org");
URLConnuction uc = u.openConnection();
uc.setConnectTimeout(30000);
uc.setReadTimeout(45000);
```

Configuring the Client Request HTTP Header

An HTTP client (e.g., a browser) sends the server a request line and a header. For example, here's an HTTP header that Chrome sends:

```
Accept:text/html,application/xhtml+xml,application/xml;q=0.9,*/*;q=0.8
Accept-Charset:ISO-8859-1,utf-8;q=0.7,*;q=0.3
Accept-Encoding:gzip,deflate,sdch
Accept-Language:en-US,en;q=0.8
Cache-Control:max-age=0
Connection:keep-alive
Cookie:reddit_first=%7B%22firsttime%22%3A%20%22first%22%7D
DNT:1
Host:lesswrong.com
User-Agent:Mozilla/5.0 (Macintosh; Intel Mac OS X 10_8_3) AppleWebKit/537.31
    (KHTML, like Gecko) Chrome/26.0.1410.65 Safari/537.31
```

A web server can use this information to serve different pages to different clients, to get and set cookies, to authenticate users through passwords, and more. Placing different fields in the header that the client sends and the server responds with does all of this.

 It's important to understand that this is *not the HTTP header that the server sends to the client* that is read by the various getHeader Field() and getHeaderFieldKey() methods discussed previously. This is the *HTTP header that the client sends to the server.*

Each URLConnection sets a number of different name-value pairs in the header by default. Here's the HTTP header that a connection from the SourceViewer2 program of Example 7-1 sends:

```
User-Agent: Java/1.7.0_17
Host: httpbin.org
Accept: text/html, image/gif, image/jpeg, *; q=.2, */*; q=.2
Connection: close
```

As you can see, it's a little simpler than the one Chrome sends, and it has a different user agent and accepts different kinds of files. However, you can modify these and add new fields before connecting.

You add headers to the HTTP header using the setRequestProperty() method before you open the connection:

```
public void setRequestProperty(String name, String value)
```

The setRequestProperty() method adds a field to the header of this URLConnection with a specified name and value. This method can be used only before the connection is opened. It throws an IllegalStateException if the connection is already open. The `getRequestProperty()` method returns the value of the named field of the HTTP header used by this `URLConnection`.

HTTP allows a single named request property to have multiple values. In this case, the separate values will be separated by commas. For example, the Accept header sent by Java 7 in the previous code snippet has the four values text/html, image/gif, image/jpeg, and *.

 These methods only really have meaning when the URL being connected to is an *HTTP* URL, because only the HTTP protocol makes use of headers like this. Though they could possibly have other meanings in other protocols, such as NNTP, this is really just an example of poor API design. These methods should be part of the more specific `HttpURLConnection` class, not the generic `URLConnection` class.

For instance, web servers and clients store some limited persistent information with cookies. A cookie is a collection of name-value pairs. The server sends a cookie to a client using the response HTTP header. From that point forward, whenever the client requests a URL from that server, it includes a Cookie field in the HTTP request header that looks like this:

```
Cookie: username=elharo; password=ACD0X9F23JJJn6G; session=100678945
```

This particular Cookie field sends three name-value pairs to the server. There's no limit to the number of name-value pairs that can be included in any one cookie. Given a `URLConnection` object uc, you could add this cookie to the connection, like this:

```
uc.setRequestProperty("Cookie",
    "username=elharo; password=ACD0X9F23JJJn6G; session=100678945");
```

You can set the same property to a new value, but this changes the existing property value. To add an additional property value, use the `addRequestProperty()` method instead:

```
public void addRequestProperty(String name, String value)
```

There's no fixed list of legal headers. Servers usually ignore any headers they don't recognize. HTTP does put a few restrictions on the content of the names and values of header fields. For instance, the names can't contain whitespace and the values can't contain any line breaks. Java enforces the restrictions on fields containing line breaks, but not much else. If a field contains a line break, `setRequestProperty()` and `addRequestProperty()` throw an `IllegalArgumentException`. Otherwise, it's quite easy to make a `URLConnection` send malformed headers to the server, so be careful. Some servers will handle the malformed headers gracefully. Some will ignore the bad header and return the requested document anyway, but some will reply with an HTTP 400, Bad Request error.

If, for some reason, you need to inspect the headers in a URLConnection, there's a standard getter method:

```
public String getRequestProperty(String name)
```

Java also includes a method to get all the request properties for a connection as a Map:

```
public Map<String,List<String>> getRequestProperties()
```

The keys are the header field names. The values are lists of property values. Both names and values are stored as strings.

Writing Data to a Server

Sometimes you need to write data to a URLConnection, for example, when you submit a form to a web server using POST or upload a file using PUT. The getOutputStream() method returns an OutputStream on which you can write data for transmission to a server:

```
public OutputStream getOutputStream()
```

A URLConnection doesn't allow output by default, so you have to call setDoOutput(true) before asking for an output stream. When you set doOutput to true for an *http* URL, the request method is changed from GET to POST. In Chapter 5, you saw how to send data to server-side programs with GET. However, GET should be limited to safe operations, such as search requests or page navigation, and not used for unsafe operations that create or modify a resource, such as posting a comment on a web page or ordering a pizza. Safe operations can be bookmarked, cached, spidered, prefetched, and so on. Unsafe operations should not be.

Once you have an OutputStream, buffer it by chaining it to a BufferedOutputStream or a BufferedWriter. You may also chain it to a DataOutputStream, an OutputStream Writer, or some other class that's more convenient to use than a raw OutputStream. For example:

```
try {
  URL u = new URL("http://www.somehost.com/cgi-bin/acgi");
  // open the connection and prepare it to POST
  URLConnection uc = u.openConnection();
  uc.setDoOutput(true);

  OutputStream raw = uc.getOutputStream();
  OutputStream buffered = new BufferedOutputStream(raw);
  OutputStreamWriter out = new OutputStreamWriter(buffered, "8859_1");
  out.write("first=Julie&middle=&last=Harting&work=String+Quartet\r\n");
  out.flush();
  out.close();
} catch (IOException ex) {
```

```
    System.err.println(ex);
  }
```

Sending data with POST is almost as easy as with GET. Invoke setDoOutput(true) and use the URLConnection's getOutputStream() method to write the query string rather than attaching it to the URL. Java buffers all the data written onto the output stream until the stream is closed. This enables it to calculate the value for the Content-length header. The complete transaction, including client request and server response, looks something like this:

```
% telnet www.cafeaulait.org 80
Trying 152.19.134.41...
Connected to www.cafeaulait.org.
Escape character is '^]'.
POST /books/jnp3/postquery.phtml HTTP/1.0
Accept: text/plain
Content-type: application/x-www-form-urlencoded
Content-length: 63
Connection: close
Host: www.cafeaulait.org

username=Elliotte+Rusty+Harold&email=elharo%40ibiblio%2eorg
HTTP/1.1 200 OK
Date: Sat, 04 May 2013 13:27:24 GMT
Server: Apache
Content-Style-Type: text/css
Content-Length: 864
Connection: close
Content-Type: text/html; charset=utf-8

<html xmlns="http://www.w3.org/1999/xhtml">
<head>
  <title>Query Results</title>
</head>
<body>

<h1>Query Results</h1>

<p>You submitted the following name/value pairs:</p>

<ul>
<li>username = Elliotte Rusty Harold</li>
<li>email = elharo@ibiblio.org</li>
</ul>

<hr />
Last Modified July 25, 2012

</body>
</html>
Connection closed by foreign host.
```

For that matter, as long as you control both the client and the server, you can use any other sort of data encoding you like. For instance, SOAP and XML-RPC both POST data to web servers as XML rather than an x-www-form-url-encoded query string.

Example 7-14 is a program called FormPoster that uses the URLConnection class and the QueryString class from Chapter 5 to post form data. The constructor sets the URL. The query string is built using the add() method. The post() method actually sends the data to the server by opening a URLConnection to the specified URL, setting its doOutput field to true, and writing the query string on the output stream. It then returns the input stream containing the server's response.

The main() method is a simple test for this program that sends the name "Elliotte Rusty Harold" and the email address *elharo@biblio.org* to the resource at *http://www.cafeau-lait.org/books/jnp4/postquery.phtml*. This resource is a simple form tester that accepts any input using either the POST or GET method and returns an HTML page showing the names and values that were submitted. The data returned is HTML; this example simply displays the HTML rather than attempting to parse it. It would be easy to extend this program by adding a user interface that lets you enter the name and email address to be posted—but because doing that triples the size of the program while showing nothing more of network programming, it is left as an exercise for the reader. Once you understand this example, it should be easy to write Java programs that communicate with other server-side scripts.

Example 7-14. Posting a form

```
import java.io.*;
import java.net.*;

public class FormPoster {

  private URL url;
  // from Chapter 5, Example 5-8
  private QueryString query = new QueryString();

  public FormPoster (URL url) {
    if (!url.getProtocol().toLowerCase().startsWith("http")) {
      throw new IllegalArgumentException(
          "Posting only works for http URLs");
    }
    this.url = url;
  }

  public void add(String name, String value) {
    query.add(name, value);
  }

  public URL getURL() {
    return this.url;
  }
```

```java
public InputStream post() throws IOException {

  // open the connection and prepare it to POST
  URLConnection uc = url.openConnection();
  uc.setDoOutput(true);
  try (OutputStreamWriter out
      = new OutputStreamWriter(uc.getOutputStream(), "UTF-8")) {

    // The POST line, the Content-type header,
    // and the Content-length headers are sent by the URLConnection.
    // We just need to send the data
    out.write(query.toString());
    out.write("\r\n");
    out.flush();
  }

  // Return the response
  return uc.getInputStream();
}

public static void main(String[] args) {
  URL url;
  if (args.length > 0) {
    try {
      url = new URL(args[0]);
    } catch (MalformedURLException ex) {
      System.err.println("Usage: java FormPoster url");
      return;
    }
  } else {
    try {
      url = new URL(
          "http://www.cafeaulait.org/books/jnp4/postquery.phtml");
    } catch (MalformedURLException ex) { // shouldn't happen
      System.err.println(ex);
      return;
    }
  }

  FormPoster poster = new FormPoster(url);
  poster.add("name", "Elliotte Rusty Harold");
  poster.add("email", "elharo@ibiblio.org");

  try (InputStream in = poster.post()) {
    // Read the response
    Reader r = new InputStreamReader(in);
    int c;
    while((c = r.read()) != -1) {
      System.out.print((char) c);
    }
    System.out.println();
```

```
    } catch (IOException ex) {
      System.err.println(ex);
    }
  }
}
```

Here's the response from the server:

```
% java -classpath .:jnp4e.jar FormPoster
<html xmlns="http://www.w3.org/1999/xhtml">
<head>
        <title>Query Results</title>
</head>
<body>

<h1>Query Results</h1>

<p>You submitted the following name/value pairs:</p>

<ul>
<li>name = Elliotte Rusty Harold</li>
<li>email = elharo@ibiblio.org
</li>
</ul>

<hr />
Last Modified May 10, 2013

</body>
</html>
```

The main() method tries to read the first command-line argument from args[0]. The argument is optional; if there is an argument, it is assumed to be a URL that can be POSTed to. If there are no arguments, main() initializes url with a default URL, *http:// www.cafeaulait.org/books/jnp4/postquery.phtml*. main() then constructs a FormPost er object. Two name-value pairs are added to this FormPoster object. Next, the post() method is invoked and its response read and printed on System.out.

The post() method is the heart of the class. It first opens a connection to the URL stored in the url field. It sets the doOutput field of this connection to true because this URL Connection needs to send output and chains the OutputStream for this URL to an ASCII OutputStreamWriter that sends the data, then flushes and closes the stream. *Do not forget to close the stream!* If the stream isn't closed, no data will be sent. Finally, the URLConnection's InputStream is returned.

To summarize, posting data to a form requires these steps:

  1. Decide what name-value pairs you'll send to the server-side program.

2. Write the server-side program that will accept and process the request. If it doesn't use any custom data encoding, you can test this program using a regular HTML form and a web browser.

3. Create a query string in your Java program. The string should look like this:

    ```
    name1=value1&name2=value2&name3=value3
    ```

    Pass each name and value in the query string to URLEncoder.encode() before adding it to the query string.

4. Open a URLConnection to the URL of the program that will accept the data.

5. Set doOutput to true by invoking setDoOutput(true).

6. Write the query string onto the URLConnection's OutputStream.

7. Close the URLConnection's OutputStream.

8. Read the server response from the URLConnection's InputStream.

GET should only be used for safe operations that can be bookmarked and linked to. POST should be used for unsafe operations that should not be bookmarked or linked to.

The getOutputStream() method is also used for the PUT request method, a means of storing files on a web server. The data to be stored is written onto the OutputStream that getOutputStream() returns. However, this can be done only from within the HttpURLConnection subclass of URLConnection, so discussion of PUT will have to wait a little while.

Security Considerations for URLConnections

URLConnection objects are subject to all the usual security restrictions about making network connections, reading or writing files, and so forth. For instance, a URLConnection can be created by an untrusted applet only if the URLConnection is pointing to the host that the applet came from. However, the details can be a little tricky because different URL schemes and their corresponding connections can have different security implications. For example, a *jar* URL that points into the applet's own *jar* file should be fine. However, a file URL that points to a local hard drive should not be.

Before attempting to connect a URL, you may want to know whether the connection will be allowed. For this purpose, the URLConnection class has a getPermission() method:

```
public Permission getPermission() throws IOException
```

This returns a java.security.Permission object that specifies what permission is needed to connect to the URL. It returns null if no permission is needed (e.g., there's no security manager in place). Subclasses of URLConnection return different subclasses of `java.security.Permission`. For instance, if the underlying URL points to *www.gwbush.com*, `getPermission()` returns a `java.net.SocketPermission` for the host *www.gwbush.com* with the connect and resolve actions.

Guessing MIME Media Types

If this were the best of all possible worlds, every protocol and every server would use standard MIME types to correctly specify the type of file being transferred. Unfortunately, that's not the case. Not only do we have to deal with older protocols such as FTP that predate MIME, but many HTTP servers that should use MIME don't provide MIME headers at all or lie and provide headers that are incorrect (usually because the server has been misconfigured). The `URLConnection` class provides two static methods to help programs figure out the MIME type of some data; you can use these if the content type just isn't available or if you have reason to believe that the content type you're given isn't correct. The first of these is `URLConnection.guessContentTypeFromName()`:

```
public static String guessContentTypeFromName(String name)
```

This method tries to guess the content type of an object based upon the extension in the filename portion of the object's URL. It returns its best guess about the content type as a `String`. This guess is likely to be correct; people follow some fairly regular conventions when thinking up filenames.

The guesses are determined by the *content-types.properties* file, normally located in the *jre/lib* directory. On Unix, Java may also look at the *mailcap* file to help it guess.

This method is not infallible by any means. For instance, it omits various XML applications such as RDF (*.rdf*), XSL (*.xsl*), and so on that should have the MIME type `application/xml`. It also doesn't provide a MIME type for CSS stylesheets (*.css*). However, it's a good start.

The second MIME type guesser method is `URLConnection.guessContentTypeFrom Stream()`:

```
public static String guessContentTypeFromStream(InputStream in)
```

This method tries to guess the content type by looking at the first few bytes of data in the stream. For this method to work, the `InputStream` must support marking so that you can return to the beginning of the stream after the first bytes have been read. Java inspects the first 16 bytes of the `InputStream`, although sometimes fewer bytes are needed to make an identification. These guesses are often not as reliable as the guesses made by `guessContentTypeFromName()`. For example, an XML document that begins with a comment rather than an XML declaration would be mislabeled as an HTML file. This method should be used only as a last resort.

HttpURLConnection

The `java.net.HttpURLConnection` class is an abstract subclass of `URLConnection`; it provides some additional methods that are helpful when working specifically with *http* URLs. In particular, it contains methods to get and set the request method, decide whether to follow redirects, get the response code and message, and figure out whether a proxy server is being used. It also includes several dozen mnemonic constants matching the various HTTP response codes. Finally, it overrides the `getPermission()` method from the `URLConnection` superclass, although it doesn't change the semantics of this method at all.

Because this class is abstract and its only constructor is protected, you can't directly create instances of `HttpURLConnection`. However, if you construct a URL object using an *http* URL and invoke its `openConnection()` method, the `URLConnection` object returned will be an instance of `HttpURLConnection`. Cast that `URLConnection` to `HttpURL Connection` like this:

```
URL u = new URL("http://lesswrong.com/");
URLConnection uc = u.openConnection();
HttpURLConnection http = (HttpURLConnection) uc;
```

Or, skipping a step, like this:

```
URL u = new URL("http://lesswrong.com/");
HttpURLConnection http = (HttpURLConnection) u.openConnection();
```

The Request Method

When a web client contacts a web server, the first thing it sends is a request line. Typically, this line begins with `GET` and is followed by the path of the resource that the client wants to retrieve and the version of the HTTP protocol that the client understands. For example:

```
GET /catalog/jfcnut/index.html HTTP/1.0
```

However, web clients can do more than simply `GET` files from web servers. They can `POST` responses to forms. They can `PUT` a file on a web server or `DELETE` a file from a server. And they can ask for just the HEAD of a document. They can ask the web server for a list of the `OPTIONS` supported at a given URL. They can even `TRACE` the request itself. All of these are accomplished by changing the request method from `GET` to a different keyword. For example, here's how a browser asks for just the header of a document using `HEAD`:

```
HEAD /catalog/jfcnut/index.html HTTP/1.1
Host: www.oreilly.com
Accept: text/html, image/gif, image/jpeg, *; q=.2, */*; q=.2
Connection: close
```

By default, `HttpURLConnection` uses the `GET` method. However, you can change this with the `setRequestMethod()` method:

```
public void setRequestMethod(String method) throws ProtocolException
```

The method argument should be one of these seven case-sensitive strings:

- GET
- POST
- HEAD
- PUT
- DELETE
- OPTIONS
- TRACE

If it's some other method, then a `java.net.ProtocolException`, a subclass of `IOException`, is thrown. However, it's generally not enough to simply set the request method. Depending on what you're trying to do, you may need to adjust the HTTP header and provide a message body as well. For instance, `POST`ing a form requires you to provide a Content-length header. We've already explored the `GET` and `POST` methods. Let's look at the other five possibilities.

 Some web servers support additional, nonstandard request methods. For instance, WebDAV requires servers to support `PROPFIND`, `PROPPATCH`, `MKCOL`, `COPY`, `MOVE`, `LOCK`, and `UNLOCK`. However, Java doesn't support any of these.

HEAD

The `HEAD` function is possibly the simplest of all the request methods. It behaves much like `GET`. However, it tells the server only to return the HTTP header, not to actually send the file. The most common use of this method is to check whether a file has been modified since the last time it was cached. Example 7-15 is a simple program that uses the `HEAD` request method and prints the last time a file on a server was modified.

Example 7-15. Get the time when a URL was last changed

```java
import java.io.*;
import java.net.*;
import java.util.*;

public class LastModified {
```

```
  public static void main(String[] args) {
    for (int i = 0; i < args.length; i++) {
      try {
        URL u = new URL(args[i]);
        HttpURLConnection http = (HttpURLConnection) u.openConnection();
        http.setRequestMethod("HEAD");
        System.out.println(u + " was last modified at "
            + new Date(http.getLastModified()));
      } catch (MalformedURLException ex) {
        System.err.println(args[i] + " is not a URL I understand");
      } catch (IOException ex) {
        System.err.println(ex);
      }
      System.out.println();
    }
  }
}
```

Here's the output from one run:

```
$ java LastModified http://www.ibiblio.org/xml/
http://www.ibiblio.org/xml/ was last modified at Tue Apr 06 07:45:29 EDT 2010
```

It wasn't absolutely necessary to use the HEAD method here. You'd have gotten the same results with GET. But if you used GET, the entire file at *http://www.ibiblio.org/xml/* would have been sent across the network, whereas all you cared about was one line in the header. When you can use HEAD, it's much more efficient to do so.

DELETE

The DELETE method removes a file at a specified URL from a web server. Because this request is an obvious security risk, not all servers will be configured to support it, and those that are will generally demand some sort of authentication. A typical DELETE request looks like this:

```
DELETE /javafaq/2008march.html HTTP/1.1
Host: www.ibiblio.org
Accept: text/html, image/gif, image/jpeg, *; q=.2, */*; q=.2
Connection: close
```

The server is free to refuse this request or ask for authorization. For example:

```
HTTP/1.1 405 Method Not Allowed
Date: Sat, 04 May 2013 13:22:12 GMT
Server: Apache
Allow: GET,HEAD,POST,OPTIONS,TRACE
Content-Length: 334
Connection: close
Content-Type: text/html; charset=iso-8859-1

<!DOCTYPE HTML PUBLIC "-//IETF//DTD HTML 2.0//EN">
<html><head>
```

```
<title>405 Method Not Allowed</title>
</head><body>
<h1>Method Not Allowed</h1>
<p>The requested method DELETE is not allowed for the URL
   /javafaq/2008march.html.</p>
<hr>
<address>Apache Server at www.ibiblio.org Port 80</address>
</body></html>
```

Even if the server accepts this request, its response is implementation dependent. Some servers may delete the file; others simply move it to a trash directory. Others simply mark it as not readable. Details are left up to the server vendor.

PUT

Many HTML editors and other programs that want to store files on a web server use the PUT method. It allows clients to place documents in the abstract hierarchy of the site without necessarily knowing how the site maps to the actual local filesystem. This contrasts with FTP, where the user has to know the actual directory structure as opposed to the server's virtual directory structure. Here's a how an editor might PUT a file on a web server:

```
PUT /blog/wp-app.php/service/pomdoros.html HTTP/1.1
Host: www.elharo.com
Authorization: Basic ZGFmZnk6c2VjcmJldA==
Content-Type: application/atom+xml;type=entry
Content-Length: 329
If-Match: "e180ee84f0671b1"

<?xml version="1.0" ?>
<entry xmlns="http://www.w3.org/2005/Atom">
 <title>The Power of Pomodoros</title>
 <id>urn:uuid:1225c695-cfb8-4ebb-aaaa-80da344efa6a</id>
 <updated>2013-02-23T19:22:11Z</updated>
 <author><name>Elliotte Harold</name></author>
 <content>Until recently, I hadn't paid much attention to...</content>
</entry>
```

As with deleting files, some sort of authentication is usually required and the server must be specially configured to support PUT. The details vary from server to server. Most web servers do not support PUT out of the box.

OPTIONS

The OPTIONS request method asks what options are supported for a particular URL. If the request URL is an asterisk (*), the request applies to the server as a whole rather than to one particular URL on the server. For example:

```
OPTIONS /xml/ HTTP/1.1
Host: www.ibiblio.org
```

```
Accept: text/html, image/gif, image/jpeg, *; q=.2, */*; q=.2
Connection: close
```

The server responds to an OPTIONS request by sending an HTTP header with a list of the commands allowed on that URL. For example, when the previous command was sent, here's what Apache responded with:

```
HTTP/1.1 200 OK
Date: Sat, 04 May 2013 13:52:53 GMT
Server: Apache
Allow: GET,HEAD,POST,OPTIONS,TRACE
Content-Style-Type: text/css
Content-Length: 0
Connection: close
Content-Type: text/html; charset=utf-8
```

The list of legal commands is found in the Allow field. However, in practice these are just the commands the server understands, not necessarily the ones it will actually perform on that URL.

TRACE

The TRACE request method sends the HTTP header that the server received from the client. The main reason for this information is to see what any proxy servers between the server and client might be changing. For example, suppose this TRACE request is sent:

```
TRACE /xml/ HTTP/1.1
Hello: Push me
Host: www.ibiblio.org
Accept: text/html, image/gif, image/jpeg, *; q=.2, */*; q=.2
Connection: close
```

The server should respond like this:

```
HTTP/1.1 200 OK
Date: Sat, 04 May 2013 14:41:40 GMT
Server: Apache
Connection: close
Content-Type: message/http

TRACE /xml/ HTTP/1.1
Hello: Push me
Host: www.ibiblio.org
Accept: text/html, image/gif, image/jpeg, *; q=.2, */*; q=.2
Connection: close
```

The first five lines are the server's normal response HTTP header. The lines from TRACE /xml/ HTTP/1.1 on are the echo of the original client request. In this case, the echo is faithful. However, if there were a proxy server between the client and server, it might not be.

Disconnecting from the Server

HTTP 1.1 supports persistent connections that allow multiple requests and responses to be sent over a single TCP socket. However, when Keep-Alive is used, the server won't immediately close a connection simply because it has sent the last byte of data to the client. The client may, after all, send another request. Servers will time out and close the connection in as little as 5 seconds of inactivity. However, it's still preferred for the client to close the connection as soon as it knows it's done.

The HttpURLConnection class transparently supports HTTP Keep-Alive unless you explicitly turn it off. That is, it will reuse sockets if you connect to the same server again before the server has closed the connection. Once you know you're done talking to a particular host, the disconnect() method enables a client to break the connection:

```
public abstract void disconnect()
```

If any streams are still open on this connection, disconnect() closes them. However, the reverse is not true. Closing a stream on a persistent connection does not close the socket and disconnect.

Handling Server Responses

The first line of an HTTP server's response includes a numeric code and a message indicating what sort of response is made. For instance, the most common response is 200 OK, indicating that the requested document was found. For example:

```
HTTP/1.1 200 OK
Cache-Control:max-age=3, must-revalidate
Connection:Keep-Alive
Content-Type:text/html; charset=UTF-8
Date:Sat, 04 May 2013 14:01:16 GMT
Keep-Alive:timeout=5, max=200
Server:Apache
Transfer-Encoding:chunked
Vary:Accept-Encoding,Cookie
WP-Super-Cache:Served supercache file from PHP

<HTML>
<HEAD>
rest of document follows...
```

Another response that you're undoubtedly all too familiar with is 404 Not Found, indicating that the URL you requested no longer points to a document. For example:

```
HTTP/1.1 404 Not Found
Date: Sat, 04 May 2013 14:05:43 GMT
Server: Apache
Last-Modified: Sat, 12 Jan 2013 00:19:15 GMT
ETag: "375933-2b9e-4d30c5cb0c6c0;4d02eaff53b80"
Accept-Ranges: bytes
```

```
Content-Length: 11166
Connection: close
Content-Type: text/html; charset=ISO-8859-1

<html>
<head>
<title>Lost ... and lost</title>
<meta http-equiv="Content-Type" content="text/html; charset=iso-8859-1">
</head>

<body bgcolor="#FFFFFF">
  <h1>404 FILE NOT FOUND</h1>
Rest of error message follows...
```

There are many other, less common responses. For instance, code 301 indicates that the resource has permanently moved to a new location and the browser should redirect itself to the new location and update any bookmarks that point to the old location. For example:

```
HTTP/1.1 301 Moved Permanently
Connection: Keep-Alive
Content-Length: 299
Content-Type: text/html; charset=iso-8859-1
Date: Sat, 04 May 2013 14:20:58 GMT
Keep-Alive: timeout=5, max=200
Location: http://www.cafeaulait.org/
Server: Apache
```

Often all you need from the response message is the numeric response code. HttpURL Connection also has a getResponseCode() method to return this as an int:

```
public int getResponseCode() throws IOException
```

The text string that follows the response code is called the *response message* and is returned by the aptly named getResponseMessage() method:

```
public String getResponseMessage() throws IOException
```

HTTP 1.0 defined 16 response codes. HTTP 1.1 expanded this to 40 different codes. Although some numbers, notably 404, have become slang almost synonymous with their semantic meaning, most of them are less familiar. The HttpURLConnection class includes 36 named constants such as HttpURLConnection.OK and HttpURLConnec tion.NOT_FOUND representing the most common response codes. These are summarized in Table 6-1. Example 7-16 is a revised source viewer program that now includes the response message.

Example 7-16. A SourceViewer that includes the response code and message

```
import java.io.*;
import java.net.*;

public class SourceViewer3 {
```

```java
public static void main (String[] args) {
  for (int i = 0; i < args.length; i++) {
    try {
      // Open the URLConnection for reading
      URL u = new URL(args[i]);
      HttpURLConnection uc = (HttpURLConnection) u.openConnection();
      int code = uc.getResponseCode();
      String response = uc.getResponseMessage();
      System.out.println("HTTP/1.x " + code + " " + response);
      for (int j = 1; ; j++) {
        String header = uc.getHeaderField(j);
        String key = uc.getHeaderFieldKey(j);
        if (header == null || key == null) break;
        System.out.println(uc.getHeaderFieldKey(j) + ": " + header);
      }
      System.out.println();

      try (InputStream in = new BufferedInputStream(uc.getInputStream())) {
        // chain the InputStream to a Reader
        Reader r = new InputStreamReader(in);
        int c;
        while ((c = r.read()) != -1) {
          System.out.print((char) c);
        }
      }
    } catch (MalformedURLException ex) {
      System.err.println(args[0] + " is not a parseable URL");
    } catch (IOException ex) {
      System.err.println(ex);
    }
  }
}
```

The only thing this program doesn't read that the server sends is the version of HTTP the server is using. There's currently no method to specifically return that. In this example, you just fake it as "HTTP/1.x," like this:

```
% java SourceViewer3 http://www.oreilly.com
HTTP/1.x 200 OK
Date: Sat, 04 May 2013 11:59:52 GMT
Server: Apache
Last-Modified: Sat, 04 May 2013 11:41:06 GMT
Accept-Ranges: bytes
Content-Length: 80165
Content-Type: text/html; charset=utf-8
Cache-Control: max-age=14400
Expires: Sat, 04 May 2013 15:59:52 GMT
Vary: Accept-Encoding
Keep-Alive: timeout=3, max=100
Connection: Keep-Alive
```

```
<!DOCTYPE HTML PUBLIC "-//W3C//DTD HTML 4.01 Transitional//EN"
    "http://www.w3.org/TR/html4/loose.dtd">
<html>
...
```

However, `uc.getHeaderField(0)` does return the entire first HTTP request line, version included:

```
HTTP/1.1 200 OK
```

Error conditions

On occasion, the server encounters an error but returns useful information in the message body nonetheless. For example, when a client requests a nonexistent page from the *www.ibiblio.org* website, rather than simply returning a 404 error code, the server sends the search page shown in Figure 7-2 to help the user figure out where the missing page might have gone.

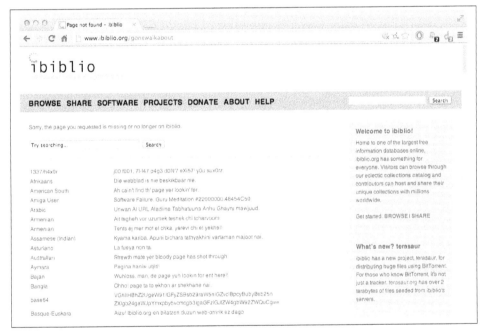

Figure 7-2. IBiblio's 404 page

The `getErrorStream()` method returns an `InputStream` containing this page or `null` if no error was encountered or no data returned:

```
public InputStream getErrorStream()
```

Generally, you'll invoke `getErrorStream()` inside a `catch` block after `getInput Stream()` has failed. Example 7-17 demonstrates with a program that reads form the input stream if possible. However, if that fails for any reason, it then reads from the error stream instead.

Example 7-17. Download a web page with a URLConnection

```
import java.io.*;
import java.net.*;

public class SourceViewer4 {

  public static void main (String[] args) {
    try {
      URL u = new URL(args[0]);
      HttpURLConnection uc = (HttpURLConnection) u.openConnection();
      try (InputStream raw = uc.getInputStream()) {
        printFromStream(raw);
      } catch (IOException ex) {
        printFromStream(uc.getErrorStream());
      }
    } catch (MalformedURLException ex) {
      System.err.println(args[0] + " is not a parseable URL");
    } catch (IOException ex) {
      System.err.println(ex);
    }
  }

  private static void printFromStream(InputStream raw) throws IOException {
    try (InputStream buffer = new BufferedInputStream(raw)) {
      Reader reader = new InputStreamReader(buffer);
      int c;
      while ((c = reader.read()) != -1) {
        System.out.print((char) c);
      }
    }
  }
}
```

Redirects

The 300-level response codes all indicate some sort of redirect; that is, the requested resource is no longer available at the expected location but it may be found at some other location. When encountering such a response, most browsers automatically load the document from its new location. However, this can be a security risk, because it has the potential to move the user from a trusted site to an untrusted one, perhaps without the user even noticing.

By default, an `HttpURLConnection` follows redirects. However, the `HttpURLConnec tion` class has two static methods that let you decide whether to follow redirects:

```
public static boolean getFollowRedirects()
public static void    setFollowRedirects(boolean follow)
```

The getFollowRedirects() method returns true if redirects are being followed, false if they aren't. With an argument of true, the setFollowRedirects() method makes HttpURLConnection objects follow redirects. With an argument of false, it prevents them from following redirects. Because these are static methods, they change the behavior of all HttpURLConnection objects constructed after the method is invoked. The setFollowRedirects() method may throw a SecurityException if the security manager disallows the change. Applets especially are not allowed to change this value.

Java has two methods to configure redirection on an instance-by-instance basis. These are:

```
public boolean getInstanceFollowRedirects()
public void    setInstanceFollowRedirects(boolean followRedirects)
```

If setInstanceFollowRedirects() is not invoked on a given HttpURLConnection, that HttpURLConnection simply follows the default behavior as set by the class method HttpURLConnection.setFollowRedirects().

Proxies

Many users behind firewalls or using AOL or other high-volume ISPs access the Web through proxy servers. The usingProxy() method tells you whether the particular HttpURLConnection is going through a proxy server:

```
public abstract boolean usingProxy()
```

It returns true if a proxy is being used, false if not. In some contexts, the use of a proxy server may have security implications.

Streaming Mode

Every request sent to an HTTP server has an HTTP header. One field in this header is the Content-length (i.e., the number of bytes in the body of the request). The header comes before the body. However, to write the header you need to know the length of the body, which you may not have yet. Normally, the way Java solves this catch-22 is by caching everything you write onto the OutputStream retrieved from the HttpURLConnection until the stream is closed. At that point, it knows how many bytes are in the body so it has enough information to write the Content-length header.

This scheme is fine for small requests sent in response to typical web forms. However, it's burdensome for responses to very long forms or some SOAP messages. It's very wasteful and slow for medium or large documents sent with HTTP PUT. It's much more efficient if Java doesn't have to wait for the last byte of data to be written before sending the first byte of data over the network. Java offers two solutions to this problem. If you know the size of your data—for instance, you're uploading a file of known size using HTTP PUT—you can tell the HttpURLConnection object the size of that data. If you don't know the size of the data in advance, you can use chunked transfer encoding instead. In chunked transfer encoding, the body of the request is sent in multiple pieces, each with its own separate content length. To turn on chunked transfer encoding, just pass the size of the chunks you want to the setChunkedStreamingMode() method before you connect the URL:

```
public void setChunkedStreamingMode(int chunkLength)
```

Java will then use a slightly different form of HTTP than the examples in this book. However, to the Java programmer, the difference is irrelevant. As long as you're using the URLConnection class instead of raw sockets and as long as the server supports chunked transfer encoding, it should all just work without any further changes to your code. However, chunked transfer encoding does get in the way of authentication and redirection. If you're trying to send chunked files to a redirected URL or one that requires password authentication, an HttpRetryException will be thrown. You'll then need to retry the request at the new URL or at the old URL with the appropriate credentials; and this all needs to be done manually without the full support of the HTTP protocol handler you normally have. Therefore, don't use chunked transfer encoding unless you really need it. As with most performance advice, this means you shouldn't implement this optimization until measurements prove the nonstreaming default is a bottleneck.

If you do happen to know the size of the request data in advance, you can optimize the connection by providing this information to the HttpURLConnection object. If you do this, Java can start streaming the data over the network immediately. Otherwise, it has to cache everything you write in order to determine the content length, and only send it over the network after you've closed the stream. If you know exactly how big your data is, pass that number to the setFixedLengthStreamingMode() method:

```
public void setFixedLengthStreamingMode(int contentLength)
public void setFixedLengthStreamingMode(long contentLength) // Java 7
```

Because this number can actually be larger than the maximum size of an int, in Java 7 and later you can use a long instead.

Java will use this number in the Content-length HTTP header field. However, if you then try to write more or less than the number of bytes given here, Java will throw an IOException. Of course, that happens later, when you're writing data, not when you first call this method. The setFixedLengthStreamingMode() method itself will throw an IllegalArgumentException if you pass in a negative number, or an IllegalStateException if the connection is connected or has already been set to chunked transfer encoding. (You can't use both chunked transfer encoding and fixed-length streaming mode on the same request.)"

Fixed-length streaming mode is transparent on the server side. Servers neither know nor care how the Content-length was set, as long as it's correct. However, like chunked transfer encoding, streaming mode does interfere with authentication and redirection. If either of these is required for a given URL, an `HttpRetryException` will be thrown; you have to manually retry. Therefore, don't use this mode unless you really need it.

CHAPTER 8

Sockets for Clients

Data is transmitted across the Internet in packets of finite size called *datagrams*. Each datagram contains a *header* and a *payload*. The header contains the address and port to which the packet is going, the address and port from which the packet came, a checksum to detect data corruption, and various other housekeeping information used to ensure reliable transmission. The payload contains the data itself. However, because datagrams have a finite length, it's often necessary to split the data across multiple packets and reassemble it at the destination. It's also possible that one or more packets may be lost or corrupted in transit and need to be retransmitted or that packets arrive out of order and need to be reordered. Keeping track of this—splitting the data into packets, generating headers, parsing the headers of incoming packets, keeping track of what packets have and haven't been received, and so on—is a lot of work and requires a lot of intricate code.

Fortunately, you don't have to do the work yourself. Sockets allow the programmer to treat a network connection as just another stream onto which bytes can be written and from which bytes can be read. Sockets shield the programmer from low-level details of the network, such as error detection, packet sizes, packet splitting, packet retransmission, network addresses, and more.

Using Sockets

A socket is a connection between two hosts. It can perform seven basic operations:

- Connect to a remote machine
- Send data
- Receive data
- Close a connection
- Bind to a port

- Listen for incoming data
- Accept connections from remote machines on the bound port

Java's `Socket` class, which is used by both clients and servers, has methods that correspond to the first four of these operations. The last three operations are needed only by servers, which wait for clients to connect to them. They are implemented by the `ServerSocket` class, which is discussed in the next chapter. Java programs normally use client sockets in the following fashion:

- The program creates a new socket with a constructor.
- The socket attempts to connect to the remote host.

Once the connection is established, the local and remote hosts get input and output streams from the socket and use those streams to send data to each other. This connection is *full-duplex*. Both hosts can send and receive data simultaneously. What the data means depends on the protocol; different commands are sent to an FTP server than to an HTTP server. There will normally be some agreed-upon handshaking followed by the transmission of data from one to the other.

When the transmission of data is complete, one or both sides close the connection. Some protocols, such as HTTP 1.0, require the connection to be closed after each request is serviced. Others, such as FTP and HTTP 1.1, allow multiple requests to be processed in a single connection.

Investigating Protocols with Telnet

In this chapter, you'll see clients that use sockets to communicate with a number of well-known Internet services such as time, dict, and more. The sockets themselves are simple enough; however, the protocols to communicate with different servers make life complex.

To get a feel for how a protocol operates, you can use Telnet to connect to a server, type different commands to it, and watch its responses. By default, Telnet attempts to connect to port 23. To connect to servers on different ports, specify the port you want to connect to like this:

```
$ telnet localhost 25
```

This requests a connection to port 25, the SMTP port, on the local machine; SMTP is the protocol used to transfer email between servers or between a mail client and a server. If you know the commands to interact with an SMTP server, you can send email without going through a mail program. This trick can be used to forge email. For example, some years ago, the summer students at the National Solar Observatory in Sunspot, New Mexico, made it appear that the party one of the scientists was throwing after the annual volleyball match between the staff and the students was in fact a victory party for the students. (Of course, the author of this book had absolutely nothing to do with such despicable behavior. ;-)) The interaction with the SMTP server went something like this; input the user types is shown in bold (the names have been changed to protect the gullible):

```
flare% telnet localhost 25
Trying 127.0.0.1 ...
Connected to localhost.sunspot.noao.edu.
Escape character is '^]'.
220 flare.sunspot.noao.edu Sendmail 4.1/SMI-4.1 ready at
Fri, 5 Jul 93 13:13:01 MDT
HELO sunspot.noao.edu
250 flare.sunspot.noao.edu Hello localhost [127.0.0.1], pleased to meet you
MAIL FROM: bart
250 bart... Sender ok
RCPT TO: local@sunspot.noao.edu
250 local@sunspot.noao.edu... Recipient ok
DATA
354 Enter mail, end with "." on a line by itself

In a pitiful attempt to reingratiate myself with the students
after their inevitable defeat of the staff on the volleyball
court at 4:00 P.M., July 24, I will be throwing a victory
party for the students at my house that evening at 7:00.
Everyone is invited.

Beer and Ben-Gay will be provided so the staff may drown
their sorrows and assuage their aching muscles after their
public humiliation.

Sincerely,

Bart
.
250 Mail accepted
QUIT
221 flare.sunspot.noao.edu delivering mail
Connection closed by foreign host.
```

Several members of the staff asked Bart why he, a staff member, was throwing a victory party for the students. The moral of this story is that you should never trust email, especially patently ridiculous email like this, without independent verification.

In the 20 years since this happened, most SMTP servers have added a little more security than shown here. They tend to require usernames and passwords, and only accept connections from clients in the local networks and other trusted mail servers. However, it's still the case that you can use Telnet to simulate a client, see how the client and the server interact, and thus learn what your Java program needs to do. Although this session doesn't demonstrate all the features of the SMTP protocol, it's sufficient to enable you to deduce how a simple email client talks to a server.

Reading from Servers with Sockets

Let's begin with a simple example. You're going to connect to the daytime server at the National Institute for Standards and Technology (NIST) and ask it for the current time. This protocol is defined in RFC 867 (*https://tools.ietf.org/html/rfc867*). Reading that, you see that the daytime server listens on port 13, and that the server sends the time in a human-readable format and closes the connection. You can test the daytime server with Telnet like this:

```
$ telnet time.nist.gov 13
Trying 129.6.15.28...
Connected to time.nist.gov.
Escape character is '^]'.

56375 13-03-24 13:37:50 50 0 0 888.8 UTC(NIST) *
Connection closed by foreign host.
```

The line "56375 13-03-24 13:37:50 50 0 0 888.8 UTC(NIST)" is sent by the daytime server. When you read the Socket's InputStream, this is what you will get. The other lines are produced either by the Unix shell or by the Telnet program.

RFC 867 does not specify any particular format for the output other than that it be human readable. In this case, you can see this connection was made on March 24, 2013, at 1:37: 50 P.M., Greenwich Meantime. More specifically, the format (*http://bit.ly/nist-format*) is defined as *JJJJJ YY-MM-DD HH:MM:SS TT L H msADV UTC(NIST) OTM* where:

- *JJJJJ* is the "Modified Julian Date" (i.e., it is the number of whole days since midnight on November 17, 1858).

- *YY-MM-DD* is the last two digits of the year, the month, and the current day of month.

- *HH:MM:SS* is the time in hours, minutes, and seconds in Coordinated Universal Time (UTC, essentially Greenwich Mean Time).

- *TT* indicates whether the United States is currently observing on Standard Time or Daylight Savings Time: 00 means standard time; 50 means daylight savings time. Other values count down the number of days until the switchover.

- *L* is a one-digit code that indicates whether a leap second will be added or subtracted at midnight on the last day of the current month: 0 for no leap second, 1 to add a leap second, and 2 to subtract a leap second.

- *H* represents the health of the server: 0 means healthy, 1 means up to 5 seconds off, 2 means more than 5 seconds off, 3 means an unknown amount of inaccuracy, and 4 is maintenance mode.

- *msADV* is a number of milliseconds that NIST adds to the time it sends to roughly compensate for network delays. In the preceding code, you can see that it added

888.8 milliseconds to this result, because that's how long it estimates it's going to take for the response to return.

- The string *UTC(NIST)* is a constant, and the *OTM* is almost a constant (an asterisk unless something really weird has happened).

These details are all NIST specific. They are not part of the daytime standard. Although they do offer a lot of data, if you have a real programmatic need to sync with a network time server, you're better off using the NTP (*http://www.ntp.org/*) protocol defined in RFC 5905 (*https://tools.ietf.org/html/rfc5905*) instead.

I'm not sure how long this example is going to work as shown here. These servers are overloaded, and I did have intermittent problems connecting while writing this chapter. In early 2013, NIST announced (*http://tf.nist.gov/tf-cgi/servers.cgi*), "Users of the NIST *DAY-TIME* protocol on tcp port 13 are also strongly encouraged to upgrade to the network time protocol, which provides greater accuracy and requires less network bandwidth. The NIST time client (nistime-32bit.exe) supports both protocols. We expect to replace the tcp version of this protocol with a udp-based version near the end of 2013." I'll show you how to access this service over UDP in Chapter 11.

Now let's see how to retrieve this same data programmatically using sockets. First, open a socket to *time.nist.gov* on port 13:

```
Socket socket = new Socket("time.nist.gov", 13);
```

This doesn't just create the object. It actually makes the connection across the network. If the connection times out or fails because the server isn't listening on port 13, then the constructor throws an IOException, so you'll usually wrap this in a try block. In Java 7, Socket implements Autocloseable so you can use try-with-resources:

```
try (Socket socket = new Socket("time.nist.gov", 13)) {
  // read from the socket...
} catch (IOException ex) {
  System.err.println("Could not connect to time.nist.gov");
}
```

In Java 6 and earlier, you'll want to explicitly close the socket in a finally block to release resources the socket holds:

```
Socket socket = null;
try {
  socket = new Socket(hostname, 13);
  // read from the socket...
} catch (IOException ex) {
  System.err.println(ex);
```

```
    } finally {
      if (socket != null) {
        try {
          socket.close();
        } catch (IOException ex) {
          // ignore
        }
      }
    }
}
```

The next step is optional but highly recommended. Set a timeout on the connection using the setSoTimeout() method. Timeouts are measured in milliseconds, so this statement sets the socket to time out after 15 seconds of nonresponsiveness:

```
socket.setSoTimeout(15000);
```

Although a socket should throw a ConnectException pretty quickly if the server rejects the connection, or a NoRouteToHostException if the routers can't figure out how to send your packets to the server, neither of these help you with the case where a misbehaving server accepts the connection and then stops talking to you without actively closing the connection. Setting a timeout on the socket means that each read from or write to the socket will take at most a certain number of milliseconds. If a server hangs while you're connected to it, you will be notified with a SocketTimeoutException. Exactly how long a timeout to set depends on the needs of your application and how responsive you expect the server to be. Fifteen seconds is a long time for a local intranet server to respond, but it's rather short for an overloaded public server like *time.nist.gov*.

Once you've opened the socket and set its timeout, call getInputStream() to return an InputStream you can use to read bytes from the socket. In general, a server can send any bytes at all; but in this specific case, the protocol specifies that those bytes must be ASCII:

```
InputStream in = socket.getInputStream();
StringBuilder time = new StringBuilder();
InputStreamReader reader = new InputStreamReader(in, "ASCII");
for (int c = reader.read(); c != -1; c = reader.read()) {
  time.append((char) c);
}
System.out.println(time);
```

Here I've stored the bytes in a StringBuilder. You can, of course, use any data structure that fits your problem to hold the data that comes off the network.

Example 8-1 puts this all together in a program that also allows you to choose a different daytime server.

Example 8-1. A daytime protocol client

```
import java.net.*;
import java.io.*;
```

```java
public class DaytimeClient {

  public static void main(String[] args) {

    String hostname = args.length > 0 ? args[0] : "time.nist.gov";
    Socket socket = null;
    try {
      socket = new Socket(hostname, 13);
      socket.setSoTimeout(15000);
      InputStream in = socket.getInputStream();
      StringBuilder time = new StringBuilder();
      InputStreamReader reader = new InputStreamReader(in, "ASCII");
      for (int c = reader.read(); c != -1; c = reader.read()) {
        time.append((char) c);
      }
      System.out.println(time);
    } catch (IOException ex) {
      System.err.println(ex);
    } finally {
      if (socket != null) {
        try {
          socket.close();
        } catch (IOException ex) {
          // ignore
        }
      }
    }
  }
}
```

Typical output is much the same as if you connected with Telnet:

```
$ java DaytimeClient
56375 13-03-24 15:05:42 50 0 0 843.6 UTC(NIST) *
```

As far as network-specific code goes, that's pretty much it. In most network programs like this, the real effort is in speaking the protocol and comprehending the data formats. For instance, rather than simply printing out the text the server sends you, you might want to parse it into a `java.util.Date` object instead. Example 8-2 shows you how to do this. For variety, I also wrote this example taking advantage of Java 7's `AutoCloseable` and try-with-resources.

Example 8-2. Construct a Date by talking to time.nist.gov

```java
import java.net.*;
import java.text.*;
import java.util.Date;
import java.io.*;

public class Daytime {
```

```java
  public Date getDateFromNetwork() throws IOException, ParseException {
    try (Socket socket = new Socket("time.nist.gov", 13)) {
      socket.setSoTimeout(15000);
      InputStream in = socket.getInputStream();
      StringBuilder time = new StringBuilder();
      InputStreamReader reader = new InputStreamReader(in, "ASCII");
      for (int c = reader.read(); c != -1; c = reader.read()) {
        time.append((char) c);
      }
      return parseDate(time.toString());
    }
  }

  static Date parseDate(String s) throws ParseException {
    String[] pieces = s.split(" ");
    String dateTime = pieces[1] + " " + pieces[2] + " UTC";
    DateFormat format = new SimpleDateFormat("yy-MM-dd hh:mm:ss z");
    return format.parse(dateTime);
  }
}
```

Notice, however, this class doesn't actually do anything with the network that Example 8-1 didn't do. It just added a bunch of code to turn strings into dates.

When reading data from the network, it's important to keep in mind that not all protocols use ASCII or even text. For example, the time protocol specified in RFC 868 (*http://tools.ietf.org/html/rfc868*) specifies that the time be sent as the number of seconds since midnight, January 1, 1900, Greenwich Mean Time. However, this is not sent as an ASCII string like 2,524,521,600 or –1297728000. Rather, it is sent as a 32-bit, unsigned, big-endian binary number.

 The RFC never actually comes out and says that this is the format used. It specifies 32 bits and assumes you know that all network protocols use big-endian numbers. The fact that the number is unsigned can be determined only by calculating the wraparound date for signed and unsigned integers and comparing it to the date given in the specification (2036). To make matters worse, the specification gives an example of a negative time that can't actually be sent by time servers that follow the protocol. Time is a relatively old protocol, standardized in the early 1980s before the IETF was as careful about such issues as it is today. Nonetheless, if you find yourself implementing a not particularly well-specified protocol, you may have to do a significant amount of testing against existing implementations to figure out what you need to do. In the worst case, different implementations may behave differently.

Because the time protocol doesn't send back text, you can't easily use Telnet to test such a service, and your program can't read the server response with a Reader or any sort of readLine() method. A Java program that connects to time servers must read the raw bytes and interpret them appropriately. In this example, that job is complicated by Java's lack of a 32-bit unsigned integer type. Consequently, you have to read the bytes one at a time and manually convert them into a long using the bitwise operators << and |. Example 8-3 demonstrates. When speaking other protocols, you may encounter data formats even more alien to Java. For instance, a few network protocols use 64-bit fixed-point numbers. There's no shortcut to handle all possible cases. You simply have to grit your teeth and code the math you need to handle the data in whatever format the server sends.

Example 8-3. A time protocol client

```
import java.net.*;
import java.text.*;
import java.util.Date;
import java.io.*;

public class Time {

  private static final String HOSTNAME = "time.nist.gov";

  public static void main(String[] args) throws IOException, ParseException {
    Date d = Time.getDateFromNetwork();
    System.out.println("It is " + d);
  }

  public static Date getDateFromNetwork() throws IOException, ParseException {
    // The time protocol sets the epoch at 1900,
    // the Java Date class at 1970. This number
    // converts between them.

    long differenceBetweenEpochs = 2208988800L;

    // If you'd rather not use the magic number, uncomment
    // the following section which calculates it directly.
    /*
    TimeZone gmt = TimeZone.getTimeZone("GMT");
    Calendar epoch1900 = Calendar.getInstance(gmt);
    epoch1900.set(1900, 01, 01, 00, 00, 00);
    long epoch1900ms = epoch1900.getTime().getTime();
    Calendar epoch1970 = Calendar.getInstance(gmt);
    epoch1970.set(1970, 01, 01, 00, 00, 00);
    long epoch1970ms = epoch1970.getTime().getTime();

    long differenceInMS = epoch1970ms - epoch1900ms;
    long differenceBetweenEpochs = differenceInMS/1000;
    */
```

```
    Socket socket = null;
    try {
      socket = new Socket(HOSTNAME, 37);
      socket.setSoTimeout(15000);

      InputStream raw = socket.getInputStream();

      long secondsSince1900 = 0;
      for (int i = 0; i < 4; i++) {
        secondsSince1900 = (secondsSince1900 << 8) | raw.read();
      }

      long secondsSince1970
              = secondsSince1900 - differenceBetweenEpochs;
      long msSince1970 = secondsSince1970 * 1000;
      Date time = new Date(msSince1970);

      return time;
    } finally {
      try {
        if (socket != null) socket.close();
      }
      catch (IOException ex) {}
    }
  }
}
```

Here's the output of this program from a sample run:

```
$ java Time
It is Sun Mar 24 12:22:17 EDT 2013
```

The time protocol actually specifies Greenwich Mean Time, but the toString() method in Java's Date class, implicitly invoked by System.out.println(), converts this into the time zone of the local host, Eastern Daylight Time in this case.

Writing to Servers with Sockets

Writing to a server is not noticeably harder than reading from one. You simply ask the socket for an output stream as well as an input stream. Although it's possible to send data over the socket using the output stream at the same time you're reading data over the input stream, most protocols are designed so that the client is either reading or writing over a socket, not both at the same time. In the most common pattern, the client sends a request. Then the server responds. The client may send another request, and the server responds again. This continues until one side or the other is done, and closes the connection.

One simple bidirectional TCP protocol is *dict*, defined in RFC 2229. In this protocol, the client opens a socket to port 2628 on the dict server and sends commands such as "DEFINE eng-lat gold". This tells the server to send a definition of the word *gold* using its English-to-Latin dictionary. (Different servers have different dictionaries installed.) After the first definition is received, the client can ask for another. When it's done it sends the command "quit". You can explore dict with Telnet like this:

```
$ telnet dict.org 2628
Trying 216.18.20.172...
Connected to dict.org.
Escape character is '^]'.
220 pan.alephnull.com dictd 1.12.0/rf on Linux 3.0.0-14-server
    <auth.mime> <499772.29595.1364340382@pan.alephnull.com>
DEFINE eng-lat gold
150 1 definitions retrieved
151 "gold" eng-lat "English-Latin Freedict dictionary"
gold [gould]
   aurarius; aureus; chryseus
   aurum; chrysos

.
250 ok [d/m/c = 1/0/10; 0.000r 0.000u 0.000s]
DEFINE eng-lat computer
552 no match [d/m/c = 0/0/9; 0.000r 0.000u 0.000s]
quit
221 bye [d/m/c = 0/0/0; 42.000r 0.000u 0.000s]
```

You can see that control response lines begin with a three-digit code. The actual definition is plain text, terminated with a period on a line by itself. If the dictionary doesn't contain the word you asked for, it returns 552 no match. Of course, you could also find this out, and a lot more, by reading the RFC.

It's not hard to implement this protocol in Java. First, open a socket to a dict server—_dict.org__ is a good one—on port 2628:

```
Socket socket = new Socket("dict.org", 2628);
```

Once again you'll want to set a timeout in case the server hangs while you're connected to it:

```
socket.setSoTimeout(15000);
```

In the dict protocol, the client speaks first, so ask for the output stream using getOutputStream():

```
OutputStream out = socket.getOutputStream();
```

The getOutputStream() method returns a raw OutputStream for writing data from your application to the other end of the socket. You usually chain this stream to a more convenient class like DataOutputStream or OutputStreamWriter before using it. For performance reasons, it's a good idea to buffer it as well. Because the dict protocol is text based, more specifically UTF-8 based, it's convenient to wrap this in a Writer:

```
Writer writer = new OutputStreamWriter(out, "UTF-8");
```

Now write the command over the socket:

```
writer.write("DEFINE eng-lat gold\r\n");
```

Finally, flush the output so you'll be sure the command is sent over the network:

```
writer.flush();
```

The server should now respond with a definition. You can read that using the socket's input stream:

```
InputStream in = socket.getInputStream();
BufferedReader reader = new BufferedReader(
  new InputStreamReader(in, "UTF-8"));
for (String line = reader.readLine();
  !line.equals(".");
  line = reader.readLine()) {
    System.out.println(line);
}
```

When you see a period on a line by itself, you know the definition is complete. You can then send the quit over the output stream:

```
writer.write("quit\r\n");
writer.flush();
```

Example 8-4 shows a complete dict client. It connects to *dict.org*, and translates any words the user enters on the command line into Latin. It filters out all the metadata lines that begin with response codes such as 150 or 220. However, it does specifically check for a line that begins "552 no match" in case the server doesn't recognize the word.

Example 8-4. A network-based English-to-Latin translator

```
import java.io.*;
import java.net.*;

public class DictClient {

  public static final String SERVER = "dict.org";
  public static final int PORT = 2628;
  public static final int TIMEOUT = 15000;

  public static void main(String[] args) {

    Socket socket = null;
    try {
      socket = new Socket(SERVER, PORT);
      socket.setSoTimeout(TIMEOUT);
      OutputStream out = socket.getOutputStream();
      Writer writer = new OutputStreamWriter(out, "UTF-8");
      writer = new BufferedWriter(writer);
      InputStream in = socket.getInputStream();
      BufferedReader reader = new BufferedReader(
          new InputStreamReader(in, "UTF-8"));
```

```
      for (String word : args) {
        define(word, writer, reader);
      }

      writer.write("quit\r\n");
      writer.flush();
    } catch (IOException ex) {
      System.err.println(ex);
    } finally { // dispose
      if (socket != null) {
        try {
          socket.close();
        } catch (IOException ex) {
          // ignore
        }
      }
    }
  }
}

  static void define(String word, Writer writer, BufferedReader reader)
      throws IOException, UnsupportedEncodingException {
    writer.write("DEFINE eng-lat " + word + "\r\n");
    writer.flush();

    for (String line = reader.readLine(); line != null; line = reader.readLine()) {
      if (line.startsWith("250 ")) { // OK
        return;
      } else if (line.startsWith("552 ")) { // no match
        System.out.println("No definition found for " + word);
        return;
      }
      else if (line.matches("\\d\\d\\d .*")) continue;
      else if (line.trim().equals(".")) continue;
      else System.out.println(line);
    }
  }
}
```

Here's a sample run:

```
$ java DictClient gold uranium silver copper lead
gold [gould]
    aurarius; aureus; chryseus
    aurum; chrysos

No definition found for uranium
silver [silvər]
    argenteus
    argentum

copper [kɔpər]
    æneus; aheneus; ærarius; chalceus
```

æs

```
lead [led]
   ducere
   molybdus; plumbum
```

Example 8-4 is line oriented. It reads a line of input from the console, sends it to the server, and waits to read a line of output it gets back.

Half-closed sockets

The close() method shuts down both input and output from the socket. On occasion, you may want to shut down only half of the connection, either input or output. The shutdownInput() and shutdownOutput() methods close only half the connection:

```
public void shutdownInput() throws IOException
public void shutdownOutput() throws IOException
```

Neither actually closes the socket. Instead, they adjust the stream connected to the socket so that it thinks it's at the end of the stream. Further reads from the input stream after shutting down input return –1. Further writes to the socket after shutting down output throw an IOException.

Many protocols, such as finger, whois, and HTTP, begin with the client sending a request to the server, then reading the response. It would be possible to shut down the output after the client has sent the request. For example, this code fragment sends a request to an HTTP server and then shuts down the output, because it won't need to write anything else over this socket:

```
try (Socket connection = new Socket("www.oreilly.com", 80)) {
  Writer out = new OutputStreamWriter(
          connection.getOutputStream(), "8859_1");
  out.write("GET / HTTP 1.0\r\n\r\n");
  out.flush();
  connection.shutdownOutput();
  // read the response...
} catch (IOException ex) {
  ex.printStackTrace();
}
```

Notice that even though you shut down half or even both halves of a connection, you still need to close the socket when you're through with it. The shutdown methods simply affect the socket's streams. They don't release the resources associated with the socket, such as the port it occupies.

The isInputShutdown() and isOutputShutdown() methods tell you whether the input and output streams are open or closed, respectively. You can use these (rather than isConnected() and isClosed()) to more specifically ascertain whether you can read from or write to a socket:

```
public boolean isInputShutdown()
public boolean isOutputShutdown()
```

Constructing and Connecting Sockets

The `java.net.Socket` class is Java's fundamental class for performing client-side TCP operations. Other client-oriented classes that make TCP network connections such as URL, URLConnection, Applet, and JEditorPane all ultimately end up invoking the methods of this class. This class itself uses native code to communicate with the local TCP stack of the host operating system.

Basic Constructors

Each `Socket` constructor specifies the host and the port to connect to. Hosts may be specified as an `InetAddress` or a `String`. Remote ports are specified as int values from 1 to 65535:

```
public Socket(String host, int port) throws UnknownHostException, IOException
public Socket(InetAddress host, int port) throws IOException
```

These constructors connect the socket (i.e., before the constructor returns, an active network connection is established to the remote host). If the connection can't be opened for some reason, the constructor throws an IOException or an UnknownHostException. For example:

```
try {
  Socket toOReilly = new Socket("www.oreilly.com", 80);
  // send and receive data...
} catch (UnknownHostException ex) {
  System.err.println(ex);
} catch (IOException ex) {
  System.err.println(ex);
}
```

In this constructor, the host argument is just a hostname expressed as a String. If the domain name server cannot resolve the hostname or is not functioning, the constructor throws an UnknownHostException. If the socket cannot be opened for some other reason, the constructor throws an IOException. There are many reasons a connection attempt might fail: the host you're trying to reach may not accept connections on that port, the hotel WiFi service may be blocking you until you log in to its website and pay $14.95, or routing problems may be preventing your packets from reaching their destination.

Because this constructor doesn't just create a Socket object but also tries to connect the socket to the remote host, you can use the object to determine whether connections to a particular port are allowed, as in Example 8-5.

Example 8-5. Find out which of the first 1024 ports seem to be hosting TCP servers on a specified host

```java
import java.net.*;
import java.io.*;

public class LowPortScanner {

  public static void main(String[] args) {

    String host = args.length > 0 ? args[0] : "localhost";

    for (int i = 1; i < 1024; i++) {
      try {
        Socket s = new Socket(host, i);
        System.out.println("There is a server on port " + i + " of "
         + host);
        s.close();
      } catch (UnknownHostException ex) {
        System.err.println(ex);
        break;
      } catch (IOException ex) {
        // must not be a server on this port
      }
    }
  }
}
```

Here's the output this program produces on my local host (your results will vary, depending on which ports are occupied):

```
$ java LowPortScanner
There is a server on port 21 of localhost
There is a server on port 22 of localhost
There is a server on port 23 of localhost
There is a server on port 25 of localhost
There is a server on port 37 of localhost
There is a server on port 111 of localhost
There is a server on port 139 of localhost
There is a server on port 210 of localhost
There is a server on port 515 of localhost
There is a server on port 873 of localhost
```

If you're curious about what servers are running on these ports, try experimenting with Telnet. On a Unix system, you may be able to find out which services reside on which ports by looking in the file */etc/services*. If LowPortScanner finds any ports that are running servers but are not listed in */etc/services*, then that's interesting.

Although this program looks simple, it's not without its uses. The first step to securing a system is understanding it. This program helps you understand what your system is doing so you can find (and close) possible entrance points for attackers. You may also find rogue servers: for example, `LowPortScanner` might tell you that there's a server on port 800, which, on further investigation, turns out to be an HTTP server somebody is running to serve MP3 files, and which is saturating your T1.

Three constructors create unconnected sockets. These provide more control over exactly how the underlying socket behaves, for instance by choosing a different proxy server or an encryption scheme:

```
public Socket()
public Socket(Proxy proxy)
protected Socket(SocketImpl impl)
```

Picking a Local Interface to Connect From

Two constructors specify both the host and port to connect *to* and the interface and port to connect *from*:

```
public Socket(String host, int port, InetAddress interface, int localPort)
        throws IOException, UnknownHostException
public Socket(InetAddress host, int port, InetAddress interface, int localPort)
        throws IOException
```

This socket connects *to* the host and port specified in the first two arguments. It connects *from* the local network interface and port specified by the last two arguments. The network interface may be either physical (e.g., an Ethernet card) or virtual (a multi-homed host with more than one IP address). If 0 is passed for the `localPort` argument, Java chooses a random available port between 1024 and 65535.

Selecting a particular network interface from which to send data is uncommon, but a need does come up occasionally. One situation where you might want to explicitly choose the local address would be on a router/firewall that uses dual Ethernet ports. Incoming connections would be accepted on one interface, processed, and forwarded to the local network from the other interface. Suppose you were writing a program to periodically dump error logs to a printer or send them over an internal mail server. You'd want to make sure you used the inward-facing network interface instead of the outward-facing network interface. For example:

```
try {
  InetAddress inward = InetAddress.getByName("router");
  Socket socket = new Socket("mail", 25, inward, 0);
  // work with the sockets...
} catch (IOException ex) {
  System.err.println(ex);
}
```

By passing 0 for the local port number, I say that I don't care which port is used but I do want to use the network interface bound to the local hostname *router*.

This constructor can throw an IOException or an UnknownHostException for the same reasons as the previous constructors. In addition, it throws an IOException (probably a BindException, although again that's just a subclass of IOException and not specifically declared in the throws clause of this method) if the socket is unable to bind to the requested local network interface. For instance, a program running on *a.example.com* can't connect from *b.example.org*. You could take deliberate advantage of this to restrict a compiled program to run on only a predetermined host. It would require customizing distributions for each computer and is certainly overkill for cheap products. Furthermore, Java programs are so easy to disassemble, decompile, and reverse engineer that this scheme is far from foolproof. Nonetheless, it might be part of a scheme to enforce a software license.

Constructing Without Connecting

All the constructors we've talked about so far both create the socket object and open a network connection to a remote host. Sometimes you want to split those operations. If you give no arguments to the Socket constructor, it has nowhere to connect to:

```
public Socket()
```

You can connect later by passing a SocketAddress to one of the connect() methods. For example:

```
try {
  Socket socket = new Socket();
  // fill in socket options
  SocketAddress address = new InetSocketAddress("time.nist.gov", 13);
  socket.connect(address);
  // work with the sockets...
} catch (IOException ex) {
  System.err.println(ex);
}
```

You can pass an int as the second argument to specify the number of milliseconds to wait before the connection times out:

```
public void connect(SocketAddress endpoint, int timeout) throws IOException
```

The default, 0, means wait forever.

The raison d'être for this constructor is to enable different kinds of sockets. You also need to use it to set a socket option that can only be changed before the socket connects. I'll discuss this in "Setting Socket Options" on page 263. However, the prime benefit I find is that it enables me to clean up the code in try-catch-finally blocks, especially prior to Java 7. The noargs constructor throws no exceptions so it enables you to avoid the annoying null check when closing a socket in a finally block. With the original constructor, most code looks like this:

```
Socket socket = null;
try {
  socket = new Socket(SERVER, PORT);
  // work with the socket...
} catch (IOException ex) {
  System.err.println(ex);
} finally {
  if (socket != null) {
    try {
      socket.close();
    } catch (IOException ex) {
      // ignore
    }
  }
}
```

With the noargs constructor, it looks like this:

```
Socket socket = new Socket();
SocketAddress address = new InetSocketAddress(SERVER, PORT);
try {
  socket.connect(address);
  // work with the socket...
} catch (IOException ex) {
  System.err.println(ex);
} finally {
  try {
    socket.close();
  } catch (IOException ex) {
    // ignore
  }
}
```

That's not quite as nice as the autoclosing version in Java 7, but it is an improvement.

Socket Addresses

The SocketAddress class represents a connection endpoint. It is an empty abstract class with no methods aside from a default constructor. At least theoretically, the SocketAddress class can be used for both TCP and non-TCP sockets. In practice, only TCP/IP sockets are currently supported and the socket addresses you actually use are all instances of InetSocketAddress.

The primary purpose of the SocketAddress class is to provide a convenient store for transient socket connection information such as the IP address and port that can be reused to create new sockets, even after the original socket is disconnected and garbage collected. To this end, the Socket class offers two methods that return SocketAddress objects (getRemoteSocketAddress() returns the address of the system being connected to and getLocalSocketAddress() returns the address from which the connection is made):

```
public SocketAddress getRemoteSocketAddress()
public SocketAddress getLocalSocketAddress()
```

Both of these methods return null if the socket is not yet connected. For example, first you might connect to Yahoo! then store its address:

```
Socket socket = new Socket("www.yahoo.com", 80);
SocketAddress yahoo = socket.getRemoteSocketAddress();
socket.close();
```

Later, you could reconnect to Yahoo! using this address:

```
Socket socket2 = new Socket();
socket2.connect(yahoo);
```

The InetSocketAddress class (which is the only subclass of SocketAddress in the JDK, and the only subclass I've ever encountered) is usually created with a host and a port (for clients) or just a port (for servers):

```
public InetSocketAddress(InetAddress address, int port)
public InetSocketAddress(String host, int port)
public InetSocketAddress(int port)
```

You can also use the static factory method InetSocketAddress.createUnresolved() to skip looking up the host in DNS:

```
public static InetSocketAddress createUnresolved(String host, int port)
```

InetSocketAddress has a few getter methods you can use to inspect the object:

```
public final InetAddress getAddress()
public final int         getPort()
public final String      getHostName()
```

Proxy Servers

The last constructor creates an unconnected socket that connects through a specified proxy server:

```
public Socket(Proxy proxy)
```

Normally, the proxy server a socket uses is controlled by the socksProxyHost and socksProxyPort system properties, and these properties apply to all sockets in the system. However, a socket created by this constructor will use the specified proxy server instead. Most notably, you can pass Proxy.NO_PROXY for the argument to bypass all proxy servers completely and connect directly to the remote host. Of course, if a firewall prevents direct connections, there's nothing Java can do about it; and the connection will fail.

To use a particular proxy server, specify it by address. For example, this code fragment uses the SOCKS proxy server at *myproxy.example.com* to connect to the host *login.ibi-blio.org*:

```
SocketAddress proxyAddress = new InetSocketAddress("myproxy.example.com", 1080);
Proxy proxy = new Proxy(Proxy.Type.SOCKS, proxyAddress);
Socket s = new Socket(proxy);
SocketAddress remote = new InetSocketAddress("login.ibiblio.org", 25);
s.connect(remote);
```

SOCKS is the only low-level proxy type Java understands. There's also a high-level `Proxy.Type.HTTP` that works in the application layer rather than the transport layer and a `Proxy.Type.DIRECT` that represents proxyless connections.

Getting Information About a Socket

Socket objects have several properties that are accessible through getter methods:

- Remote address
- Remote port
- Local address
- Local port

Here are the getter methods for accessing these properties:

```
public InetAddress getInetAddress()
public int getPort()
public InetAddress getLocalAddress()
public int getLocalPort()
```

There are no setter methods. These properties are set as soon as the socket connects, and are fixed from there on.

The `getInetAddress()` and `getPort()` methods tell you the remote host and port the `Socket` is connected to; or, if the connection is now closed, which host and port the `Socket` was connected to when it was connected. The `getLocalAddress()` and `getLocalPort()` methods tell you the network interface and port the `Socket` is connected from.

Unlike the remote port, which (for a client socket) is usually a "well-known port" that has been preassigned by a standards committee, the local port is usually chosen by the system at runtime from the available unused ports. This way, many different clients on a system can access the same service at the same time. The local port is embedded in outbound IP packets along with the local host's IP address, so the server can send data back to the right port on the client.

Example 8-6 reads a list of hostnames from the command line, attempts to open a socket to each one, and then uses these four methods to print the remote host, the remote port, the local address, and the local port.

Example 8-6. Get a socket's information

```
import java.net.*;
import java.io.*;

public class SocketInfo {

  public static void main(String[] args) {

    for (String host : args) {
      try {
        Socket theSocket = new Socket(host, 80);
        System.out.println("Connected to " + theSocket.getInetAddress()
            + " on port "  + theSocket.getPort() + " from port "
            + theSocket.getLocalPort() + " of "
            + theSocket.getLocalAddress());
      } catch (UnknownHostException ex) {
        System.err.println("I can't find " + host);
      } catch (SocketException ex) {
        System.err.println("Could not connect to " + host);
      } catch (IOException ex) {
        System.err.println(ex);
      }
    }
  }
}
```

Here's the result of a sample run. I included *www.oreilly.com* on the command line twice in order to demonstrate that each connection was assigned a different local port, regardless of the remote host; the local port assigned to any connection is unpredictable and depends mostly on what other ports are in use. The connection to *login.ibiblio.org* failed because that machine does not run any servers on port 80:

```
$ java SocketInfo www.oreilly.com www.oreilly.com www.elharo.com
  login.ibiblio.org
Connected to www.oreilly.com/208.201.239.37 on port 80 from port 49156 of
/192.168.254.25
Connected to www.oreilly.com/208.201.239.37 on port 80 from port 49157 of
/192.168.254.25
Connected to www.elharo.com/216.254.106.198 on port 80 from port 49158 of
/192.168.254.25
Could not connect to login.ibiblio.org
```

Closed or Connected?

The isClosed() method returns true if the socket is closed, false if it isn't. If you're uncertain about a socket's state, you can check it with this method rather than risking an IOException. For example:

```
if (socket.isClosed()) {
    // do something...
```

```
} else {
  // do something else...
}
```

However, this is not a perfect test. If the socket has never been connected in the first place, isClosed() returns false, even though the socket isn't exactly open.

The Socket class also has an isConnected() method. The name is a little misleading. It does not tell you if the socket is currently connected to a remote host (like if it is unclosed). Instead, it tells you whether the socket has ever been connected to a remote host. If the socket was able to connect to the remote host at all, this method returns true, even after that socket has been closed. To tell if a socket is currently open, you need to check that isConnected() returns true and isClosed() returns false. For example:

```
boolean connected = socket.isConnected() && ! socket.isClosed();
```

Finally, the isBound() method tells you whether the socket successfully bound to the outgoing port on the local system. Whereas isConnected() refers to the remote end of the socket, isBound() refers to the local end. This isn't very important yet. Binding will become more important when we discuss server sockets in Chapter 9.

toString()

The Socket class overrides only one of the standard methods from java.lang.Object: toString(). The toString() method produces a string that looks like this:

```
Socket[addr=www.oreilly.com/198.112.208.11,port=80,localport=50055]
```

This is useful primarily for debugging. Don't rely on this format; it may change in the future. All parts of this string are accessible directly through other methods (specifically getInetAddress(), getPort(), and getLocalPort()).

 Because sockets are transitory objects that typically last only as long as the connection they represent, there's not much reason to store them in hash tables or compare them to each other. Therefore, Socket does not override equals() or hashCode(), and the semantics for these methods are those of the Object class. Two Socket objects are equal to each other if and only if they are the same object.

Setting Socket Options

Socket options specify how the native sockets on which the Java Socket class relies send and receive data. Java supports nine options for client-side sockets:

- TCP_NODELAY
- SO_BINDADDR

- SO_TIMEOUT
- SO_LINGER
- SO_SNDBUF
- SO_RCVBUF
- SO_KEEPALIVE
- OOBINLINE
- IP_TOS

The funny-looking names for these options are taken from the named constants in the C header files used in Berkeley Unix where sockets were invented. Thus, they follow classic Unix C naming conventions rather than the more legible Java naming conventions. For instance, SO_SNDBUF really means "Socket Option Send Buffer Size."

TCP_NODELAY

```
public void setTcpNoDelay(boolean on) throws SocketException
public boolean getTcpNoDelay() throws SocketException
```

Setting TCP_NODELAY to true ensures that packets are sent as quickly as possible regardless of their size. Normally, small (one-byte) packets are combined into larger packets before being sent. Before sending another packet, the local host waits to receive acknowledgment of the previous packet from the remote system. This is known as *Nagle's algorithm*. The problem with Nagle's algorithm is that if the remote system doesn't send acknowledgments back to the local system fast enough, applications that depend on the steady transfer of small parcels of information may slow down. This issue is especially problematic for GUI programs such as games or network computer applications where the server needs to track client-side mouse movement in real time. On a really slow network, even simple typing can be too slow because of the constant buffering. Setting TCP_NODELAY to true defeats this buffering scheme, so that all packets are sent as soon as they're ready.

setTcpNoDelay(true) turns off buffering for the socket. setTcpNoDelay(false) turns it back on. getTcpNoDelay() returns true if buffering is off and false if buffering is on. For example, the following fragment turns off buffering (that is, it turns on TCP_NODELAY) for the socket s if it isn't already off:

```
if (!s.getTcpNoDelay()) s.setTcpNoDelay(true);
```

These two methods are each declared to throw a SocketException, which will happen if the underlying socket implementation doesn't support the TCP_ NODELAY option.

SO_LINGER

```
public void setSoLinger(boolean on, int seconds) throws SocketException
public int getSoLinger() throws SocketException
```

The SO_LINGER option specifies what to do with datagrams that have not yet been sent when a socket is closed. By default, the `close()` method returns immediately; but the system still tries to send any remaining data. If the linger time is set to zero, any unsent packets are thrown away when the socket is closed. If SO_LINGER is turned on and the linger time is any positive value, the `close()` method blocks while waiting the specified number of seconds for the data to be sent and the acknowledgments to be received. When that number of seconds has passed, the socket is closed and any remaining data is not sent, acknowledgment or no.

These two methods each throw a `SocketException` if the underlying socket implementation does not support the SO_LINGER option. The `setSoLinger()` method can also throw an `IllegalArgumentException` if you try to set the linger time to a negative value. However, the `getSoLinger()` method may return –1 to indicate that this option is disabled, and as much time as is needed is taken to deliver the remaining data; for example, to set the linger timeout for the `Socket s` to four minutes, if it's not already set to some other value:

```
if (s.getTcpSoLinger() == -1) s.setSoLinger(true, 240);
```

The maximum linger time is 65,535 seconds, and may be smaller on some platforms. Times larger than that will be reduced to the maximum linger time. Frankly, 65,535 seconds (more than 18 hours) is much longer than you actually want to wait. Generally, the platform default value is more appropriate.

SO_TIMEOUT

```
public void setSoTimeout(int milliseconds) throws SocketException
public int getSoTimeout() throws SocketException
```

Normally when you try to read data from a socket, the `read()` call blocks as long as necessary to get enough bytes. By setting SO_TIMEOUT, you ensure that the call will not block for more than a fixed number of milliseconds. When the timeout expires, an `InterruptedIOException` is thrown, and you should be prepared to catch it. However, the socket is still connected. Although this `read()` call failed, you can try to read from the socket again. The next call may succeed.

Timeouts are given in milliseconds. Zero is interpreted as an infinite timeout; it is the default value. For example, to set the timeout value of the `Socket` object `s` to 3 minutes if it isn't already set, specify 180,000 milliseconds:

```
if (s.getSoTimeout() == 0) s.setSoTimeout(180000);
```

These two methods each throw a `SocketException` if the underlying socket implementation does not support the SO_TIMEOUT option. The `setSoTimeout()` method also throws an `IllegalArgumentException` if the specified timeout value is negative.

SO_RCVBUF and SO_SNDBUF

TCP uses buffers to improve network performance. Larger buffers tend to improve performance for reasonably fast (say, 10Mbps and up) connections whereas slower, dial-up connections do better with smaller buffers. Generally, transfers of large, continuous blocks of data, which are common in file transfer protocols such as FTP and HTTP, benefit from large buffers, whereas the smaller transfers of interactive sessions, such as Telnet and many games, do not. Relatively old operating systems designed in the age of small files and slow networks, such as BSD 4.2, use two-kilobyte buffers. Windows XP used 17,520 byte buffers. These days, 128 kilobytes is a common default.

Maximum achievable bandwidth equals buffer size divided by latency. For example, on Windows XP suppose the latency between two hosts is half a second (500 ms). Then the bandwidth is 17520 bytes / 0.5 seconds = 35040 bytes / second = 273.75 kilobits / second. That's the *maximum* speed of any socket, regardless of how fast the network is. That's plenty fast for a dial-up connection, and not bad for ISDN, but not really adequate for a DSL line or FIOS.

You can increase speed by decreasing latency. However, latency is a function of the network hardware and other factors outside the control of your application. On the other hand, you do control the buffer size. For example, if you increase the buffer size from 17,520 bytes to 128 kilobytes, the maximum bandwidth increases to 2 megabits per second. Double the buffer size again to 256 kilobytes, and the maximum bandwidth doubles to 4 megabits per second. Of course, the network itself has limits on maximum bandwidth. Set the buffer too high and your program will try to send and receive data faster than the network can handle, leading to congestion, dropped packets, and slower performance. Thus, when you want maximum bandwidth, you need to match the buffer size to the latency of the connection so it's a little less than the bandwidth of the network.

You can use ping to check the latency to a particular host manually, or you can time a call to `InetAddress.isReachable()` from inside your program.

The SO_RCVBUF option controls the suggested send buffer size used for network input. The SO_SNDBUF option controls the suggested send buffer size used for network output:

```
public void setReceiveBufferSize(int size)
    throws SocketException, IllegalArgumentException
```

```
public int getReceiveBufferSize() throws SocketException
public void setSendBufferSize(int size)
    throws SocketException, IllegalArgumentException
public int getSendBufferSize() throws SocketException
```

Although it looks like you should be able to set the send and receive buffers independently, the buffer is usually set to the smaller of these two. For instance, if you set the send buffer to 64K and the receive buffer to 128K, you'll have 64K as both the send and receive buffer size. Java will report that the receive buffer is 128K, but the underlying TCP stack will really be using 64K.

The setReceiveBufferSize()/setSendBufferSize methods suggest a number of bytes to use for buffering output on this socket. However, the underlying implementation is free to ignore or adjust this suggestion. In particular, Unix and Linux systems often specify a maximum buffer size, typically 64K or 256K, and do not allow any socket to have a larger one. If you attempt to set a larger value, Java will just pin it to the maximum possible buffer size. On Linux, it's not unheard of for the underlying implementation to double the requested size. For example, if you ask for a 64K buffer, you may get a 128K buffer instead.

These methods throw an IllegalArgumentException if the argument is less than or equal to zero. Although they're also declared to throw SocketException, they probably won't in practice, because a SocketException is thrown for the same reason as IllegalArgumentException and the check for the IllegalArgumentException is made first.

In general, if you find your application is not able to fully utilize the available bandwidth (e.g., you have a 25 Mbps Internet connection, but your data is transferring at a piddling 1.5 Mbps) try increasing the buffer sizes. By contrast, if you're dropping packets and experiencing congestion, try decreasing the buffer size. However, most of the time, unless you're really taxing the network in one direction or the other, the defaults are fine. In particular, modern operating systems use TCP window scaling (not controllable from Java) to dynamically adjust buffer sizes to fit the network. As with almost any performance tuning advice, the rule of thumb is not to do it until you've measured a problem. And even then you may well get more speed by increasing the maximum allowed buffer size at the operating system level than by adjusting the buffer sizes of individual sockets.

SO_KEEPALIVE

If SO_KEEPALIVE is turned on, the client occasionally sends a data packet over an idle connection (most commonly once every two hours), just to make sure the server hasn't crashed. If the server fails to respond to this packet, the client keeps trying for a little more than 11 minutes until it receives a response. If it doesn't receive a response within 12 minutes, the client closes the socket. Without SO_KEEPALIVE, an inactive client could live more or less forever without noticing that the server had crashed. These methods turn SO_KEEPALIVE on and off and determine its current state:

```
public void setKeepAlive(boolean on) throws SocketException
public boolean getKeepAlive() throws SocketException
```

The default for SO_KEEPALIVE is false. This code fragment turns SO_KEEPALIVE off, if it's turned on:

```
if (s.getKeepAlive()) s.setKeepAlive(false);
```

OOBINLINE

TCP includes a feature that sends a single byte of "urgent" data out of band. This data is sent immediately. Furthermore, the receiver is notified when the urgent data is received and may elect to process the urgent data before it processes any other data that has already been received. Java supports both sending and receiving such urgent data. The sending method is named, obviously enough, sendUrgentData():

```
public void sendUrgentData(int data) throws IOException
```

This method sends the lowest-order byte of its argument almost immediately. If necessary, any currently cached data is flushed first.

How the receiving end responds to urgent data is a little confused, and varies from one platform and API to the next. Some systems receive the urgent data separately from the regular data. However, the more common, more modern approach is to place the urgent data in the regular received data queue in its proper order, tell the application that urgent data is available, and let it hunt through the queue to find it.

By default, Java ignores urgent data received from a socket. However, if you want to receive urgent data inline with regular data, you need to set the OOBINLINE option to true using these methods:

```
public void setOOBInline(boolean on) throws SocketException
public boolean getOOBInline() throws SocketException
```

The default for OOBINLINE is false. This code fragment turns OOBINLINE on, if it's turned off:

```
if (!s.getOOBInline()) s.setOOBInline(true);
```

Once OOBINLINE is turned on, any urgent data that arrives will be placed on the socket's input stream to be read in the usual way. Java does not distinguish it from nonurgent data. That makes it less than ideally useful, but if you have a particular byte (e.g., a Ctrl-C) that has special meaning to your program and never shows up in the regular data stream, then this would enable you to send it more quickly.

SO_REUSEADDR

When a socket is closed, it may not immediately release the local port, especially if a connection was open when the socket was closed. It can sometimes wait for a small amount of time to make sure it receives any lingering packets that were addressed to the port that were still crossing the network when the socket was closed. The system won't do anything with any of the late packets it receives. It just wants to make sure they don't accidentally get fed into a new process that has bound to the same port.

This isn't a big problem on a random port, but it can be an issue if the socket has bound to a well-known port because it prevents any other socket from using that port in the meantime. If the SO_REUSEADDR is turned on (it's turned off by default), another socket is allowed to bind to the port even while data may be outstanding for the previous socket.

In Java this option is controlled by these two methods:

```
public void setReuseAddress(boolean on) throws SocketException
public boolean getReuseAddress() throws SocketException
```

For this to work, `setReuseAddress()` must be called *before* the new socket binds to the port. This means the socket must be created in an unconnected state using the noargs constructor; then `setReuseAddress(true)` is called, and the socket is connected using the `connect()` method. Both the socket that was previously connected and the new socket reusing the old address must set SO_REUSEADDR to true for it to take effect.

IP_TOS Class of Service

Different types of Internet service have different performance needs. For instance, video chat needs relatively high bandwidth and low latency for good performance, whereas email can be passed over low-bandwidth connections and even held up for several hours without major harm. VOIP needs less bandwidth than video but minimum jitter. It might be wise to price the different classes of service differentially so that people won't ask for the highest class of service automatically. After all, if sending an overnight letter cost the same as sending a package via media mail, we'd all just use FedEx overnight, which would quickly become congested and overwhelmed. The Internet is no different.

The class of service is stored in an eight-bit field called IP_TOS in the IP header. Java lets you inspect and set the value a socket places in this field using these two methods:

```
public int getTrafficClass() throws SocketException
public void setTrafficClass(int trafficClass) throws SocketException
```

The traffic class is given as an `int` between 0 and 255. Because this value is copied to an eight-bit field in the TCP header, only the low order byte of this `int` is used; and values outside this range cause `IllegalArgumentExceptions`.

In 21st-century TCP stacks, the high-order six bits of this byte contain a Differentiated Services Code Point (DSCP) value and the low-order two bits contain an Explicit Congestion Notification (ECN) value. The DSCP thus has room for up to 2^6 different traffic classes. However, it's up to individual networks and routers to specify exactly what the 64 different possible DSCP values mean. The four values shown in Table 8-1 are fairly common.

Table 8-1. Common DSCP values and interpretations

PHB (Per Hop Behavior)	Binary value	Purpose
Default	00000	Best-effort traffic.
Expedited Forwarding (EF)	101110	Low-loss, low-delay, low-jitter traffic. Often limited to 30% or less of network capacity.
Assured Forwarding (AF)	*multiple*	Assured delivery up to a specified rate.
Class Selector	xxx000	Backward compatibility with the IPv4 TOS header, as stored in the first three bits.

For example, the Expedited Forwarding PHB is a good choice for for VOIP. EF traffic is often given strict priority queuing above all other traffic classes. This code fragment sets a socket to use Expedited Forwarding by setting the traffic class to 10111000:

```
Socket s = new Socket("www.yahoo.com", 80);
s.setTrafficClass(0xB8); // 10111000 in binary
```

Remember the low-order two bits of this number are Explicit Congestion Notification, and should be set to zero.

Assured Forwarding is actually 12 different DSCP values divided into four classes as shown in Table 8-2. The purpose here is to allow a sender to express relative preferences for which packets to drop when the network is congested. Within a class, packets with lower priority are dropped before packets with a higher priority. Between classes, packest from a higher-priority class are given preference, though lower-priority classes are not starved completely.

Table 8-2. Assured forwarding priority classes

	Class 1 (lowest priority)	Class 2	Class 3	Class 4 (highest priority)
Low Drop Rate	AF11 (001010)	AF21 (010010)	AF31 (011010)	AF41 (100010)
Medium Drop Rate	AF12 (001100)	AF22 (010100)	AF32 (011100)	AF42 (100100)
High Drop Rate	AF13 (001110)	AF23 (010110)	AF33 (011110)	AF43 (100110)

For example, the following code fragment sets up three sockets with different forwarding characteristics. If the network gets congested enough, socket 3, in class 4 with a high drop rate, will send most of its data. Socket 1, in class 1 with a low drop rate, will also get to send data, though not as quickly as socket 1; and socket 3, with a high drop rate also in class 1 will be blocked completely until the congestion eases up enough that socket 2 is no longer dropping packets:

```
Socket s1 = new Socket("www.example.com", 80);
s1.setTrafficClass(0x26); // 00100110 in binary
Socket s2 = new Socket("www.example.com", 80);
s2.setTrafficClass(0x0A); // 00001010 in binary
Socket s3 = new Socket("www.example.com", 80);
s3.setTrafficClass(0x0E); // 00001110 in binary
```

DSCP values are not hard and fast guarantees of service. In practice, although DSCP values are respected on some networks internally, any time a packet crosses ISPs, this information is almost always ignored.

 The JavaDoc for these options is severely out of date, and describes a quality of service scheme based on bit fields for four traffic classes: low cost, high reliability, maximum throughput, and minimum delay. This scheme was never widely implemented and probably hasn't been used in this century. The specific TCP header where these values were stored has been repurposed for the DSCP and EN values described here. However, in the unlikely event you need it, you can put these values in the high-order three bits of a class selector PHB, followed by zero bits.

The underlying socket implementation is not required to respect any of these requests. They only provide a hint to the TCP stack about the desired policy. Many implementations ignore these values completely. Android in particular treats the setTraffic Class() method as a no-op. If the TCP stack is unable to provide the requested class of service, it may, but is not required to, throw a SocketException.

As an alternative way to express preferences, the setPerformancePreferences() method assigns relative preferences to connection time, latency, and bandwidth:

```
public void setPerformancePreferences(int connectionTime,
    int latency, int bandwidth)
```

For instance, if connectionTime is 2, latency is 1, and bandwidth is 3, then maximum bandwidth is the most important characteristic, minimum latency is the least important, and connection time is in the middle. If connectionTime is 2, latency is 2, and band width is 3, then maximum bandwidth is the most important characteristic, while minimum latency and connection time are equally important. Exactly how any given VM implements this is implementation dependent. Indeed, it may be a no-op in some implementations.

Socket Exceptions

Most methods of the Socket class are declared to throw IOException or its subclass, java.net.SocketException:

```
public class SocketException extends IOException
```

However, knowing that a problem occurred is often not sufficient to deal with the problem. Did the remote host refuse the connection because it was busy? Did the remote host refuse the connection because no service was listening on the port? Did the connection attempt timeout because of network congestion or because the host was down? There are several subclasses of SocketException that provide more information about what went wrong and why:

```
public class BindException extends SocketException
public class ConnectException extends SocketException
public class NoRouteToHostException extends SocketException
```

A BindException is thrown if you try to construct a Socket or ServerSocket object on a local port that is in use or that you do not have sufficient privileges to use. A Connec tException is thrown when a connection is refused at the remote host, which usually happens because the host is busy or no process is listening on that port. Finally, a NoRouteToHostException indicates that the connection has timed out.

The java.net package also includes ProtocolException, which is a direct subclass of IOException:

```
public class ProtocolException extends IOException
```

This is thrown when data is received from the network that somehow violates the TCP/IP specification.

None of these exception classes have any special methods you wouldn't find in any other exception class, but you can take advantage of these subclasses to provide more informative error messages or to decide whether retrying the offending operation is likely to be successful.

Sockets in GUI Applications

The HotJava web browser was the first large-scale Java GUI network client. HotJava has been discontinued, but there are still numerous network-aware client applications written in Java, including the Eclipse IDE and the Frostwire BitTorrent client. It is completely possible to write commercial-quality client applications in Java; and it is especially possible to write network-aware applications, both clients and servers. This section demonstrates a network client, whois, to illustrate this point; and to discuss the special considerations that arise when integrating networking code with Swing applications. The example stops short of what could be done, but only in the user interface. All the necessary networking code is present. Indeed, once again you find out that network code is easy; it's user interfaces that are hard.

Whois

Whois is a simple directory service protocol defined in RFC 954; it was originally designed to keep track of administrators responsible for Internet hosts and domains. A whois client connects to one of several central servers and requests directory information for a person or persons; it can usually give you a phone number, an email address, and a snail mail address (not necessarily current ones, though). With the explosive growth of the Internet, flaws have become apparent in the whois protocol, most notably its centralized nature. A more complex replacement called whois++ is documented in RFCs 1913 and 1914 but has not been widely implemented.whois directory service protocol)

Let's begin with a simple client to connect to a whois server. The basic structure of the whois protocol is:

1. The client opens a TCP socket to port 43 on the server.
2. The client sends a search string terminated by a carriage return/linefeed pair (\r\n). The search string can be a name, a list of names, or a special command, as discussed shortly. You can also search for domain names, like *www.oreilly.com* or *netscape.com*, which give you information about a network.
3. The server sends an unspecified amount of human-readable information in response to the command and closes the connection.
4. The client displays this information to the user.

The search string the client sends has a fairly simple format. At its most basic, it's just the name of the person you're searching for. Here's a simple whois search for "Harold":

```
$ telnet whois.internic.net 43
Trying 199.7.50.74...
Connected to whois.internic.net.
Escape character is '^]'.
Harold

Whois Server Version 2.0

Domain names in the .com and .net domains can now be registered
with many different competing registrars. Go to http://www.internic.net
for detailed information.

HAROLD.LUCKYLAND.ORG
HAROLD.FRUGAL.COM
HAROLD.NET
HAROLD.COM

To single out one record, look it up with "xxx", where xxx is one of the
of the records displayed above. If the records are the same, look them up
with "=xxx" to receive a full display for each record.
```

```
>>> Last update of whois database: Sat, 30 Mar 2013 15:15:05 UTC <<<
...
Connection closed by foreign host.
```

Although the previous input has a pretty clear format, that format is regrettably non-standard. Different whois servers can and do send decidedly different output. For example, here are the first couple of results from the same search at the main French whois server, *whois.nic.fr*:

```
% telnet whois.nic.fr 43
telnet whois.nic.fr 43
Trying 192.134.4.18...
Connected to winter.nic.fr.
Escape character is '^]'.
Harold

Tous droits reserves par copyright.
Voir http://www.nic.fr/outils/dbcopyright.html
Rights restricted by copyright.
See http://www.nic.fr/outils/dbcopyright.html

person:     Harold Potier
address:    ARESTE
address:    154 Avenue Du Brezet
address:    63000 Clermont-Ferrand
address:    France
phone:      +33 4 73 42 67 67
fax-no:     +33 4 73 42 67 67
nic-hdl:    HP4305-FRNIC
mnt-by:     OLEANE-NOC
changed:    hostmaster@oleane.net 20000510
changed:    migration-dbm@nic.fr 20001015
source:     FRNIC

person:     Harold Israel
address:    LE PARADIS LATIN
address:    28 rue du Cardinal Lemoine
address:    Paris, France 75005 FR
phone:      +33 1 43252828
fax-no:     +33 1 43296363
e-mail:     info@cie.fr
nic-hdl:    HI68-FRNIC
notify:     info@cie.fr
changed:    registrar@ns.il 19991011
changed:    migration-dbm@nic.fr 20001015
source:     FRNIC
```

Here each complete record is returned rather than just a list of sites. Other whois servers may use still other formats. This protocol is not at all designed for machine processing. You pretty much have to write new code to handle the output of each different whois server. However, regardless of the output format, each response likely contains a *han-*

dle, which in the Internic output is a domain name, and in the nic.fr output is in the nic-hdl field. Handles are guaranteed to be unique, and are used to get more specific information about a person or a network. If you search for a handle, you will get at most one match. If your search only has one match, either because you're lucky or you're searching for a handle, the server returns a more detailed record. Here's a search for *oreilly.com*. Because there is only one *oreilly.com* in the database, the server returns all the information it has on this domain:

```
% telnet whois.internic.net 43
Trying 198.41.0.6...
Connected to whois.internic.net.
Escape character is '^]'.
oreilly.com

Whois Server Version 1.3

Domain names in the .com and .net domains can now be registered
with many different competing registrars. Go to http://www.internic.net
for detailed information.

    Domain Name: OREILLY.COM
    Registrar: BULKREGISTER, LLC.
    Whois Server: whois.bulkregister.com
    Referral URL: http://www.bulkregister.com
    Name Server: NS1.SONIC.NET
    Name Server: NS.OREILLY.COM
    Status: ACTIVE
    Updated Date: 17-oct-2002
    Creation Date: 27-may-1997
    Expiration Date: 26-may-2004


>>> Last update of whois database: Tue, 16 Dec 2003 18:36:16 EST <<<
...
Connection closed by foreign host.
```

The whois protocol supports several flags you can use to restrict or expand your search. For example, if you know you want to search for a person named "Elliott" but you aren't sure whether he spells his name "Elliot," "Elliott," or perhaps even something as unlikely as "Elliotte," you would type:

```
% whois Person Partial Elliot
```

This tells the whois server that you want only matches for people (not domains, gateways, groups, or the like) whose names begin with the letters "Elliot." Unfortunately, you need to do a separate search if you want to find someone who spells his name "Eliot." The rules for modifying a search are summarized in Table 8-3. Each prefix should be placed before the search string on the command line.

Table 8-3. Whois prefixes

Prefix	Meaning
Domain	Find only domain records.
Gateway	Find only gateway records.
Group	Find only group records.
Host	Find only host records.
Network	Find only network records.
Organization	Find only organization records.
Person	Find only person records.
ASN	Find only autonomous system number records.
Handle or !	Search only for matching handles.
Mailbox or @	Search only for matching email addresses.
Name or :	Search only for matching names.
Expand or *	Search only for group records and show all individuals in that group.
Full or =	Show complete record for each match.
Partial or suffix	Match records that start with the given string.
Summary or $	Show just the summary, even if there's only one match.
SUBdisplay or %	Show the users of the specified host, the hosts on the specified network, etc.

These keywords are all useful, but they're way too much trouble to remember. In fact, most people don't even know that they exist. They just type "whois Harold" at the command line and sort through the mess that comes back. A good whois client doesn't rely on users remembering arcane keywords; rather, it shows them the options. Supplying this requires a graphical user interface for end users and a better API for client programmers.

A Network Client Library

It's best to think of network protocols like whois in terms of the bits and bytes that move across the network, whether as packets, datagrams, or streams. No network protocol neatly fits into a GUI (with the arguable exception of the Remote Framebuffer Protocol used by VNC and X11). It's usually best to encapsulate the network code into a separate library that the GUI code can invoke as needed.

Example 8-7 is a reusable Whois class. Two fields define the state of each Whois object: host, an InetAddress object, and port, an int. Together, these define the server that this particular Whois object connects to. Five constructors set these fields from various combinations of arguments. Furthermore, the host can be changed using the se tHost() method.

The main functionality of the class is in one method, lookUpNames(). The lookUp Names() method returns a String containing the whois response to a given query. The arguments specify the string to search for, what kind of record to search for, which database to search in, and whether an exact match is required. I could have used strings or int constants to specify the kind of record to search for and the database to search in, but because there are only a small number of valid values, lookUpNames() defines enums with a fixed number of members instead. This solution provides much stricter compile-time type-checking and guarantees the Whois class won't have to handle an unexpected value.

Example 8-7. The Whois class

```
import java.net.*;
import java.io.*;

public class Whois {

  public final static int DEFAULT_PORT = 43;
  public final static String DEFAULT_HOST = "whois.internic.net";

  private int port = DEFAULT_PORT;
  private InetAddress host;

  public Whois(InetAddress host, int port) {
    this.host = host;
    this.port = port;
  }

  public Whois(InetAddress host) {
    this(host, DEFAULT_PORT);
  }

  public Whois(String hostname, int port)
   throws UnknownHostException {
    this(InetAddress.getByName(hostname), port);
  }

  public Whois(String hostname) throws UnknownHostException {
    this(InetAddress.getByName(hostname), DEFAULT_PORT);
  }

  public Whois() throws UnknownHostException {
    this(DEFAULT_HOST, DEFAULT_PORT);
  }

  // Items to search for
  public enum SearchFor {
    ANY("Any"), NETWORK("Network"), PERSON("Person"), HOST("Host"),
    DOMAIN("Domain"), ORGANIZATION("Organization"), GROUP("Group"),
    GATEWAY("Gateway"), ASN("ASN");
```

```java
    private String label;

    private SearchFor(String label) {
      this.label = label;
    }
  }

  // Categories to search in
  public enum SearchIn {
    ALL(""), NAME("Name"), MAILBOX("Mailbox"), HANDLE("!");

    private String label;

    private SearchIn(String label) {
      this.label = label;
    }
  }

  public String lookUpNames(String target, SearchFor category,
      SearchIn group, boolean exactMatch) throws IOException {

    String suffix = "";
    if (!exactMatch) suffix = ".";

    String prefix = category.label + " " + group.label;
    String query = prefix + target + suffix;

    Socket socket = new Socket();
    try {
      SocketAddress address = new InetSocketAddress(host, port);
      socket.connect(address);
      Writer out
          = new OutputStreamWriter(socket.getOutputStream(), "ASCII");
      BufferedReader in = new BufferedReader(new
          InputStreamReader(socket.getInputStream(), "ASCII"));
      out.write(query + "\r\n");
      out.flush();

      StringBuilder response = new StringBuilder();
      String theLine = null;
      while ((theLine = in.readLine()) != null) {
        response.append(theLine);
        response.append("\r\n");
      }
      return response.toString();
    } finally {
      socket.close();
    }
  }

  public InetAddress getHost() {
```

```
      return this.host;
  }

  public void setHost(String host)
      throws UnknownHostException {
    this.host = InetAddress.getByName(host);
  }
}
```

Figure 8-1 shows one possible interface for a graphical whois client that depends on Example 8-7 for the actual network connections. This interface has a text field to enter the name to be searched for and a checkbox to determine whether the match should be exact or partial. A group of radio buttons lets users specify which group of records they want to search. Another group of radio buttons chooses the fields that should be searched. By default, this client searches all fields of all records for an exact match.

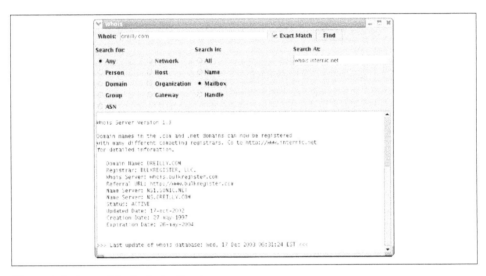

Figure 8-1. A graphical whois client

When a user enters a string in the Whois: search box and presses Enter or clicks the Find button, the program makes a connection to the whois server and retrieves records that match that string. These are placed in the text area in the bottom of the window. Initially, the server is set to *whois.internic.net*, but the user is free to change this setting. Example 8-8 is the program that produces this interface.

Example 8-8. A graphical Whois client interface

```
import java.awt.*;
import java.awt.event.*;
import java.net.*;
import javax.swing.*;
```

```java
public class WhoisGUI extends JFrame {

  private JTextField searchString = new JTextField(30);
  private JTextArea names = new JTextArea(15, 80);
  private JButton findButton = new JButton("Find");;
  private ButtonGroup searchIn = new ButtonGroup();
  private ButtonGroup searchFor = new ButtonGroup();
  private JCheckBox exactMatch = new JCheckBox("Exact Match", true);
  private JTextField chosenServer = new JTextField();
  private Whois server;

  public WhoisGUI(Whois whois) {
    super("Whois");
    this.server = whois;
    Container pane = this.getContentPane();

    Font f = new Font("Monospaced", Font.PLAIN, 12);
    names.setFont(f);
    names.setEditable(false);

    JPanel centerPanel = new JPanel();
    centerPanel.setLayout(new GridLayout(1, 1, 10, 10));
    JScrollPane jsp = new JScrollPane(names);
    centerPanel.add(jsp);
    pane.add("Center", centerPanel);

    // You don't want the buttons in the south and north
    // to fill the entire sections so add Panels there
    // and use FlowLayouts in the Panel
    JPanel northPanel = new JPanel();
    JPanel northPanelTop = new JPanel();
    northPanelTop.setLayout(new FlowLayout(FlowLayout.LEFT));
    northPanelTop.add(new JLabel("Whois: "));
    northPanelTop.add("North", searchString);
    northPanelTop.add(exactMatch);
    northPanelTop.add(findButton);
    northPanel.setLayout(new BorderLayout(2,1));
    northPanel.add("North", northPanelTop);
    JPanel northPanelBottom = new JPanel();
    northPanelBottom.setLayout(new GridLayout(1,3,5,5));
    northPanelBottom.add(initRecordType());
    northPanelBottom.add(initSearchFields());
    northPanelBottom.add(initServerChoice());
    northPanel.add("Center", northPanelBottom);

    pane.add("North", northPanel);

    ActionListener al = new LookupNames();
    findButton.addActionListener(al);
    searchString.addActionListener(al);
  }
```

```
private JPanel initRecordType() {
  JPanel p = new JPanel();
  p.setLayout(new GridLayout(6, 2, 5, 2));
  p.add(new JLabel("Search for:"));
  p.add(new JLabel(""));

  JRadioButton any = new JRadioButton("Any", true);
  any.setActionCommand("Any");
  searchFor.add(any);
  p.add(any);

  p.add(this.makeRadioButton("Network"));
  p.add(this.makeRadioButton("Person"));
  p.add(this.makeRadioButton("Host"));
  p.add(this.makeRadioButton("Domain"));
  p.add(this.makeRadioButton("Organization"));
  p.add(this.makeRadioButton("Group"));
  p.add(this.makeRadioButton("Gateway"));
  p.add(this.makeRadioButton("ASN"));

  return p;
}

private JRadioButton makeRadioButton(String label) {
  JRadioButton button = new JRadioButton(label, false);
  button.setActionCommand(label);
  searchFor.add(button);
  return button;
}

private JRadioButton makeSearchInRadioButton(String label) {
  JRadioButton button = new JRadioButton(label, false);
  button.setActionCommand(label);
  searchIn.add(button);
  return button;
}

private JPanel initSearchFields() {
  JPanel p = new JPanel();
  p.setLayout(new GridLayout(6, 1, 5, 2));
  p.add(new JLabel("Search In: "));

  JRadioButton all = new JRadioButton("All", true);
  all.setActionCommand("All");
  searchIn.add(all);
  p.add(all);

  p.add(this.makeSearchInRadioButton("Name"));
  p.add(this.makeSearchInRadioButton("Mailbox"));
  p.add(this.makeSearchInRadioButton("Handle"));
```

```
      return p;
    }

    private JPanel initServerChoice() {
      final JPanel p = new JPanel();
      p.setLayout(new GridLayout(6, 1, 5, 2));
      p.add(new JLabel("Search At: "));

      chosenServer.setText(server.getHost().getHostName());
      p.add(chosenServer);
      chosenServer.addActionListener( new ActionListener() {
        @Override
        public void actionPerformed(ActionEvent event) {
          try {
            server = new Whois(chosenServer.getText());
          } catch (UnknownHostException ex) {
            JOptionPane.showMessageDialog(p,
              ex.getMessage(), "Alert", JOptionPane.ERROR_MESSAGE);
          }
        }
      } );

      return p;
    }

    private class LookupNames implements ActionListener {

      @Override
      public void actionPerformed(ActionEvent event) {
        names.setText("");
        SwingWorker<String, Object> worker = new Lookup();
        worker.execute();
      }
    }

    private class Lookup extends SwingWorker<String, Object> {

      @Override
      protected String doInBackground() throws Exception {
        Whois.SearchIn group = Whois.SearchIn.ALL;
        Whois.SearchFor category = Whois.SearchFor.ANY;

        String searchForLabel = searchFor.getSelection().getActionCommand();
        String searchInLabel = searchIn.getSelection().getActionCommand();

        if (searchInLabel.equals("Name")) group = Whois.SearchIn.NAME;
        else if (searchInLabel.equals("Mailbox")) {
          group = Whois.SearchIn.MAILBOX;
        } else if (searchInLabel.equals("Handle")) {
          group = Whois.SearchIn.HANDLE;
        }
```

```java
    if (searchForLabel.equals("Network")) {
      category = Whois.SearchFor.NETWORK;
    } else if (searchForLabel.equals("Person")) {
      category = Whois.SearchFor.PERSON;
    } else if (searchForLabel.equals("Host")) {
      category = Whois.SearchFor.HOST;
    } else if (searchForLabel.equals("Domain")) {
      category = Whois.SearchFor.DOMAIN;
    } else if (searchForLabel.equals("Organization")) {
      category = Whois.SearchFor.ORGANIZATION;
    } else if (searchForLabel.equals("Group")) {
      category = Whois.SearchFor.GROUP;
    } else if (searchForLabel.equals("Gateway")) {
      category = Whois.SearchFor.GATEWAY;
    } else if (searchForLabel.equals("ASN")) {
      category = Whois.SearchFor.ASN;
    }

    server.setHost(chosenServer.getText());
    return server.lookUpNames(searchString.getText(),
        category, group, exactMatch.isSelected());
  }

  @Override
  protected void done() {
    try {
      names.setText(get());
    } catch (Exception ex) {
      JOptionPane.showMessageDialog(WhoisGUI.this,
          ex.getMessage(), "Lookup Failed", JOptionPane.ERROR_MESSAGE);
    }
  }
}

public static void main(String[] args) {
  try {
    Whois server = new Whois();
    WhoisGUI a = new WhoisGUI(server);
    a.setDefaultCloseOperation(WindowConstants.EXIT_ON_CLOSE);
    a.pack();
    EventQueue.invokeLater(new FrameShower(a));
  } catch (UnknownHostException ex) {
    JOptionPane.showMessageDialog(null, "Could not locate default host "
        + Whois.DEFAULT_HOST, "Error", JOptionPane.ERROR_MESSAGE);
  }
}

private static class FrameShower implements Runnable {

  private final Frame frame;

  FrameShower(Frame frame) {
```

```
      this.frame = frame;
    }

    @Override
    public void run() {
     frame.setVisible(true);
    }
  }
}
```

The `main()` method is the usual block of code to start up a standalone application. It constructs a `Whois` object and then uses that to construct a `WhoisGUI` object. Then the `WhoisGUI()` constructor sets up the Swing interface. There's a lot of redundant code here, so it's broken out into the private methods `initSearchFields()`, `initServer Choice()`, `makeSearchInRadioButton()`, and `makeSearchForRadioButton()`. As usual with `LayoutManager`-based interfaces, the setup is fairly involved. Because you'd probably use a visual designer to build such an application, I won't describe it in detail here.

When the constructor returns, the `main()` method attaches an anonymous inner class to the window that will close the application when the window is closed. (This isn't in the constructor because other programs that use this class may not want to exit the program when the window closes.) `main()` then packs and shows the window. To avoid an obscure race condition that can lead to deadlock this needs to be done in the event dispatch thread; hence the `FrameShower` inner class that implements `Runnable` and the call to `EventQueue.invokeLater()`. From that point on, all activity takes place in the event dispatch thread.

The first event this program must respond to is the user typing a name in the Whois: search box and either clicking the Find button or hitting Enter. In this case, the `Lookup Names` inner class sets the main text to the empty string and executes a `SwingWorker` to make the network connection. `SwingWorker` (introduced in Java 6) is a really important class to learn if you're going to write GUI applications that access the network, or for that matter perform any I/O at all.

The problem `SwingWorker` solves is this. In any Java GUI application there are two rules you must follow in order to avoid deadlock and slowness:

- All updates to Swing components happen on the event dispatch thread.
- No slow blocking operations, especially I/O, happen on the event dispatch thread. Otherwise a slow-to-respond server can hang the entire application.

These two rules are at loggerheads for network- and I/O-heavy code because the part of the code that performs the I/O can't update the GUI and vice versa. These have to happen in two different threads.

There are several ways to sidestep this paradox, but prior to Java 6 they're all quite complex. In Java 6 and later, however, the solution is easy. Define a subclass of Swing Worker and override two methods:

1. The doInBackground() method performs the long-running, I/O-heavy operation. It does not interact with the GUI. It can return any convenient type and throw any exception.
2. The done() method is automatically invoked on the event dispatch thread after the doInBackground() method returns, so it can update the GUI. This method can call the get() method to retrieve the return value calculated by doInBackground().

Example 8-8 uses an inner class named Lookup as its SwingWorker. The doInBack ground() method talks to the whois server, and returns the server's response as a String. The done() method updates the names text area with the server's response.

The second event this program must respond to is the user typing a new host in the server text field. In this case, an anonymous inner class tries to construct a new Whois object and stores it in the server field. If it fails (e.g., because the user mistyped the hostname), the old server is restored. An alert box informs the user of this event.

This is not a perfect client by any means. The most glaring omission is that it doesn't provide a way to save the data and quit the program. However, it does demonstrate how to safely make network connections from a GUI program without blocking the event dispatch thread.

CHAPTER 9

Sockets for Servers

The previous chapter discussed sockets from the standpoint of *clients*: programs that open a socket to a server that's listening for connections. However, client sockets themselves aren't enough; clients aren't much use unless they can talk to a server, and the Socket class discussed in the previous chapter is not sufficient for writing servers. To create a Socket, you need to know the Internet host to which you want to connect. When you're writing a server, you don't know in advance who will contact you; and even if you did, you wouldn't know when that host wanted to contact you. In other words, servers are like receptionists who sit by the phone and wait for incoming calls. They don't know who will call or when, only that when the phone rings, they have to pick it up and talk to whoever is there. You can't program that behavior with the Socket class alone.

For servers that accept connections, Java provides a ServerSocket class that represents server sockets. In essence, a server socket's job is to sit by the phone and wait for incoming calls. More technically, a server socket runs on the server and listens for incoming TCP connections. Each server socket listens on a particular port on the server machine. When a client on a remote host attempts to connect to that port, the server wakes up, negotiates the connection between the client and the server, and returns a regular Socket object representing the socket between the two hosts. In other words, server sockets wait for connections while client sockets initiate connections. Once a ServerSocket has set up the connection, the server uses a regular Socket object to send data to the client. Data always travels over the regular socket.

Using ServerSockets

The ServerSocket class contains everything needed to write servers in Java. It has constructors that create new ServerSocket objects, methods that listen for connections on a specified port, methods that configure the various server socket options, and the usual miscellaneous methods such as toString().

In Java, the basic life cycle of a server program is this:

1. A new ServerSocket is created on a particular port using a ServerSocket() constructor.

2. The ServerSocket listens for incoming connection attempts on that port using its accept() method. accept() blocks until a client attempts to make a connection, at which point accept() returns a Socket object connecting the client and the server.

3. Depending on the type of server, either the Socket's getInputStream() method, getOutputStream() method, or both are called to get input and output streams that communicate with the client.

4. The server and the client interact according to an agreed-upon protocol until it is time to close the connection.

5. The server, the client, or both close the connection.

6. The server returns to step 2 and waits for the next connection.

Let's demonstrate with one of the simpler protocols, daytime. Recall from the Chapter 8 that a daytime server listens on port 13. When a client connects, the server sends the time in a human-readable format and closes the connection. For example, here's a connection to the daytime server at *time-a.nist.gov*:

```
$ telnet time-a.nist.gov 13
Trying 129.6.15.28...
Connected to time-a.nist.gov.
Escape character is '^]'.

56375 13-03-24 13:37:50 50 0 0 888.8 UTC(NIST) *
Connection closed by foreign host.
```

Implementing your own daytime server is easy. First, create a server socket that listens on port 13:

```
ServerSocket server = new ServerSocket(13);
```

Next, accept a connection:

```
Socket connection = server.accept();
```

The accept() call *blocks*. That is, the program stops here and waits, possibly for hours or days, until a client connects on port 13. When a client does connect, the accept() method returns a Socket object.

Note that the connection is returned a `java.net.Socket` object, the same as you used for clients in the previous chapter. The daytime protocol requires the server (and only the server) to talk, so get an `OutputStream` from the socket. Because the daytime protocol requires text, chain this to an `OutputStreamWriter`:

```
OutputStream out = connection.getOutputStream();
Writer writer = new OutputStreamWriter(writer, "ASCII");
```

Now get the current time and write it onto the stream. The daytime protocol doesn't require any particular format other than that it be human readable, so let Java pick for you:

```
Date now = new Date();
out.write(now.toString() +"\r\n");
```

Do note, however, the use of a carriage return/linefeed pair to terminate the line. This is almost always what you want in a network server. You should explicitly choose this rather than using the system line separator, whether explicitly with `System.getProper` `ty("line.separator")` or implicitly via a method such as `println()`.

Finally, flush the connection and close it:

```
out.flush();
connection.close();
```

You won't always have to close the connection after just one write. Many protocols, dict and HTTP 1.1 for instance, allow clients to send multiple requests over a single socket and expect the server to send multiple responses. Some protocols such as FTP can even hold a socket open indefinitely. However, the daytime protocol only allows a single response.

If the client closes the connection while the server is still operating, the input and/or output streams that connect the server to the client throw an `InterruptedIOExcep` `tion` on the next read or write. In either case, the server should then get ready to process the next incoming connection.

Of course, you'll want to do all this repeatedly, so you'll put this all inside a loop. Each pass through the loop invokes the `accept()` method once. This returns a `Socket` object representing the connection between the remote client and the local server. Interaction with the client takes place through this `Socket` object. For example:

```
ServerSocket server = new ServerSocket(port);
while (true) {
  try (Socket connection = server.accept()) {
    Writer out = new OutputStreamWriter(connection.getOutputStream());
    Date now = new Date();
    out.write(now.toString() +"\r\n");
    out.flush();
  } catch (IOException ex) {
    // problem with one client; don't shut down the server
```

```
      System.err.println(ex.getMessage());
    }
  }
}
```

This is called an *iterative* server. There's one big loop, and in each pass through the loop a single connection is completely processed. This works well for a very simple protocol with very small requests and responses like daytime, though even with this simple a protocol it's possible for one slow client to delay other faster clients. Upcoming examples will address this with multiple threads or asynchronous I/O.

When exception handling is added, the code becomes somewhat more convoluted. It's important to distinguish between exceptions that should probably shut down the server and log an error message, and exceptions that should just close that active connection. Exceptions within the scope of a particular connection should close that connection, but not affect other connections or shut down the server. Exceptions outside the scope of an individual request probably should shut down the server. To organize this, nest the try blocks:

```
ServerSocket server = null;
try {
  server = new ServerSocket(port);
  while (true) {
    Socket connection = null;
    try {
      connection = server.accept();
      Writer out = new OutputStreamWriter(connection.getOutputStream());
      Date now = new Date();
      out.write(now.toString() +"\r\n");
      out.flush();
      connection.close();
    } catch (IOException ex) {
      // this request only; ignore
    } finally {
      try {
        if (connection != null) connection.close();
      } catch (IOException ex) {}
    }
  }
} catch (IOException ex) {
  ex.printStackTrace();
} finally {
  try {
    if (server != null) server.close();
  } catch (IOException ex) {}
}
```

Always close a socket when you're finished with it. In Chapter 8, I said that a client shouldn't rely on the other side of a connection to close the socket; that goes triple for servers. Clients time out or crash; users cancel transactions; networks go down in high-traffic periods; hackers launch denial-of-service attacks. For any of these or a hundred

---

more reasons, you cannot rely on clients to close sockets, even when the protocol requires them to, which this one doesn't.

Example 9-1 puts this all together. It uses Java 7's try-with-resources to autoclose the sockets.

Example 9-1. A daytime server

```java
import java.net.*;
import java.io.*;
import java.util.Date;

public class DaytimeServer {

  public final static int PORT = 13;

  public static void main(String[] args) {
    try (ServerSocket server = new ServerSocket(PORT)) {
      while (true) {
        try (Socket connection = server.accept()) {
          Writer out = new OutputStreamWriter(connection.getOutputStream());
          Date now = new Date();
          out.write(now.toString() +"\r\n");
          out.flush();
          connection.close();
        } catch (IOException ex) {}
      }
    } catch (IOException ex) {
      System.err.println(ex);
    }
  }
}
```

The class has a single method, main(), which does all the work. The outer try block traps any IOExceptions that may arise while the ServerSocket object server is constructed on the daytime port. The inner try block watches for exceptions thrown while the connections are accepted and processed. The accept() method is called within an infinite loop to watch for new connections; like many servers, this program never terminates but continues listening until an exception is thrown or you stop it manually.

 The command for stopping a program manually depends on your system; under Unix, Windows, and many other systems, Ctrl-C will do the job. If you are running the server in the background on a Unix system, stop it by finding the server's process ID and killing it with the kill command (**kill** *pid*).

When a client connects, accept() returns a Socket, which is stored in the local variable connection, and the program continues. It calls getOutputStream() to get the output

stream associated with that Socket and then chains that output stream to a new Out
putStreamWriter, out. A new Date object provides the current time. The content is
sent to the client by writing its string representation on out with write().

Connecting from Telnet, you should see something like this:

```
$ telnet localhost 13
Trying 127.0.0.1...
Connected to localhost.
Escape character is '^]'.
Sat Mar 30 16:15:10 EDT 2013
Connection closed by foreign host
```

 If you run this program on Unix (including Linux and Mac OS X),
you need to run it as root in order to connect to port 13. If you don't
want to or can't run it as root, change the port number to something above 1024—say, 1313.

Serving Binary Data

Sending binary, nontext data is not significantly harder. You just use an Output
Stream that writes a byte array rather than a Writer that writes a String. Example 9-2
demonstrates with an iterative time server that follows the time protocol outlined in
RFC 868. When a client connects, the server sends a 4-byte, big-endian, unsigned integer
specifying the number of seconds that have passed since 12:00 A.M., January 1, 1900,
GMT (the epoch). Once again, the current time is found by creating a new Date object.
However, because Java's Date class counts milliseconds since 12:00 A.M., January 1,
1970, GMT rather than seconds since 12:00 A.M., January 1, 1900, GMT, some conversion is necessary.

Example 9-2. A time server

```
import java.io.*;
import java.net.*;
import java.util.Date;

public class TimeServer {

  public final static int PORT = 37;

  public static void main(String[] args) {

    // The time protocol sets the epoch at 1900,
    // the Date class at 1970. This number
    // converts between them.
    long differenceBetweenEpochs = 2208988800L;

    try (ServerSocket server = new ServerSocket(PORT)) {
```

```
  while (true) {
    try (Socket connection = server.accept()) {
      OutputStream out = connection.getOutputStream();
      Date now = new Date();
      long msSince1970 = now.getTime();
      long secondsSince1970 = msSince1970/1000;
      long secondsSince1900 = secondsSince1970
          + differenceBetweenEpochs;
      byte[] time = new byte[4];
      time[0]
          = (byte) ((secondsSince1900 & 0x00000000FF000000L) >> 24);
      time[1]
          = (byte) ((secondsSince1900 & 0x0000000000FF0000L) >> 16);
      time[2]
          = (byte) ((secondsSince1900 & 0x000000000000FF00L) >> 8);
      time[3] = (byte) (secondsSince1900 & 0x00000000000000FFL);
      out.write(time);
      out.flush();
    } catch (IOException ex) {
      System.err.println(ex.getMessage());
    }
  }
  } catch (IOException ex) {
    System.err.println(ex);
  }
 }
}
```

As with the TimeClient of the previous chapter, most of the effort here goes into working with a data format (32-bit unsigned integers) that Java doesn't natively support.

Multithreaded Servers

Daytime and time are both very quick protocols. The server sends a few dozen bytes at most and then closes the connection. It's plausible here to process each connection fully before moving on to the next one. Even in that case, though, it is possible that a slow or crashed client might hang the server for a few seconds until it notices the socket is broken. If the sending of data can take a significant amount of time even when client and server are behaving, you really don't want each connection to wait for the next.

Old-fashioned Unix servers such as wu-ftpd create a new process to handle each connection so that multiple clients can be serviced at the same time. Java programs should spawn a thread to interact with the client so that the server can be ready to process the next connection sooner. A thread places a far smaller load on the server than a complete child process. In fact, the overhead of forking too many processes is why the typical Unix FTP server can't handle more than roughly 400 connections without slowing to a crawl. On the other hand, if the protocol is simple and quick and allows the server to close the connection when it's through, it will be more efficient for the server to process the client request immediately without spawning a thread.

The operating system stores incoming connection requests addressed to a particular port in a first-in, first-out queue. By default, Java sets the length of this queue to 50, although it can vary from operating system to operating system. Some operating systems (not Solaris) have a maximum queue length. For instance, on FreeBSD, the default maximum queue length is 128. On these systems, the queue length for a Java server socket will be the largest operating-system allowed value less than or equal to 50. After the queue fills to capacity with unprocessed connections, the host refuses additional connections on that port until slots in the queue open up. Many (though not all) clients will try to make a connection multiple times if their initial attempt is refused. Several ServerSocket constructors allow you to change the length of the queue if its default length isn't large enough. However, you won't be able to increase the queue beyond the maximum size that the operating system supports. Whatever the queue size, though, you want to be able to empty it faster than new connections are coming in, even if it takes a while to process each connection.

The solution here is to give each connection its own thread, separate from the thread that accepts incoming connections into the queue. For instance, Example 9-3 is a daytime server that spawns a new thread to handle each incoming connection. This prevents one slow client from blocking all the other clients. This is a *thread per connection* design.

Example 9-3. A multithreaded daytime server

```java
import java.net.*;
import java.io.*;
import java.util.Date;

public class MultithreadedDaytimeServer {

  public final static int PORT = 13;

  public static void main(String[] args) {
    try (ServerSocket server = new ServerSocket(PORT)) {
      while (true) {
        try {
          Socket connection = server.accept();
          Thread task = new DaytimeThread(connection);
          task.start();
        } catch (IOException ex) {}
      }
    } catch (IOException ex) {
      System.err.println("Couldn't start server");
    }
  }

  private static class DaytimeThread extends Thread {
```

```
    private Socket connection;

    DaytimeThread(Socket connection) {
      this.connection = connection;
    }

    @Override
    public void run() {
      try {
        Writer out = new OutputStreamWriter(connection.getOutputStream());
        Date now = new Date();
        out.write(now.toString() +"\r\n");
        out.flush();
      } catch (IOException ex) {
        System.err.println(ex);
      } finally {
        try {
          connection.close();
        } catch (IOException e) {
          // ignore;
        }
      }
    }
  }
}
```

Example 9-3 uses try-with-resources to autoclose the server socket. However, it deliberately does not use try-with-resources for the client sockets accepted by the server socket. This is because the client socket escapes from the try block into a separate thread. If you used try-with-resources, the main thread would close the socket as soon as it got to the end of the while loop, likely before the spawned thread had finished using it.

There's actually a denial-of-service attack on this server though. Because Example 9-3 spawns a new thread for each connection, numerous roughly simultaneous incoming connections can cause it to spawn an indefinite number of threads. Eventually, the Java virtual machine will run out of memory and crash. A better approach is to use a fixed thread pool as described in Chapter 3 to limit the potential resource usage. Fifty threads should be plenty. Example 9-4 shouldn't crash no matter what load it's under. It may start refusing connections, but it won't crash.

Example 9-4. A daytime server using a thread pool

```
import java.io.*;
import java.net.*;
import java.util.*;
import java.util.concurrent.*;

public class PooledDaytimeServer {

  public final static int PORT = 13;
```

```
  public static void main(String[] args) {

    ExecutorService pool = Executors.newFixedThreadPool(50);

    try (ServerSocket server = new ServerSocket(PORT)) {
      while (true) {
        try {
          Socket connection = server.accept();
          Callable<Void> task = new DaytimeTask(connection);
          pool.submit(task);
        } catch (IOException ex) {}
      }
    } catch (IOException ex) {
      System.err.println("Couldn't start server");
    }
  }

  private static class DaytimeTask implements Callable<Void> {

    private Socket connection;

    DaytimeTask(Socket connection) {
      this.connection = connection;
    }

    @Override
    public Void call() {
      try {
        Writer out = new OutputStreamWriter(connection.getOutputStream());
        Date now = new Date();
        out.write(now.toString() +"\r\n");
        out.flush();
      } catch (IOException ex) {
        System.err.println(ex);
      } finally {
        try {
          connection.close();
        } catch (IOException e) {
          // ignore;
        }
      }
      return null;
    }
  }
}
```

Example 9-4 is structured much like Example 9-3. The single difference is that it uses a
Callable rather than a Thread subclass, and rather than starting threads it submits these
callables to an executor service preconfigured with 50 threads.

Writing to Servers with Sockets

In the examples so far, the server has only written to client sockets. It hasn't read from them. Most protocols, however, require the server to do both. This isn't hard. You'll accept a connection as before, but this time ask for both an `InputStream` and an `Out putStream`. Read from the client using the `InputStream` and write to it using the `Out putStream`. The main trick is understanding the protocol: when to write and when to read.

The echo protocol, defined in RFC 862, is one of the simplest interactive TCP services. The client opens a socket to port 7 on the echo server and sends data. The server sends the data back. This continues until the client closes the connection. The echo protocol is useful for testing the network to make sure that data is not mangled by a misbehaving router or firewall. You can test echo with Telnet like this:

```
$ telnet rama.poly.edu 7
Trying 128.238.10.212...
Connected to rama.poly.edu.
Escape character is '^]'.
This is a test
This is a test
This is another test
This is another test
9876543210
9876543210
^]
telnet> close
Connection closed.
```

This sample is line oriented because that's how Telnet works. It reads a line of input from the console, sends it to the server, then waits to read a line of output it gets back. However, the echo protocol doesn't require this. It echoes each byte as it receives it. It doesn't really care whether those bytes represent characters in some encoding or are divided into lines. Unlike many protocols, echo does not specify lockstep behavior where the client sends a request but then waits for the full server response before sending any more data.

Unlike daytime and time, in the echo protocol the client is responsible for closing the connection. This makes it even more important to support asynchronous operation with many threads because a single client can remain connected indefinitely. In Example 9-5, the server spawns up to 500 threads.

Example 9-5. An echo server

```
import java.net.*;
import java.io.*;
import java.util.concurrent.*;

public class EchoServer {
```

```java
  public final static int PORT = 7;

  public static void main(String[] args) {

    ExecutorService pool = Executors.newFixedThreadPool(500);

    try (ServerSocket server = new ServerSocket(PORT)) {
      while (true) {
        try {
          Socket connection = server.accept();
          Callable<Void> task = new EchoTask(connection);
          pool.submit(task);
        } catch (IOException ex) {}
      }
    } catch (IOException ex) {
      System.err.println("Couldn't start server");
    }
  }

  private static class EchoTask implements Callable<Void> {

    private Socket connection;

    EchoTask(Socket connection) {
      this.connection = connection;
    }

    @Override
    public Void call() throws IOException {
      try {
        InputStream in = new BufferedInputStream(connection.getInputStream());
        OutputStream out = connection.getOutputStream();
        int c;
        while ((c = in.read()) != -1) {
          out.write(c);
          out.flush();
        }
      } catch (IOException ex) {
        System.err.println(ex);
      } finally {
        connection.close();
      }
      return null;
    }
  }
}
```

Closing Server Sockets

If you're finished with a server socket, you should close it, especially if the program is going to continue to run for some time. This frees up the port for other programs that may wish to use it. Closing a `ServerSocket` should not be confused with closing a `Socket`. Closing a `ServerSocket` frees a port on the local host, allowing another server to bind to the port; it also breaks all currently open sockets that the `ServerSocket` has accepted.

Server sockets are closed automatically when a program dies, so it's not absolutely necessary to close them in programs that terminate shortly after the `ServerSocket` is no longer needed. Nonetheless, it doesn't hurt. Programmers often follow the same close-if-not-null pattern in a `try-finally` block that you're already familiar with from streams and client-side sockets:

```
ServerSocket server = null;
try {
  server = new ServerSocket(port);
  // ... work with the server socket
} finally {
  if (server != null) {
    try {
      server.close();
    } catch (IOException ex) {
    // ignore
    }
  }
}
```

You can improve this slightly by using the noargs `ServerSocket()` constructor, which does not throw any exceptions and does not bind to a port. Instead, you call the `bind()` method to bind to a socket address after the `ServerSocket()` object has been constructed:

```
ServerSocket server = new ServerSocket();
try {
  SocketAddress address = new InetSocketAddress(port);
  server.bind(address);
  // ... work with the server socket
} finally {
  try {
    server.close();
  } catch (IOException ex) {
  // ignore
  }
}
```

In Java 7, `ServerSocket` implements `AutoCloseable` so you can take advantage of try-with-resources instead:

```
try (ServerSocket server = new ServerSocket(port)) {
  // ... work with the server socket
}
```

After a server socket has been closed, it cannot be reconnected, even to the same port.

The isClosed() method returns true if the ServerSocket has been closed, false if it hasn't:

```
public boolean isClosed()
```

ServerSocket objects that were created with the noargs ServerSocket() constructor and not yet bound to a port are not considered to be closed. Invoking isClosed() on these objects returns false. The isBound() method tells you whether the ServerSock et has been bound to a port:

```
public boolean isBound()
```

As with the isBound() method of the Socket class discussed in the Chapter 8, the name is a little misleading. isBound() returns true if the ServerSocket has ever been bound to a port, even if it's currently closed. If you need to test whether a ServerSocket is open, you must check both that isBound() returns true and that isClosed() returns false. For example:

```
public static boolean isOpen(ServerSocket ss) {
  return ss.isBound() && !ss.isClosed();
}
```

Logging

Servers run unattended for long periods of time. It's often important to debug what happened when in a server long after the fact. For this reason, it's advisable to store server logs for at least some period of time.

What to Log

There are two primary things you want to store in your logs:

- Requests
- Server errors

Indeed, servers often keep two different logfiles for these two different items. The audit log usually contains one entry for each connection made to the server. Servers that perform multiple operations per connection may have one entry per operation instead. For instance, a dict server might log one entry for each word a client looks up.

The error log contains mostly unexpected exceptions that occurred while the server was running. For instance, any NullPointerException that happens should be logged here because it indicates a bug in the server you'll need to fix. The error log does not contain client errors, such as a client that unexpectedly disconnects or sends a malformed request. These go into the request log. The error log is exclusively for unexpected exceptions.

The general rule of thumb for error logs is that every line in the error log should be looked at and resolved. The ideal number of entries in an error log is zero. Every entry in this log represents a bug to be investigated and resolved. If investigation of an error log entry ends with the decision that that exception is not really a problem, and the code is working as intended, remove the log statement. Error logs that fill up with too many false alarms rapidly become ignored and useless.

For the same reason, do not keep debug logs in production. Do not log every time you enter a method, every time a condition is met, and so on. No one ever looks at these logs. They just waste space and hide real problems. If you need method-level logging for debugging, put it in a separate file, and turn it off in the global properties file when running in production.

More advanced logging systems provide log analysis tools that enable you to do things like show only messages with priority INFO or higher, or only show messages that originated from a certain part of the code. These tools make it more feasible to keep a single logfile or database, perhaps even share one log among many different binaries or programs. Nonetheless, the principle still applies that a log record no one will ever look at is worthless at best and more often than not distracting or confusing.

Do not follow the common antipattern of logging everything you can think of just in case someone might need it someday. In practice, programmers are terrible at guessing in advance which log messages they might need for debugging production problems. Once a problem occurs, it is sometimes obvious what messages you need; but it is rare to be able to anticipate this in advance. Adding "just in case" messages to logfiles usually means that when a problem does occur, you're frantically hunting for the relevant messages in an even bigger sea of irrelevant data.

How to Log

Many legacy programs dating back to Java 1.3 and earlier still use third-party logging libraries such as log4j or Apache Commons Logging, but the java.util.logging package available since Java 1.4 suffices for most needs. Choosing it avoids a lot of complex third-party dependencies.

Although you can load a logger on demand, it's usually easiest to just create one per class like so:

```
private final static Logger auditLogger = Logger.getLogger("requests");
```

Loggers are thread safe, so there's no problem storing them in a shared static field. Indeed, they almost have to be because even if the Logger object were not shared between threads, the logfile or database would be. This is important in highly multithreaded servers.

This example outputs to a log named "requests." Multiple Logger objects can output to the same log, but each logger always logs to exactly one log. What and where the log is depends on external configuration. Most commonly it's a file, which may or may not be named "requests"; but it can be a database, a SOAP service running on a different server, another Java program on the same host, or something else.

Once you have a logger, you can write to it using any of several methods. The most basic is log(). For example, this catch block logs an unexpected runtime exception at the highest level:

```
catch (RuntimeException ex) {
  logger.log(Level.SEVERE, "unexpected error " + ex.getMessage(), ex);
}
```

Including the exception instead of just a message is optional but customary when logging from a catch block.

There are seven levels defined as named constants in java.util.logging.Level in descending order of seriousness:

- Level.SEVERE (highest value)
- Level.WARNING
- Level.INFO
- Level.CONFIG
- Level.FINE
- Level.FINER
- Level.FINEST (lowest value)

I use info for audit logs and warning or severe for error logs. Lower levels are for debugging only and should not be used in production systems. Info, severe, and warning all have convenience helper methods that log at that level. For example, this statement logs a hit including the date and the remote address:

```
logger.info(new Date() + " " + connection.getRemoteSocketAddress());
```

You can use any format that's convenient for the individual log records. Generally, each record should contain a timestamp, the client address, and any information specific to the request that was being processed. If the log message represents an error, include the specific exception that was thrown. Java fills in the location in the code where the message was logged automatically, so you don't need to worry about that.

Example 9-6 demonstrates by adding logging to the daytime server.

Example 9-6. A daytime server that logs requests and errors

```java
import java.io.*;
import java.net.*;
import java.util.Date;
import java.util.concurrent.*;
import java.util.logging.*;

public class LoggingDaytimeServer {

  public final static int PORT = 13;
  private final static Logger auditLogger = Logger.getLogger("requests");
  private final static Logger errorLogger = Logger.getLogger("errors");

  public static void main(String[] args) {

   ExecutorService pool = Executors.newFixedThreadPool(50);

   try (ServerSocket server = new ServerSocket(PORT)) {
     while (true) {
       try {
         Socket connection = server.accept();
         Callable<Void> task = new DaytimeTask(connection);
         pool.submit(task);
       } catch (IOException ex) {
         errorLogger.log(Level.SEVERE, "accept error", ex);
       } catch (RuntimeException ex) {
         errorLogger.log(Level.SEVERE, "unexpected error " + ex.getMessage(), ex);
       }
     }
    } catch (IOException ex) {
      errorLogger.log(Level.SEVERE, "Couldn't start server", ex);
    } catch (RuntimeException ex) {
      errorLogger.log(Level.SEVERE, "Couldn't start server: " + ex.getMessage(), ex);
    }
  }

  private static class DaytimeTask implements Callable<Void> {

    private Socket connection;

    DaytimeTask(Socket connection) {
      this.connection = connection;
    }

    @Override
    public Void call() {
      try {
        Date now = new Date();
        // write the log entry first in case the client disconnects
        auditLogger.info(now + " " + connection.getRemoteSocketAddress());
        Writer out = new OutputStreamWriter(connection.getOutputStream());
        out.write(now.toString() +"\r\n");
```

```
      out.flush();
    } catch (IOException ex) {
      // client disconnected; ignore;
    } finally {
      try {
        connection.close();
      } catch (IOException ex) {
        // ignore;
      }
    }
    return null;
  }
 }
}
```

As well as logging, Example 9-6 has also added catch blocks for RuntimeException that cover most of the code and all of the network connections. This is strongly advisable in network servers. The last thing you want is for your entire server to fall down just because one request went down an unplanned code path and threw an IllegalArgumentExcep tion. Usually when this happens that request is going to fail, but you can continue processing other requests. If you're even more careful, you can send the client the appropriate error response. In HTTP, this would be a 500 internal server error.

Not every exception automatically turns into an error log entry. For example, if a client disconnects while you're writing the time, that's an IOException. However, it's not a bug or a server error, so it isn't written to the error log. In some situations, you might want to log it in the audit log, or a third location. However, remember the golden rule of logging: if no one's going to look at it, don't log it. Unless you really plan to investigate and do something about client disconnects, don't bother to record them.

By default, the logs are just output to the console. For example, here's the output from the preceding server when I connected to it a few times in quick succession:

```
Apr 13, 2013 8:54:50 AM LoggingDaytimeServer$DaytimeTask call
INFO: Sat Apr 13 08:54:50 EDT 2013 /0:0:0:0:0:0:0:1:56665
Apr 13, 2013 8:55:08 AM LoggingDaytimeServer$DaytimeTask call
INFO: Sat Apr 13 08:55:08 EDT 2013 /0:0:0:0:0:0:0:1:56666
Apr 13, 2013 8:55:16 AM LoggingDaytimeServer$DaytimeTask call
INFO: Sat Apr 13 08:55:16 EDT 2013 /0:0:0:0:0:0:0:1:56667
```

You'll want to configure the runtime environment such that logs go to a more permanent destination. Although you can specify this in code, it's usually advisable to set this up in a configuration file so log locations can be changed without recompiling.

The java.util.logging.config.file system property points to a file in the normal properties format that controls the logging. You set this property by passing the -Djava.util.logging.config.file=_filename_ argument when launching the virtual machine. For instance, in Mac OS X, it might be set in the VMOptions in the *Info.plist* file:

```
<key>Java</key>
<dict>
  <key>VMOptions</key>
  <array>
    <string>-Djava.util.logging.config.file=/opt/daytime/logging.properties
          </string>
  </array>
</dict>
```

Example 9-7 is a sample logging properties file that specifies:

- Logs should be written to a file.
- The requests log should be in */var/logs/daytime/requests.log* at level Info.
- The errors log should be in */var/logs/daytime/requests.log* at level Severe.
- Limit the log size to about 10 megabytes, then rotate.
- Keep two logs: the current one and the previous one.
- Use the basic text formatter (not XML).
- Each line of the logfile should be in the form *level message timestamp*.

Example 9-7. A logging properties file

```
handlers=java.util.logging.FileHandler
java.util.logging.FileHandler.pattern = /var/logs/daytime/requests.log
java.util.logging.FileHandler.limit = 10000000
java.util.logging.FileHandler.count = 2
java.util.logging.FileHandler.formatter = java.util.logging.SimpleFormatter
java.util.logging.FileHandler.append = true
java.util.logging.SimpleFormatter.format=%4$s: %5$s [%1$tc]%n

requests.level = INFO
audit.level = SEVERE
```

Here's some typical log output (note that it looks like the timestamp is doubled in request messages because the log message also includes the current time; this would not typically be the case for a server whose purpose was anything other than serving the current time):

```
SEVERE: Couldn't start server [Sat Apr 13 10:07:01 EDT 2013]
INFO: Sat Apr 13 10:08:05 EDT 2013 /0:0:0:0:0:0:0:1:57275
      [Sat Apr 13 10:08:05 EDT 2013]
INFO: Sat Apr 13 10:08:06 EDT 2013 /0:0:0:0:0:0:0:1:57276
      [Sat Apr 13 10:08:06 EDT 2013]
```

The one thing I don't like about the Java Logging API is that it doesn't give you an easy way to specify by configuration alone that different messages belong in different logs. For instance, you can't easily separate your error and your audit log. It can be done, but it requires you to define a new subclass of `FileHandler` for each separate log so you can assign it a new file.

Finally, once you've configured your servers with logging, don't forget to look in them, especially the error logs. There's no point to a logfile no one ever looks at. You'll also want to plan for and implement log rotation and retention policies. Hard drives get bigger every year, but it's still possible for a high-volume server to fill up a filesystem with log data if you aren't paying attention. Murphy's law says this is most likely to happen at 4:00 A.M. on New Year's Day when you're on vacation halfway around the world.

Constructing Server Sockets

There are four public `ServerSocket` constructors:

```
public ServerSocket(int port) throws BindException, IOException
public ServerSocket(int port, int queueLength)
    throws BindException, IOException
public ServerSocket(int port, int queueLength, InetAddress bindAddress)
    throws IOException
public ServerSocket() throws IOException
```

These constructors specify the port, the length of the queue used to hold incoming connection requests, and the local network interface to bind to. They pretty much all do the same thing, though some use default values for the queue length and the address to bind to.

For example, to create a server socket that would be used by an HTTP server on port 80, you would write:

```
ServerSocket httpd = new ServerSocket(80);
```

To create a server socket that would be used by an HTTP server on port 80 and queues up to 50 unaccepted connections at a time:

```
ServerSocket httpd = new ServerSocket(80, 50);
```

If you try to expand the queue past the operating system's maximum queue length, the maximum queue length is used instead.

By default, if a host has multiple network interfaces or IP addresses, the server socket listens on the specified port on all the interfaces and IP addresses. However, you can add a third argument to bind only to one particular local IP address. That is, the server socket only listens for incoming connections on the specified address; it won't listen for connections that come in through the host's other addresses.

For example, *login.ibiblio.org* is a particular Linux box in North Carolina. It's connected to the Internet with the IP address 152.2.210.122. The same box has a second Ethernet card with the local IP address 192.168.210.122 that is not visible from the public Internet, only from the local network. If, for some reason, you wanted to run a server on this host that only responded to local connections from within the same network, you could create a server socket that listens on port 5776 of 192.168.210.122 but not on port 5776 of 152.2.210.122, like so:

```
InetAddress local = InetAddress.getByName("192.168.210.122");
ServerSocket httpd = new ServerSocket(5776, 10, local);
```

In all three constructors, you can pass 0 for the port number so the system will select an available port for you. A port chosen by the system like this is sometimes called an *anonymous port* because you don't know its number in advance (though you can find out after the port has been chosen). This is often useful in multisocket protocols such as FTP. In passive FTP the client first connects to a server on the well-known port 21, so the server has to specify that port. However, when a file needs to be transferred, the server starts listening on any available port. The server then tells the client what other port it should connect to for data using the command connection already open on port 21. Thus, the data port can change from one session to the next and does not need to be known in advance. (Active FTP is similar except the client listens on an ephemeral port for the server to connect to it, rather than the other way around.)

All these constructors throw an `IOException`, specifically, a `BindException`, if the socket cannot be created and bound to the requested port. An `IOException` when creating a `ServerSocket` almost always means one of two things. Either another server socket, possibly from a completely different program, is already using the requested port, or you're trying to connect to a port from 1 to 1023 on Unix (including Linux and Mac OS X) without root (superuser) privileges.

You can take advantage of this to write a variation on the `LowPortScanner` program of the previous chapter. Rather than attempting to connect to a server running on a given port, you instead attempt to open a server on that port. If it's occupied, the attempt will fail. Example 9-8 checks for ports on the local machine by attempting to create `Server Socket` objects on them and seeing on which ports that fails. If you're using Unix and are not running as root, this program works only for ports 1024 and above.

Example 9-8. Look for local ports

```
import java.io.*;
import java.net.*;

public class LocalPortScanner {
```

```
  public static void main(String[] args) {

    for (int port = 1; port <= 65535; port++) {
      try {
        // the next line will fail and drop into the catch block if
        // there is already a server running on the port
        ServerSocket server = new ServerSocket(port);
      } catch (IOException ex) {
        System.out.println("There is a server on port " + port + ".");
      }
    }
  }
}
```

Here's the output I got when running `LocalPortScanner` on my Windows workstation:

```
D:\JAVA\JNP4\examples\9>java LocalPortScanner
There is a server on port 135.
There is a server on port 1025.
There is a server on port 1026.
There is a server on port 1027.
There is a server on port 1028.
```

Constructing Without Binding

The noargs constructor creates a `ServerSocket` object but does not actually bind it to a port, so it cannot initially accept any connections. It can be bound later using the `bind()` methods:

```
public void bind(SocketAddress endpoint) throws IOException
public void bind(SocketAddress endpoint, int queueLength) throws IOException
```

The primary use for this feature is to allow programs to set server socket options before binding to a port. Some options are fixed after the server socket has been bound. The general pattern looks like this:

```
ServerSocket ss = new ServerSocket();
// set socket options...
SocketAddress  http = new InetSocketAddress(80);
ss.bind(http);
```

You can also pass null for the `SocketAddress` to select an arbitrary port. This is like passing 0 for the port number in the other constructors.

Getting Information About a Server Socket

The `ServerSocket` class provides two getter methods that tell you the local address and port occupied by the server socket. These are useful if you've opened a server socket on an anonymous port and/or an unspecified network interface. This would be the case, for one example, in the data connection of an FTP session:

```
public InetAddress getInetAddress()
```

This method returns the address being used by the server (the local host). If the local host has a single IP address (as most do), this is the address returned by `InetAd` `dress.getLocalHost()`. If the local host has more than one IP address, the specific address returned is one of the host's IP addresses. You can't predict which address you will get. For example:

```
ServerSocket httpd = new ServerSocket(80);
InetAddress ia = httpd.getInetAddress();
```

If the `ServerSocket` has not yet bound to a network interface, this method returns null:

```
public int getLocalPort()
```

The `ServerSocket` constructors allow you to listen on an unspecified port by passing 0 for the port number. This method lets you find out what port you're listening on. You might use this in a peer-to-peer multisocket program where you already have a means to inform other peers of your location. Or a server might spawn several smaller servers to perform particular operations. The well-known server could inform clients on what ports they can find the smaller servers. Of course, you can also use `getLocalPort()` to find a nonanonymous port, but why would you need to? Example 9-9 demonstrates.

Example 9-9. A random port

```
import java.io.*;
import java.net.*;

public class RandomPort {

  public static void main(String[] args) {
    try {
      ServerSocket server = new ServerSocket(0);
      System.out.println("This server runs on port "
          + server.getLocalPort());
    } catch (IOException ex) {
      System.err.println(ex);
    }
  }
}
```

Here's the output of several runs:

```
$ java RandomPort
This server runs on port 1154
D:\JAVA\JNP4\examples\9>java RandomPort
This server runs on port 1155
D:\JAVA\JNP4\examples\9>java RandomPort
This server runs on port 1156
```

At least on this system, the ports aren't truly random, but they are indeterminate until runtime.

If the ServerSocket has not yet bound to a port, getLocalPort() returns –1.

As with most Java objects, you can also just print out a ServerSocket using its to
String() method. A String returned by a ServerSocket's toString() method looks
like this:

```
ServerSocket[addr=0.0.0.0,port=0,localport=5776]
```

addr is the address of the local network interface to which the server socket is bound.
This will be 0.0.0.0 if it's bound to all interfaces, as is commonly the case. port is always
0. The localport is the local port on which the server is listening for connections. This
method is sometimes useful for debugging, but not much more. Don't rely on it.

Socket Options

Socket options specify how the native sockets on which the ServerSocket class relies
send and receive data. For server sockets, Java supports three options:

- SO_TIMEOUT
- SO_REUSEADDR
- SO_RCVBUF

It also allows you to set performance preferences for the socket's packets.

SO_TIMEOUT

SO_TIMEOUT is the amount of time, in milliseconds, that accept() waits for an incoming connection before throwing a java.io.InterruptedIOException. If
SO_TIMEOUT is 0, accept() will never time out. The default is to never time out.

Setting SO_TIMEOUT is uncommon. You might need it if you were implementing a
complicated and secure protocol that required multiple connections between the client
and the server where responses needed to occur within a fixed amount of time. However,
most servers are designed to run for indefinite periods of time and therefore just use
the default timeout value, 0 (never time out). If you want to change this, the setSoTi
meout() method sets the SO_TIMEOUT field for this server socket object:

```
public void setSoTimeout(int timeout) throws SocketException
public int  getSoTimeout() throws IOException
```

The countdown starts when accept() is invoked. When the timeout expires, ac
cept() throws a SocketTimeoutException, a subclass of IOException. You need to set
this option before calling accept(); you cannot change the timeout value while ac
cept() is waiting for a connection. The timeout argument must be greater than or equal
to zero; if it isn't, the method throws an IllegalArgumentException. For example:

```
try (ServerSocket server = new ServerSocket(port)) {
  server.setSoTimeout(30000); // block for no more than 30 seconds
  try {
    Socket s = server.accept();
    // handle the connection
    // ...
  } catch (SocketTimeoutException ex) {
    System.err.println("No connection within 30 seconds");
  }
} catch (IOException ex) {
  System.err.println("Unexpected IOException: " + e);
}
```

The getSoTimeout() method returns this server socket's current SO_TIMEOUT value.
For example:

```
public void printSoTimeout(ServerSocket server) {
  int timeout = server.getSoTimeOut();
  if (timeout > 0) {
    System.out.println(server + " will time out after "
        + timeout + "milliseconds.");
  } else if (timeout == 0) {
    System.out.println(server + " will never time out.");
  } else {
    System.out.println("Impossible condition occurred in " + server);
    System.out.println("Timeout cannot be less than zero." );
  }
}
```

SO_REUSEADDR

The SO_REUSEADDR option for server sockets is very similar to the same option for
client sockets, discussed in the previous chapter. It determines whether a new socket
will be allowed to bind to a previously used port while there might still be data traversing
the network addressed to the old socket. As you probably expect, there are two methods
to get and set this option:

```
public boolean getReuseAddress() throws SocketException
public void setReuseAddress(boolean on) throws SocketException
```

The default value is platform dependent. This code fragment determines the default
value by creating a new ServerSocket and then calling getReuseAddress():

```
ServerSocket ss = new ServerSocket(10240);
System.out.println("Reusable: " + ss.getReuseAddress());
```

On the Linux and Mac OS X boxes where I tested this code, server sockets were reusable
by default.

SO_RCVBUF

The SO_RCVBUF option sets the default receive buffer size for client sockets accepted by the server socket. It's read and written by these two methods:

```
public int  getReceiveBufferSize() throws SocketException
public void setReceiveBufferSize(int size) throws SocketException
```

Setting SO_RCVBUF on a server socket is like calling `setReceiveBufferSize()` on each individual socket returned by `accept()` (except that you can't change the receive buffer size after the socket has been accepted). Recall from the previous chapter that this option suggests a value for the size of the individual IP packets in the stream. Faster connections will want to use larger buffers, although most of the time the default value is fine.

You can set this option before or after the server socket is bound, unless you want to set a receive buffer size larger than 64K. In that case, you must set the option on an unbound `ServerSocket` before binding it. For example:

```
ServerSocket ss = new ServerSocket();
int receiveBufferSize = ss.getReceiveBufferSize();
if (receiveBufferSize < 131072) {
  ss.setReceiveBufferSize(131072);
}
ss.bind(new InetSocketAddress(8000));
//...
```

Class of Service

As you learned in the previous chapter, different types of Internet services have different performance needs. For instance, live streaming video of sports needs relatively high bandwidth. On the other hand, a movie might still need high bandwidth but be able to tolerate more delay and latency. Email can be passed over low-bandwidth connections and even held up for several hours without major harm.

Four general traffic classes are defined for TCP:

- Low cost
- High reliability
- Maximum throughput
- Minimum delay

These traffic classes can be requested for a given `Socket`. For instance, you can request the minimum delay available at low cost. These measures are all fuzzy and relative, not guarantees of service. Not all routers and native TCP stacks support these classes.

The `setPerformancePreferences()` method expresses the relative preferences given to connection time, latency, and bandwidth for sockets accepted on this server:

```
public void setPerformancePreferences(int connectionTime, int latency,
    int bandwidth)
```

For instance, by setting `connectionTime` to 2, `latency` to 1, and `bandwidth` to 3, you indicate that maximum bandwidth is the most important characteristic, minimum latency is the least important, and connection time is in the middle:

```
ss.setPerformancePreferences(2, 1, 3);
```

Exactly how any given VM implements this is implementation dependent. The underlying socket implementation is not required to respect any of these requests. They only provide a hint to the TCP stack about the desired policy. Many implementations including Android ignore these values completely.

HTTP Servers

This section shows several different HTTP servers you can build with server sockets, each with a different special purpose and each slightly more complex than the previous one.

HTTP is a large protocol. As you saw in Chapter 5, a full-featured HTTP server must respond to requests for files, convert URLs into filenames on the local system, respond to POST and GET requests, handle requests for files that don't exist, interpret MIME types, and much, much more. However, many HTTP servers don't need all of these features. For example, many sites simply display an "under construction" message. Clearly, Apache is overkill for a site like this. Such a site is a candidate for a custom server that does only one thing. Java's network class library makes writing simple servers like this almost trivial.

Custom servers aren't useful only for small sites. High-traffic sites like Yahoo! are also candidates for custom servers because a server that does only one thing can often be much faster than a general-purpose server such as Apache or Microsoft IIS. It is easy to optimize a special-purpose server for a particular task; the result is often much more efficient than a general-purpose server that needs to respond to many different kinds of requests. For instance, icons and images that are used repeatedly across many pages or on high-traffic pages might be better handled by a server that read all the image files into memory on startup and then served them straight out of RAM, rather than having to read them off disk for each request. Furthermore, this server could avoid wasting time on logging if you didn't want to track the image requests separately from the requests for the pages in which they were included.

Finally, Java isn't a bad language for full-featured web servers meant to compete with the likes of Apache or IIS. Even if you believe CPU-intensive Java programs are slower than CPU-intensive C and C++ programs (something I very much doubt is true in modern VMs), most HTTP servers are limited by network bandwidth and latency, not by CPU speed. Consequently, Java's other advantages, such as its half-compiled/half-interpreted nature, dynamic class loading, garbage collection, and memory protection really get a chance to shine. In particular, sites that make heavy use of dynamic content through servlets, PHP pages, or other mechanisms can often run much faster when reimplemented on top of a pure or mostly pure Java web server. Indeed, there are several production web servers written in Java, such as the Eclipse Foundation's Jetty (*http://eclipse.org/jetty/$$*). Many other web servers written in C now include substantial Java components to support the Java Servlet API and Java Server Pages. These largely replaced traditional CGIs, ASPs, and server-side includes, mostly because the Java equivalents are faster and less resource intensive. I'm not going to explore these technologies here because they easily deserve a book of their own. I refer interested readers to Jason Hunter's Java Servlet Programming (O'Reilly). However, it is important to note that servers in general and web servers in particular are one area where Java really is competitive with C for real-world performance.

A Single-File Server

Our investigation of HTTP servers begins with a server that always sends out the same file, no matter what the request. It's called `SingleFileHTTPServer` and is shown in Example 9-10. The filename, local port, and content encoding are read from the command line. If the port is omitted, port 80 is assumed. If the encoding is omitted, ASCII is assumed.

Example 9-10. An HTTP server that serves a single file

```java
import java.io.*;
import java.net.*;
import java.nio.charset.Charset;
import java.nio.file.*;
import java.util.concurrent.*;
import java.util.logging.*;

public class SingleFileHTTPServer {

  private static final Logger logger = Logger.getLogger("SingleFileHTTPServer");

  private final byte[] content;
  private final byte[] header;
  private final int port;
  private final String encoding;

  public SingleFileHTTPServer(String data, String encoding,
      String mimeType, int port) throws UnsupportedEncodingException {
    this(data.getBytes(encoding), encoding, mimeType, port);
  }
```

```java
public SingleFileHTTPServer(
    byte[] data, String encoding, String mimeType, int port) {
  this.content = data;
  this.port = port;
  this.encoding = encoding;
  String header = "HTTP/1.0 200 OK\r\n"
      + "Server: OneFile 2.0\r\n"
      + "Content-length: " + this.content.length + "\r\n"
      + "Content-type: " + mimeType + "; charset=" + encoding + "\r\n\r\n";
  this.header = header.getBytes(Charset.forName("US-ASCII"));
}

public void start() {
  ExecutorService pool = Executors.newFixedThreadPool(100);
  try (ServerSocket server = new ServerSocket(this.port)) {
    logger.info("Accepting connections on port " + server.getLocalPort());
    logger.info("Data to be sent:");
    logger.info(new String(this.content, encoding));

    while (true) {
      try {
        Socket connection = server.accept();
        pool.submit(new HTTPHandler(connection));
      } catch (IOException ex) {
        logger.log(Level.WARNING, "Exception accepting connection", ex);
      } catch (RuntimeException ex) {
        logger.log(Level.SEVERE, "Unexpected error", ex);
      }
    }
  } catch (IOException ex) {
    logger.log(Level.SEVERE, "Could not start server", ex);
  }
}

private class HTTPHandler implements Callable<Void> {
  private final Socket connection;

  HTTPHandler(Socket connection) {
    this.connection = connection;
  }

  @Override
  public Void call() throws IOException {
    try {
      OutputStream out = new BufferedOutputStream(
                            connection.getOutputStream()
                         );
      InputStream in = new BufferedInputStream(
                            connection.getInputStream()
                         );
      // read the first line only; that's all we need
      StringBuilder request = new StringBuilder(80);
```

```
      while (true) {
        int c = in.read();
        if (c == '\r' || c == '\n' || c == -1) break;
        request.append((char) c);
      }
      // If this is HTTP/1.0 or later send a MIME header
      if (request.toString().indexOf("HTTP/") != -1) {
        out.write(header);
      }
      out.write(content);
      out.flush();
    } catch (IOException ex) {
      logger.log(Level.WARNING, "Error writing to client", ex);
    } finally {
      connection.close();
    }
    return null;
  }
}

public static void main(String[] args) {

  // set the port to listen on
  int port;
  try {
    port = Integer.parseInt(args[1]);
    if (port < 1 || port > 65535) port = 80;
  } catch (RuntimeException ex) {
    port = 80;
  }

  String encoding = "UTF-8";
  if (args.length > 2) encoding = args[2];

  try {
    Path path = Paths.get(args[0]);;
    byte[] data = Files.readAllBytes(path);

    String contentType = URLConnection.getFileNameMap().getContentTypeFor(args[0]);
    SingleFileHTTPServer server = new SingleFileHTTPServer(data, encoding,
        contentType, port);
    server.start();

  } catch (ArrayIndexOutOfBoundsException ex) {
    System.out.println(
        "Usage: java SingleFileHTTPServer filename port encoding");
  } catch (IOException ex) {
    logger.severe(ex.getMessage());
  }
}
}
```

The constructors set up the data to be sent along with an HTTP header that includes information about content length and content encoding. The header and the body of the response are stored in byte arrays in the desired encoding so that they can be blasted to clients very quickly.

The SingleFileHTTPServer class holds the content to send, the header to send, and the port to bind to. The start() method creates a ServerSocket on the specified port, then enters an infinite loop that continually accepts connections and processes them.

Each incoming socket is processed by a runnable Handler object that is submitted to a thread pool. Thus, one slow client can't starve other clients. Each Handler gets an InputStream from it which it reads the client request. It looks at the first line to see whether it contains the string HTTP. If it sees this string, the server assumes that the client understands HTTP/1.0 or later and therefore sends a MIME header for the file; then it sends the data. If the client request doesn't contain the string HTTP, the server omits the header, sending the data by itself. Finally, the handler closes the connection.

The main() method just reads parameters from the command line. The name of the file to be served is read from the first command-line argument. If no file is specified or the file cannot be opened, an error message is printed and the program exits. Assuming the file can be read, its contents are read into the byte array data using the Path and Files classes introduced in Java 7. The URLConnection class makes a reasonable guess about the content type of the file, and that guess is stored in the contentType variable. Next, the port number is read from the second command-line argument. If no port is specified or if the second argument is not an integer from 1 to 65,535, port 80 is used. The encoding is read from the third command-line argument, if present. Otherwise, UTF-8 is assumed. Then these values are used to construct a SingleFileHTTPServer object and start it.

The main() method is only one possible interface. You could easily use this class as part of some other program. If you added a setter method to change the content, you could easily use it to provide simple status information about a running server or system. However, that would raise some additional issues of thread safety that Example 9-10 doesn't have to address because the data is immutable.

Here's what you see when you connect to this server via Telnet (the specifics depend on the exact server and file):

```
% telnet macfaq.dialup.cloud9.net 80
Trying 168.100.203.234...
Connected to macfaq.dialup.cloud9.net.
Escape character is '^]'.
GET / HTTP/1.0
HTTP/1.0 200 OK
Server: OneFile 2.0
Content-length: 959
```

```
Content-type: text/html; charset=UTF-8

<!DOCTYPE HTML PUBLIC "-//W3C//DTD HTML 3.2//EN">
<HTML>
<HEAD>;
<TITLE>Under Construction</TITLE>
</HEAD>

<BODY>
...
```

A Redirector

Redirection is another simple but useful application for a special-purpose HTTP server. In this section, you develop a server that redirects users from one website to another—for example, from *cnet.com* to *www.cnet.com*. Example 9-11 reads a URL and a port number from the command line, opens a server socket on the port, and redirects all requests that it receives to the site indicated by the new URL using a 302 FOUND code. In this example, I chose to use a new thread rather than a thread pool for each connection. This is perhaps a little simpler to code and understand but somewhat less efficient.

Example 9-11. An HTTP redirector

```java
import java.io.*;
import java.net.*;
import java.util.*;
import java.util.logging.*;

public class Redirector {

  private static final Logger logger = Logger.getLogger("Redirector");

  private final int port;
  private final String newSite;

  public Redirector(String newSite, int port) {
    this.port = port;
    this.newSite = newSite;
  }

  public void start() {
    try (ServerSocket server = new ServerSocket(port)) {
      logger.info("Redirecting connections on port "
          + server.getLocalPort() + " to " + newSite);

      while (true) {
        try {
          Socket s = server.accept();
          Thread t = new RedirectThread(s);
          t.start();
        } catch (IOException ex) {
```

```
        logger.warning("Exception accepting connection");
      } catch (RuntimeException ex) {
        logger.log(Level.SEVERE, "Unexpected error", ex);
      }
    }
  } catch (BindException ex) {
    logger.log(Level.SEVERE, "Could not start server.", ex);
  } catch (IOException ex) {
    logger.log(Level.SEVERE, "Error opening server socket", ex);
  }
}

private class RedirectThread extends Thread {

  private final Socket connection;

  RedirectThread(Socket s) {
    this.connection = s;
  }

  public void run() {
    try {
      Writer out = new BufferedWriter(
                    new OutputStreamWriter(
                     connection.getOutputStream(), "US-ASCII"
                    )
                   );
      Reader in = new InputStreamReader(
                    new BufferedInputStream(
                     connection.getInputStream()
                    )
                   );

      // read the first line only; that's all we need
      StringBuilder request = new StringBuilder(80);
      while (true) {
        int c = in.read();
        if (c == '\r' || c == '\n' || c == -1) break;
        request.append((char) c);
      }

      String get = request.toString();
      String[] pieces = get.split("\\w*");
      String theFile = pieces[1];

      // If this is HTTP/1.0 or later send a MIME header
      if (get.indexOf("HTTP") != -1) {
        out.write("HTTP/1.0 302 FOUND\r\n");
        Date now = new Date();
        out.write("Date: " + now + "\r\n");
        out.write("Server: Redirector 1.1\r\n");
        out.write("Location: " + newSite + theFile + "\r\n");
```

```
        out.write("Content-type: text/html\r\n\r\n");
        out.flush();
      }
      // Not all browsers support redirection so we need to
      // produce HTML that says where the document has moved to.
      out.write("<HTML><HEAD><TITLE>Document moved</TITLE></HEAD>\r\n");
      out.write("<BODY><H1>Document moved</H1>\r\n");
      out.write("The document " + theFile
          + " has moved to\r\n<A HREF=\"" + newSite + theFile + "\">"
          + newSite  + theFile
          + "</A>.\r\n Please update your bookmarks<P>");
      out.write("</BODY></HTML>\r\n");
      out.flush();
      logger.log(Level.INFO,
          "Redirected " + connection.getRemoteSocketAddress());
    } catch(IOException ex) {
      logger.log(Level.WARNING,
          "Error talking to " + connection.getRemoteSocketAddress(), ex);
    } finally {
      try {
        connection.close();
      } catch (IOException ex) {}
    }
  }
}

public static void main(String[] args) {

  int thePort;
  String theSite;

  try {
    theSite = args[0];
    // trim trailing slash
    if (theSite.endsWith("/")) {
      theSite = theSite.substring(0, theSite.length() - 1);
    }
  } catch (RuntimeException ex) {
    System.out.println(
        "Usage: java Redirector http://www.newsite.com/ port");
    return;
  }

  try {
    thePort = Integer.parseInt(args[1]);
  } catch (RuntimeException ex) {
    thePort = 80;
  }

  Redirector redirector = new Redirector(theSite, thePort);
  redirector.start();
```

```
    }
}
```

In order to start the redirector on port 80 and redirect incoming requests to *http://www.cafeconleche.org/*, type:

```
D:\JAVA\JNP4\examples\09> java Redirector http://www.cafeconleche.org/
Redirecting connections on port 80 to http://www.cafeconleche.org/
```

If you connect to this server via Telnet, this is what you'll see:

```
% telnet macfaq.dialup.cloud9.net 80
Trying 168.100.203.234...
Connected to macfaq.dialup.cloud9.net.
Escape character is '^]'.
GET / HTTP/1.0
HTTP/1.0 302 FOUND
Date: Sun Mar 31 12:38:42 EDT 2013
Server: Redirector 1.1
Location: http://www.cafeconleche.org/
Content-type: text/html

<HTML><HEAD><TITLE>Document moved</TITLE></HEAD>
<BODY><H1>Document moved</H1>
The document / has moved to
<A HREF="http://www.cafeconleche.org/">http://www.cafeconleche.
 org/</A>.
 Please update your bookmarks<P></BODY></HTML>
Connection closed by foreign host.
```

If, however, you connect with a web browser, you should be sent to *http://www.cafeconleche.org/* with only a slight delay. You should never see the HTML added after the response code; this is only provided to support very old browsers that don't do redirection automatically, as well as a few security paranoids who have configured their browsers not to redirect automatically.

The main() method provides a very simple interface that reads the URL of the new site to redirect connections to and the local port to listen on. It uses this information to construct a Redirector object. Then it invokes start(). If the port is not specified, Redirector listens on port 80. If the site is omitted, Redirector prints an error message and exits.

The start() method of Redirector binds the server socket to the port, prints a brief status message, and then enters an infinite loop in which it listens for connections. Every time a connection is accepted, the resulting Socket object is used to construct a Redi rectThread. This RedirectThread is then started. All further interaction with the client takes place in this new thread. The start() method then simply waits for the next incoming connection.

The run() method of RedirectThread does most of the work. It begins by chaining a Writer to the Socket's output stream and a Reader to the Socket's input stream. Both input and output are buffered. Then the run() method reads the first line the client sends. Although the client will probably send a whole MIME header, you can ignore that. The first line contains all the information you need. The line looks something like this:

```
GET /directory/filename.html HTTP/1.0
```

It is possible that the first word will be POST or PUT instead or that there will be no HTTP version. The second "word" is the file the client wants to retrieve. This *must* begin with a slash (/). Browsers are responsible for converting relative URLs to absolute URLs that begin with a slash; the server does not do this. The third word is the version of the HTTP protocol the browser understands. Possible values are nothing at all (pre-HTTP/1.0 browsers), HTTP/1.0, or HTTP/1.1.

To handle a request like this, Redirector ignores the first word. The second word is attached to the URL of the target server (stored in the field newSite) to give a full redirected URL. The third word is used to determine whether to send a MIME header; MIME headers are not used for old browsers that do not understand HTTP/1.0. If there is a version, a MIME header is sent; otherwise, it is omitted.

Sending the data is almost trivial. The Writer out is used. Because all the data you send is pure ASCII, the exact encoding isn't too important. The only trick here is that the end-of-line character for HTTP requests is \r\n–a carriage return followed by a line-feed.

The next lines each send one line of text to the client. The first line printed is:

```
HTTP/1.0 302 FOUND
```

This is an HTTP/1.0 response code that tells the client to expect to be redirected. The second line is a Date: header that gives the current time at the server. This line is optional. The third line is the name and version of the server; this line is also optional but is used by spiders that try to keep statistics about the most popular web servers. The next line is the Location: header, which is required for this response type. It tells the client where it is being redirected to. Last is the standard Content-type: header. You send the content type text/html to indicate that the client should expect to see HTML. Finally, a blank line is sent to signify the end of the header data.

Everything after this will be HTML, which is processed by the browser and displayed to the user. The next several lines print a message for browsers that do not support redirection, so those users can manually jump to the new site. That message looks like:

```
<HTML><HEAD><TITLE>Document moved</TITLE></HEAD>
<BODY><H1>Document moved</H1>
The document / has moved to
```

```
<A HREF="http://www.cafeconleche.org/">http://www.cafeconleche.org/</A>.
   Please update your bookmarks<P></BODY></HTML>
```

Finally, the connection is closed and the thread dies.

A Full-Fledged HTTP Server

Enough special-purpose HTTP servers. This next section develops a full-blown HTTP server, called JHTTP, that can serve an entire document tree, including images, applets, HTML files, text files, and more. It will be very similar to the SingleFileHTTPServer, except that it pays attention to the GET requests. This server is still fairly lightweight; after looking at the code, we'll discuss other features you might want to add.

Because this server may have to read and serve large files from the filesystem over potentially slow network connections, you'll change its approach. Rather than processing each request as it arrives in the main thread of execution, you'll place incoming connections in a pool. Separate instances of a RequestProcessor class will remove the connections from the pool and process them. Example 9-12 shows the main JHTTP class. As in the previous two examples, the main() method of JHTTP handles initialization, but other programs can use this class to run basic web servers.

Example 9-12. The JHTTP web server

```java
import java.io.*;
import java.net.*;
import java.util.concurrent.*;
import java.util.logging.*;

public class JHTTP {

  private static final Logger logger = Logger.getLogger(
      JHTTP.class.getCanonicalName());
  private static final int NUM_THREADS = 50;
  private static final String INDEX_FILE = "index.html";

  private final File rootDirectory;
  private final int port;

  public JHTTP(File rootDirectory, int port) throws IOException {

    if (!rootDirectory.isDirectory()) {
      throw new IOException(rootDirectory
          + " does not exist as a directory");
    }
    this.rootDirectory = rootDirectory;
    this.port = port;
  }

  public void start() throws IOException {
    ExecutorService pool = Executors.newFixedThreadPool(NUM_THREADS);
```

```
      try (ServerSocket server = new ServerSocket(port)) {
        logger.info("Accepting connections on port " + server.getLocalPort());
        logger.info("Document Root: " + rootDirectory);

        while (true) {
          try {
            Socket request = server.accept();
            Runnable r = new RequestProcessor(
                rootDirectory, INDEX_FILE, request);
            pool.submit(r);
          } catch (IOException ex) {
            logger.log(Level.WARNING, "Error accepting connection", ex);
          }
        }
      }
  }

  public static void main(String[] args) {

    // get the Document root
    File docroot;
    try {
      docroot = new File(args[0]);
    } catch (ArrayIndexOutOfBoundsException ex) {
      System.out.println("Usage: java JHTTP docroot port");
      return;
    }

    // set the port to listen on
    int port;
    try {
      port = Integer.parseInt(args[1]);
      if (port < 0 || port > 65535) port = 80;
    } catch (RuntimeException ex) {
      port = 80;
    }

    try {
      JHTTP webserver = new JHTTP(docroot, port);
      webserver.start();
    } catch (IOException ex) {
      logger.log(Level.SEVERE, "Server could not start", ex);
    }
  }
}
```

The main() method of the JHTTP class sets the document root directory from
args[0]. The port is read from args[1] or 80 is used for a default. Then a new JHTTP
object is constructed and started. JHTTP creates a thread pool to handle requests and
repeatedly accepts incoming connections. You submit one RequestProcessor thread
per incoming connection into the pool.

Each connection is handled by the run() method of the RequestProcessor class shown in Example 9-13. It gets input and output streams from the socket and chains them to a reader and a writer. The reader reads the first line of the client request to determine the version of HTTP that the client supports—you want to send a MIME header only if this is HTTP/1.0 or later—and the requested file. Assuming the method is GET, the file that is requested is converted to a filename on the local filesystem. If the file requested is a directory (i.e., its name ends with a slash), you add the name of an index file. You use the canonical path to make sure that the requested file doesn't come from outside the document root directory. Otherwise, a sneaky client could walk all over the local filesystem by including .. in URLs to walk up the directory hierarchy. This is all you'll need from the client, although a more advanced web server, especially one that logged hits, would read the rest of the MIME header the client sends.

Next, the requested file is opened and its contents are read into a byte array. If the HTTP version is 1.0 or later, you write the appropriate MIME headers on the output stream. To figure out the content type, you call the URLConnection.getFileNameMap().get ContentTypeFor(fileName) method to map file extensions such as *.html* onto MIME types such as text/html. The byte array containing the file's contents is written onto the output stream and the connection is closed. If the file cannot be found or opened, you send the client a 404 response instead. If the client sends a method you don't support, such as POST, you send back a 501 error. If an exception occurs, you log it, close the connection, and continue.

Example 9-13. The runnable class that handles HTTP requests

```
import java.io.*;
import java.net.*;
import java.nio.file.Files;
import java.util.*;
import java.util.logging.*;

public class RequestProcessor implements Runnable {

  private final static Logger logger = Logger.getLogger(
      RequestProcessor.class.getCanonicalName());

  private File rootDirectory;
  private String indexFileName = "index.html";
  private Socket connection;

  public RequestProcessor(File rootDirectory,
      String indexFileName, Socket connection) {

    if (rootDirectory.isFile()) {
      throw new IllegalArgumentException(
          "rootDirectory must be a directory, not a file");
    }
    try {
```

```
      rootDirectory = rootDirectory.getCanonicalFile();
    } catch (IOException ex) {
    }
    this.rootDirectory = rootDirectory;

    if (indexFileName != null) this.indexFileName = indexFileName;
    this.connection = connection;
  }

  @Override
  public void run() {
    // for security checks
    String root = rootDirectory.getPath();
    try {
      OutputStream raw = new BufferedOutputStream(
                          connection.getOutputStream()
                        );
      Writer out = new OutputStreamWriter(raw);
      Reader in = new InputStreamReader(
                    new BufferedInputStream(
                     connection.getInputStream()
                    ),"US-ASCII"
                  );
      StringBuilder requestLine = new StringBuilder();
      while (true) {
        int c = in.read();
        if (c == '\r' || c == '\n') break;
        requestLine.append((char) c);
      }

      String get = requestLine.toString();

      logger.info(connection.getRemoteSocketAddress() + " " + get);

      String[] tokens = get.split("\\s+");
      String method = tokens[0];
      String version = "";
      if (method.equals("GET")) {
        String fileName = tokens[1];
        if (fileName.endsWith("/")) fileName += indexFileName;
        String contentType =
            URLConnection.getFileNameMap().getContentTypeFor(fileName);
        if (tokens.length > 2) {
          version = tokens[2];
        }

        File theFile = new File(rootDirectory,
            fileName.substring(1, fileName.length()));

        if (theFile.canRead()
            // Don't let clients outside the document root
            && theFile.getCanonicalPath().startsWith(root)) {
```

```
      byte[] theData = Files.readAllBytes(theFile.toPath());
      if (version.startsWith("HTTP/")) { // send a MIME header
        sendHeader(out, "HTTP/1.0 200 OK", contentType, theData.length);
      }

      // send the file; it may be an image or other binary data
      // so use the underlying output stream
      // instead of the writer
      raw.write(theData);
      raw.flush();
    } else { // can't find the file
      String body = new StringBuilder("<HTML>\r\n")
          .append("<HEAD><TITLE>File Not Found</TITLE>\r\n")
          .append("</HEAD>\r\n")
          .append("<BODY>")
          .append("<H1>HTTP Error 404: File Not Found</H1>\r\n")
          .append("</BODY></HTML>\r\n").toString();
      if (version.startsWith("HTTP/")) { // send a MIME header
        sendHeader(out, "HTTP/1.0 404 File Not Found",
            "text/html; charset=utf-8", body.length());
      }
      out.write(body);
      out.flush();
    }
  } else { // method does not equal "GET"
    String body = new StringBuilder("<HTML>\r\n")
        .append("<HEAD><TITLE>Not Implemented</TITLE>\r\n")
        .append("</HEAD>\r\n")
        .append("<BODY>")
        .append("<H1>HTTP Error 501: Not Implemented</H1>\r\n")
        .append("</BODY></HTML>\r\n").toString();
    if (version.startsWith("HTTP/")) { // send a MIME header
      sendHeader(out, "HTTP/1.0 501 Not Implemented",
              "text/html; charset=utf-8", body.length());
    }
    out.write(body);
    out.flush();
  }
  } catch (IOException ex) {
    logger.log(Level.WARNING,
        "Error talking to " + connection.getRemoteSocketAddress(), ex);
  } finally {
    try {
      connection.close();
    }
    catch (IOException ex) {}
  }
}

private void sendHeader(Writer out, String responseCode,
    String contentType, int length)
    throws IOException {
```

```
    out.write(responseCode + "\r\n");
    Date now = new Date();
    out.write("Date: " + now + "\r\n");
    out.write("Server: JHTTP 2.0\r\n");
    out.write("Content-length: " + length + "\r\n");
    out.write("Content-type: " + contentType + "\r\n\r\n");
    out.flush();
  }
}
```

This server is functional but still rather austere. Here are a few features that could be added:

- A server administration interface
- Support for the Java Servlet API
- Support for other request methods, such as POST, HEAD, and PUT
- Support for multiple document roots so individual users can have their own sites

Finally, spend a little time thinking about ways to optimize this server. If you really want to use JHTTP to run a high-traffic site, there are a couple of things that can speed this server up. The first thing to do is implement smart caching. Keep track of the requests you've received and store the data from the most frequently requested files in a Map so that they're kept in memory. Use a low-priority thread to update this cache. You can also try using nonblocking I/O and channels instead of threads and streams. We'll explore this possibility in Chapter 11.

CHAPTER 10

Secure Sockets

AT&T has provided the United States National Security Agency with full access to all of its customers' Internet traffic by copying packets to data-mining equipment installed in secret rooms in its switching centers.[1] Britain's GCHQ taps into the fiber-optic cables that carry most of the world's phone calls and Internet traffic.[2] In Sweden, the National Defence Radio Establishment requires fiber-optic cable owners to install fiber mirroring equipment on their premises. And this is just a small sampling of government sponsored eavesdropping we know about.

As an Internet user, you do have defenses against snooping bureaucrats. To make Internet connections more fundamentally secure, sockets can be encrypted. This allows transactions to be confidential, authenticated, and accurate.

However, encryption is a complex subject. Performing it properly requires a detailed understanding not only of the mathematical algorithms used to encrypt data, but also of the protocols used to exchange keys and encrypted data. Even a small mistake can open a large hole in your armor and reveal your communications to an eavesdropper. Consequently, writing encryption software is a task best left to experts. Fortunately, nonexperts with only a layperson's understanding of the underlying protocols and algorithms can secure their communications with software designed by experts. Every time you order something from an online store, chances are the transaction is encrypted and authenticated using protocols and algorithms you need to know next to nothing about. As a programmer who wants to write network client software that talks to online stores, you need to know a little more about the protocols and algorithms involved, but not a lot more, provided you can use a class library written by experts who do understand

---

1. Ryan Singel, "Whistle-Blower Outs NSA Spy Room," *Wired*. April 7, 2006. (*http://bit.ly/whistleblower-wired-article*)

2. Ewen MacAskill, Julian Borger, Nick Hopkins, Nick Davies, and James Ball, "GCHQ taps fibre-optic cables for secret access to world's communications," *The Guardian*. June 21, 2013. (*http://bit.ly/guardian-fibre-optic*)

the details. If you want to write the server software that runs the online store, you need to know a little bit more but still not as much as you would if you were designing all this from scratch without reference to other work.

The Java Secure Sockets Extension (JSSE) can secure network communications using the Secure Sockets Layer (SSL) Version 3 and Transport Layer Security (TLS) protocols and their associated algorithms. SSL is a security protocol that enables web browsers and other TCP clients to talk to HTTP and other TCP servers using various levels of confidentiality and authentication.

Secure Communications

Confidential communication through an open channel such as the public Internet absolutely requires that data be encrypted. Most encryption schemes that lend themselves to computer implementation are based on the notion of a key, a slightly more general kind of password that's not limited to text. The plain-text message is combined with the bits of the key according to a mathematical algorithm to produce the encrypted cipher-text. Using keys with more bits makes messages exponentially more difficult to decrypt by brute-force guessing of the key.

In traditional secret key (or symmetric) encryption, the same key is used to encrypt and decrypt the data. Both the sender and the receiver have to know the single key. Imagine Angela wants to send Gus a secret message. She first sends Gus the key they'll use to exchange the secret. But the key can't be encrypted because Gus doesn't have the key yet, so Angela has to send the key unencrypted. Now suppose Edgar is eavesdropping on the connection between Angela and Gus. He will get the key at the same time that Gus does. From that point forward, he can read anything Angela and Gus say to each other using that key.

In *public key* (or *asymmetric*) encryption, different keys are used to encrypt and decrypt the data. One key, called the public key, encrypts the data. This key can be given to anyone. A different key, called the private key, is used to decrypt the data. This must be kept secret but needs to be possessed by only one of the correspondents. If Angela wants to send a message to Gus, she asks Gus for his public key. Gus sends it to her over an unencrypted connection. Angela uses Gus's public key to encrypt her message and sends it to him. If Edgar is eavesdropping when Gus sends Angela his key, Edgar also gets Gus's public key. However, this doesn't allow Edgar to decrypt the message Angela sends Gus, because decryption requires Gus's private key. The message is safe even if the public key is detected in transit.

Asymmetric encryption can also be used for authentication and message integrity checking. For this use, Angela would encrypt a message with her private key before sending it. When Gus received it, he'd decrypt it with Angela's public key. If the decryption succeeded, Gus would know that the message came from Angela. After all, no one else could have produced a message that would decrypt properly with her public key. Gus would also know that the message wasn't changed en route, either maliciously by Edgar or unintentionally by buggy software or network noise, because any such change would have screwed up the decryption. With a little more effort, Angela can double-encrypt the message, once with her private key, once with Gus's public key, thus getting all three benefits of privacy, authentication, and integrity.

In practice, public-key encryption is much more CPU-intensive and much slower than secret-key encryption. Therefore, instead of encrypting the entire transmission with Gus's public key, Angela encrypts a traditional secret key and sends it to Gus. Gus decrypts it with his private key. Now Angela and Gus both know the secret key, but Edgar doesn't. Therefore, Gus and Angela can now use faster secret-key encryption to communicate privately without Edgar listening in.

Edgar still has one good attack on this protocol, however. (Important: the attack is on the protocol used to send and receive messages, *not* on the encryption algorithms used. This attack does not require Edgar to break Gus and Angela's encryption and is completely independent of key length.) Edgar can not only read Gus's public key when he sends it to Angela, but he can also replace it with his own public key! Then when Angela thinks she's encrypting a message with Gus's public key, she's really using Edgar's. When she sends a message to Gus, Edgar intercepts it, decrypts it using his private key, encrypts it using Gus's public key, and sends it on to Gus. This is called a *man-in-the-middle attack*. Working alone on an insecure channel, Gus and Angela have no easy way to protect against this. The solution used in practice is for both Gus and Angela to store and verify their public keys with a trusted third-party certification authority. Rather than sending each other their public keys, Gus and Angela retrieve each other's public key from the certification authority. This scheme still isn't perfect—Edgar may be able to place himself in between Gus and the certification authority, Angela and the certification authority, and Gus and Angela—but it makes life harder for Edgar.

As this example indicates, the theory and practice of encryption and authentication, both algorithms and protocols, is a challenging field that's fraught with mines and pitfalls to surprise the amateur cryptographer. It is much easier to design a bad encryption algorithm or protocol than a good one. And it's not always obvious which algorithms and protocols are good and which aren't. Fortunately, you don't have to be a cryptography expert to use strong cryptography in Java network programs. JSSE shields you from the low-level details of how algorithms are negotiated, keys are exchanged, correspondents are authenticated, and data is encrypted. JSSE allows you to create sockets and server sockets that transparently handle the negotiations and encryption necessary for secure communication. All you have to do is send your data over the same streams and sockets you're familiar with from previous chapters. The Java Secure Socket Extension is divided into four packages:

`javax.net.ssl`

The abstract classes that define Java's API for secure network communication.

`javax.net`

The abstract socket factory classes used instead of constructors to create secure sockets.

`java.security.cert`

The classes for handling the public-key certificates needed for SSL.

`com.sun.net.ssl`

The concrete classes that implement the encryption algorithms and protocols in Sun's reference implementation of the JSSE. Technically, these are not part of the JSSE standard. Other implementers may replace this package with one of their own; for instance, one that uses native code to speed up the CPU-intensive key generation and encryption process.

Creating Secure Client Sockets

If you don't care very much about the underlying details, using an encrypted SSL socket to talk to an existing secure server is truly straightforward. Rather than constructing a `java.net.Socket` object with a constructor, you get one from a `javax.net.ssl.SSLSocketFactory` using its `createSocket()` method. `SSLSocketFactory` is an abstract class that follows the abstract factory design pattern. You get an instance of it by invoking the static `SSLSocketFactory.getDefault()` method:

```
SocketFactory factory = SSLSocketFactory.getDefault();
Socket socket = factory.createSocket("login.ibiblio.org", 7000);
```

This either returns an instance of `SSLSocketFactory` or throws an `InstantiationEx ception` if no concrete subclass can be found. Once you have a reference to the factory, use one of these five overloaded `createSocket()` methods to build an `SSLSocket`:

```
public abstract Socket createSocket(String host, int port)
    throws IOException, UnknownHostException
public abstract Socket createSocket(InetAddress host, int port)
    throws IOException
public abstract Socket createSocket(String host, int port,
    InetAddress interface, int localPort)
    throws IOException, UnknownHostException
public abstract Socket createSocket(InetAddress host, int port,
    InetAddress interface, int localPort)
    throws IOException, UnknownHostException
public abstract Socket createSocket(Socket proxy, String host, int port,
    boolean autoClose) throws IOException
```

The first two methods create and return a socket that's connected to the specified host and port or throw an `IOException` if they can't connect. The third and fourth methods connect and return a socket that's connected to the specified host and port from the specified local network interface and port. The last `createSocket()` method, however, is a little different. It begins with an existing `Socket` object that's connected to a proxy server. It returns a `Socket` that tunnels through this proxy server to the specified host and port. The `autoClose` argument determines whether the underlying `proxy` socket should be closed when this socket is closed. If `autoClose` is `true`, the underlying socket will be closed; if `false`, it won't be.

The `Socket` that all these methods return will really be a `javax.net.ssl.SSLSocket`, a subclass of `java.net.Socket`. However, you don't need to know that. Once the secure socket has been created, you use it just like any other socket, through its `getInput Stream()`, `getOutputStream()`, and other methods. For example, suppose a server that accepts orders is listening on port 7000 of *login.ibiblio.org*. Each order is sent as an ASCII string using a single TCP connection. The server accepts the order and closes the connection. (I'm leaving out a *lot* of details that would be necessary in a real-world system, such as the server sending a response code telling the client whether the order was accepted.) The orders that clients send look like this:

```
Name: John Smith
Product-ID: 67X-89
Address: 1280 Deniston Blvd, NY NY 10003
Card number: 4000-1234-5678-9017
Expires: 08/05
```

There's enough information in this message to let someone snooping packets use John Smith's credit card number for nefarious purposes. Consequently, before sending this order, you should encrypt it. The simplest way to do that without burdening either the server or the client with a lot of complicated, error-prone encryption code is to use a secure socket. The following code sends the order over a secure socket:

```
SSLSocketFactory factory
    = (SSLSocketFactory) SSLSocketFactory.getDefault();
Socket socket = factory.createSocket("login.ibiblio.org", 7000);

Writer out = new OutputStreamWriter(socket.getOutputStream(),
    "US-ASCII");
out.write("Name: John Smith\r\n");
out.write("Product-ID: 67X-89\r\n");
out.write("Address: 1280 Deniston Blvd, NY NY 10003\r\n");
out.write("Card number: 4000-1234-5678-9017\r\n");
out.write("Expires: 08/05\r\n");
out.flush();
```

Only the first three statements in the `try` block are noticeably different from what you'd do with an insecure socket. The rest of the code just uses the normal methods of the `Socket`, `OutputStream`, and `Writer` classes.

Reading input is no harder. Example 10-1 is a simple program that connects to a secure HTTP server, sends a simple GET request, and prints out the response.

Example 10-1. HTTPSClient

```
import java.io.*;
import javax.net.ssl.*;

public class HTTPSClient {

  public static void main(String[] args) {

    if (args.length == 0) {
      System.out.println("Usage: java HTTPSClient2 host");
      return;
    }

    int port = 443; // default https port
    String host = args[0];

    SSLSocketFactory factory
        = (SSLSocketFactory) SSLSocketFactory.getDefault();
    SSLSocket socket = null;
    try {
      socket = (SSLSocket) factory.createSocket(host, port);

      // enable all the suites
      String[] supported = socket.getSupportedCipherSuites();
      socket.setEnabledCipherSuites(supported);

      Writer out = new OutputStreamWriter(socket.getOutputStream(), "UTF-8");
      // https requires the full URL in the GET line
      out.write("GET http://" + host + "/ HTTP/1.1\r\n");
      out.write("Host: " + host + "\r\n");
      out.write("\r\n");
      out.flush();

      // read response
      BufferedReader in = new BufferedReader(
          new InputStreamReader(socket.getInputStream()));

      // read the header
      String s;
      while (!(s = in.readLine()).equals("")) {
        System.out.println(s);
      }
      System.out.println();

      // read the length
      String contentLength = in.readLine();
      int length = Integer.MAX_VALUE;
      try {
```

```
      length = Integer.parseInt(contentLength.trim(), 16);
    } catch (NumberFormatException ex) {
      // This server doesn't send the content-length
      // in the first line of the response body
    }
    System.out.println(contentLength);

    int c;
    int i = 0;
    while ((c = in.read()) != -1 && i++ < length) {
      System.out.write(c);
    }

    System.out.println();
  } catch (IOException ex) {
    System.err.println(ex);
  } finally {
    try {
      if (socket != null) socket.close();
    } catch (IOException e) {}
  }
  }
}
```

Here are the first few lines of output from this program when you connect to the U.S.
Postal Service's website:

```
% java HTTPSClient www.usps.com
HTTP/1.1 200 OK
Server: IBM_HTTP_Server
Cache-Control: max-age=0
Expires: Sun, 31 Mar 2013 17:29:33 GMT
Content-Type: text/html
Date: Sun, 31 Mar 2013 18:00:14 GMT
Transfer-Encoding:  chunked
Connection: keep-alive
Connection: Transfer-Encoding

00004000

<!DOCTYPE html PUBLIC "-//W3C//DTD HTML 4.01 Transitional//EN"
"http://www.w3.org/TR/html4/loose.dtd">
```

When I tested this program for the previous edition, it initially refused to connect to *www.usps.com* because it couldn't verify the iden-
tity of the remote server. The problem was that the root certificates
shipped with the version of the JDK I was using (1.4.2_02-b3) had
expired. Upgrading to the latest minor version (1.4.2_03-b2) fixed the
problem. If you see any exception messages like "No trusted certificate found," try upgrading to the latest minor version of the JDK.

When you run this program, you may notice that it's slower to respond than you expect. There's a noticeable amount of both CPU and network overhead involved in generating and exchanging the public keys. Even over a fast network, it can take a few seconds to establish a connection. Consequently, you may not want to serve all your content over HTTPS, only the content that really needs to be private and isn't latency sensitive.

Choosing the Cipher Suites

Different implementations of the JSSE support different combinations of authentication and encryption algorithms. For instance, the implementation that Oracle bundles with Java 7 only supports 128-bit AES encryption, whereas IAIK's iSaSiLk (*http://bit.ly/JCE-unlimited*) supports 256-bit AES encryption.

 The stock JSSE bundled with the JDK actually does have code for stronger 256-bit encryption, but it's disabled unless you install the JCE Unlimited Strength Jurisdiction Policy Files (*http://www.oracle.com/technetwork/java/javase/downloads/index.html*). I don't even want to begin trying to explain the legal briar patch that makes this necessary.

The getSupportedCipherSuites() method in SSLSocketFactory tells you which combination of algorithms is available on a given socket:

```
public abstract String[] getSupportedCipherSuites()
```

However, not all cipher suites that are understood are necessarily allowed on the connection. Some may be too weak and consequently disabled. The getEnabledCipher Suites() method of SSLSocketFactory tells you which suites this socket is willing to use:

```
public abstract String[] getEnabledCipherSuites()
```

The actual suite used is negotiated between the client and server at connection time. It's possible that the client and the server won't agree on any suite. It's also possible that although a suite is enabled on both client and server, one or the other or both won't have the keys and certificates needed to use the suite. In either case, the createSocket() method will throw an SSLException, a subclass of IOException. You can change the suites the client attempts to use via the setEnabledCipherSuites() method:

```
public abstract void setEnabledCipherSuites(String[] suites)
```

The argument to this method should be a list of the suites you want to use. Each name must be one of the suites listed by getSupportedCipherSuites(). Otherwise, an Ille galArgumentException will be thrown. Oracle's JDK 1.7 supports these cipher suites:

- TLS_ECDHE_ECDSA_WITH_AES_128_CBC_SHA256

- TLS_ECDHE_RSA_WITH_AES_128_CBC_SHA256
- TLS_RSA_WITH_AES_128_CBC_SHA256
- TLS_ECDH_ECDSA_WITH_AES_128_CBC_SHA256
- TLS_ECDH_RSA_WITH_AES_128_CBC_SHA256
- TLS_DHE_RSA_WITH_AES_128_CBC_SHA256
- TLS_DHE_DSS_WITH_AES_128_CBC_SHA256
- TLS_ECDHE_ECDSA_WITH_AES_128_CBC_SHA
- TLS_ECDHE_RSA_WITH_AES_128_CBC_SHA
- TLS_RSA_WITH_AES_128_CBC_SHA
- TLS_ECDH_ECDSA_WITH_AES_128_CBC_SHA
- TLS_ECDH_RSA_WITH_AES_128_CBC_SHA
- TLS_DHE_RSA_WITH_AES_128_CBC_SHA
- TLS_DHE_DSS_WITH_AES_128_CBC_SHA
- TLS_ECDHE_ECDSA_WITH_RC4_128_SHA
- TLS_ECDHE_RSA_WITH_RC4_128_SHA
- SSL_RSA_WITH_RC4_128_SHA
- TLS_ECDH_ECDSA_WITH_RC4_128_SHA
- TLS_ECDH_RSA_WITH_RC4_128_SHA
- TLS_ECDHE_ECDSA_WITH_3DES_EDE_CBC_SHA
- TLS_ECDHE_RSA_WITH_3DES_EDE_CBC_SHA
- SSL_RSA_WITH_3DES_EDE_CBC_SHA
- TLS_ECDH_ECDSA_WITH_3DES_EDE_CBC_SHA
- TLS_ECDH_RSA_WITH_3DES_EDE_CBC_SHA
- SSL_DHE_RSA_WITH_3DES_EDE_CBC_SHA
- SSL_DHE_DSS_WITH_3DES_EDE_CBC_SHA
- SSL_RSA_WITH_RC4_128_MD5
- TLS_EMPTY_RENEGOTIATION_INFO_SCSV
- TLS_DH_anon_WITH_AES_128_CBC_SHA256
- TLS_ECDH_anon_WITH_AES_128_CBC_SHA
- TLS_DH_anon_WITH_AES_128_CBC_SHA
- TLS_ECDH_anon_WITH_RC4_128_SHA
- SSL_DH_anon_WITH_RC4_128_MD5

- TLS_ECDH_anon_WITH_3DES_EDE_CBC_SHA
- SSL_DH_anon_WITH_3DES_EDE_CBC_SHA
- TLS_RSA_WITH_NULL_SHA256
- TLS_ECDHE_ECDSA_WITH_NULL_SHA
- TLS_ECDHE_RSA_WITH_NULL_SHA
- SSL_RSA_WITH_NULL_SHA
- TLS_ECDH_ECDSA_WITH_NULL_SHA
- TLS_ECDH_RSA_WITH_NULL_SHA
- TLS_ECDH_anon_WITH_NULL_SHA
- SSL_RSA_WITH_NULL_MD5
- SSL_RSA_WITH_DES_CBC_SHA
- SSL_DHE_RSA_WITH_DES_CBC_SHA
- SSL_DHE_DSS_WITH_DES_CBC_SHA
- SSL_DH_anon_WITH_DES_CBC_SHA
- SSL_RSA_EXPORT_WITH_RC4_40_MD5
- SSL_DH_anon_EXPORT_WITH_RC4_40_MD5
- SSL_RSA_EXPORT_WITH_DES40_CBC_SHA
- SSL_DHE_RSA_EXPORT_WITH_DES40_CBC_SHA
- SSL_DHE_DSS_EXPORT_WITH_DES40_CBC_SHA
- SSL_DH_anon_EXPORT_WITH_DES40_CBC_SHA
- TLS_KRB5_WITH_RC4_128_SHA
- TLS_KRB5_WITH_RC4_128_MD5
- TLS_KRB5_WITH_3DES_EDE_CBC_SHA
- TLS_KRB5_WITH_3DES_EDE_CBC_MD5
- TLS_KRB5_WITH_DES_CBC_SHA
- TLS_KRB5_WITH_DES_CBC_MD5
- TLS_KRB5_EXPORT_WITH_RC4_40_SHA
- TLS_KRB5_EXPORT_WITH_RC4_40_MD5
- TLS_KRB5_EXPORT_WITH_DES_CBC_40_SHA
- TLS_KRB5_EXPORT_WITH_DES_CBC_40_MD5

Each name has an algorithm divided into four parts: protocol, key exchange algorithm, encryption algorithm, and checksum. For example, the name SSL_DH_anon_EX-

PORT_WITH_DES40_CBC_SHA means Secure Sockets Layer Version 3; Diffie-Hellman method for key agreement; no authentication; Data Encryption Standard encryption with 40-bit keys; Cipher Block Chaining, and the Secure Hash Algorithm checksum.

By default, the JDK 1.7 implementation enables all the encrypted authenticated suites (the first 28 members of this list). If you want nonauthenticated transactions or authenticated but unencrypted transactions, you must enable those suites explicitly with the setEnabledCipherSuites() method. You should probably avoid any of these suites that contain NULL, ANON, or EXPORT in their names unless you want the NSA to read your messages.

TLS_ECDHE_ECDSA_WITH_AES_128_CBC_SHA256 is believed to be reasonably secure against all known attacks. TLS_ECDHE_ECD-SA_WITH_AES_256_CBC_SHA256 is even better if you've enabled it. In general, any suite that begins with TLS_ECDHE and ends with SHA256 or SHA384 is the strongest possible encryption widely available today. Most others are subject to attacks of varying levels of severity.

Besides key lengths, there's an important difference between DES/AES and RC4-based ciphers. DES and AES are block ciphers (i.e., they encrypt a certain number of bits at a time). DES always encrypts 64 bits. If 64 bits aren't available, the encoder has to pad the input with extra bits. AES can encrypt blocks of 128, 192, or 256 bits, but still has to pad the input if it doesn't come out to an even multiple of the block size. This isn't a problem for file transfer applications such as secure HTTP and FTP, where more or less all the data is available at once. However, it's problematic for user-centered protocols such as chat and Telnet. RC4 is a stream cipher that can encrypt one byte at a time and is more appropriate for protocols that may need to send a single byte at a time.

For example, let's suppose that Edgar has some fairly powerful parallel computers at his disposal and can quickly break any encryption that's 64 bits or less and that Gus and Angela know this. Furthermore, they suspect that Edgar can blackmail one of their ISPs or the phone company into letting him tap the line, so they want to avoid anonymous connections that are vulnerable to man-in-the-middle attacks. To be safe, Gus and Angela decide to use only the strongest suite available, which happens to be TLS_ECDHE_ECDSA_WITH_AES_128_CBC_SHA256. This code fragment limits their connection to that one suite:

```
String[] strongSuites = {"TLS_ECDHE_ECDSA_WITH_AES_128_CBC_SHA256"};
socket.setEnabledCipherSuites(strongSuites);
```

If the other side of the connection doesn't support this encryption protocol, the socket will throw an exception when they try to read from or write to it, thus ensuring that no confidential information is accidentally transmitted over a weak channel.

Event Handlers

Network communications are slow compared to the speed of most computers. Authenticated network communications are even slower. The necessary key generation and setup for a secure connection can easily take several seconds. Consequently, you may want to deal with the connection asynchronously. JSSE uses the standard Java event model to notify programs when the handshaking between client and server is complete. The pattern is a familiar one. In order to get notifications of handshake-complete events, simply implement the HandshakeCompletedListener interface:

```
public interface HandshakeCompletedListener
    extends java.util.EventListener
```

This interface declares the handshakeCompleted() method:

```
public void handshakeCompleted(HandshakeCompletedEvent event)
```

This method receives as an argument a HandshakeCompletedEvent:

```
public class HandshakeCompletedEvent extends java.util.EventObject
```

The HandshakeCompletedEvent class provides four methods for getting information about the event:

```
public SSLSession getSession()
public String getCipherSuite()
public X509Certificate[] getPeerCertificateChain()
    throws SSLPeerUnverifiedException
public SSLSocket getSocket()
```

Particular HandshakeCompletedListener objects register their interest in handshake-completed events from a particular SSLSocket via its addHandshakeCompletedListener() and removeHandshakeCompletedListener() methods:

```
public abstract void addHandshakeCompletedListener(
    HandshakeCompletedListener listener)
public abstract void removeHandshakeCompletedListener(
    HandshakeCompletedListener listener) throws IllegalArgumentException
```

Session Management

SSL is commonly used on web servers, and for good reason. Web connections tend to be transitory; every page requires a separate socket. For instance, checking out of Amazon.com on its secure server requires seven separate page loads, more if you have to edit an address or choose gift wrapping. Imagine if every one of those pages took an extra 10 seconds or more to negotiate a secure connection. Because of the high overhead involved in handshaking between two hosts for secure communications, SSL allows *sessions* to be established that extend over multiple sockets. Different sockets within the same session use the same set of public and private keys. If the secure connection to

Amazon.com takes seven sockets, all seven will be established within the same session and use the same keys. Only the first socket within that session will have to endure the overhead of key generation and exchange.

As a programmer using JSSE, you don't need to do anything extra to take advantage of sessions. If you open multiple secure sockets to one host on one port within a reasonably short period of time, JSSE will reuse the session's keys automatically. However, in high-security applications, you may want to disallow session-sharing between sockets or force reauthentication of a session. In the JSSE, sessions are represented by instances of the SSLSession interface; you can use the methods of this interface to check the times the session was created and last accessed, invalidate the session, and get various information about the session:

```
public byte[] getId()
public SSLSessionContext getSessionContext()
public long getCreationTime()
public long getLastAccessedTime()
public void invalidate()
public void putValue(String name, Object value)
public Object getValue(String name)
public void removeValue(String name)
public String[] getValueNames()
public X509Certificate[] getPeerCertificateChain()
  throws SSLPeerUnverifiedException
public String getCipherSuite()
public String getPeerHost()
```

The getSession() method of SSLSocket returns the Session this socket belongs to:

```
public abstract SSLSession getSession()
```

However, sessions are a trade-off between performance and security. It is more secure to renegotiate the key for each and every transaction. If you've got really spectacular hardware and are trying to protect your systems from an equally determined, rich, motivated, and competent adversary, you may want to avoid sessions. To prevent a socket from creating a session that passes false to setEnableSessionCreation(), use:

```
public abstract void setEnableSessionCreation(boolean allowSessions)
```

The getEnableSessionCreation() method returns true if multisocket sessions are allowed, false if they're not:

```
public abstract boolean getEnableSessionCreation()
```

On rare occasions, you may even want to reauthenticate a connection (i.e., throw away all the certificates and keys that have previously been agreed to and start over with a new session). The startHandshake() method does this:

```
public abstract void startHandshake() throws IOException
```

Client Mode

It's a rule of thumb that in most secure communications, the server is required to authenticate itself using the appropriate certificate. However, the client is not. That is, when I buy a book from Amazon using its secure server, it has to prove to my browser's satisfaction that it is indeed Amazon and not Joe Random Hacker. However, I do not have to prove to Amazon that I am Elliotte Rusty Harold. For the most part, this is as it should be, because purchasing and installing the trusted certificates necessary for authentication is a fairly user-hostile experience that readers shouldn't have to go through just to buy the latest Nutshell Handbook. However, this asymmetry can lead to credit card fraud. To avoid problems like this, sockets can be required to authenticate themselves. This strategy wouldn't work for a service open to the general public. However, it might be reasonable in certain internal, high-security applications.

The setUseClientMode() method determines whether the socket needs to use authentication in its first handshake. The name of the method is a little misleading. It can be used for both client- and server-side sockets. However, when true is passed in, it means the socket is in client mode (whether it's on the client side or not) and will not offer to authenticate itself. When false is passed, it will try to authenticate itself:

```
public abstract void setUseClientMode(boolean mode)
    throws IllegalArgumentException
```

This property can be set only once for any given socket. Attempting to set it a second time throws an IllegalArgumentException.

The getUseClientMode() method simply tells you whether this socket will use authentication in its first handshake:

```
public abstract boolean getUseClientMode()
```

A secure socket on the server side (i.e., one returned by the accept() method of an SSLServerSocket) uses the setNeedClientAuth() method to require that all clients connecting to it authenticate themselves (or not):

```
public abstract void setNeedClientAuth(boolean needsAuthentication)
    throws IllegalArgumentException
```

This method throws an IllegalArgumentException if the socket is not on the server side.

The getNeedClientAuth() method returns true if the socket requires authentication from the client side, false otherwise:

```
public abstract boolean getNeedClientAuth()
```

Creating Secure Server Sockets

Secure client sockets are only half of the equation. The other half is SSL-enabled server sockets. These are instances of the `javax.net.SSLServerSocket` class:

```
public abstract class SSLServerSocket extends ServerSocket
```

Like `SSLSocket`, all the constructors in this class are protected and instances are created by an abstract factory class, `javax.net.SSLServerSocketFactory`:

```
public abstract class SSLServerSocketFactory
    extends ServerSocketFactory
```

Also like `SSLSocketFactory`, an instance of `SSLServerSocketFactory` is returned by a static `SSLServerSocketFactory.getDefault()` method:

```
public static ServerSocketFactory getDefault()
```

And like `SSLSocketFactory`, `SSLServerSocketFactory` has three overloaded `create ServerSocket()` methods that return instances of `SSLServerSocket` and are easily understood by analogy with the `java.net.ServerSocket` constructors:

```
public abstract ServerSocket createServerSocket(int port)
    throws IOException
public abstract ServerSocket createServerSocket(int port,
    int queueLength) throws IOException
public abstract ServerSocket createServerSocket(int port,
    int queueLength, InetAddress interface) throws IOException
```

If that were all there was to creating secure server sockets, they would be quite straightforward and simple to use. Unfortunately, that's not all there is to it. The factory that `SSLServerSocketFactory.getDefault()` returns generally only supports server authentication. It does not support encryption. To get encryption as well, server-side secure sockets require more initialization and setup. Exactly how this setup is performed is implementation dependent. In Sun's reference implementation, a `com.sun.net.ssl.SSLContext` object is responsible for creating fully configured and initialized secure server sockets. The details vary from JSSE implementation to JSSE implementation, but to create a secure server socket in the reference implementation, you have to:

1. Generate public keys and certificates using *keytool*.

2. Pay money to have your certificates authenticated by a trusted third party such as Comodo.

3. Create an `SSLContext` for the algorithm you'll use.

4. Create a `TrustManagerFactory` for the source of certificate material you'll be using.

5. Create a `KeyManagerFactory` for the type of key material you'll be using.

6. Create a `KeyStore` object for the key and certificate database. (Oracle's default is JKS.)

7. Fill the `KeyStore` object with keys and certificates; for instance, by loading them from the filesystem using the passphrase they're encrypted with.

8. Initialize the `KeyManagerFactory` with the `KeyStore` and its passphrase.

9. Initialize the context with the necessary key managers from the `KeyManagerFactory`, trust managers from the `TrustManagerFactory`, and a source of randomness. (The last two can be null if you're willing to accept the defaults.)

Example 10-2 demonstrates this procedure with a complete `SecureOrderTaker` for accepting orders and printing them on `System.out`. Of course, in a real application, you'd do something more interesting with the orders.

Example 10-2. SecureOrderTaker

```java
import java.io.*;
import java.net.*;
import java.security.*;
import java.security.cert.CertificateException;
import java.util.Arrays;

import javax.net.ssl.*;

public class SecureOrderTaker {

  public final static int PORT = 7000;
  public final static String algorithm = "SSL";

  public static void main(String[] args) {
    try {
      SSLContext context = SSLContext.getInstance(algorithm);

      // The reference implementation only supports X.509 keys
      KeyManagerFactory kmf = KeyManagerFactory.getInstance("SunX509");

      // Oracle's default kind of key store
      KeyStore ks = KeyStore.getInstance("JKS");

      // For security, every key store is encrypted with a
      // passphrase that must be provided before we can load
      // it from disk. The passphrase is stored as a char[] array
      // so it can be wiped from memory quickly rather than
      // waiting for a garbage collector.
      char[] password = System.console().readPassword();
      ks.load(new FileInputStream("jnp4e.keys"), password);
      kmf.init(ks, password);
      context.init(kmf.getKeyManagers(), null, null);

      // wipe the password
```

```java
    Arrays.fill(password, '0');

    SSLServerSocketFactory factory
        = context.getServerSocketFactory();

    SSLServerSocket server
        = (SSLServerSocket) factory.createServerSocket(PORT);

    // add anonymous (non-authenticated) cipher suites
    String[] supported = server.getSupportedCipherSuites();
    String[] anonCipherSuitesSupported = new String[supported.length];
    int numAnonCipherSuitesSupported = 0;
    for (int i = 0; i < supported.length; i++) {
      if (supported[i].indexOf("_anon_") > 0) {
        anonCipherSuitesSupported[numAnonCipherSuitesSupported++] =
                                                 supported[i];
      }
    }

    String[] oldEnabled = server.getEnabledCipherSuites();
    String[] newEnabled = new String[oldEnabled.length
        + numAnonCipherSuitesSupported];
    System.arraycopy(oldEnabled, 0, newEnabled, 0, oldEnabled.length);
    System.arraycopy(anonCipherSuitesSupported, 0, newEnabled,
        oldEnabled.length, numAnonCipherSuitesSupported);

    server.setEnabledCipherSuites(newEnabled);

    // Now all the set up is complete and we can focus
    // on the actual communication.
    while (true) {
      // This socket will be secure,
      // but there's no indication of that in the code!
      try (Socket theConnection = server.accept()) {
        InputStream in = theConnection.getInputStream();
        int c;
        while ((c = in.read()) != -1) {
          System.out.write(c);
        }
      } catch (IOException ex) {
        ex.printStackTrace();
      }
    }
  } catch (IOException | KeyManagementException
      | KeyStoreException | NoSuchAlgorithmException
      | CertificateException | UnrecoverableKeyException ex) {
    ex.printStackTrace();
  }
  }
}
```

This example loads the necessary keys and certificates from a file named *jnp4e.keys* in the current working directory protected with the password "2andnotafnord". What this example doesn't show you is how that file was created. It was built with the *keytool* program that's bundled with the JDK like this:

```
$ keytool -genkey -alias ourstore -keystore jnp4e.keys
Enter keystore password:
Re-enter new password:
What is your first and last name?
  [Unknown]:  Elliotte Harold
What is the name of your organizational unit?
  [Unknown]:  Me, Myself, and I
What is the name of your organization?
  [Unknown]:  Cafe au Lait
What is the name of your City or Locality?
  [Unknown]:  Brooklyn
What is the name of your State or Province?
  [Unknown]:  New York
What is the two-letter country code for this unit?
  [Unknown]:  NY
Is <CN=Elliotte Harold, OU="Me, Myself, and I", O=Cafe au Lait, L=Brooklyn,
ST=New York, C=NY> correct?
  [no]:  y

Enter key password for <ourstore>
        (RETURN if same as keystore password):
```

When this is finished, you'll have a file named *jnp4e.keys*, which contains your public keys. However, no one will believe that these are your public keys unless you have them certified by a trusted third party such as GeoTrust or GoDaddy. If you just want to explore the JSSE before deciding whether to go through the hassle and expense of purchasing a verified certificate, Oracle includes a verified keystore file called *testkeys*, protected with the password "passphrase," that has some JSSE samples. However, this isn't good enough for real work.

Another approach is to use cipher suites that don't require authentication. There are several of these in the JDK, including:

- SSL_DH_anon_EXPORT_WITH_DES40_CBC_SHA
- SSL_DH_anon_EXPORT_WITH_RC4_40_MD5
- SSL_DH_anon_WITH_3DES_EDE_CBC_SHA
- SSL_DH_anon_WITH_DES_CBC_SHA
- SSL_DH_anon_WITH_RC4_128_MD5
- TLS_DH_anon_WITH_AES_128_CBC_SHA
- TLS_DH_anon_WITH_AES_128_CBC_SHA256
- TLS_ECDH_anon_WITH_3DES_EDE_CBC_SHA

- TLS_ECDH_anon_WITH_AES_128_CBC_SHA
- TLS_ECDH_anon_WITH_NULL_SHA
- TLS_ECDH_anon_WITH_RC4_128_SHA

These are not enabled by default because they're vulnerable to a man-in-the-middle attack, but at least they allow you to write simple programs without paying money.

Configuring SSLServerSockets

Once you've successfully created and initialized an SSLServerSocket, there are a lot of applications you can write using nothing more than the methods inherited from java.net.ServerSocket. However, there are times when you need to adjust its behavior a little. Like SSLSocket, SSLServerSocket provides methods to choose cipher suites, manage sessions, and establish whether clients are required to authenticate themselves. Most of these methods are similar to the methods of the same name in SSLSocket. The difference is that they work on the server side and set the defaults for sockets accepted by an SSLServerSocket. In some cases, once an SSLSocket has been accepted, you can still use the methods of SSLSocket to configure that one socket rather than all sockets accepted by this SSLServerSocket.

Choosing the Cipher Suites

The SSLServerSocket class has the same three methods for determining which cipher suites are supported and enabled as SSLSocket does:

```
public abstract String[] getSupportedCipherSuites()
public abstract String[] getEnabledCipherSuites()
public abstract void     setEnabledCipherSuites(String[] suites)
```

These use the same suite names as the similarly named methods in SSLSocket. The difference is that these methods apply to all sockets accepted by the SSLServerSocket rather than to just one SSLSocket. For example, the following code fragment has the effect of enabling anonymous, unauthenticated connections on the SSLServerSocket server. It relies on the names of these suites containing the string *anon*. This is true for Oracle's reference implementations, though there's no guarantee that other implementers will follow this convention:

```
String[] supported = server.getSupportedCipherSuites();
String[] anonCipherSuitesSupported = new String[supported.length];
int numAnonCipherSuitesSupported = 0;
for (int i = 0; i < supported.length; i++) {
  if (supported[i].indexOf("_anon_") > 0) {
    anonCipherSuitesSupported[numAnonCipherSuitesSupported++]
        = supported[i];
  }
```

```
    }

String[] oldEnabled = server.getEnabledCipherSuites();
String[] newEnabled = new String[oldEnabled.length
    + numAnonCipherSuitesSupported];
System.arraycopy(oldEnabled, 0, newEnabled, 0, oldEnabled.length);
System.arraycopy(anonCipherSuitesSupported, 0, newEnabled,
    oldEnabled.length, numAnonCipherSuitesSupported);

server.setEnabledCipherSuites(newEnabled);
```

This fragment retrieves the list of both supported and enabled cipher suites using `get SupportedCipherSuites()` and `getEnabledCipherSuites()`. It looks at the name of every supported suite to see whether it contains the substring "anon." If the suite name does contain this substring, the suite is added to a list of anonymous cipher suites. Once the list of anonymous cipher suites is built, it's combined in a new array with the previous list of enabled cipher suites. The new array is then passed to `setEnabledCipher Suites()` so that both the previously enabled and the anonymous cipher suites can now be used.

Session Management

Both client and server must agree to establish a session. The server side uses the `setE nableSessionCreation()` method to specify whether this will be allowed and the `ge tEnableSessionCreation()` method to determine whether this is currently allowed:

```
public abstract void setEnableSessionCreation(boolean allowSessions)
public abstract boolean getEnableSessionCreation()
```

Session creation is enabled by default. If the server disallows session creation, then a client that wants a session will still be able to connect. It just won't get a session and will have to handshake again for every socket. Similarly, if the client refuses sessions but the server allows them, they'll still be able to talk to each other but without sessions.

Client Mode

The `SSLServerSocket` class has two methods for determining and specifying whether client sockets are required to authenticate themselves to the server. By passing `true` to the `setNeedClientAuth()` method, you specify that only connections in which the client is able to authenticate itself will be accepted. By passing `false`, you specify that authentication is not required of clients. The default is `false`. If, for some reason, you need to know what the current state of this property is, the `getNeedClientAuth()` method will tell you:

```
public abstract void setNeedClientAuth(boolean flag)
public abstract boolean getNeedClientAuth()
```

The setUseClientMode() method allows a program to indicate that even though it has created an SSLServerSocket, it is and should be treated as a client in the communication with respect to authentication and other negotiations. For example, in an FTP session, the client program opens a server socket to receive data from the server, but that doesn't make it less of a client. The getUseClientMode() method returns true if the SSLServerSocket is in client mode, false otherwise:

```
public abstract void setUseClientMode(boolean flag)
public abstract boolean getUseClientMode()
```

CHAPTER 11

Nonblocking I/O

Compared to CPUs and memory or even disks, networks are slow. A high-end modern PC is capable of moving data between the CPU and main memory at speeds of around six gigabytes per second. It can move data to and from disk at the much slower but still respectable speed of about 150 megabytes per second.[1] By contrast, the theoretical maximum on today's fastest local area networks tops out at about 150 megabytes per second, though many LANs only support speeds ten to a hundred times slower than that. And the speed across the public Internet is generally at least an order of magnitude smaller than what you see across a LAN. My faster than average FIOS connection promises 6 megabytes per second down and 3 megabytes per second up, about 5% of what my LAN can support. CPUs, disks, and networks are all speeding up over time. These numbers are all substantially higher than I reported in the third edition of this book 10 years ago. Nonetheless, CPUs and disks are likely to remain several orders of magnitude faster than networks for the foreseeable future. The last thing you want to do in these circumstances is make the blazingly fast CPU wait for the (relatively) molasses-slow network.

The traditional Java solution for allowing the CPU to race ahead of the network is a combination of buffering and multithreading. Multiple threads can generate data for several different connections at once and store that data in buffers until the network is actually ready to send it; this approach works well for fairly simple servers and clients without extreme performance needs. However, the overhead of spawning multiple threads and switching between them can be nontrivial. For instance, each thread re-

---

1. These are rough, theoretical maximum numbers. Nonetheless, it's worth pointing out that I'm using megabyte to mean 1,024*1,024 bytes and gigabyte to mean 1,024 megabytes. Manufacturers often round the size of a gigabyte down to 1,000 megabytes and the size of a megabyte down to 1,000,000 bytes to make their numbers sound more impressive. Furthermore, networking speeds are often referred to in kilo/mega/giga *bits* per second rather than bytes per second. Here I'm reporting all numbers in bytes so I can compare hard drive, memory, and network bandwidths.

quires about one extra megabyte of RAM. On a large server that may be processing thousands of requests a second, you may not want to assign a thread to each connection. It's faster if one thread can take responsibility for multiple connections, pick one that's ready to receive data, fill it with as much data as that connection can manage as quickly as possible, then move on to the next ready connection.

To work well, this approach needs to be supported by the underlying operating system. Fortunately, pretty much every modern operating system you're likely to be using as a high-volume server supports such nonblocking I/O. However, it might not be well supported on some client systems of interest, such as tablets, cell phones, and the like. Indeed, the `java.nio` package that provides this support is not part of any current or planned Java ME profiles, though it is found in Android. However, the whole new I/O API is designed for and only really matters on servers, which is why I haven't done more than allude to it until we began talking about servers. Client and even peer-to-peer systems rarely need to process so many simultaneous connections that multithreaded, stream-based I/O becomes a noticeable bottleneck.

NIO Too Little, Too Late?

There was a time when properly architected nonblocking I/O dramatically outperformed multithreaded, multiprocess designs. That time was the 1990s. Unfortunately, Java didn't get nonblocking I/O until Java 1.4 in 2002. By the time Java 5 was released in 2004 and certainly by the time Java 6 was released in 2006, the continuing improvements to native threading in operating systems had eliminated almost all context switching and uncontested synchronization overhead. Furthermore, server memory had grown to the point where 10,000 simultaneous threads could easily fit in memory on commodity hardware; and multicore/multi-CPU systems that required multiple threads for maximum utilization were becoming common. On today's Java 7 and Java 8 64-bit VMs that's even more true. In 2013, it's really hard to justify the added complexity of a NIO-based architecture compared to a much simpler thread-per-request or thread-per-connection design.

But isn't NIO faster? Not necessarily. In actual measurements in Java 6 on Linux (*http:// bit.ly/Java-measurements*), multi-threaded classic I/O designs outperform NIO by 30% or so.

Are there any situations in which asynchronous I/O does beat classic I/O? Maybe. The one situation I can still imagine is a server that needs to support a colossal number of long-lived, simultaneous connections, say 10,000+, but where each client doesn't send very much data very frequently. For instance, imagine a central server in the home office collecting transactions from each cash register in a nationwide chain of convenience stores. This scenario is tailor-made for NIO, and can probably be implemented much more efficiently with asynchronous or nonblocking on-demand processing in just a few threads.

But always remember the two golden rules of optimization:

1. Don't do it.
2. (For experts only) OK, do it but only after you have clear and unambiguous measurements proving you have a problem, and that will clearly show whether your changes have fixed the problem.

An Example Client

Although the new I/O APIs aren't specifically designed for clients, they do work for them. I'm going to begin with a client program using the new I/O APIs because it's a little simpler. In particular, many clients can be implemented with one connection at a time, so I can introduce channels and buffers before talking about selectors and non-blocking I/O.

A simple client for the character generator protocol defined in RFC 864 will demonstrate the basics. This protocol is designed for testing clients. The server listens for connections on port 19. When a client connects, the server sends a continuous sequence of characters until the client disconnects. Any input from the client is ignored. The RFC does not specify which character sequence to send, but recommends that the server use a recognizable pattern. One common pattern is rotating, 72-character carriage return/line-feed delimited lines of the 95 ASCII printing characters, like this:

```
 !"#$%&'()*+,-./0123456789:;<=>?@ABCDEFGHIJKLMNOPQRSTUVWXYZ[\]^_`abcdefgh
"#$%&'()*+,-./0123456789:;<=>?@ABCDEFGHIJKLMNOPQRSTUVWXYZ[\]^_`abcdefghi
#$%&'()*+,-./0123456789:;<=>?@ABCDEFGHIJKLMNOPQRSTUVWXYZ[\]^_`abcdefghij
$%&'()*+,-./0123456789:;<=>?@ABCDEFGHIJKLMNOPQRSTUVWXYZ[\]^_`abcdefghijk
%&'()*+,-./0123456789:;<=>?@ABCDEFGHIJKLMNOPQRSTUVWXYZ[\]^_`abcdefghijkl
&'()*+,-./0123456789:;<=>?@ABCDEFGHIJKLMNOPQRSTUVWXYZ[\]^_`abcdefghijklm
```

I picked this protocol for the examples in this chapter because both the protocol for transmitting the data and the algorithm to generate the data are simple enough that they won't obscure the I/O. However, chargen can transmit a lot of data over a relatively few connections and quickly saturate a network. It's thus a good candidate for the new I/O APIs.

Chargen is not commonly used these days, and may be blocked by local firewalls even if it's turned on. It's vulnerable to a "ping-pong" denial-of-service attack, in which spoofed Internet packets cause two hosts to spew an unlimited amount of data at each other. Furthermore, because it's almost infinitely asymmetric—the server sends an unlimited amount of data in response to the smallest of client requests—it's very easy for even a few dozen compromised hosts, much less a large botnet, to convince a chargen server to saturate its local bandwidth.

When implementing a client that takes advantage of the new I/O APIs, begin by invoking the static factory method `SocketChannel.open()` to create a new `java.nio.chan nels.SocketChannel` object. The argument to this method is a `java.net.SocketAd dress` object indicating the host and port to connect to. For example, this fragment connects the channel to *rama.poly.edu* on port 19:

```
SocketAddress rama = new InetSocketAddress("rama.poly.edu", 19);
SocketChannel client = SocketChannel.open(rama);
```

The channel is opened in blocking mode, so the next line of code won't execute until the connection is established. If the connection can't be established, an `IOException` is thrown.

If this were a traditional client, you'd now ask for the socket's input and/or output streams. However, it's not. With a channel you write directly to the channel itself. Rather than writing byte arrays, you write `ByteBuffer` objects. You've got a pretty good idea that the lines of text are 74 ASCII characters long (72 printable characters followed by a carriage return/linefeed pair) so you'll create a `ByteBuffer` that has a 74-byte capacity using the static `allocate()` method:

```
ByteBuffer buffer = ByteBuffer.allocate(74);
```

Pass this `ByteBuffer` object to the channel's `read()` method. The channel fills this buffer with the data it reads from the socket. It returns the number of bytes it successfully read and stored in the buffer:

```
int bytesRead = client.read(buffer);
```

By default, this will read at least one byte or return –1 to indicate the end of the data, exactly as an `InputStream` does. It will often read more bytes if more bytes are available to be read. Shortly you'll see how to put this client in nonblocking mode where it will return 0 immediately if no bytes are available, but for the moment this code blocks just like an `InputStream`. As you could probably guess, this method can also throw an `IOException` if anything goes wrong with the read.

Assuming there is some data in the buffer—that is, n > 0—this data can be copied to `System.out`. There are ways to extract a byte array from a `ByteBuffer` that can then be written on a traditional `OutputStream` such as `System.out`. However, it's more informative to stick with a pure, channel-based solution. Such a solution requires wrapping the `OutputStream` `System.out` in a channel using the `Channels` utility class, specifically, its `newChannel()` method:

```
WritableByteChannel output = Channels.newChannel(System.out);
```

You can then write the data that was read onto this output channel connected to `System.out`. However, before you do that, you have to *flip* the buffer so that the output channel starts from the beginning of the data that was read rather than the end:

```
buffer.flip();
output.write(buffer);
```

You don't have to tell the output channel how many bytes to write. Buffers keep track of how many bytes they contain. However, in general, the output channel is not guaranteed to write all the bytes in the buffer. In this specific case, though, it's a blocking channel and it will either do so or throw an `IOException`.

You shouldn't create a new buffer for each read and write. That would kill the performance. Instead, reuse the existing buffer. You'll need to clear the buffer before reading into it again:

```
buffer.clear();
```

This is a little different than flipping. Flipping leaves the data in the buffer intact, but prepares it for writing rather than reading. Clearing resets the buffer to a pristine state. (Actually that's a tad simplistic. The old data is still present; it's not overwritten, but it will be overwritten with new data read from the source as soon as possible.)

Example 11-1 puts this together into a complete client. Because chargen is by design an endless protocol, you'll need to kill the program using Ctrl-C.

Example 11-1. A channel-based chargen client

```java
import java.nio.*;
import java.nio.channels.*;
import java.net.*;
import java.io.IOException;

public class ChargenClient {

  public static int DEFAULT_PORT = 19;

  public static void main(String[] args) {

    if (args.length == 0) {
      System.out.println("Usage: java ChargenClient host [port]");
      return;
    }
```

```
  int port;
  try {
    port = Integer.parseInt(args[1]);
  } catch (RuntimeException ex) {
    port = DEFAULT_PORT;
  }

  try {
    SocketAddress address = new InetSocketAddress(args[0], port);
    SocketChannel client = SocketChannel.open(address);

    ByteBuffer buffer = ByteBuffer.allocate(74);
    WritableByteChannel out = Channels.newChannel(System.out);

    while (client.read(buffer) != -1) {
      buffer.flip();
      out.write(buffer);
      buffer.clear();
    }
  } catch (IOException ex) {
    ex.printStackTrace();
  }
}
}
```

Here's the output from a sample run:

```
$ java ChargenClient rama.poly.edu
 !"#$%&'()*+,-./0123456789:;<=>?@ABCDEFGHIJKLMNOPQRSTUVWXYZ[\]^_`abcdefg
!"#$%&'()*+,-./0123456789:;<=>?@ABCDEFGHIJKLMNOPQRSTUVWXYZ[\]^_`abcdefgh
"#$%&'()*+,-./0123456789:;<=>?@ABCDEFGHIJKLMNOPQRSTUVWXYZ[\]^_`abcdefghi
#$%&'()*+,-./0123456789:;<=>?@ABCDEFGHIJKLMNOPQRSTUVWXYZ[\]^_`abcdefghij
$%&'()*+,-./0123456789:;<=>?@ABCDEFGHIJKLMNOPQRSTUVWXYZ[\]^_`abcdefghijk
%&'()*+,-./0123456789:;<=>?@ABCDEFGHIJKLMNOPQRSTUVWXYZ[\]^_`abcdefghijkl
&'()*+,-./0123456789:;<=>?@ABCDEFGHIJKLMNOPQRSTUVWXYZ[\]^_`abcdefghijklm
...
```

So far, this is just an alternate vision of a program that could have easily been written using streams. The really new feature comes if you want the client to do something besides copying all input to output. You can run this connection in either blocking or nonblocking mode in which read() returns immediately even if no data is available. This allows the program to do something else before it attempts to read. It doesn't have to wait for a slow network connection. To change the blocking mode, pass true (block) or false (don't block) to the configureBlocking() method. Let's make this connection nonblocking:

```
client.configureBlocking(false);
```

In nonblocking mode, read() may return 0 because it doesn't read anything. Therefore, the loop needs to be a little different:

```
while (true) {
  // Put whatever code here you want to run every pass through the loop
  // whether anything is read or not
  int n = client.read(buffer);
  if (n > 0) {
    buffer.flip();
    out.write(buffer);
    buffer.clear();
  } else if (n == -1) {
    // This shouldn't happen unless the server is misbehaving.
    break;
  }
}
```

There's not a lot of call for this in a one-connection client like this one. Perhaps you could check to see if the user has done something to cancel input, for example. However, as you'll see in the next section, when a program is processing multiple connections, this enables code to run very quickly on the fast connections and more slowly on the slow ones. Each connection gets to run at its own speed without being held up behind the slowest driver on the one-lane road.

An Example Server

Clients are well and good, but channels and buffers are really intended for server systems that need to process many simultaneous connections efficiently. Handling servers requires a third new piece in addition to the buffers and channels used for the client. Specifically, you need selectors that allow the server to find all the connections that are ready to receive output or send input.

To demonstrate the basics, this example implements a simple server for the character generator protocol. When implementing a server that takes advantage of the new I/O APIs, begin by calling the static factory method ServerSocketChannel.open() method to create a new ServerSocketChannel object:

```
ServerSocketChannel serverChannel = ServerSocketChannel.open();
```

Initially, this channel is not actually listening on any port. To bind it to a port, retrieve its ServerSocket peer object with the socket() method and then use the bind() method on that peer. For example, this code fragment binds the channel to a server socket on port 19:

```
ServerSocket ss = serverChannel.socket();
ss.bind(new InetSocketAddress(19));
```

In Java 7 and later, you can bind directly without retrieving the underlying java.net.ServerSocket:

```
serverChannel.bind(new InetSocketAddress(19));
```

As with regular server sockets, binding to port 19 requires you to be root on Unix (including Linux and Mac OS X). Nonroot users can only bind to ports 1024 and higher.

The server socket channel is now listening for incoming connections on port 19. To accept one, call the `accept()` method, which returns a `SocketChannel` object:

```
SocketChannel clientChannel = serverChannel.accept();
```

On the server side, you'll definitely want to make the client channel nonblocking to allow the server to process multiple simultaneous connections:

```
clientChannel.configureBlocking(false);
```

You may also want to make the `ServerSocketChannel` nonblocking. By default, this `accept()` method blocks until there's an incoming connection, like the `accept()` method of `ServerSocket`. To change this, simply call `configureBlocking(false)` before calling `accept()`:

```
serverChannel.configureBlocking(false);
```

A nonblocking `accept()` returns null almost immediately if there are no incoming connections. Be sure to check for that or you'll get a nasty `NullPointerException` when trying to use the socket.

There are now two open channels: a server channel and a client channel. Both need to be processed. Both can run indefinitely. Furthermore, processing the server channel will create more open client channels. In the traditional approach, you assign each connection a thread, and the number of threads climbs rapidly as clients connect. Instead, in the new I/O API, you create a `Selector` that enables the program to iterate over all the connections that are ready to be processed. To construct a new `Selector`, just call the static `Selector.open()` factory method:

```
Selector selector = Selector.open();
```

Next, you need to register each channel with the selector that monitors it using the channel's `register()` method. When registering, specify the operation you're interested in using a named constant from the `SelectionKey` class. For the server socket, the only operation of interest is OP_ACCEPT; that is, is the server socket channel ready to accept a new connection?

```
serverChannel.register(selector, SelectionKey.OP_ACCEPT);
```

For the client channels, you want to know something a little different—specifically, whether they're ready to have data written onto them. For this, use the OP_WRITE key:

```
SelectionKey key = clientChannel.register(selector, SelectionKey.OP_WRITE);
```

Both `register()` methods return a `SelectionKey` object. However, you're only going to need to use that key for the client channels, because there can be more than one of them. Each `SelectionKey` has an attachment of arbitrary `Object` type. This is normally used to hold an object that indicates the current state of the connection. In this case, you can store the buffer that the channel writes onto the network. Once the buffer is fully drained, you'll refill it. Fill an array with the data that will be copied into each buffer. Rather than writing to the end of the buffer, and then rewinding to the beginning of the buffer and writing again, it's easier just to start with two sequential copies of the data so every line is available as a contiguous sequence in the array:

```
byte[] rotation = new byte[95*2];
for (byte i = ' '; i <= '~'; i++) {
  rotation[i - ' '] = i;
  rotation[i + 95 - ' '] = i;
}
```

Because this array will only be read from after it's been initialized, you can reuse it for multiple channels. However, each channel will get its own buffer filled with the contents of this array. You'll stuff the buffer with the first 72 bytes of the rotation array, then add a carriage return/linefeed pair to break the line. Then you'll flip the buffer so it's ready for draining, and attach it to the channel's key:

```
ByteBuffer buffer = ByteBuffer.allocate(74);
buffer.put(rotation, 0, 72);
buffer.put((byte) '\r');
buffer.put((byte) '\n');
buffer.flip();
key2.attach(buffer);
```

To check whether anything is ready to be acted on, call the selector's select() method. For a long-running server, this normally goes in an infinite loop:

```
while (true) {
  selector.select ();
  // process selected keys...
}
```

Assuming the selector does find a ready channel, its selectedKeys() method returns a java.util.Set containing one SelectionKey object for each ready channel. Otherwise, it returns an empty set. In either case, you can loop through this with a java.util.Iterator:

```
Set<SelectionKey> readyKeys = selector.selectedKeys();
Iterator iterator = readyKeys.iterator();
while (iterator.hasNext()) {
  SelectionKey key = iterator.next();
  // Remove key from set so we don't process it twice
  iterator.remove();
  // operate on the channel...
}
```

Removing the key from the set tells the Selector that you've dealt with it, and the Selector doesn't need to keep giving it back every time you call select(). The Selec tor will add the channel back into the ready set when `select()` is called again if the channel becomes ready again. It's really important to remove the key from the ready set here, though.

If the ready channel is the server channel, the program accepts a new socket channel and adds it to the selector. If the ready channel is a socket channel, the program writes as much of the buffer as it can onto the channel. If no channels are ready, the selector waits for one. One thread, the main thread, processes multiple simultaneous connections.

In this case, it's easy to tell whether a client or a server channel has been selected because the server channel will only be ready for accepting and the client channels will only be ready for writing. Both of these are I/O operations, and both can throw `IOExceptions` for a variety of reasons, so you'll want to wrap this all in a `try` block:

```
try {
  if (key.isAcceptable()) {
    ServerSocketChannel server = (ServerSocketChannel) key.channel();
    SocketChannel connection = server.accept();
    connection.configureBlocking(false);
    connection.register(selector, SelectionKey.OP_WRITE);
    // set up the buffer for the client...
  } else if (key.isWritable()) {
    SocketChannel client = (SocketChannel) key.channel();
    // write data to client...
  }
}
```

Writing the data onto the channel is easy. Retrieve the key's attachment, cast it to `Byte Buffer`, and call `hasRemaining()` to check whether there's any unwritten data left in the buffer. If there is, write it. Otherwise, refill the buffer with the next line of data from the `rotation` array and write that.

```
ByteBuffer buffer = (ByteBuffer) key.attachment();
if (!buffer.hasRemaining()) {
  // Refill the buffer with the next line
  // Figure out where the last line started
  buffer.rewind();
  int first = buffer.get();
  // Increment to the next character
  buffer.rewind();
  int position = first - ' ' + 1;
  buffer.put(rotation, position, 72);
  buffer.put((byte) '\r');
  buffer.put((byte) '\n');
  buffer.flip();
}
client.write(buffer);
```

The algorithm that figures out where to grab the next line of data relies on the characters being stored in the rotation array in ASCII order. buffer.get() reads the first byte of data from the buffer. From this number you subtract the space character (32) because that's the first character in the rotation array. This tells you which index in the array the buffer currently starts at. You add 1 to find the start of the next line and refill the buffer.

In the chargen protocol, the server never closes the connection. It waits for the client to break the socket. When this happens, an exception will be thrown. Cancel the key and close the corresponding channel:

```
catch (IOException ex) {
  key.cancel();
  try {
    key.channel().close();
  } catch (IOException cex) {
    // ignore
  }
}
```

Example 11-2 puts this all together in a complete chargen server that processes multiple connections efficiently in a single thread.

Example 11-2. A nonblocking chargen server

```
import java.nio.*;
import java.nio.channels.*;
import java.net.*;
import java.util.*;
import java.io.IOException;

public class ChargenServer {

  public static int DEFAULT_PORT = 19;

  public static void main(String[] args) {

    int port;
    try {
      port = Integer.parseInt(args[0]);
    } catch (RuntimeException ex) {
      port = DEFAULT_PORT;
    }
    System.out.println("Listening for connections on port " + port);

    byte[] rotation = new byte[95*2];
    for (byte i = ' '; i <= '~'; i++) {
      rotation[i -' '] = i;
      rotation[i + 95 - ' '] = i;
    }
```

```
ServerSocketChannel serverChannel;
Selector selector;
try {
  serverChannel = ServerSocketChannel.open();
  ServerSocket ss = serverChannel.socket();
  InetSocketAddress address = new InetSocketAddress(port);
  ss.bind(address);
  serverChannel.configureBlocking(false);
  selector = Selector.open();
  serverChannel.register(selector, SelectionKey.OP_ACCEPT);
} catch (IOException ex) {
  ex.printStackTrace();
  return;
}

while (true) {
  try {
    selector.select();
  } catch (IOException ex) {
    ex.printStackTrace();
    break;
  }

  Set<SelectionKey> readyKeys = selector.selectedKeys();
  Iterator<SelectionKey> iterator = readyKeys.iterator();
  while (iterator.hasNext()) {

    SelectionKey key = iterator.next();
    iterator.remove();
    try {
      if (key.isAcceptable()) {
        ServerSocketChannel server = (ServerSocketChannel) key.channel();
        SocketChannel client = server.accept();
        System.out.println("Accepted connection from " + client);
        client.configureBlocking(false);
        SelectionKey key2 = client.register(selector, SelectionKey.
                                                        OP_WRITE);
        ByteBuffer buffer = ByteBuffer.allocate(74);
        buffer.put(rotation, 0, 72);
        buffer.put((byte) '\r');
        buffer.put((byte) '\n');
        buffer.flip();
        key2.attach(buffer);
      } else if (key.isWritable()) {
        SocketChannel client = (SocketChannel) key.channel();
        ByteBuffer buffer = (ByteBuffer) key.attachment();
        if (!buffer.hasRemaining()) {
          // Refill the buffer with the next line
          buffer.rewind();
          // Get the old first character
          int first = buffer.get();
          // Get ready to change the data in the buffer
```

```
          buffer.rewind();
          // Find the new first characters position in rotation
          int position = first - ' ' + 1;
          // copy the data from rotation into the buffer
          buffer.put(rotation, position, 72);
          // Store a line break at the end of the buffer
          buffer.put((byte) '\r');
          buffer.put((byte) '\n');
          // Prepare the buffer for writing
          buffer.flip();
        }
        client.write(buffer);
      }
    } catch (IOException ex) {
      key.cancel();
      try {
        key.channel().close();
      }
      catch (IOException cex) {}
    }
  }
 }
 }
}
```

This example only uses one thread. There are situations where you might still want to use multiple threads, especially if different operations have different priorities. For instance, you might want to accept new connections in one high-priority thread and service existing connections in a lower-priority thread. However, you're no longer required to have a 1:1 ratio between threads and connections, which improves the scalability of servers written in Java.

It may also be important to use multiple threads for maximum performance. Multiple threads allow the server to take advantage of multiple CPUs. Even with a single CPU, it's often a good idea to separate the accepting thread from the processing threads. The thread pools discussed in Chapter 3 are still relevant even with the new I/O model. The thread that accepts the connections can add the connections it's accepted into the queue for processing by the threads in the pool. This is still faster than doing the same thing without selectors because `select()` ensures you're never wasting any time on connections that aren't ready to receive data. On the other hand, the synchronization issues here are tricky, so don't attempt this until profiling proves there is a bottleneck.

Buffers

In Chapter 2, I recommended that you always buffer your streams. Almost nothing has a greater impact on the performance of network programs than a big enough buffer. In the new I/O model, you're no longer given the choice. All I/O is buffered. Indeed, the buffers are fundamental parts of the API. Instead of writing data onto output streams and reading data from input streams, you read and write data from buffers. Buffers may appear to be just an array of bytes as in buffered streams. However, native implementations can connect them directly to hardware or memory or use other, very efficient implementations.

From a programming perspective, the key difference between streams and channels is that streams are byte-based whereas channels are block-based. A stream is designed to provide one byte after the other, in order. Arrays of bytes can be passed for performance. However, the basic notion is to pass data one byte at a time. By contrast, a channel passes blocks of data around in buffers. Before bytes can be read from or written to a channel, the bytes have to be stored in a buffer, and the data is written or read one buffer at a time.

The second key difference between streams and channels/buffers is that channels and buffers tend to support both reading and writing on the same object. This isn't always true. For instance, a channel that points to a file on a CD-ROM can be read but not written. A channel connected to a socket that has shutdown input could be written but not read. If you try to write to a read-only channel or read from a write-only channel, an UnsupportedOperationException will be thrown. However, more often than not network programs can read from and write to the same channels.

Without worrying too much about the underlying details (which can vary hugely from one implementation to the next, mostly as a result of being tuned very closely to the host operating system and hardware), you can think of a buffer as a fixed-size list of elements of a particular, normally primitive data type, like an array. However, it's not necessarily an array behind the scenes. Sometimes it is; sometimes it isn't. There are specific subclasses of Buffer for all of Java's primitive data types except boolean: Byte Buffer, CharBuffer, ShortBuffer, IntBuffer, LongBuffer, FloatBuffer, and Double Buffer. The methods in each subclass have appropriately typed return values and argument lists. For example, the DoubleBuffer class has methods to put and get doubles. The IntBuffer class has methods to put and get ints. The common Buffer superclass only provides methods that don't need to know the type of the data the buffer contains. (The lack of primitive-aware generics really hurts here.) Network programs use Byte Buffer almost exclusively, although occasionally one program might use a view that overlays the ByteBuffer with one of the other types.

Besides its list of data, each buffer tracks four key pieces of information. All buffers have the same methods to set and get these values, regardless of the buffer's type:

position

The next location in the buffer that will be read from or written to. This starts counting at 0 and has a maximum value equal to the size of the buffer. It can be set or gotten with these two methods:

```
public final int     position()
public final Buffer position(int newPosition)
```

capacity

The maximum number of elements the buffer can hold. This is set when the buffer is created and cannot be changed thereafter. It can be read with this method:

```
public final int capacity()
```

limit

The end of accessible data in the buffer. You cannot write or read at or past this point without changing the limit, even if the buffer has more capacity. It is set and gotten with these two methods:

```
public final int     limit()
public final Buffer limit(int newLimit)
```

mark

A client-specified index in the buffer. It is set at the current position by invoking the mark() method. The current position is set to the marked position by invoking reset():

```
public final Buffer mark()
public final Buffer reset()
```

If the position is set below an existing mark, the mark is discarded.

Unlike reading from an InputStream, reading from a buffer does not actually change the buffer's data in any way. It's possible to set the position either forward or backward so you can start reading from a particular place in the buffer. Similarly, a program can adjust the limit to control the end of the data that will be read. Only the capacity is fixed.

The common Buffer superclass also provides a few other methods that operate by reference to these common properties.

The clear() method "empties" the buffer by setting the position to zero and the limit to the capacity. This allows the buffer to be completely refilled:

```
public final Buffer clear()
```

However, the clear() method does not remove the old data from the buffer. It's still present and could be read using absolute get methods or changing the limit and position again.

The rewind() method sets the position to zero, but does not change the limit:

```
public final Buffer rewind()
```

This allows the buffer to be reread.

The flip() method sets the limit to the current position and the position to zero:

```
public final Buffer flip()
```

It is called when you want to drain a buffer you've just filled.

Finally, there are two methods that return information about the buffer but don't change it. The remaining() method returns the number of elements in the buffer between the current position and the limit. The hasRemaining() method returns true if the number of remaining elements is greater than zero:

```
public final int     remaining()
public final boolean hasRemaining()
```

Creating Buffers

The buffer class hierarchy is based on inheritance but not really on polymorphism, at least not at the top level. You normally need to know whether you're dealing with an IntBuffer or a ByteBuffer or a CharBuffer or something else. You write code to one of these subclasses, not to the common Buffer superclass.

Each typed buffer class has several factory methods that create implementation-specific subclasses of that type in various ways. Empty buffers are normally created by *allocate* methods. Buffers that are prefilled with data are created by *wrap* methods. The allocate methods are often useful for input, and the wrap methods are normally used for output.

Allocation

The basic allocate() method simply returns a new, empty buffer with a specified fixed capacity. For example, these lines create byte and int buffers, each with a size of 100:

```
ByteBuffer buffer1 = ByteBuffer.allocate(100);
IntBuffer  buffer2 = IntBuffer.allocate(100);
```

The cursor is positioned at the beginning of the buffer (i.e., the position is 0). A buffer created by allocate() will be implemented on top of a Java array, which can be accessed by the array() and arrayOffset() methods. For example, you could read a large chunk of data into a buffer using a channel and then retrieve the array from the buffer to pass to other methods:

```
byte[] data1 = buffer1.array();
int[]  data2 = buffer2.array();
```

The array() method does expose the buffer's private data, so use it with caution. Changes to the backing array are reflected in the buffer and vice versa. The normal pattern here is to fill the buffer with data, retrieve its backing array, and then operate on the array. This isn't a problem as long as you don't write to the buffer after you've started working with the array.

Direct allocation

The `ByteBuffer` class (but not the other buffer classes) has an additional `allocateDir ect()` method that may not create a backing array for the buffer. The VM may implement a directly allocated `ByteBuffer` using direct memory access to the buffer on an Ethernet card, kernel memory, or something else. It's not required, but it's allowed, and this can improve performance for I/O operations. From an API perspective, `allocate Direct()` is used exactly like `allocate()`:

```
ByteBuffer buffer = ByteBuffer.allocateDirect(100);
```

Invoking `array()` and `arrayOffset()` on a direct buffer will throw an `UnsupportedO perationException`. Direct buffers may be faster on some virtual machines, especially if the buffer is large (roughly a megabyte or more). However, direct buffers are more expensive to create than indirect buffers, so they should only be allocated when the buffer is expected to be around for a while. The details are highly VM dependent. As is generally true for most performance advice, you probably shouldn't even consider using direct buffers until measurements prove performance is an issue.

Wrapping

If you already have an array of data that you want to output, you'll normally wrap a buffer around it, rather than allocating a new buffer and copying its components into the buffer one at a time. For example:

```
byte[] data = "Some data".getBytes("UTF-8");
ByteBuffer buffer1 = ByteBuffer.wrap(data);
char[] text = "Some text".toCharArray();
CharBuffer buffer2 = CharBuffer.wrap(text);
```

Here, the buffer contains a reference to the array, which serves as its backing array. Buffers created by wrapping are never direct. Again, changes to the array are reflected in the buffer and vice versa, so don't wrap the array until you're finished with it.

Filling and Draining

Buffers are designed for sequential access. Recall that each buffer has a curent position identified by the `position()` method that is somewhere between zero and the number of elements in the buffer, inclusive. The buffer's position is incremented by one when an element is read from or written to the buffer. For example, suppose you allocate a `CharBuffer` with capacity 12, and fill it by putting five characters into it:

```
CharBuffer buffer = CharBuffer.allocate(12);
buffer.put('H');
buffer.put('e');
buffer.put('l');
buffer.put('l');
buffer.put('o');
```

The position of the buffer is now 5. This is called *filling* the buffer.

You can only fill the buffer up to its capacity. If you tried to fill it past its initially set capacity, the put() method would throw a BufferOverflowException.

If you now tried to get() from the buffer, you'd get the null character (\u0000) that Java initializes char buffers with that's found at position 5. Before you can read the data you wrote in out again, you need to flip the buffer:

```
buffer.flip();
```

This sets the limit to the position (5 in this example) and resets the position to 0, the start of the buffer. Now you can drain it into a new string:

```
String result = "";
while (buffer.hasRemaining()) {
  result += buffer.get();
}
```

Each call to get() moves the position forward one. When the position reaches the limit, hasRemaining() returns false. This is called *draining* the buffer.

Buffer classes also have *absolute* methods that fill and drain at specific positions within the buffer without updating the position. For example, ByteBuffer has these two:

```
public abstract byte       get(int index)
public abstract ByteBuffer put(int index, byte b)
```

These both throw an IndexOutOfBoundsException if you try to access a position at or past the limit of the buffer. For example, using absolute methods, you can put the same text into a buffer like this:

```
CharBuffer buffer = CharBuffer.allocate(12);
buffer.put(0, 'H');
buffer.put(1, 'e');
buffer.put(2, 'l');
buffer.put(3, 'l');
buffer.put(4, 'o');
```

However, you no longer need to flip before reading it out, because the absolute methods don't change the position. Furthermore, order no longer matters. This produces the same end result:

```
CharBuffer buffer = CharBuffer.allocate(12);
buffer.put(1, 'e');
buffer.put(4, 'o');
buffer.put(0, 'H');
buffer.put(3, 'l');
buffer.put(2, 'l');
```

Bulk Methods

Even with buffers, it's often faster to work with blocks of data rather than filling and draining one element at a time. The different buffer classes have bulk methods that fill and drain an array of their element type.

For example, ByteBuffer has put() and get() methods that fill and drain a ByteBuffer from a preexisting byte array or subarray:

```
public ByteBuffer get(byte[] dst, int offset, int length)
public ByteBuffer get(byte[] dst)
public ByteBuffer put(byte[] array, int offset, int length)
public ByteBuffer put(byte[] array)
```

These put methods insert the data from the specified array or subarray, beginning at the current position. The get methods read the data into the argument array or subarray beginning at the current position. Both put and get increment the position by the length of the array or subarray. The put methods throw a BufferOverflowException if the buffer does not have sufficient space for the array or subarray. The get methods throw a BufferUnderflowException if the buffer does not have enough data remaining to fill the array or subarrray. These are runtime exceptions.

Data Conversion

All data in Java ultimately resolves to bytes. Any primitive data type—int, double, float, etc.—can be written as bytes. Any sequence of bytes of the right length can be interpreted as a primitive datum. For example, any sequence of four bytes corresponds to an int or a float (actually both, depending on how you want to read it). A sequence of eight bytes corresponds to a long or a double. The ByteBuffer class (and only the ByteBuffer class) provides relative and absolute put methods that fill a buffer with the bytes corresponding to an argument of primitive type (except boolean) and relative and absolute get methods that read the appropriate number of bytes to form a new primitive datum:

```
public abstract char       getChar()
public abstract ByteBuffer putChar(char value)
public abstract char       getChar(int index)
public abstract ByteBuffer putChar(int index, char value)
public abstract short      getShort()
public abstract ByteBuffer putShort(short value)
public abstract short      getShort(int index)
public abstract ByteBuffer putShort(int index, short value)
public abstract int        getInt()
public abstract ByteBuffer putInt(int value)
public abstract int        getInt(int index)
public abstract ByteBuffer putInt(int index, int value)
public abstract long       getLong()
public abstract ByteBuffer putLong(long value)
```

```
public abstract long       getLong(int index)
public abstract ByteBuffer putLong(int index, long value)
public abstract float      getFloat()
public abstract ByteBuffer putFloat(float value)
public abstract float      getFloat(int index)
public abstract ByteBuffer putFloat(int index, float value)
public abstract double     getDouble()
public abstract ByteBuffer putDouble(double value)
public abstract double     getDouble(int index)
public abstract ByteBuffer putDouble(int index, double value)
```

In the world of new I/O, these methods do the job performed by `DataOutputStream` and `DataInputStream` in traditional I/O. These methods do have an additional ability not present in `DataOutputStream` and `DataInputStream`. You can choose whether to interpret the byte sequences as big-endian or little-endian `ints`, `floats`, `doubles`, and so on. By default, all values are read and written as big endian (i.e., most significant byte first. The two `order()` methods inspect and set the buffer's byte order using the named constants in the `ByteOrder` class. For example, you can change the buffer to little-endian interpretation like so:

```
if (buffer.order().equals(ByteOrder.BIG_ENDIAN)) {
  buffer.order(ByteOrder.LITTLE_ENDIAN);
}
```

Suppose instead of a chargen protocol, you want to test the network by generating binary data. This test can highlight problems that aren't apparent in the ASCII chargen protocol, such as an old gateway configured to strip off the high-order bit of every byte, throw away every 2^{30} byte, or put into diagnostic mode by an unexpected sequence of control characters. These are not theoretical problems. I've seen variations on all of these at one time or another.

You could test the network for such problems by sending out every possible `int`. This would, after almost 4.3 billion iterations, test every possible four-byte sequence. On the receiving end, you could easily test whether the data received is expected with a simple numeric comparison. If any problems are found, it is easy to tell exactly where they occurred. In other words, this protocol (call it `Intgen`) behaves like this:

1. The client connects to the server.
2. The server immediately begins sending four-byte, big-endian integers, starting with 0 and incrementing by 1 each time. The server will eventually wrap around into the negative numbers.
3. The server runs indefinitely. The client closes the connection when it's had enough.

The server would store the current int in a four-byte-long direct `ByteBuffer`. One buffer would be attached to each channel. When the channel becomes available for writing, the buffer is drained onto the channel. Then the buffer is rewound and the content of the buffer is read with `getInt()`. The program then clears the buffer, increments the previous value by one, and fills the buffer with the new value using `putInt()`. Finally, it flips the buffer so it will be ready to be drained the next time the channel becomes writable. Example 11-3 demonstrates.

Example 11-3. Intgen server

```java
import java.nio.*;
import java.nio.channels.*;
import java.net.*;
import java.util.*;
import java.io.IOException;

public class IntgenServer {

  public static int DEFAULT_PORT = 1919;

  public static void main(String[] args) {

    int port;
    try {
      port = Integer.parseInt(args[0]);
    } catch (RuntimeException ex) {
      port = DEFAULT_PORT;
    }
    System.out.println("Listening for connections on port " + port);

    ServerSocketChannel serverChannel;
    Selector selector;
    try {
      serverChannel = ServerSocketChannel.open();
      ServerSocket ss = serverChannel.socket();
      InetSocketAddress address = new InetSocketAddress(port);
      ss.bind(address);
      serverChannel.configureBlocking(false);
      selector = Selector.open();
      serverChannel.register(selector, SelectionKey.OP_ACCEPT);
    } catch (IOException ex) {
      ex.printStackTrace();
      return;
    }

    while (true) {
      try {
        selector.select();
      } catch (IOException ex) {
        ex.printStackTrace();
        break;
      }

      Set<SelectionKey> readyKeys = selector.selectedKeys();
      Iterator<SelectionKey> iterator = readyKeys.iterator();
```

```
    while (iterator.hasNext()) {
      SelectionKey key = iterator.next();
      iterator.remove();
      try {
        if (key.isAcceptable()) {
          ServerSocketChannel server = (ServerSocketChannel) key.channel();
          SocketChannel client = server.accept();
          System.out.println("Accepted connection from " + client);
          client.configureBlocking(false);
          SelectionKey key2 = client.register(selector, SelectionKey.
                                                             OP_WRITE);

          ByteBuffer output = ByteBuffer.allocate(4);
          output.putInt(0);
          output.flip();
          key2.attach(output);
        } else if (key.isWritable()) {
          SocketChannel client = (SocketChannel) key.channel();
          ByteBuffer output = (ByteBuffer) key.attachment();
          if (! output.hasRemaining()) {
            output.rewind();
            int value = output.getInt();
            output.clear();
            output.putInt(value + 1);
            output.flip();
          }
          client.write(output);
        }
      } catch (IOException ex) {
        key.cancel();
        try {
          key.channel().close();
        }
        catch (IOException cex) {}
      }
    }
  }
 }
}
```

View Buffers

If you know the ByteBuffer read from a SocketChannel contains nothing but elements
of one particular primitive data type, it may be worthwhile to create a *view buffer*. This
is a new Buffer object of appropriate type (e.g., DoubleBuffer, IntBuffer, etc.), that
draws its data from an underlying ByteBuffer beginning with the current position.
Changes to the view buffer are reflected in the underlying buffer and vice versa. However, each buffer has its own independent limit, capacity, mark, and position. View
buffers are created with one of these six methods in ByteBuffer:

```
public abstract ShortBuffer  asShortBuffer()
public abstract CharBuffer   asCharBuffer()
```

```
public abstract IntBuffer    asIntBuffer()
public abstract LongBuffer   asLongBuffer()
public abstract FloatBuffer  asFloatBuffer()
public abstract DoubleBuffer asDoubleBuffer()
```

For example, consider a client for the Intgen protocol. This protocol is only going to read ints, so it may be helpful to use an IntBuffer rather than a ByteBuffer. Example 11-4 demonstrates. For variety, this client is synchronous and blocking, but it still uses channels and buffers.

Example 11-4. Intgen client

```
import java.nio.*;
import java.nio.channels.*;
import java.net.*;
import java.io.IOException;

public class IntgenClient {

  public static int DEFAULT_PORT = 1919;

  public static void main(String[] args) {

    if (args.length == 0) {
      System.out.println("Usage: java IntgenClient host [port]");
      return;
    }

    int port;
    try {
      port = Integer.parseInt(args[1]);
    } catch (RuntimeException ex) {
      port = DEFAULT_PORT;
    }

    try {
      SocketAddress address = new InetSocketAddress(args[0], port);
      SocketChannel client  = SocketChannel.open(address);
      ByteBuffer    buffer  = ByteBuffer.allocate(4);
      IntBuffer     view    = buffer.asIntBuffer();

      for (int expected = 0; ; expected++) {
        client.read(buffer);
        int actual = view.get();
        buffer.clear();
        view.rewind();

        if (actual != expected) {
          System.err.println("Expected " + expected + "; was " + actual);
          break;
        }
        System.out.println(actual);
```

```
      }
    } catch(IOException ex) {
      ex.printStackTrace();
    }
  }
}
```

There's one thing to note here. Although you can fill and drain the buffers using the methods of the IntBuffer class exclusively, data must be read from and written to the channel using the original ByteBuffer of which the IntBuffer is a view. The SocketCh annel class only has methods to read and write ByteBuffers. It cannot read or write any other kind of buffer. This also means you need to clear the ByteBuffer on each pass through the loop or the buffer will fill up and the program will halt. The positions and limits of the two buffers are independent and must be considered separately. Finally, if you're working in nonblocking mode, be careful that all the data in the underlying ByteBuffer is drained before reading or writing from the overlaying view buffer. Nonblocking mode provides no guarantee that the buffer will still be aligned on an int, double, or char. boundary following a drain. It's completely possible for a nonblocking channel to write half the bytes of an int or a double. When using nonblocking I/O, be sure to check for this problem before putting more data in the view buffer.

Compacting Buffers

Most writable buffers support a compact() method:

```
public abstract ByteBuffer    compact()
public abstract IntBuffer     compact()
public abstract ShortBuffer   compact()
public abstract FloatBuffer   compact()
public abstract CharBuffer    compact()
public abstract DoubleBuffer  compact()
```

(If it weren't for invocation chaining, these six methods could have been replaced by one method in the common Buffer superclass.) Compacting shifts any remaining data in the buffer to the start of the buffer, freeing up more space for elements. Any data that was in those positions will be overwritten. The buffer's position is set to the end of the data so it's ready for writing more data.

Compacting is an especially useful operation when you're *copying*—reading from one channel and writing the data to another using nonblocking I/O. You can read some data into a buffer, write the buffer out again, then compact the data so all the data that wasn't written is at the beginning of the buffer, and the position is at the end of the data remaining in the buffer, ready to receive more data. This allows the reads and writes to be interspersed more or less at random with only one buffer. Several reads can take place in a row, or several writes follow consecutively. If the network is ready for immediate output but not input (or vice versa), the program can take advantage of that. This technique can be used to implement an echo server as shown in Example 11-5. The echo protocol simply responds to the client with whatever data the client sent. Like chargen, it's useful for network testing. Also like chargen, echo relies on the client to close the connection. Unlike chargen, however, an echo server must both read and write from the connection.

Example 11-5. Echo server

```java
import java.nio.*;
import java.nio.channels.*;
import java.net.*;
import java.util.*;
import java.io.IOException;

public class EchoServer {

  public static int DEFAULT_PORT = 7;

  public static void main(String[] args) {

    int port;
    try {
      port = Integer.parseInt(args[0]);
    } catch (RuntimeException ex) {
      port = DEFAULT_PORT;
    }
    System.out.println("Listening for connections on port " + port);

    ServerSocketChannel serverChannel;
    Selector selector;
    try {
      serverChannel = ServerSocketChannel.open();
      ServerSocket ss = serverChannel.socket();
      InetSocketAddress address = new InetSocketAddress(port);
      ss.bind(address);
      serverChannel.configureBlocking(false);
      selector = Selector.open();
      serverChannel.register(selector, SelectionKey.OP_ACCEPT);
    } catch (IOException ex) {
      ex.printStackTrace();
      return;
    }

    while (true) {
      try {
        selector.select();
      } catch (IOException ex) {
        ex.printStackTrace();
        break;
      }

      Set<SelectionKey> readyKeys = selector.selectedKeys();
```

```
    Iterator<SelectionKey> iterator = readyKeys.iterator();
    while (iterator.hasNext()) {
      SelectionKey key = iterator.next();
      iterator.remove();
      try {
        if (key.isAcceptable()) {
          ServerSocketChannel server = (ServerSocketChannel) key.channel();
          SocketChannel client = server.accept();
          System.out.println("Accepted connection from " + client);
          client.configureBlocking(false);
          SelectionKey clientKey = client.register(
              selector, SelectionKey.OP_WRITE | SelectionKey.OP_READ);
          ByteBuffer buffer = ByteBuffer.allocate(100);
          clientKey.attach(buffer);
        }
        if (key.isReadable()) {
          SocketChannel client = (SocketChannel) key.channel();
          ByteBuffer output = (ByteBuffer) key.attachment();
          client.read(output);
        }
        if (key.isWritable()) {
          SocketChannel client = (SocketChannel) key.channel();
          ByteBuffer output = (ByteBuffer) key.attachment();
          output.flip();
          client.write(output);
          output.compact();
        }
      } catch (IOException ex) {
        key.cancel();
        try {
          key.channel().close();
        } catch (IOException cex) {}
      }
    }
  }
 }
}
```

One thing I noticed while writing and debugging this program: the buffer size makes a
big difference, although perhaps not in the way you might think. A big buffer can hide
a lot of bugs. If the buffer is large enough to hold complete test cases without being
flipped or drained, it's very easy to not notice that the buffer isn't being flipped or com-
pacted at the right times because the test cases never actually need to do that. Before
shipping your program, try turning the buffer size down to something significantly
lower than the input you're expecting. In this case, I tested with a buffer size of 10. This
test degrades performance, so you shouldn't ship with such a ridiculously small buffer,
but you absolutely should test your code with small buffers to make sure it behaves
properly when the buffer fills up.

Duplicating Buffers

It's often desirable to make a copy of a buffer to deliver the same information to two or more channels. The duplicate() methods in each of the six typed buffer classes do this:

```
public abstract ByteBuffer   duplicate()
public abstract IntBuffer    duplicate()
public abstract ShortBuffer  duplicate()
public abstract FloatBuffer  duplicate()
public abstract CharBuffer   duplicate()
public abstract DoubleBuffer duplicate()
```

The return values are not clones. The duplicated buffers share the same data, including the same backing array if the buffer is indirect. Changes to the data in one buffer are reflected in the other buffer. Thus, you should mostly use this method when you're only going to read from the buffers. Otherwise, it can be tricky to keep track of where the data is being modified.

The original and duplicated buffers do have independent marks, limits, and positions even though they share the same data. One buffer can be ahead of or behind the other buffer.

Duplication is useful when you want to transmit the same data over multiple channels, roughly in parallel. You can make duplicates of the main buffer for each channel and allow each channel to run at its own speed. For example, recall the single-file HTTP server in Example 9-10. Reimplemented with channels and buffers as shown in Example 11-6, NonblockingSingleFileHTTPServer, the single file to serve is stored in one constant, read-only buffer. Every time a client connects, the program makes a duplicate of this buffer just for that channel, which is stored as the channel's attachment. Without duplicates, one client has to wait until the other finishes so the original buffer can be rewound. Duplicates enable simultaneous buffer reuse.

Example 11-6. A nonblocking HTTP server that serves one file

```
import java.io.*;
import java.nio.*;
import java.nio.channels.*;
import java.nio.charset.*;
import java.nio.file.*;
import java.util.*;
import java.net.*;

public class NonblockingSingleFileHTTPServer {

  private ByteBuffer contentBuffer;
  private int port = 80;

  public NonblockingSingleFileHTTPServer(
      ByteBuffer data, String encoding, String MIMEType, int port) {
```

```
    this.port = port;
    String header = "HTTP/1.0 200 OK\r\n"
        + "Server: NonblockingSingleFileHTTPServer\r\n"
        + "Content-length: " + data.limit() + "\r\n"
        + "Content-type: " + MIMEType + "\r\n\r\n";
    byte[] headerData = header.getBytes(Charset.forName("US-ASCII"));

    ByteBuffer buffer = ByteBuffer.allocate(
        data.limit() + headerData.length);
    buffer.put(headerData);
    buffer.put(data);
    buffer.flip();
    this.contentBuffer = buffer;
}

public void run() throws IOException {
  ServerSocketChannel serverChannel = ServerSocketChannel.open();
  ServerSocket  serverSocket = serverChannel.socket();
  Selector selector = Selector.open();
  InetSocketAddress localPort = new InetSocketAddress(port);
  serverSocket.bind(localPort);
  serverChannel.configureBlocking(false);
  serverChannel.register(selector, SelectionKey.OP_ACCEPT);

  while (true) {
    selector.select();
    Iterator<SelectionKey> keys = selector.selectedKeys().iterator();
    while (keys.hasNext()) {
      SelectionKey key = keys.next();
      keys.remove();
      try {
        if (key.isAcceptable()) {
          ServerSocketChannel server = (ServerSocketChannel) key.channel();
          SocketChannel channel = server.accept();
          channel.configureBlocking(false);
          channel.register(selector, SelectionKey.OP_READ);
        } else if (key.isWritable()) {
          SocketChannel channel = (SocketChannel) key.channel();
          ByteBuffer buffer = (ByteBuffer) key.attachment();
          if (buffer.hasRemaining()) {
             channel.write(buffer);
          } else { // we're done
             channel.close();
          }
        } else if (key.isReadable()) {
          // Don't bother trying to parse the HTTP header.
          // Just read something.
          SocketChannel channel = (SocketChannel) key.channel();
          ByteBuffer buffer = ByteBuffer.allocate(4096);
          channel.read(buffer);
          // switch channel to write-only mode
          key.interestOps(SelectionKey.OP_WRITE);
```

```
            key.attach(contentBuffer.duplicate());
          }
        } catch (IOException ex) {
          key.cancel();
          try {
            key.channel().close();
          }
          catch (IOException cex) {}
        }
      }
    }
  }

  public static void main(String[] args) {
    if (args.length == 0) {
      System.out.println(
        "Usage: java NonblockingSingleFileHTTPServer file port encoding");
      return;
    }

    try {
      // read the single file to serve
      String contentType =
          URLConnection.getFileNameMap().getContentTypeFor(args[0]);
      Path file = FileSystems.getDefault().getPath(args[0]);
      byte[] data = Files.readAllBytes(file);
      ByteBuffer input = ByteBuffer.wrap(data);

      // set the port to listen on
      int port;
      try {
        port = Integer.parseInt(args[1]);
        if (port < 1 || port > 65535) port = 80;
      } catch (RuntimeException ex) {
        port = 80;
      }

      String encoding = "UTF-8";
      if (args.length > 2) encoding = args[2];

      NonblockingSingleFileHTTPServer server
          = new NonblockingSingleFileHTTPServer(
          input, encoding, contentType, port);
      server.run();
    } catch (IOException ex) {
      System.err.println(ex);
    }
  }
}
```

The constructors set up the data to be sent along with an HTTP header that includes information about content length and content encoding. The header and the body of the response are stored in a single `ByteBuffer` so that they can be blasted to clients very quickly. However, although all clients receive the same content, they may not receive it at the same time. Different parallel clients will be at different locations in the file. This is why we duplicate the buffer, so each channel has its own buffer. The overhead is small because all channels do share the same content. They just have different indexes into that content.

All incoming connections are handled by a single `Selector` in the `run()` method. The initial setup here is very similar to the earlier chargen server. The `run()` method opens a `ServerSocketChannel` and binds it to the specified port. Then it creates the `Selec tor` and registers it with the `ServerSocketChannel`. When a `SocketChannel` is accepted, the same `Selector` object is registered with it. Initially it's registered for reading because the HTTP protocol requires the client to send a request before the server responds.

The response to a read is simplistic. The program reads as many bytes of input as it can up to 4K. Then it resets the interest operations for the channel to writability. (A more complete server would actually attempt to parse the HTTP header request here and choose the file to send based on that information.) Next, the content buffer is duplicated and attached to the channel.

The next time the program passes through the `while` loop, this channel should be ready to receive data (or if not the next time, the time after that; the asynchronous nature of the connection means we won't see it until it's ready). At this point, you get the buffer out of the attachment, and write as much of the buffer as you can onto the channel. It's no big deal if you don't write it all this time. You'll just pick up where you left off the next pass through the loop. The buffer keeps track of its own position. Although many incoming clients might result in the creation of many buffer objects, the real overhead is minimal because they'll all share the same underlying data.

The `main()` method reads parameters from the command line. The name of the file to be served is read from the first command-line argument. If no file is specified or the file cannot be opened, an error message is printed and the program exits. Assuming the file can be read, its contents are read into a `ByteBuffer` using the convenient `Path` and `Files` classes from Java 7. A reasonable guess is made about the content type of the file, and that guess is stored in the `contentType` variable. Next, the port number is read from the second command-line argument. If no port is specified, or if the second argument is not an integer from 1 to 65,535, port 80 is used. The encoding is read from the third command-line argument if present. Otherwise, UTF-8 is assumed. Then these values are used to construct a `NonblockingSingleFileHTTPServer` object and start it running.

Slicing Buffers

Slicing a buffer is a slight variant of duplicating. Slicing also creates a new buffer that shares data with the old buffer. However, the slice's zero position is the current position of the original buffer, and its capacity only goes up to the source buffer's limit. That is, the slice is a subsequence of the original buffer that only contains the elements from the current position to the limit. Rewinding the slice only moves it back to the position of the original buffer when the slice was created. The slice can't see anything in the original buffer before that point. Again, there are separate slice() methods in each of the six typed buffer classes:

```
public abstract ByteBuffer    slice()
public abstract IntBuffer     slice()
public abstract ShortBuffer   slice()
public abstract FloatBuffer   slice()
public abstract CharBuffer    slice()
public abstract DoubleBuffer  slice()
```

This is useful when you have a long buffer of data that is easily divided into multiple parts such as a protocol header followed by the data. You can read out the header, then slice the buffer and pass the new buffer containing only the data to a separate method or class.

Marking and Resetting

Like input streams, buffers can be marked and reset if you want to reread some data. Unlike input streams, this can be done to all buffers, not just some of them. For a change, the relevant methods are declared once in the Buffer superclass and inherited by all the various subclasses:

```
public final Buffer mark()
public final Buffer reset()
```

The reset() method throws an InvalidMarkException, a runtime exception, if the mark is not set. The mark is also unset when the position is set to a point before the mark.

Object Methods

The buffer classes all provide the usual equals(), hashCode(), and toString() methods. They also implement Comparable, and therefore provide compareTo() methods. However, buffers are not Serializable or Cloneable.

Two buffers are considered to be equal if:

- They have the same type (e.g., a ByteBuffer is never equal to an IntBuffer but may be equal to another ByteBuffer).
- They have the same number of elements remaining in the buffer.
- The remaining elements at the same relative positions are equal to each other.

Note that equality does not consider the buffers' elements that precede the position, the buffers' capacity, limits, or marks. For example, this code fragment prints true even though the first buffer is twice the size of the second:

```
CharBuffer buffer1 = CharBuffer.wrap("12345678");
CharBuffer buffer2 = CharBuffer.wrap("5678");
buffer1.get();
buffer1.get();
buffer1.get();
buffer1.get();
System.out.println(buffer1.equals(buffer2));
```

The hashCode() method is implemented in accordance with the contract for equality. That is, two equal buffers will have equal hash codes and two unequal buffers are very unlikely to have equal hash codes. However, because the buffer's hash code changes every time an element is added to or removed from the buffer, buffers do not make good hash table keys.

Comparison is implemented by comparing the remaining elements in each buffer, one by one. If all the corresponding elements are equal, the buffers are equal. Otherwise, the result is the outcome of comparing the first pair of unequal elements. If one buffer runs out of elements before an unequal element is found and the other buffer still has elements, the shorter buffer is considered to be less than the longer buffer.

The toString() method returns strings that look something like this:

```
java.nio.HeapByteBuffer[pos=0 lim=62 cap=62]
```

These are primarily useful for debugging. The notable exception is CharBuffer, which returns a string containing the remaining chars in the buffer.

Channels

Channels move blocks of data into and out of buffers to and from various I/O sources such as files, sockets, datagrams, and so forth. The channel class hierarchy is rather convoluted, with multiple interfaces and many optional operations. However, for purposes of network programming there are only three really important channel classes, SocketChannel, ServerSocketChannel, and DatagramChannel; and for the TCP connections we've talked about so far you only need the first two.

SocketChannel

The SocketChannel class reads from and writes to TCP sockets. The data must be encoded in ByteBuffer objects for reading and writing. Each SocketChannel is associated with a peer Socket object that can be used for advanced configuration, but this requirement can be ignored for applications where the default options are fine.

Connecting

The SocketChannel class does not have any public constructors. Instead, you create a new SocketChannel object using one of the two static open() methods:

```
public static SocketChannel open(SocketAddress remote) throws IOException
public static SocketChannel open() throws IOException
```

The first variant makes the connection. This method blocks (i.e., the method will not return until the connection is made or an exception is thrown). For example:

```
SocketAddress address = new InetSocketAddress("www.cafeaulait.org",  80);
SocketChannel channel = SocketChannel.open(address);
```

The noargs version does not immediately connect. It creates an initially unconnected socket that must be connected later using the connect() method. For example:

```
SocketChannel channel = SocketChannel.open();
SocketAddress address = new InetSocketAddress("www.cafeaulait.org",  80);
channel.connect(address);
```

You might choose this more roundabout approach in order to configure various options on the channel and/or the socket before connecting. Specifically, use this approach if you want to open the channel without blocking:

```
SocketChannel channel = SocketChannel.open();
SocketAddress address = new InetSocketAddress("www.cafeaulait.org",  80);
channel.configureBlocking(false);
channel.connect();
```

With a nonblocking channel, the connect() method returns immediately, even before the connection is established. The program can do other things while it waits for the operating system to finish the connection. However, before it can actually use the connection, the program must call finishConnect():

```
public abstract boolean finishConnect() throws IOException
```

(This is only necessary in nonblocking mode. For a blocking channel, this method returns true immediately.) If the connection is now ready for use, finishConnect() returns true. If the connection has not been established yet, finishConnect() returns false. Finally, if the connection could not be established, for instance because the network is down, this method throws an exception.

If the program wants to check whether the connection is complete, it can call these two methods:

```
public abstract boolean isConnected()
public abstract boolean isConnectionPending()
```

The isConnected() method returns true if the connection is open. The isConnection Pending() method returns true if the connection is still being set up but is not yet open.

Reading

To read from a SocketChannel, first create a ByteBuffer the channel can store data in. Then pass it to the read() method:

```
public abstract int read(ByteBuffer dst) throws IOException
```

The channel fills the buffer with as much data as it can, then returns the number of bytes it put there. When it encounters the end of stream, the channel fills the buffer with any remaining bytes and then returns –1 on the next call to read(). If the channel is blocking, this method will read at least one byte or return –1 or throw an exception. If the channel is nonblocking, however, this method may return 0.

Because the data is stored into the buffer at the current position, which is updated automatically as more data is added, you can keep passing the same buffer to the read() method until the buffer is filled. For example, this loop will read until the buffer is filled or the end of stream is detected:

```
while (buffer.hasRemaining() && channel.read(buffer) != -1) ;
```

It is sometimes useful to be able to fill several buffers from one source. This is called a *scatter*. These two methods accept an array of ByteBuffer objects as arguments and fill each one in turn:

```
public final long read(ByteBuffer[] dsts) throws IOException
public final long read(ByteBuffer[] dsts, int offset, int length)
    throws IOException
```

The first variant fills all the buffers. The second method fills length buffers, starting with the one at offset.

To fill an array of buffers, just loop while the last buffer in the list has space remaining. For example:

```
ByteBuffer[] buffers = new ByteBuffer[2];
buffers[0] = ByteBuffer.allocate(1000);
buffers[1] = ByteBuffer.allocate(1000);
while (buffers[1].hasRemaining() && channel.read(buffers) != -1) ;
```

Writing

Socket channels have both read and write methods. In general, they are full duplex. In order to write, simply fill a ByteBuffer, flip it, and pass it to one of the write methods, which drains it while copying the data onto the output—pretty much the reverse of the reading process.

The basic write() method takes a single buffer as an argument:

```
public abstract int write(ByteBuffer src) throws IOException
```

As with reads (and unlike OutputStreams), this method is not guaranteed to write the complete contents of the buffer if the channel is nonblocking. Again, however, the cursor-based nature of buffers enables you to easily call this method again and again until the buffer is fully drained and the data has been completely written:

```
while (buffer.hasRemaining() && channel.write(buffer) != -1) ;
```

It is often useful to be able to write data from several buffers onto one socket. This is called a *gather*. For example, you might want to store the HTTP header in one buffer and the HTTP body in another buffer. The implementation might even fill the two buffers simultaneously using two threads or overlapped I/O. These two methods accept an array of ByteBuffer objects as arguments, and drain each one in turn:

```
public final long write(ByteBuffer[] dsts) throws IOException
public final long write(ByteBuffer[] dsts, int offset, int length)
    throws IOException
```

The first variant drains all the buffers. The second method drains length buffers, starting with the one at offset.

Closing

Just as with regular sockets, you should close a channel when you're done with it to free up the port and any other resources it may be using:

```
public void close() throws IOException
```

Closing an already closed channel has no effect. Attempting to write data to or read data from a closed channel throws an exception. If you're uncertain whether a channel has been closed, check with isOpen():

```
public boolean isOpen()
```

Naturally, this returns false if the channel is closed, true if it's open (close() and isOpen() are the only two methods declared in the Channel interface and shared by all channel classes).

Starting in Java 7, SocketChannel implements AutoCloseable, so you can use it in try-with-resources.

ServerSocketChannel

The ServerSocketChannel class has one purpose: to accept incoming connections. You cannot read from, write to, or connect a ServerSocketChannel. The only operation it supports is accepting a new incoming connection. The class itself only declares four methods, of which accept() is the most important. ServerSocketChannel also inherits several methods from its superclasses, mostly related to registering with a Selector for notification of incoming connections. And finally, like all channels, it has a `close()` method that shuts down the server socket.

Creating server socket channels

The static factory method `ServerSocketChannel.open()` creates a new `ServerSock etChannel` object. However, the name is a little deceptive. This method does not actually open a new server socket. Instead, it just creates the object. Before you can use it, you need to call the `socket()` method to get the corresponding peer `ServerSocket`. At this point, you can configure any server options you like, such as the receive buffer size or the socket timeout, using the various setter methods in `ServerSocket`. Then connect this `ServerSocket` to a `SocketAddress` for the port you want to bind to. For example, this code fragment opens a `ServerSocketChannel` on port 80:

```
try {
  ServerSocketChannel server = ServerSocketChannel.open();
  ServerSocket socket = serverChannel.socket();
  SocketAddress address = new InetSocketAddress(80);
  socket.bind(address);
} catch (IOException ex) {
  System.err.println("Could not bind to port 80 because " + ex.getMessage());
}
```

In Java 7, this gets a little simpler because `ServerSocketChannel` now has a `bind()` method of its own:

```
try {
  ServerSocketChannel server = ServerSocketChannel.open();
  SocketAddress address = new InetSocketAddress(80);
  server.bind(address);
} catch (IOException ex) {
  System.err.println("Could not bind to port 80 because " + ex.getMessage());
}
```

A factory method is used here rather than a constructor so that different virtual machines can provide different implementations of this class, more closely tuned to the local hardware and OS. However, this factory is not user configurable. The `open()` method always returns an instance of the same class when running in the same virtual machine.

Accepting connections

Once you've opened and bound a `ServerSocketChannel` object, the `accept()` method can listen for incoming connections:

```
public abstract SocketChannel accept() throws IOException
```

`accept()` can operate in either blocking or nonblocking mode. In blocking mode, the `accept()` method waits for an incoming connection. It then accepts that connection and returns a SocketChannel object connected to the remote client. The thread cannot do anything until a connection is made. This strategy might be appropriate for simple servers that can respond to each request immediately. Blocking mode is the default.

A ServerSocketChannel can also operate in nonblocking mode. In this case, the ac cept() method returns null if there are no incoming connections. Nonblocking mode is more appropriate for servers that need to do a lot of work for each connection and thus may want to process multiple requests in parallel. Nonblocking mode is normally used in conjunction with a Selector. To make a ServerSocketChannel nonblocking, pass false to its configureBlocking() method.

The accept() method is declared to throw an IOException if anything goes wrong. There are several subclasses of IOException that indicate more detailed problems, as well as a couple of runtime exceptions:

ClosedChannelException
> You cannot reopen a ServerSocketChannel after closing it.

AsynchronousCloseException
> Another thread closed this ServerSocketChannel while accept() was executing.

ClosedByInterruptException
> Another thread interrupted this thread while a blocking ServerSocketChannel was waiting.

NotYetBoundException
> You called open() but did not bind the ServerSocketChannel's peer ServerSock et to an address before calling accept(). This is a runtime exception, not an IOException.

SecurityException
> The security manager refused to allow this application to bind to the requested port.

The Channels Class

Channels is a simple utility class for wrapping channels around traditional I/O-based streams, readers, and writers, and vice versa. It's useful when you want to use the new I/O model in one part of a program for performance, but still interoperate with legacy APIs that expect streams. It has methods that convert from streams to channels and methods that convert from channels to streams, readers, and writers:

```
public static InputStream newInputStream(ReadableByteChannel ch)
public static OutputStream newOutputStream(WritableByteChannel ch)
public static ReadableByteChannel newChannel(InputStream in)
public static WritableByteChannel newChannel(OutputStream out)
public static Reader newReader (ReadableByteChannel channel,
    CharsetDecoder decoder, int minimumBufferCapacity)
```

```
public static Reader newReader (ReadableByteChannel ch, String encoding)
public static Writer newWriter (WritableByteChannel ch, String encoding)
```

The SocketChannel class discussed in this chapter implements both the ReadableByte Channel and WritableByteChannel interfaces seen in these signatures. ServerSock etChannel implements neither of these because you can't read from or write to it.

For example, all current XML APIs use streams, files, readers, and other traditional I/O APIs to read the XML document. If you're writing an HTTP server designed to process SOAP requests, you may want to read the HTTP request bodies using channels and parse the XML using SAX for performance. In this case, you'd need to convert these channels into streams before passing them to XMLReader's parse() method:

```
SocketChannel channel = server.accept();
processHTTPHeader(channel);
XMLReader parser = XMLReaderFactory.createXMLReader();
parser.setContentHandler(someContentHandlerObject);
InputStream in = Channels.newInputStream(channel);
parser.parse(in);
```

Asynchronous Channels (Java 7)

Java 7 introduces the AsynchronousSocketChannel and AsynchronousServerSock etChannel classes. These behave like and have almost the same interface as SocketCh annel and ServerSocketChannel (though they are not subclasses of those classes). However, unlike SocketChannel and ServerSocketChannel, reads from and writes to asynchronous channels return immediately, even before the I/O is complete. The data read or written is further processed by a Future or a CompletionHandler. The con nect() and accept() methods also execute asynchronously and return Futures. Se lectors are not used.

For example, suppose a program needs to perform a lot of initialization at startup. Some of that involves network connections that are going to take several seconds each. You can start several asynchronous operations in parallel, then perform your local initializations, and then request the results of the network operations:

```
SocketAddress address = new InetSocketAddress(args[0], port);
AsynchronousSocketChannel client = AsynchronousSocketChannel.open();
Future<Void> connected = client.connect(address);

ByteBuffer buffer = ByteBuffer.allocate(74);

// wait for the connection to finish
connected.get();

// read from the connection
Future<Integer> future = client.read(buffer);

// do other things...
```

```
// wait for the read to finish...
future.get();

// flip and drain the buffer
buffer.flip();
WritableByteChannel out = Channels.newChannel(System.out);
out.write(buffer);
```

The advantage of this approach is that the network connections run in parallel while the program does other things. When you're ready to process the data from the network, but not before, you stop and wait for it by calling Future.get(). You could achieve the same effect with thread pools and callables, but this is perhaps a little simpler, especially if buffers are a natural fit for your application.

This approach fits the situation where you want to get results back in a very particular order. However, if you don't care about order, if you can process each network read independently of the others, then you may be better off using a CompletionHandler instead. For example, imagine you're writing a search engine web spider that feeds pages into some backend. Because you don't care about the order of the responses returned, you can spawn a large number of AsynchronousSocketChannel requests and give each one a CompletionHandler that stores the results in the backend.

The generic CompletionHandler interface declares two methods: completed(), which is invoked if the read finishes successfully; and failed(), which is invoked on an I/O error. For example, here's a simple CompletionHandler that prints whatever it received on System.out:

```
class LineHandler implements CompletionHandler<Integer, ByteBuffer> {

  @Override
  public void completed(Integer result, ByteBuffer buffer) {
    buffer.flip();
    WritableByteChannel out = Channels.newChannel(System.out);
    try {
      out.write(buffer);
    } catch (IOException ex) {
      System.err.println(ex);
    }
  }

  @Override
  public void failed(Throwable ex, ByteBuffer attachment) {
    System.err.println(ex.getMessage());
  }
}
```

When you read from the channel you pass a buffer, an attachment, and a Completion Handler to the read() method:

```
ByteBuffer buffer = ByteBuffer.allocate(74);
CompletionHandler<Integer, ByteBuffer> handler = new LineHandler();
channel.read(buffer, buffer, handler);
```

Here I've made the attachment the buffer itself. This is one way to push the data read from the network into the `CompletionHandler` where it can handle it. Another common pattern is to make the `CompletionHandler` an anonymous inner class and the buffer a final local variable so it's in scope inside the completion handler.

Although you can safely share an `AsynchronousSocketChannel` or `AsynchronousServerSocketChannel` between multiple threads, no more than one thread can read from this channel at a time and no more than one thread can write to the channel at a time. (One thread can read and another thread can write simultaneously, though.) If a thread attempts to read while another thread has a pending read, the `read()` method throws a `ReadPendingException`. Similarly, if a thread attempts to write while another thread has a pending write, the `write()` method throws a `WritePendingException`.

Socket Options (Java 7)

Beginning in Java 7, `SocketChannel`, `ServerSocketChannel`, `AsynchronousServerSocketChannel`, `AsynchronousSocketChannel`, and `DatagramChannel` all implement the new `NetworkChannel` interface. The primary purpose of this interface is to support the various TCP options such as TCP_NODELAY, SO_TIMEOUT, SO_LINGER, SO_SNDBUF, SO_RCVBUF, and SO_KEEPALIVE discussed in Chapter 8 and Chapter 9. The options have the same meaning in the underlying TCP stack whether set on a socket or a channel. However, the interface to these options is a little different. Rather than individual methods for each supported option, the channel classes each have just three methods to get, set, and list the supported options:

```
<T> T getOption(SocketOption<T> name) throws IOException
<T> NetworkChannel setOption(SocketOption<T> name, T value) throws IOException
Set<SocketOption<?>> supportedOptions()
```

The `SocketOption` class is a generic class specifying the name and type of each option. The type parameter <T> determines whether the option is a `boolean`, `Integer`, or `NetworkInterface`. The `StandardSocketOptions` class provides constants for each of the 11 options Java recognizes:

- `SocketOption<NetworkInterface>` `StandardSocketOptions.IP_MULTICAST_IF`

- `SocketOption<Boolean>` `StandardSocketOptions.IP_MULTICAST_LOOP`

- `SocketOption<Integer>` `StandardSocketOptions.IP_MULTICAST_TTL`

- `SocketOption<Integer>` `StandardSocketOptions.IP_TOS`

- `SocketOption<Boolean>` `StandardSocketOptions.SO_BROADCAST`

- `SocketOption<Boolean>` `StandardSocketOptions.SO_KEEPALIVE`

- SocketOption<Integer> StandardSocketOptions.SO_LINGER

- SocketOption<Integer> StandardSocketOptions.SO_RCVBUF

- SocketOption<Boolean> StandardSocketOptions.SO_REUSEADDR

- SocketOption<Integer> StandardSocketOptions.SO_SNDBUF

- SocketOption<Boolean> StandardSocketOptions.TCP_NODELAY

For example, this code fragment opens a client network channel and sets SO_LINGER to 240 seconds:

```
NetworkChannel channel = SocketChannel.open();
channel.setOption(StandardSocketOptions.SO_LINGER, 240);
```

Different channels and sockets support different options. For instance, ServerSock etChannel supports SO_REUSEADDR and SO_RCVBUF but not SO_SNDBUF. Trying to set an option the channel doesn't support throws an UnsupportedOperationEx ception.

Example 11-7 is a simple program to list all supported socket options for the different types of network channels.

Example 11-7. Listing supported options

```
import java.io.*;
import java.net.*;
import java.nio.channels.*;

public class OptionSupport {

  public static void main(String[] args) throws IOException {
    printOptions(SocketChannel.open());
    printOptions(ServerSocketChannel.open());
    printOptions(AsynchronousSocketChannel.open());
    printOptions(AsynchronousServerSocketChannel.open());
    printOptions(DatagramChannel.open());
  }

  private static void printOptions(NetworkChannel channel) throws IOException {
    System.out.println(channel.getClass().getSimpleName() + " supports:");
    for (SocketOption<?> option : channel.supportedOptions()) {
      System.out.println(option.name() + ": " + channel.getOption(option));
    }
    System.out.println();
    channel.close();
  }

}
```

Here's the output showing which options are supported by which types of channels, and what the default values are:

```
SocketChannelImpl supports:
SO_OOBINLINE: false
SO_REUSEADDR: false
SO_LINGER: -1
SO_KEEPALIVE: false
IP_TOS: 0
SO_SNDBUF: 131072
SO_RCVBUF: 131072
TCP_NODELAY: false

ServerSocketChannelImpl supports:
SO_REUSEADDR: true
SO_RCVBUF: 131072

UnixAsynchronousSocketChannelImpl supports:
SO_KEEPALIVE: false
SO_REUSEADDR: false
SO_SNDBUF: 131072
TCP_NODELAY: false
SO_RCVBUF: 131072

UnixAsynchronousServerSocketChannelImpl supports:
SO_REUSEADDR: true
SO_RCVBUF: 131072

DatagramChannelImpl supports:
IP_MULTICAST_TTL: 1
SO_BROADCAST: false
SO_REUSEADDR: false
IP_MULTICAST_IF: null
IP_TOS: 0
IP_MULTICAST_LOOP: true
SO_SNDBUF: 9216
SO_RCVBUF: 196724
```

Readiness Selection

For network programming, the second part of the new I/O APIs is readiness selection, the ability to choose a socket that will not block when read or written. This is primarily of interest to servers, although clients running multiple simultaneous connections with several windows open—such as a web spider or a browser—can take advantage of it as well.

In order to perform readiness selection, different channels are registered with a Selec tor object. Each channel is assigned a SelectionKey. The program can then ask the Selector object for the set of keys to the channels that are ready to perform the operation you want to perform without blocking.

The Selector Class

The only constructor in `Selector` is protected. Normally, a new selector is created by invoking the static factory method `Selector.open()`:

```
public static Selector open() throws IOException
```

The next step is to add channels to the selector. There are no methods in the `Selec` tor class to add a channel. The `register()` method is declared in the `SelectableChan` nel class. Not all channels are selectable—in particular, `FileChannels` aren't selectable —but all network channels are. Thus, the channel is registered with a selector by passing the selector to one of the channel's register methods:

```
public final SelectionKey register(Selector sel, int ops)
    throws ClosedChannelException
public final SelectionKey register(Selector sel, int ops, Object att)
    throws ClosedChannelException
```

This approach feels backward to me, but it's not hard to use. The first argument is the selector the channel is registering with. The second argument is a named constant from the `SelectionKey` class identifying the operation the channel is registering for. The `SelectionKey` class defines four named bit constants used to select the type of the operation:

- `SelectionKey.OP_ACCEPT`
- `SelectionKey.OP_CONNECT`
- `SelectionKey.OP_READ`
- `SelectionKey.OP_WRITE`

These are bit-flag int constants (1, 2, 4, etc.). Therefore, if a channel needs to register for multiple operations in the same selector (e.g., for both reading and writing on a socket), combine the constants with the bitwise or operator (|) when registering:

```
channel.register(selector,  SelectionKey.OP_READ | SelectionKey.OP_WRITE);
```

The optional third argument is an attachment for the key. This object is often used to store state for the connection. For example, if you were implementing a web server, you might attach a `FileInputStream` or `FileChannel` connected to the local file the server streams to the client.

After the different channels have been registered with the selector, you can query the selector at any time to find out which channels are ready to be processed. Channels may be ready for some operations and not others. For instance, a channel could be ready for reading but not writing.

There are three methods that select the ready channels. They differ in how long they wait to find a ready channel. The first, selectNow(), performs a nonblocking select. It returns immediately if no connections are ready to be processed now:

```
public abstract int selectNow() throws IOException
```

The other two select methods are blocking:

```
public abstract int select() throws IOException
public abstract int select(long timeout) throws IOException
```

The first method waits until at least one registered channel is ready to be processed before returning. The second waits no longer than timeout milliseconds for a channel to be ready before returning 0. These methods are useful if your program doesn't have anything to do when no channels are ready to be processed.

When you know the channels are ready to be processed, retrieve the ready channels using selectedKeys():

```
public abstract Set<SelectionKey> selectedKeys()
```

You iterate through the returned set, processing each SelectionKey in turn. You'll also want to remove the key from the iterator to tell the selector that you've handled it. Otherwise, the selector will keep telling you about it on future passes through the loop.

Finally, when you're ready to shut down the server or when you no longer need the selector, you should close it:

```
public abstract void close() throws IOException
```

This step releases any resources associated with the selector. More importantly, it cancels all keys registered with the selector and interrupts up any threads blocked by one of this selector's select methods.

The SelectionKey Class

SelectionKey objects serve as pointers to channels. They can also hold an object attachment, which is how you normally store the state for the connection on that channel.

SelectionKey objects are returned by the register() method when registering a channel with a selector. However, you don't usually need to retain this reference. The selectedKeys() method returns the same objects again inside a Set. A single channel can be registered with multiple selectors.

When retrieving a SelectionKey from the set of selected keys, you often first test what that key is ready to do. There are four possibilities:

```
public final boolean isAcceptable()
public final boolean isConnectable()
public final boolean isReadable()
public final boolean isWritable()
```

This test isn't always necessary. In some cases, the selector is only testing for one possibility and will only return keys to do that one thing. But if the selector does test for multiple readiness states, you'll want to test which one kicked the channel into the ready state before operating on it. It's also possible that a channel is ready to do more than one thing.

Once you know what the channel associated with the key is ready to do, retrieve the channel with the channel() method:

```
public abstract SelectableChannel channel()
```

If you've stored an object in the SelectionKey to hold state information, you can retrieve it with the attachment() method:

```
public final Object attachment()
```

Finally, when you're finished with a connection, deregister its SelectionKey object so the selector doesn't waste any resources querying it for readiness. I don't know that this is absolutely essential in all cases, but it doesn't hurt. You do this by invoking the key's cancel() method:

```
public abstract void cancel()
```

However, this step is only necessary if you haven't closed the channel. Closing a channel automatically deregisters all keys for that channel in all selectors. Similarly, closing a selector invalidates all keys in that selector.

CHAPTER 12

UDP

Previous chapters discussed network applications that run on top of the TCP transport layer protocol. TCP is designed for reliable transmission of data. If data is lost or damaged in transmission, TCP ensures that the data is resent. If packets of data arrive out of order, TCP puts them back in the correct order. If the data is coming too fast for the connection, TCP throttles the speed back so that packets won't be lost. A program never needs to worry about receiving data that is out of order or incorrect. However, this reliability comes at a price. That price is speed. Establishing and tearing down TCP connections can take a fair amount of time, particularly for protocols such as HTTP, which tend to require many short transmissions.

The User Datagram Protocol (UDP) is an alternative transport layer protocol for sending data over IP that is very quick, but not reliable. When you send UDP data, you have no way of knowing whether it arrived, much less whether different pieces of data arrived in the order in which you sent them. However, the pieces that do arrive generally arrive quickly.

The UDP Protocol

The obvious question to ask is why anyone would ever use an unreliable protocol. Surely, if you have data worth sending, you care about whether the data arrives correctly? Clearly, UDP isn't a good match for applications like FTP that require reliable transmission of data over potentially unreliable networks. However, there are many kinds of applications in which raw speed is more important than getting every bit right. For example, in real-time audio or video, lost or swapped packets of data simply appear as static. Static is tolerable, but awkward pauses in the audio stream, when TCP requests a retransmission or waits for a wayward packet to arrive, are unacceptable. In other applications, reliability tests can be implemented in the application layer. For example, if a client sends a short UDP request to a server, it may assume that the packet is lost if no response is returned within an established period of time; this is one way the Domain

Name System (DNS) works. (DNS can also operate over TCP.) In fact, you could implement a reliable file transfer protocol using UDP, and many people have: Network File System (NFS), Trivial FTP (TFTP), and FSP, a more distant relative of FTP, all use UDP. (The latest version of NFS can use either UDP or TCP.) In these protocols, the application is responsible for reliability; UDP doesn't take care of it (the application must handle missing or out-of-order packets). This is a lot of work, but there's no reason it can't be done—although if you find yourself writing this code, think carefully about whether you might be better off with TCP.

The difference between TCP and UDP is often explained by analogy with the phone system and the post office. TCP is like the phone system. When you dial a number, the phone is answered and a connection is established between the two parties. As you talk, you know that the other party hears your words in the order in which you say them. If the phone is busy or no one answers, you find out right away. UDP, by contrast, is like the postal system. You send packets of mail to an address. Most of the letters arrive, but some may be lost on the way. The letters probably arrive in the order in which you sent them, but that's not guaranteed. The farther away you are from your recipient, the more likely it is that mail will be lost on the way or arrive out of order. If this is a problem, you can write sequential numbers on the envelopes, then ask the recipients to arrange them in the correct order and send you mail telling you which letters arrived so that you can resend any that didn't get there the first time. However, you and your correspondent need to agree on this protocol in advance. The post office will not do it for you.

Both the phone system and the post office have their uses. Although either one could be used for almost any communication, in some cases one is definitely superior to the other. The same is true of UDP and TCP. The past several chapters have all focused on TCP applications, which are more common than UDP applications. However, UDP also has its place; in this chapter, we'll look at what you can do with UDP. If you want to go further, the next chapter describes multicasting over UDP. A multicast socket is a fairly simple variation on a standard UDP socket.

Java's implementation of UDP is split into two classes: DatagramPacket and Datagram Socket. The DatagramPacket class stuffs bytes of data into UDP packets called *datagrams* and lets you unstuff datagrams that you receive. A DatagramSocket sends as well as receives UDP datagrams. To send data, you put the data in a DatagramPacket and send the packet using a DatagramSocket. To receive data, you take a DatagramPacket object from a DatagramSocket and then inspect the contents of the packet. The sockets themselves are very simple creatures. In UDP, everything about a datagram, including the address to which it is directed, is included in the packet itself; the socket only needs to know the local port on which to listen or send.

This division of labor contrasts with the Socket and ServerSocket classes used by TCP. First, UDP doesn't have any notion of a unique connection between two hosts. One socket sends and receives all data directed to or from a port without any concern for who the remote host is. A single `DatagramSocket` can send data to and receive data from many independent hosts. The socket isn't dedicated to a single connection, as it is in TCP. In fact, UDP doesn't have any concept of a connection between two hosts; it only knows about individual datagrams. Figuring out who sent what data is the application's responsibility. Second, TCP sockets treat a network connection as a stream: you send and receive data with input and output streams that you get from the socket. UDP doesn't support this; you always work with individual datagram packets. All the data you stuff into a single datagram is sent as a single packet and is either received or lost as a group. One packet is not necessarily related to the next. Given two packets, there is no way to determine which packet was sent first and which was sent second. Instead of the orderly queue of data that's necessary for a stream, datagrams try to crowd into the recipient as quickly as possible, like a crowd of people pushing their way onto a bus. And occasionally, if the bus is crowded enough, a few packets, like people, may not squeeze on and will be left waiting at the bus stop.

UDP Clients

Let's begin with a simple example. As in "Reading from Servers with Sockets" on page 244 we will connect to the daytime server at the National Institute for Standards and Technology (NIST) and ask it for the current time. However, this time you'll use UDP instead of TCP. Recall that the daytime server listens on port 13, and that the server sends the time in a human-readable format and closes the connection.

Now let's see how to retrieve this same data programmatically using UDP. First, open a socket on port 0:

```
DatagramSocket socket = new DatagramSocket(0);
```

This is very different than a TCP socket. You only specify a local port to connect to. The socket does not know the remote host or address. By specifying port 0 you ask Java to pick a random available port for you, much as with server sockets.

The next step is optional but highly recommended. Set a timeout on the connection using the `setSoTimeout()` method. Timeouts are measured in milliseconds, so this statement sets the socket to time out after 10 seconds of nonresponsiveness:

```
socket.setSoTimeout(10000);
```

Timeouts are even more important for UDP than TCP because many problems that would cause an `IOException` in TCP silently fail in UDP. For example, if the remote host is not listening on the targeted port, you'll never hear about it.

Next you need to set up the packets. You'll need two, one to send and one to receive. For the daytime protocol it doesn't matter what data you put in the packet, but you do need to tell it the remote host and remote port to connect to:

```
InetAddress host = InetAddress.getByName("time.nist.gov");
DatagramPacket request = new DatagramPacket(new byte[1], 1, host, 13);
```

The packet that receives the server's response just contains an empty byte array. This needs to be large enough to hold the entire response. If it's too small, it will be silently truncated—1k should be enough space:

```
byte[] data = new byte[1024];
DatagramPacket response = new DatagramPacket(data, data.length);
```

Now you're ready. First send the packet over the socket and then receive the response:

```
socket.send(request);
socket.receive(response);
```

Finally, extract the bytes from the response and convert them to a string you can show to the end user:

```
String daytime = new String(response.getData(), 0, response.getLength(),
    "US-ASCII");
System.out.println(daytime);
```

The constructor and send() and receive() methods can each throw an IOException, so you'll usually wrap all this in a try block. In Java 7, DatagramSocket implements Autocloseable so you can use try-with-resources:

```
try (DatagramSocket socket = new DatagramSocket(0)) {
  // connect to the server...
} catch (IOException ex) {
  System.err.println("Could not connect to time.nist.gov");
}
```

In Java 6 and earlier, you'll want to explicitly close the socket in a finally block to release resources the socket holds:

```
DatagramSocket socket = null;
try {
  socket = new DatagramSocket(0);
  // connect to the server...
} catch (IOException ex) {
  System.err.println(ex);
} finally {
  if (socket != null) {
    try {
      socket.close();
    } catch (IOException ex) {
      // ignore
    }
  }
}
```

Example 12-1 puts this all together.

Example 12-1. A daytime protocol client

```java
import java.io.*;
import java.net.*;

public class DaytimeUDPClient {

  private final static int PORT = 13;
  private static final String HOSTNAME = "time.nist.gov";

  public static void main(String[] args) {
    try (DatagramSocket socket = new DatagramSocket(0)) {
      socket.setSoTimeout(10000);
      InetAddress host = InetAddress.getByName(HOSTNAME);
      DatagramPacket request = new DatagramPacket(new byte[1], 1, host , PORT);
      DatagramPacket response = new DatagramPacket(new byte[1024], 1024);
      socket.send(request);
      socket.receive(response);
      String result = new String(response.getData(), 0, response.getLength(),
                          "US-ASCII");
      System.out.println(result);
    } catch (IOException ex) {
      ex.printStackTrace();
    }
  }
}
```

Typical output is much the same as if you connected with TCP:

```
$ java DaytimeUDPClient
56375 13-04-11 19:55:22 50 0 0 843.6 UTC(NIST) *
```

UDP Servers

A UDP server follows almost the same pattern as a UDP client, except that you usually receive before sending and don't choose an anonymous port to bind to. Unlike TCP, there's no separate DatagramServerSocket class.

For example, let's implement a daytime server over UDP. Begin by opening a datagram socket on a well-known port. For daytime, this port is 13:

```
DatagramSocket socket = new DatagramSocket(13);
```

As with TCP sockets, on Unix systems (including Linux and Mac OS X) you need to be running as root in order to bind to a port below 1024. You can either use sudo to run the program or simply change the port to something 1024 or higher.

Next, create a packet into which to receive a request. You need to supply both a byte array in which to store incoming data, the offset into the array, and the number of bytes to store. Here you set up a packet with space for 1,024 bytes starting at 0:

```
DatagramPacket request = new DatagramPacket(new byte[1024], 0, 1024);
```

Then receive it:

```
socket.receive(request);
```

This call blocks indefinitely until a UDP packet arrives on port 13. When it does, Java fills the byte array with data and the receive() method returns.

Next, create a response packet. This has four parts: the raw data to send, the number of bytes of the raw data to send, the host to send to, and the port on that host to address. In this example, the raw data comes from a String form of the current time, and the host and the port are simply the host and port of the incoming packet:

```
String daytime = new Date().toString() + "\r\n";
byte[] data = daytime.getBytes("US-ASCII");
InetAddress host = request.getAddress();
int port = request.getPort();
DatagramPacket response = new DatagramPacket(data, data.length, host, port);
```

Finally, send the response back over the same socket that received it:

```
socket.send(response);
```

Example 12-2 wraps this sequence up in a while loop, complete with logging and exception handling, so that it can process many incoming requests.

Example 12-2. A daytime protocol server

```
import java.net.*;
import java.util.Date;
import java.util.logging.*;
import java.io.*;

public class DaytimeUDPServer {

  private final static int PORT = 13;
  private final static Logger audit = Logger.getLogger("requests");
  private final static Logger errors = Logger.getLogger("errors");

  public static void main(String[] args) {
    try (DatagramSocket socket = new DatagramSocket(PORT)) {
      while (true) {
        try {
          DatagramPacket request = new DatagramPacket(new byte[1024], 1024);
          socket.receive(request);

          String daytime = new Date().toString();
          byte[] data = daytime.getBytes("US-ASCII");
          DatagramPacket response = new DatagramPacket(data, data.length,
              request.getAddress(), request.getPort());
          socket.send(response);
          audit.info(daytime + " " + request.getAddress());
        } catch (IOException | RuntimeException ex) {
```

```
                errors.log(Level.SEVERE, ex.getMessage(), ex);
            }
        }
    } catch (IOException ex) {
        errors.log(Level.SEVERE, ex.getMessage(), ex);
    }
  }
}
```

As you can see in this example, UDP servers tend not to be as multithreaded as TCP servers. They usually don't do a lot of work for any one client, and they can't get blocked waiting for the other end to respond because UDP never reports errors. Unless a lot of time-consuming work is required to prepare the response, an iterative approach works just fine for UDP servers.

The DatagramPacket Class

UDP datagrams add very little to the IP datagrams they sit on top of. Figure 12-1 shows a typical UDP datagram. The UDP header adds only eight bytes to the IP header. The UDP header includes source and destination port numbers, the length of everything that follows the IP header, and an optional checksum. Because port numbers are given as two-byte unsigned integers, 65,536 different possible UDP ports are available per host. These are distinct from the 65,536 different TCP ports per host. Because the length is also a two-byte unsigned integer, the number of bytes in a datagram is limited to 65,536 minus the eight bytes for the header. However, this is redundant with the datagram length field of the IP header, which limits datagrams to between 65,467 and 65,507 bytes. (The exact number depends on the size of the IP header.) The checksum field is optional and not used in or accessible from application layer programs. If the checksum for the data fails, the native network software silently discards the datagram; neither the sender nor the receiver is notified. UDP is an unreliable protocol, after all.

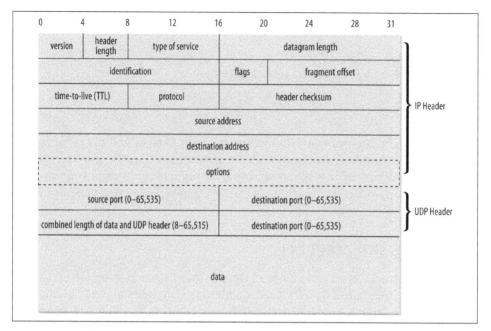

Figure 12-1. The structure of a UDP datagram

Although the theoretical maximum amount of data in a UDP datagram is 65,507 bytes, in practice there is almost always much less. On many platforms, the actual limit is more likely to be 8,192 bytes (8K). And implementations are not required to accept datagrams with more than 576 total bytes, including data and headers. Consequently, you should be extremely wary of any program that depends on sending or receiving UDP packets with more than 8K of data. Most of the time, larger packets are simply truncated to 8K of data. For maximum safety, the data portion of a UDP packet should be kept to 512 bytes or less, although this limit can negatively affect performance compared to larger packet sizes. (This is a problem for TCP datagrams too, but the stream-based API provided by `Socket` and `ServerSocket` completely shields programmers from these details.)

In Java, a UDP datagram is represented by an instance of the `DatagramPacket` class:

```
public final class DatagramPacket extends Object
```

This class provides methods to get and set the source or destination address from the IP header, to get and set the source or destination port, to get and set the data, and to get and set the length of the data. The remaining header fields are inaccessible from pure Java code.

The Constructors

DatagramPacket uses different constructors depending on whether the packet will be used to send data or to receive data. This is a little unusual. Normally, constructors are overloaded to let you provide different kinds of information when you create an object, not to create objects of the same class that will be used in different contexts. In this case, all six constructors take as arguments a byte array that holds the datagram's data and the number of bytes in that array to use for the datagram's data. When you want to receive a datagram, these are the only arguments you provide. When the socket receives a datagram from the network, it stores the datagram's data in the DatagramPacket object's buffer array, up to the length you specified.

The second set of DatagramPacket constructors is used to create datagrams you will send over the network. Like the first, these constructors require a buffer array and a length, but they also require an address and port to which the packet will be sent. In this case, you pass to the constructor a byte array containing the data you want to send and the destination address and port to which the packet is to be sent. The DatagramSock et reads the destination address and port from the packet; the address and port aren't stored within the socket, as they are in TCP.

Constructors for receiving datagrams

These two constructors create new DatagramPacket objects for receiving data from the network:

```
public DatagramPacket(byte[] buffer, int length)
public DatagramPacket(byte[] buffer, int offset, int length)
```

If the first constructor is used, when a socket receives a datagram, it stores the datagram's data part in buffer beginning at buffer[0] and continuing until the packet is completely stored or until length bytes have been written into the buffer. For example, this code fragment creates a new DatagramPacket for receiving a datagram of up to 8,192 bytes:

```
byte[] buffer = new byte[8192];
DatagramPacket dp = new DatagramPacket(buffer, buffer.length);
```

If the second constructor is used, storage begins at buffer[offset] instead. Otherwise, these two constructors are identical. length must be less than or equal to buffer.length - offset. If you try to construct a DatagramPacket with a length that will overflow the buffer, the constructor throws an IllegalArgumentException. This is a RuntimeEx ception, so your code is not required to catch it. It is OK to construct a DatagramPack et with a length less than buffer.length - offset. In this case, at most the first length bytes of buffer will be filled when the datagram is received.

The constructor doesn't care how large the buffer is and would happily let you create a DatagramPacket with megabytes of data. However, the underlying native network software is less forgiving, and most native UDP implementations don't support more than 8,192 bytes of data per datagram. The theoretical limit for an IPv4 datagram is 65,507 bytes of data, and a DatagramPacket with a 65,507-byte buffer can receive any possible IPv4 datagram without losing data. IPv6 datagrams raise the theoretical limit to 65,536 bytes. In practice, however, many UDP-based protocols such as DNS and TFTP use packets with 512 bytes of data per datagram or fewer. The largest data size in common usage is 8,192 bytes for NFS. Almost all UDP datagrams you're likely to encounter will have 8K of data or fewer. In fact, many operating systems don't support UDP datagrams with more than 8K of data and either truncate, split, or discard larger datagrams. If a large datagram is too big and as a result the network truncates or drops it, your Java program won't be notified of the problem. Consequently, you shouldn't create Data gramPacket objects with more than 8,192 bytes of data.

Constructors for sending datagrams

These four constructors create new DatagramPacket objects used to send data across the network:

```
public DatagramPacket(byte[] data, int length,
    InetAddress destination, int port)
public DatagramPacket(byte[] data, int offset, int length,
    InetAddress destination, int port)
public DatagramPacket(byte[] data, int length,
    SocketAddress destination)
public DatagramPacket(byte[] data, int offset, int length,
    SocketAddress destination)
```

Each constructor creates a new DatagramPacket to be sent to another host. The packet is filled with length bytes of the data array starting at offset or 0 if offset is not used. If you try to construct a DatagramPacket with a length that is greater than data.length (or greater than data.length - offset), the constructor throws an IllegalArgumen tException. It's OK to construct a DatagramPacket object with an offset and a length that will leave extra, unused space at the end of the data array. In this case, only length bytes of data will be sent over the network. The InetAddress or SocketAddress object destination points to the host you want the packet delivered to; the int argument port is the port on that host.

Choosing a Datagram Size

The correct amount of data to stuff into one packet depends on the situation. Some protocols dictate the size of the packet. For example, *rlogin* transmits each character to the remote system almost as soon as the user types it. Therefore, packets tend to be short: a single byte of data, plus a few bytes of headers. Other applications aren't so picky. For

---

example, file transfer is more efficient with large buffers; the only requirement is that you split files into packets no larger than the maximum allowable packet size.

Several factors are involved in choosing the optimal packet size. If the network is highly unreliable, such as a packet radio network, smaller packets are preferable because they're less likely to be corrupted in transit. On the other hand, very fast and reliable LANs should use the largest packet size possible. Eight kilobytes—that is, 8,192 bytes—is a good compromise for many types of networks.

It's customary to convert the data to a byte array and place it in data *before* creating the DatagramPacket, but it's not absolutely necessary. Changing data *after* the datagram has been constructed and *before* it has been sent changes the data in the datagram; the data isn't copied into a private buffer. In some applications, you can take advantage of this. For example, you could store data that changes over time in data and send out the current datagram (with the most recent data) every minute. However, it's more important to make sure that the data doesn't change when you don't want it to. This is especially true if your program is multithreaded, and different threads may write into the data buffer. If this is the case, copy the data into a temporary buffer before you construct the DatagramPacket.

For instance, this code fragment creates a new DatagramPacket filled with the data "This is a test" in UTF-8. The packet is directed at port 7 (the echo port) of *www.ibiblio.org*:

```
String s = "This is a test";
byte[] data = s.getBytes("UTF-8");

try {
  InetAddress ia = InetAddress.getByName("www.ibiblio.org");
  int port = 7;
  DatagramPacket dp = new DatagramPacket(data, data.length, ia, port);
  // send the packet...
} catch (IOException ex)
}
```

Most of the time, the hardest part of creating a new DatagramPacket is translating the data into a byte array. Because this code fragment wants to send a string, it uses the getBytes() method of java.lang.String. The java.io.ByteArrayOutputStream class can also be very useful for preparing data for inclusion in datagrams.

The get Methods

DatagramPacket has six methods that retrieve different parts of a datagram: the actual data plus several fields from its header. These methods are mostly used for datagrams received from the network.

public InetAddress getAddress()

The getAddress() method returns an InetAddress object containing the address of the remote host. If the datagram was received from the Internet, the address returned is the address of the machine that sent it (the source address). On the other hand, if the datagram was created locally to be sent to a remote machine, this method returns the address of the host to which the datagram is addressed (the destination address). This method is most commonly used to determine the address of the host that sent a UDP datagram, so that the recipient can reply.

public int getPort()

The getPort() method returns an integer specifying the remote port. If this datagram was received from the Internet, this is the port on the host that sent the packet. If the datagram was created locally to be sent to a remote host, this is the port to which the packet is addressed on the remote machine.

public SocketAddress getSocketAddress()

The getSocketAddress() method returns a SocketAddress object containing the IP address and port of the remote host. As is the case for getInetAddress(), if the datagram was received from the Internet, the address returned is the address of the machine that sent it (the source address). On the other hand, if the datagram was created locally to be sent to a remote machine, this method returns the address of the host to which the datagram is addressed (the destination address). You typically invoke this method to determine the address and port of the host that sent a UDP datagram before you reply. The net effect is not noticeably different than calling getAddress() and getPort(). Also, if you're using nonblocking I/O, the DatagramChannel class accepts a SocketAddress but not an InetAddress and port.

public byte[] getData()

The getData() method returns a byte array containing the data from the datagram. It's often necessary to convert the bytes into some other form of data before they'll be useful to your program. One way to do this is to change the byte array into a String. For example, given a DatagramPacket dp received from the network, you can convert it to a UTF-8 String like this:

```
String s = new String(dp.getData(), "UTF-8");
```

If the datagram does not contain text, converting it to Java data is more difficult. One approach is to convert the byte array returned by getData() into a ByteArrayInputStream. For example:

```
InputStream in = new ByteArrayInputStream(packet.getData(),
    packet.getOffset(), packet.getLength());
```

You *must* specify the offset and the length when constructing the ByteArrayInput Stream. Do not use the ByteArrayInputStream() constructor that takes only an array as an argument. The array returned by packet.getData() probably has extra space in it that was not filled with data from the network. This space will contain whatever random values those components of the array had when the DatagramPacket was constructed.

The ByteArrayInputStream can then be chained to a DataInputStream:

```
DataInputStream din = new DataInputStream(in);
```

The data can then be read using the DataInputStream's readInt(), readLong(), read Char(), and other methods. Of course, this assumes that the datagram's sender uses the same data formats as Java; it's probably the case when the sender is written in Java, and is often (though not necessarily) the case otherwise. (Most modern computers use the same floating-point format as Java, and most network protocols specify two's complement integers in network byte order, which also matches Java's formats.)

public int getLength()

The getLength() method returns the number of bytes of data in the datagram. This is *not* necessarily the same as the length of the array returned by getData() (i.e., getDa ta().length). The int returned by getLength() may be less than the length of the array returned by getData().

public int getOffset()

This method simply returns the point in the array returned by getData() where the data from the datagram begins.

Example 12-3 uses all the methods covered in this section to print the information in the DatagramPacket. This example is a little artificial; because the program creates a DatagramPacket, it already knows what's in it. More often, you'll use these methods on a DatagramPacket received from the network, but that will have to wait for the introduction of the DatagramSocket class in the next section.

Example 12-3. Construct a DatagramPacket to receive data

```
import java.io.*;
import java.net.*;

public class DatagramExample {

  public static void main(String[] args) {

    String s = "This is a test.";

    try {
```

```
    byte[] data = s.getBytes("UTF-8");
    InetAddress ia = InetAddress.getByName("www.ibiblio.org");
    int port = 7;
    DatagramPacket dp
        = new DatagramPacket(data, data.length, ia, port);
    System.out.println("This packet is addressed to "
        + dp.getAddress() + " on port " + dp.getPort());
    System.out.println("There are " + dp.getLength()
        + " bytes of data in the packet");
    System.out.println(
        new String(dp.getData(), dp.getOffset(), dp.getLength(), "UTF-8"));
  } catch (UnknownHostException | UnsupportedEncodingException ex) {
    System.err.println(ex);
  }
 }
}
```

Here's the output:

```
% java DatagramExample
This packet is addressed to www.ibiblio.org/152.2.254.81 on port 7
There are 15 bytes of data in the packet
This is a test.
```

The setter Methods

Most of the time, the six constructors are sufficient for creating datagrams. However, Java also provides several methods for changing the data, remote address, and remote port after the datagram has been created. These methods might be important in a situation where the time to create and garbage collect new DatagramPacket objects is a significant performance hit. In some situations, reusing objects can be significantly faster than constructing new ones: for example, in a networked twitch game that sends a datagram for every bullet fired or every centimeter of movement. However, you would have to use a very speedy connection for the improvement to be noticeable relative to the slowness of the network itself.

public void setData(byte[] data)

The setData() method changes the payload of the UDP datagram. You might use this method if you are sending a large file (where large is defined as "bigger than can comfortably fit in one datagram") to a remote host. You could repeatedly send the same DatagramPacket object, just changing the data each time.

public void setData(byte[] data, int offset, int length)

This overloaded variant of the setData() method provides an alternative approach to sending a large quantity of data. Instead of sending lots of new arrays, you can put all the data in one array and send it a piece at a time. For instance, this loop sends a large array in 512-byte chunks:

```
int offset = 0;
DatagramPacket dp = new DatagramPacket(bigarray, offset, 512);
int bytesSent = 0;
while (bytesSent < bigarray.length) {
  socket.send(dp);
  bytesSent += dp.getLength();
  int bytesToSend = bigarray.length - bytesSent;
  int size = (bytesToSend > 512) ? 512 : bytesToSend;
  dp.setData(bigarray, bytesSent, size);
}
```

On the other hand, this strategy requires either a lot of confidence that the data will in fact arrive or, alternatively, a disregard for the consequences of its not arriving. It's relatively difficult to attach sequence numbers or other reliability tags to individual packets when you take this approach.

public void setAddress(InetAddress remote)

The setAddress() method changes the address a datagram packet is sent to. This might allow you to send the same datagram to many different recipients. For example:

```
String s = "Really Important Message";
byte[] data = s.getBytes("UTF-8");
DatagramPacket dp = new DatagramPacket(data, data.length);
dp.setPort(2000);
int network = "128.238.5.";
for (int host = 1; host < 255; host++) {
  try {
    InetAddress remote = InetAddress.getByName(network + host);
    dp.setAddress(remote);
    socket.send(dp);
  } catch (IOException ex) {
    // skip it; continue with the next host
  }
}
```

Whether this is a sensible choice depends on the application. If you're trying to send to all the stations on a network segment, as in this fragment, you'd probably be better off using the local broadcast address and letting the network do the work. The local broadcast address is determined by setting all bits of the IP address after the network and subnet IDs to 1. For example, Polytechnic University's network address is 128.238.0.0. Consequently, its broadcast address is 128.238.255.255. Sending a datagram to 128.238.255.255 copies it to every host on that network (although some routers and firewalls may block it, depending on its origin).

For more widely separated hosts, you're probably better off using multicasting. Multicasting actually uses the same DatagramPacket class described here. However, it uses different IP addresses and a `MulticastSocket` instead of a `DatagramSocket`. We'll discuss this further in Chapter 13.

public void setPort(int port)

The `setPort()` method changes the port a datagram is addressed to. I honestly can't think of many uses for this method. It could be used in a port scanner application that tried to find open ports running particular UDP-based services such as FSP. Another possibility might be some sort of networked game or conferencing server where the clients that need to receive the same information are all running on different ports as well as different hosts. In this case, `setPort()` could be used in conjunction with `setAddress()` to change destinations before sending the same datagram out again.

public void setAddress(SocketAddress remote)

The `setSocketAddress()` method changes the address and port a datagram packet is sent to. You can use this when replying. For example, this code fragment receives a datagram packet and responds to the same address with a packet containing the string "Hello there":

```
DatagramPacket input = new DatagramPacket(new byte[8192], 8192);
socket.receive(input);
DatagramPacket output = new DatagramPacket(
    "Hello there".getBytes("UTF-8"), 11);
SocketAddress address = input.getSocketAddress();
output.setAddress(address);
socket.send(output);
```

You could certainly write the same code using `InetAddress` objects and ports instead of a `SocketAddress`. The code would be just a few lines longer.

public void setLength(int length)

The `setLength()` method changes the number of bytes of data in the internal buffer that are considered to be part of the datagram's data as opposed to merely unfilled space. This method is useful when receiving datagrams, as we'll explore later in this chapter. When a datagram is received, its length is set to the length of the incoming data. This means that if you try to receive another datagram into the same `DatagramPacket`, it's limited to no more than the number of bytes in the first. That is, once you've received a 10-byte datagram, all subsequent datagrams will be truncated to 10 bytes; once you've received a 9-byte datagram, all subsequent datagrams will be truncated to 9 bytes; and so on. This method lets you reset the length of the buffer so that subsequent datagrams aren't truncated.

The DatagramSocket Class

To send or receive a `DatagramPacket`, you must open a datagram socket. In Java, a datagram socket is created and accessed through the `DatagramSocket` class:

```
public class DatagramSocket extends Object
```

All datagram sockets bind to a local port, on which they listen for incoming data and which they place in the header of outgoing datagrams. If you're writing a client, you don't care what the local port is, so you call a constructor that lets the system assign an unused port (an anonymous port). This port number is placed in any outgoing datagrams and will be used by the server to address any response datagrams. If you're writing a server, clients need to know on which port the server is listening for incoming datagrams; therefore, when a server constructs a `DatagramSocket`, it specifies the local port on which it will listen. However, the sockets used by clients and servers are otherwise identical: they differ only in whether they use an anonymous (system-assigned) or a well-known port. There's no distinction between client sockets and server sockets, as there is with TCP. There's no such thing as a `DatagramServerSocket`.

The Constructors

The `DatagramSocket` constructors are used in different situations, much like the `Data gramPacket` constructors. The first constructor opens a datagram socket on an anonymous local port. The second constructor opens a datagram socket on a well-known local port that listens to all local network interfaces. The last two constructors open a datagram socket on a well-known local port on a specific network interface. All constructors deal only with the local address and port. The remote address and port are stored in the `DatagramPacket`, not the `DatagramSocket`. Indeed, one `DatagramSocket` can send and receive datagrams from multiple remote hosts and ports.

public DatagramSocket() throws SocketException

This constructor creates a socket that is bound to an anonymous port. For example:

```
try {
  DatagramSocket client = new DatagramSocket();
  // send packets...
} catch (SocketException ex) {
  System.err.println(ex);
}
```

Pick this constructor for a client that initiates a conversation with a server. In this scenario, you don't care what port the socket is bound to because the server will send its response to the port from which the datagram originated. Letting the system assign a port means that you don't have to worry about finding an unused port. If, for some reason, you need to know the local port, you can find out with the `getLocalPort()` method described later in this chapter.

The same socket can receive the datagrams that a server sends back to it. The constructor throws a `SocketException` if the socket can't bind to a port. It's unusual for this constructor to throw an exception; it's hard to imagine situations in which the socket could not be opened, because the system gets to choose an available port.

public DatagramSocket(int port) throws SocketException

This constructor creates a socket that listens for incoming datagrams on a particular port, specified by the `port` argument. Use this constructor to write a server that listens on a well-known port. A `SocketException` is thrown if the socket can't be created. There are two common reasons for the constructor to fail: the specified port is already occupied, or you are trying to connect to a port below 1024 and you don't have sufficient privileges (i.e., you are not root on a Unix system; for better or worse, other platforms allow anyone to connect to low-numbered ports).

TCP ports and UDP ports are not related. Two different programs can use the same port number if one uses UDP and the other uses TCP. Example 12-4 is a port scanner that looks for UDP ports in use on the local host. It decides that the port is in use if the `DatagramSocket` constructor throws an exception. As written, it looks at ports from 1024 and up to avoid Unix's requirement that it run as root to bind to ports below 1024. You can easily extend it to check ports below 1024, however, if you have root access or are running it on Windows.

Example 12-4. Look for local UDP ports

```
import java.net.*;

public class UDPPortScanner {

  public static void main(String[] args) {
    for (int port = 1024; port <= 65535; port++) {
      try {
        // the next line will fail and drop into the catch block if
        // there is already a server running on port i
        DatagramSocket server = new DatagramSocket(port);
        server.close();
      } catch (SocketException ex) {
        System.out.println("There is a server on port " + port + ".");
      }
    }
  }
}
```

Here are the results from the Linux workstation on which much of the code in this book was written:

```
% java UDPPortScanner
There is a server on port 2049.
There is a server on port 32768.
There is a server on port 32770.
There is a server on port 32771.
```

The first port, 2049, is an NFS server. The high-numbered ports in the 30,000 range are Remote Procedure Call (RPC) services. Along with RPC, common protocols that use UDP include NFS, TFTP, and FSP.

It's much harder to scan UDP ports on a remote system than to scan for remote TCP ports. Whereas there's always some indication that a listening port, regardless of application layer protocol, has received your TCP packet, UDP provides no such guarantees. To determine that a UDP server is listening, you have to send it a packet it will recognize and respond to.

public DatagramSocket(int port, InetAddress interface) throws SocketException

This constructor is primarily used on multihomed hosts; it creates a socket that listens for incoming datagrams on a specific port and network interface. The `port` argument is the port on which this socket listens for datagrams. As with TCP sockets, you need to be root on a Unix system to create a `DatagramSocket` on a port below 1024. The `address` argument is an `InetAddress` object matching one of the host's network addresses. A `SocketException` is thrown if the socket can't be created. There are three common reasons for this constructor to fail: the specified port is already occupied, you are trying to connect to a port below 1024 and you're not root on a Unix system, or `address` is not the address of one of the system's network interfaces.

public DatagramSocket(SocketAddress interface) throws SocketException

This constructor is similar to the previous one except that the network interface address and port are read from a `SocketAddress`. For example, this code fragment creates a socket that only listens on the local loopback address:

```
SocketAddress address = new InetSocketAddress("127.0.0.1", 9999);
DatagramSocket socket = new DatagramSocket(address);
```

protected DatagramSocket(DatagramSocketImpl impl) throws SocketException

This constructor enables subclasses to provide their own implementation of the UDP protocol, rather than blindly accepting the default. Unlike sockets created by the other four constructors, this socket is not initially bound to a port. Before using it, you have to bind it to a `SocketAddress` using the `bind()` method:

```
public void bind(SocketAddress addr) throws SocketException
```

You can pass null to this method, binding the socket to any available address and port.

Sending and Receiving Datagrams

The primary task of the DatagramSocket class is to send and receive UDP datagrams. One socket can both send and receive. Indeed, it can send and receive to and from multiple hosts at the same time.

public void send(DatagramPacket dp) throws IOException

Once a DatagramPacket is created and a DatagramSocket is constructed, send the packet by passing it to the socket's send() method. For example, if theSocket is a Datagram Socket object and theOutput is a DatagramPacket object, send theOutput using the Socket like this:

```
theSocket.send(theOutput);
```

If there's a problem sending the data, this method may throw an IOException. However, this is less common with DatagramSocket than Socket or ServerSocket, because the unreliable nature of UDP means you won't get an exception just because the packet doesn't arrive at its destination. You may get an IOException if you're trying to send a larger datagram than the host's native networking software supports, but then again you may not. This depends heavily on the native UDP software in the OS and the native code that interfaces between this and Java's DatagramSocketImpl class. This method may also throw a SecurityException if the SecurityManager won't let you communicate with the host to which the packet is addressed. This is primarily a problem for applets and other remotely loaded code.

Example 12-5 is a UDP-based discard client. It reads lines of user input from Sys tem.in and sends them to a discard server, which simply discards all the data. Each line is stuffed in a DatagramPacket. Many of the simpler Internet protocols, such as discard and echo, have both TCP and UDP implementations.

Example 12-5. A UDP discard client

```
import java.net.*;
import java.io.*;

public class UDPDiscardClient {

  public final static int PORT = 9;

  public static void main(String[] args) {

    String hostname = args.length > 0 ?  args[0] : "localhost";

    try (DatagramSocket theSocket = new DatagramSocket()) {
      InetAddress server = InetAddress.getByName(hostname);
      BufferedReader userInput
          = new BufferedReader(new InputStreamReader(System.in));
      while (true) {
```

```
        String theLine = userInput.readLine();
        if (theLine.equals(".")) break;
        byte[] data = theLine.getBytes();
        DatagramPacket theOutput
            = new DatagramPacket(data, data.length, server, PORT);
        theSocket.send(theOutput);
      } // end while
    } catch (IOException ex) {
      System.err.println(ex);
    }
  }
}
```

The UDPDiscardClient class should look familiar. It has a single static field, PORT, which is set to the standard port for the discard protocol (port 9), and a single method, main(). The main() method reads a hostname from the command line and converts that hostname to the InetAddress object called server. A BufferedReader is chained to System.in to read user input from the keyboard. Next, a DatagramSocket object called theSocket is constructed. After creating the socket, the program enters an infinite while loop that reads user input line by line using readLine(). Example 12-5 is careful, however, to use only readLine() to read data from the console, the one place where it is guaranteed to work as advertised. Because the discard protocol deals only with raw bytes, it can ignore character encoding issues.

In the while loop, each line is converted to a byte array using the getBytes() method, and the bytes are stuffed in a new DatagramPacket, theOutput. Finally, theOutput is sent over theSocket, and the loop continues. If at any point the user types a period on a line by itself, the program exits. The DatagramSocket constructor may throw a SocketException, so that needs to be caught. Because this is a discard client, you don't need to worry about data coming back from the server.

public void receive(DatagramPacket dp) throws IOException

This method receives a single UDP datagram from the network and stores it in the preexisting DatagramPacket object dp. Like the accept() method in the ServerSocket class, this method blocks the calling thread until a datagram arrives. If your program does anything besides wait for datagrams, you should call receive() in a separate thread.

The datagram's buffer should be large enough to hold the data received. If it's not, receive() places as much data in the buffer as it can hold; the rest is lost. Remember that the maximum size of the data portion of a UDP datagram is 65,507 bytes. (That's the 65,536-byte maximum size of an IP datagram minus the 20-byte size of the IP header and the 8-byte size of the UDP header.) Some application protocols that use UDP further restrict the maximum number of bytes in a packet; for instance, NFS uses a maximum packet size of 8,192 bytes.

If there's a problem receiving the data, `receive()` may throw an `IOException`. In practice, this is rare because problems like dropped packets that would shut down a TCP stream are silently discarded by the network or network stack before Java ever sees them.

Example 12-6 shows a UDP discard server that receives incoming datagrams. Just for fun, it logs the data in each datagram to `System.out` so that you can see who's sending what to your discard server.

Example 12-6. The UDPDiscardServer

```
import java.net.*;
import java.io.*;

public class UDPDiscardServer {

  public final static int PORT = 9;
  public final static int MAX_PACKET_SIZE = 65507;

  public static void main(String[] args) {

    byte[] buffer = new byte[MAX_PACKET_SIZE];

    try (DatagramSocket server = new DatagramSocket(PORT)) {
      DatagramPacket packet = new DatagramPacket(buffer, buffer.length);
      while (true) {
        try {
          server.receive(packet);
          String s = new String(packet.getData(), 0, packet.getLength(), "8859_1");
          System.out.println(packet.getAddress() + " at port "
              + packet.getPort() + " says " + s);
          // reset the length for the next packet
          packet.setLength(buffer.length);
        } catch (IOException ex) {
          System.err.println(ex);
        }
      } // end while
    } catch (SocketException  ex) {
      System.err.println(ex);
    }
  }
}
```

This is a simple class with a single method, `main()`. It reads the port the server listens to from the command line. If the port is not specified on the command line, it listens on port 9. It then opens a `DatagramSocket` on that port and creates a `DatagramPacket` with a 65,507-byte buffer—large enough to receive any possible packet. Then the server enters an infinite loop that receives packets and prints the contents and the originating host on the console. There's no particular encoding expected for discard packets. Indeed, there's no particular reason these packets have to be text at all. I somewhat arbitrarily picked the Latin-1 ISO 8859-1 encoding because it's ASCII compatible and defines a character for every byte.

As each datagram is received, the length of packet is set to the length of the data in that datagram. Consequently, as the last step of the loop, the length of the packet is reset to the maximum possible value. Otherwise, the incoming packets would be limited to the minimum size of all previous packets. You can run the discard client on one machine and connect to the discard server on a second machine to verify that the network is working.

public void close()

Calling a DatagramSocket object's close() method frees the port occupied by that socket. As with streams and TCP sockets, you'll want to take care to close the datagram socket in a finally block:

```
DatagramSocket server = null
try {
  server = new DatagramSocket();
  // use the socket...
} catch (IOException ex) {
  System.err.println(ex);
} finally {
  try {
    if (server != null) server.close();
  } catch (IOException ex) {
  }
}
```

In Java 7, DatagramSocket implements AutoCloseable so you can use try-with-resources:

```
try (DatagramSocket server = new DatagramSocket()) {
  // use the socket...
}
```

It's never a bad idea to close a DatagramSocket when you're through with it; it's particularly important to close an unneeded socket if the program will continue to run for a significant amount of time. For example, the close() method was essential in Example 12-4, UDPPortScanner: if this program did not close the sockets it opened, it would tie up every UDP port on the system for a significant amount of time. On the other hand, if the program ends as soon as you're through with the DatagramSocket, you don't need to close the socket explicitly; the socket is automatically closed upon garbage collection. However, Java won't run the garbage collector just because you've run out of ports or sockets, unless by lucky happenstance you run out of memory at the same time. Closing unneeded sockets never hurts and is good programming practice.

public int getLocalPort()

A `DatagramSocket`'s `getLocalPort()` method returns an `int` that represents the local port on which the socket is listening. Use this method if you created a `DatagramSock et` with an anonymous port and want to find out what port the socket has been assigned. For example:

```
DatagramSocket ds = new DatagramSocket();
System.out.println("The socket is using port " + ds.getLocalPort());
```

public InetAddress getLocalAddress()

A `DatagramSocket`'s `getLocalAddress()` method returns an `InetAddress` object that represents the local address to which the socket is bound. It's rarely needed in practice. Normally, you either already know or simply don't care which address a socket is listening to.

public SocketAddress getLocalSocketAddress()

The `getLocalSocketAddress()` method returns a `SocketAddress` object that wraps the local interface and port to which the socket is bound. Like `getLocalAddress()`, it's a little hard to imagine a realistic use case here. This method probably exists mostly for parallelism with `setLocalSocketAddress()`.

Managing Connections

Unlike TCP sockets, datagram sockets aren't very picky about whom they'll talk to. In fact, by default they'll talk to anyone; but this is often not what you want. For instance, applets are only allowed to send datagrams to and receive datagrams from the applet host. An NFS or FSP client should accept packets only from the server it's talking to. A networked game should listen to datagrams only from the people playing the game. The next five methods let you choose which host you can send datagrams to and receive datagrams from, while rejecting all others' packets.

public void connect(InetAddress host, int port)

The `connect()` method doesn't really establish a connection in the TCP sense. However, it does specify that the `DatagramSocket` will only send packets to and receive packets from the specified remote host on the specified remote port. Attempts to send packets to a different host or port will throw an `IllegalArgumentException`. Packets received from a different host or a different port will be discarded without an exception or other notification.

A security check is made when the `connect()` method is invoked. If the VM is allowed to send data to that host and port, the check passes silently. If not, a `SecurityExcep` tion is thrown. However, once the connection has been made, send() and receive() on that DatagramSocket no longer make the security checks they'd normally make.

public void disconnect()

The disconnect() method breaks the "connection" of a connected DatagramSocket so that it can once again send packets to and receive packets from any host and port.

public int getPort()

If and only if a DatagramSocket is connected, the getPort() method returns the remote port to which it is connected. Otherwise, it returns –1.

public InetAddress getInetAddress()

If and only if a DatagramSocket is connected, the getInetAddress() method returns the address of the remote host to which it is connected. Otherwise, it returns null.

public InetAddress getRemoteSocketAddress()

If a DatagramSocket is connected, the getRemoteSocketAddress() method returns the address of the remote host to which it is connected. Otherwise, it returns null.

Socket Options

Java supports six socket options for UDP:

- SO_TIMEOUT
- SO_RCVBUF
- SO_SNDBUF
- SO_REUSEADDR
- SO_BROADCAST
- IP_TOS

SO_TIMEOUT

SO_TIMEOUT is the amount of time, in milliseconds, that receive() waits for an incoming datagram before throwing an InterruptedIOException, which is a subclass of IOException. Its value must be nonnegative. If SO_TIMEOUT is 0, receive() never times out. This value can be changed with the setSoTimeout() method and inspected with the getSoTimeout() method:

```
public void setSoTimeout(int timeout) throws SocketException
public int getSoTimeout() throws IOException
```

The default is to never time out, and indeed there are few situations in which you need to set SO_TIMEOUT. You might need it if you were implementing a secure protocol that required responses to occur within a fixed amount of time. You might also decide that the host you're communicating with is dead (unreachable or not responding) if you don't receive a response within a certain amount of time.

The setSoTimeout() method sets the SO_TIMEOUT field for a datagram socket. When the timeout expires, a blocked receive() method throws a SocketTimeoutException. Set this option *before* you call receive(). You cannot change it while receive() is waiting for a datagram. The timeout argument must be greater than or equal to zero. For example:

```
try {
  byte[] buffer = new byte[2056];
  DatagramPacket dp = new DatagramPacket(buffer, buffer.length);
  DatagramSocket ds = new DatagramSocket(2048);
  ds.setSoTimeout(30000); // block for no more than 30 seconds
  try {
   ds.receive(dp);
    // process the packet...
  } catch (SocketTimeoutException ex) {
    ss.close();
    System.err.println("No connection within 30 seconds");
  }
} catch (SocketException ex) {
  System.err.println(ex);
} catch (IOException ex) {
  System.err.println("Unexpected IOException: " + ex);
}
```

The getSoTimeout() method returns the current value of this DatagramSocket object's SO_TIMEOUT field. For example:

```
public void printSoTimeout(DatagramSocket ds) {
  int timeout = ds.getSoTimeOut();
  if (timeout > 0) {
    System.out.println(ds + " will time out after "
    + timeout + "milliseconds.");
  } else if (timeout == 0) {
    System.out.println(ds + " will never time out.");
  } else {
    System.out.println("Something is seriously wrong with " + ds);
  }
}
```

SO_RCVBUF

The SO_RCVBUF option of `DatagramSocket` is closely related to the SO_RCVBUF option of `Socket`. It determines the size of the buffer used for network I/O. Larger buffers tend to improve performance for reasonably fast (say, Ethernet-speed) connections because they can store more incoming datagrams before overflowing. Sufficiently large receive buffers are even more important for UDP than for TCP, because a UDP datagram that arrives when the buffer is full will be lost, whereas a TCP datagram that arrives at a full buffer will eventually be retransmitted. Furthermore, SO_RCVBUF sets the maximum size of datagram packets that can be received by the application. Packets that won't fit in the receive buffer are silently discarded.

`DatagramSocket` has methods to set and get the suggested receive buffer size used for network input:

```
public void setReceiveBufferSize(int size) throws SocketException
public int getReceiveBufferSize() throws SocketException
```

The `setReceiveBufferSize()` method suggests a number of bytes to use for buffering input from this socket. However, the underlying implementation is free to ignore this suggestion. For instance, many 4.3 BSD-derived systems have a maximum receive buffer size of about 52K and won't let you set a limit higher than this. My Linux box was limited to 64K. Other systems raise this to about 240K. The details are highly platform-dependent. Consequently, you may wish to check the actual size of the receive buffer with `getReceiveBufferSize()` after setting it. The `getReceiveBufferSize()` method returns the number of bytes in the buffer used for input from this socket.

Both methods throw a `SocketException` if the underlying socket implementation does not recognize the SO_RCVBUF option. This might happen on a non-POSIX operating system. The `setReceiveBufferSize()` method will throw an `IllegalArgumentExcep tion` if its argument is less than or equal to zero.

SO_SNDBUF

`DatagramSocket` has methods to get and set the suggested send buffer size used for network output:

```
public void setSendBufferSize(int size)  throws SocketException
public int getSendBufferSize() throws SocketException
```

The `setSendBufferSize()` method suggests a number of bytes to use for buffering output on this socket. Once again, however, the operating system is free to ignore this suggestion. Consequently, you'll want to check the result of `setSendBufferSize()` by immediately following it with a call to `getSendBufferSize()` to find out the real buffer size.

Both methods throw a `SocketException` if the underlying native network software doesn't understand the SO_SNDBUF option. The `setSendBufferSize()` method also throws an `IllegalArgumentException` if its argument is less than or equal to zero.

SO_REUSEADDR

The SO_REUSEADDR option does not mean the same thing for UDP sockets as it does for TCP sockets. For UDP, SO_REUSEADDR controls whether multiple datagram sockets can bind to the same port and address *at the same time*. If multiple sockets are bound to the same port, received packets will be copied to all bound sockets. This option is controlled by these two methods:

```
public void setReuseAddress(boolean on) throws SocketException
public boolean getReuseAddress() throws SocketException
```

For this to work reliably, `setReuseAddress()` must be called *before* the new socket binds to the port. This means the socket must be created in an unconnected state using the protected constructor that takes a `DatagramImpl` as an argument. In other words, it won't work with a plain vanilla `DatagramSocket`. Reusable ports are most commonly used for multicast sockets, which will be discussed in the next chapter. Datagram channels also create unconnected datagram sockets that can be configured to reuse ports, as you'll see later in this chapter.

SO_BROADCAST

The SO_BROADCAST option controls whether a socket is allowed to send packets to and receive packets from broadcast addresses such as 192.168.254.255, the local network broadcast address for the network with the local address 192.168.254.*. UDP broadcasting is often used for protocols such as DHCP that need to communicate with servers on the local net whose addresses are not known in advance. This option is controlled with these two methods:

```
public void setBroadcast(boolean on) throws SocketException
public boolean getBroadcast() throws SocketException
```

Routers and gateways do not normally forward broadcast messages, but they can still kick up a lot of traffic on the local network. This option is turned on by default, but if you like you can disable it thusly:

```
socket.setBroadcast(false);
```

This option can be changed after the socket has been bound.

On some implementations, sockets bound to a specific address do not receive broadcast packets. In other words, you should use the `DatagramPacket(int port)` constructor, not the `DatagramPacket(InetAddress address, int port)` constructor to listen to broadcasts. This is necessary in addition to setting the SO_BROADCAST option to true.

IP_TOS

Because the traffic class is determined by the value of the IP_TOS field in each IP packet header, it is essentially the same for UDP as it is for TCP. After all, packets are actually routed and prioritized according to IP, which both TCP and UDP sit on top of. There's really no difference between the `setTrafficClass()` and `getTrafficClass()` methods in `DatagramSocket` and those in `Socket`. They just have to be repeated here because `DatagramSocket` and `Socket` don't have a common superclass. These two methods let you inspect and set the class of service for a socket using these two methods:

```
public int getTrafficClass() throws SocketException
public void setTrafficClass(int trafficClass) throws SocketException
```

The traffic class is given as an int between 0 and 255. Because this value is copied to an eight-bit field in the TCP header, only the low-order byte of this `int` is used; and values outside this range cause `IllegalArgumentExceptions`.

 The JavaDoc for these options is severely out of date, and describes a quality of service scheme based on bit fields for four traffic classes: low cost, high reliability, maximum throughput, and minimum delay. This scheme was never widely implemented and probably hasn't been used in this century.

This code fragment sets a socket to use Expedited Forwarding by setting the traffic class to 10111000:

```
DatagramSocket s = new DatagramSocket();
s.setTrafficClass(0xB8); // 10111000 in binary
```

For details of the individual traffic classes, refer to "IP_TOS Class of Service" on page 269.

The underlying socket implementation is not required to respect any of these requests. Some implementations ignore these values completely. Android in particular treats the `setTrafficClass()` method as a noop. If the native network stack is unable to provide the requested class of service, Java may but is not required to throw a `SocketException`.

Some Useful Applications

In this section, you'll see several Internet servers and clients that use `DatagramPacket` and `DatagramSocket`. Some of these will be familiar from previous chapters because many Internet protocols have both TCP and UDP implementations. When an IP packet is received by a host, the host determines whether the packet is a TCP packet or a UDP datagram by inspecting the IP header. As I said earlier, there's no connection between UDP and TCP ports; TCP and UDP servers can share the same port number without problems. By convention, if a service has both TCP and UDP implementations, it uses the same port for both, although there's no technical reason this has to be the case.

Simple UDP Clients

Several Internet services need to know only the client's address and port; they ignore any data the client sends in its datagrams. Daytime, quote of the day, time, and chargen are four such protocols. Each of these responds the same way, regardless of the data contained in the datagram, or indeed regardless of whether there actually is any data in the datagram. Clients for these protocols simply send a UDP datagram to the server and read the response that comes back. Therefore, let's begin with a simple client called `UDPPoke`, shown in Example 12-7, which sends an empty UDP packet to a specified host and port and reads a response packet from the same host.

The `UDPPoke` class has four private fields. The `bufferSize` field specifies how large a return packet is expected. An 8,192-byte buffer is large enough for most of the protocols that `UDPPoke` is useful for, but it can be increased by passing a different value to the constructor. The `timeout` field specifies how long to wait for a response. The `host` and the `port` fields specify the remote host to connect to.

If the buffer length is not specified, 8,192 bytes is used. If the timeout is not given, 30 seconds (30,000 milliseconds) is used. The host, port, and buffer size are also used to construct the outgoing `DatagramPacket`. Although in theory you should be able to send a datagram with no data at all, bugs in some Java implementations require that you add at least one byte of data to the datagram. The simple servers we're currently considering ignore this data.

Once a `UDPPoke` object has been constructed, clients call its `poke()` method to send an empty `outgoing` datagram to the target and read its response. The response is initially set to null. When the expected datagram appears, its data is copied into the `response` field. This method returns null if the response doesn't come quickly enough or never comes at all.

The `main()` method merely reads the host and port to connect to from the command line, constructs a `UDPPoke` object, and pokes it. Most of the simple protocols that this client suits will return ASCII text, so this example attempts to convert the response to an ASCII string and print it.

Example 12-7. The UDPPoke class

```java
import java.io.*;
import java.net.*;

public class UDPPoke {

  private int bufferSize; // in bytes
  private int timeout; // in milliseconds
  private InetAddress host;
  private int port;

  public UDPPoke(InetAddress host, int port, int bufferSize, int timeout) {
    this.bufferSize = bufferSize;
    this.host = host;
    if (port < 1 || port > 65535) {
      throw new IllegalArgumentException("Port out of range");
    }

    this.port = port;
    this.timeout = timeout;
  }

  public UDPPoke(InetAddress host, int port, int bufferSize) {
    this(host, port, bufferSize, 30000);
  }

  public UDPPoke(InetAddress host, int port) {
    this(host, port, 8192, 30000);
  }

  public byte[] poke() {
    try (DatagramSocket socket = new DatagramSocket(0)) {
      DatagramPacket outgoing = new DatagramPacket(new byte[1], 1, host, port);
      socket.connect(host, port);
      socket.setSoTimeout(timeout);

      socket.send(outgoing);
      DatagramPacket incoming
          = new DatagramPacket(new byte[bufferSize], bufferSize);
      // next line blocks until the response is received
      socket.receive(incoming);
      int numBytes = incoming.getLength();
      byte[] response = new byte[numBytes];
      System.arraycopy(incoming.getData(), 0, response, 0, numBytes);
      return response;
    } catch (IOException ex) {
      return null;
    }
```

```
    }

    public static void main(String[] args) {
      InetAddress host;
      int port = 0;
      try {
        host = InetAddress.getByName(args[0]);
        port = Integer.parseInt(args[1]);
      } catch (RuntimeException | UnknownHostException ex) {
        System.out.println("Usage: java UDPPoke host port");
        return;
      }

      try {
        UDPPoke poker = new UDPPoke(host, port);
        byte[] response = poker.poke();
        if (response == null) {
          System.out.println("No response within allotted time");
          return;
        }
        String result = new String(response, "US-ASCII");
        System.out.println(result);
      } catch (UnsupportedEncodingException ex) {
        // Really shouldn't happen
        ex.printStackTrace();
      }
    }
  }
}
```

For example, this connects to a daytime server over UDP:

```
$ java UDPPoke rama.poly.edu 13
Sun Oct  3 13:04:22 2009
```

This connects to a chargen server:

```
$ java UDPPoke rama.poly.edu 19
123456789:;<=>?@ABCDEFGHIJKLMNOPQRSTUVWXYZ[\]^_`abcdefghijklmnopqrstuv
```

Given this class, UDP daytime, time, chargen, and quote of the day clients are almost
trivial. A time client is only slightly harder, and only because you need to convert the
four raw bytes returned by the server to a `java.util.Date` object. The same algorithm
as in Example 8-3 will accomplish that as demonstrated in Example 12-8.

Example 12-8. A UDP time client

```
import java.net.*;
import java.util.*;

public class UDPTimeClient {

  public final static int PORT = 37;
  public final static String DEFAULT_HOST = "time.nist.gov";
```

```
  public static void main(String[] args) {

    InetAddress host;
    try {
      if (args.length > 0) {
        host = InetAddress.getByName(args[0]);
      } else {
        host = InetAddress.getByName(DEFAULT_HOST);
      }
    } catch (RuntimeException | UnknownHostException ex) {
      System.out.println("Usage: java UDPTimeClient [host]");
      return;
    }

    UDPPoke poker = new UDPPoke(host, PORT);
    byte[] response = poker.poke();
    if (response == null) {
      System.out.println("No response within allotted time");
      return;
    } else if (response.length != 4) {
      System.out.println("Unrecognized response format");
      return;
    }

    // The time protocol sets the epoch at 1900,
    // the Java Date class at 1970. This number
    // converts between them.

    long differenceBetweenEpochs = 2208988800L;

    long secondsSince1900 = 0;
    for (int i = 0; i < 4; i++) {
      secondsSince1900
          = (secondsSince1900 << 8) | (response[i] & 0x000000FF);
    }

    long secondsSince1970
        = secondsSince1900 - differenceBetweenEpochs;
    long msSince1970 = secondsSince1970 * 1000;
    Date time = new Date(msSince1970);

    System.out.println(time);
  }
}
```

UDPServer

Clients aren't the only programs that benefit from a reusable implementation. The servers for these protocols are also very similar. They all wait for UDP datagrams on a specified port and reply to each datagram with another datagram. The servers differ only in the content of the datagram that they return. Example 12-9 is a simple iterative UDPServer class that can be subclassed to provide specific servers for different protocols.

The UDPServer class has two fields, the int bufferSize and the DatagramSocket socket, the latter of which is protected so it can be used by subclasses. The constructor opens a datagram socket on a specified local port to receive datagrams of no more than bufferSize bytes.

UDPServer implements Runnable so that multiple instances can run in parallel. Its run() method contains a loop that repeatedly receives an incoming datagram and responds by passing it to the abstract respond() method. This method will be overridden by particular subclasses in order to implement different kinds of servers.

Assuming this class may be used as part of other programs that do more than just run one server, you need a way to shut it down. This is provided by the shutDown() method, which sets a flag. The main loop checks this flag each pass to see if it should exit. Because the receive() call can block indefinitely if there's no traffic, you also set a timeout on the socket. This will wake it up once every 10 seconds to check for shutdown whether there's traffic or not.

UDPServer is a very flexible class. Subclasses can send zero, one, or many datagrams in response to each incoming datagram. If a lot of processing is required to respond to a packet, the respond() method can spawn a thread to do it. However, UDP servers tend not to have extended interactions with a client. Each incoming packet is treated independently of other packets, so the response can usually be handled directly in the respond() method without spawning a thread.

Example 12-9. The UDPServer class

```
import java.io.*;
import java.net.*;
import java.util.logging.*;

public abstract class UDPServer implements Runnable {

  private final int bufferSize; // in bytes
  private final int port;
  private final Logger logger = Logger.getLogger(UDPServer.class.getCanonicalName());
  private volatile boolean isShutDown = false;

  public UDPServer(int port, int bufferSize) {
    this.bufferSize = bufferSize;
    this.port = port;
  }

  public UDPServer(int port) {
    this(port, 8192);
  }
```

```
@Override
public void run() {
  byte[] buffer = new byte[bufferSize];
  try (DatagramSocket socket = new DatagramSocket(port)) {
    socket.setSoTimeout(10000); // check every 10 seconds for shutdown
    while (true) {
      if (isShutDown) return;
      DatagramPacket incoming = new DatagramPacket(buffer, buffer.length);
      try {
        socket.receive(incoming);
        this.respond(socket, incoming);
      } catch (SocketTimeoutException ex) {
        if (isShutDown) return;
      } catch (IOException ex) {
        logger.log(Level.WARNING, ex.getMessage(), ex);
      }
    } // end while
  } catch (SocketException ex) {
    logger.log(Level.SEVERE, "Could not bind to port: " + port, ex);
  }
}

public abstract void respond(DatagramSocket socket, DatagramPacket request)
    throws IOException;

public void shutDown() {
  this.isShutDown = true;
}

}
```

The easiest protocol to handle is discard. All that's needed is a main() method that sets the port and starts the thread. respond() is a do-nothing method. Example 12-10 is a high-performance UDP discard server that does nothing with incoming packets.

Example 12-10. A UDP discard server

```
import java.net.*;

public class FastUDPDiscardServer extends UDPServer {

  public final static int DEFAULT_PORT = 9;

  public FastUDPDiscardServer() {
    super(DEFAULT_PORT);
  }

  public static void main(String[] args) {
    UDPServer server = new FastUDPDiscardServer();
    Thread t = new Thread(server);
    t.start();
  }
```

```
  @Override
  public void respond(DatagramSocket socket, DatagramPacket request) {
  }
}
```

It isn't much harder to implement an echo server, as Example 12-11 shows. Unlike a stream-based TCP echo server, multiple threads are not required to handle multiple clients.

Example 12-11. A UDP echo server

```
import java.io.*;
import java.net.*;

public class UDPEchoServer extends UDPServer {

  public final static int DEFAULT_PORT = 7;

  public UDPEchoServer() {
    super(DEFAULT_PORT);
  }

  @Override
  public void respond(DatagramSocket socket, DatagramPacket packet)
      throws IOException {
    DatagramPacket outgoing = new DatagramPacket(packet.getData(),
        packet.getLength(), packet.getAddress(), packet.getPort());
    socket.send(outgoing);
  }

  public static void main(String[] args) {
    UDPServer server = new UDPEchoServer();
    Thread t = new Thread(server);
    t.start();
  }
}
```

A UDP Echo Client

The UDPPoke class implemented earlier isn't suitable for all protocols. In particular, protocols that require multiple datagrams require a different implementation. The echo protocol has both TCP and UDP implementations. Implementing the echo protocol with TCP is simple; it's more complex with UDP because you don't have I/O streams or the concept of a connection to work with. A TCP-based echo client can send a message and wait for a response on the same connection. However, a UDP-based echo client has no guarantee that the message it sent was received. Therefore, it cannot simply wait for the response; it needs to be prepared to send and receive data asynchronously.

This behavior is fairly simple to implement using threads, however. One thread can process user input and send it to the echo server, while a second thread accepts input from the server and displays it to the user. The client is divided into three classes: the main UDPEchoClient class, the SenderThread class, and the ReceiverThread class.

The UDPEchoClient class should look familiar. It reads a hostname from the command line and converts it to an InetAddress object. UDPEchoClient uses this object and the default echo port to construct a SenderThread object. This constructor can throw a SocketException, so the exception must be caught. Then the SenderThread starts. The same DatagramSocket that the SenderThread uses is used to construct a ReceiverTh read, which is then started. It's important to use the same DatagramSocket for both sending and receiving data because the echo server will send the response back to the port the data was sent from. Example 12-12 shows the code for the UDPEchoClient.

Example 12-12. The UDPEchoClient class

```
import java.net.*;

public class UDPEchoClient {

  public final static int PORT = 7;

  public static void main(String[] args) {

    String hostname = "localhost";
    if (args.length > 0) {
      hostname = args[0];
    }

    try {
      InetAddress ia = InetAddress.getByName(hostname);
      DatagramSocket socket = new DatagramSocket();
      SenderThread sender = new SenderThread(socket, ia, PORT);
      sender.start();
      Thread receiver = new ReceiverThread(socket);
      receiver.start();
    } catch (UnknownHostException ex) {
      System.err.println(ex);
    } catch (SocketException ex) {
      System.err.println(ex);
    }
  }
}
```

The SenderThread class reads input from the console a line at a time and sends it to the echo server. It's shown in Example 12-13. The input is provided by System.in, but a different client could include an option to read input from a different stream—perhaps opening a FileInputStream to read from a file. The fields of this class define the server to which it sends data, the port on that server, and the DatagramSocket that does the sending, all set in the single constructor. The DatagramSocket is connected to the remote server to make sure all datagrams received were in fact sent by the right server. It's rather unlikely that some other server on the Internet is going to bombard this particular port with extraneous data, so this is not a big flaw. However, it's a good habit to make sure that the packets you receive come from the right place, especially if security is a concern.

The run() method processes user input a line at a time. To do this, the BufferedRead er userInput is chained to System.in. An infinite loop reads lines of user input. Each line is stored in theLine. A period on a line by itself signals the end of user input and breaks out of the loop. Otherwise, the bytes of data are stored in the data array using the getBytes() method from java.lang.String. Next, the data array is placed in the payload part of the DatagramPacket output, along with information about the server, the port, and the data length. This packet is then sent to its destination by socket. This thread then yields to give other threads an opportunity to run.

Example 12-13. The SenderThread class

```
import java.io.*;
import java.net.*;

class SenderThread extends Thread {

  private InetAddress server;
  private DatagramSocket socket;
  private int port;
  private volatile boolean stopped = false;

  SenderThread(DatagramSocket socket, InetAddress address, int port) {
    this.server = address;
    this.port = port;
    this.socket = socket;
    this.socket.connect(server, port);
  }

  public void halt() {
    this.stopped = true;
  }

  @Override
  public void run() {
    try {
      BufferedReader userInput
          = new BufferedReader(new InputStreamReader(System.in));
      while (true) {
        if (stopped) return;
        String theLine = userInput.readLine();
        if (theLine.equals(".")) break;
        byte[] data = theLine.getBytes("UTF-8");
        DatagramPacket output
            = new DatagramPacket(data, data.length, server, port);
```

```
        socket.send(output);
        Thread.yield();
      }
    } catch (IOException ex) {
      System.err.println(ex);
    }
  }
}
```

The `ReceiverThread` class shown in Example 12-14 waits for datagrams to arrive from the network. When a datagram is received, it is converted to a `String` and printed on `System.out` for display to the user. A more advanced echo client could include an option to send the output elsewhere.

This class has two fields. The more important is the `DatagramSocket`, `theSocket`, which must be the same `DatagramSocket` used by the `SenderThread`. Data arrives on the port used by that `DatagramSocket`; any other `DatagramSocket` would not be allowed to connect to the same port. The second field, `stopped`, is a boolean used to halt this thread without invoking the deprecated `stop()` method.

The `run()` method is an infinite loop that uses `socket`'s `receive()` method to wait for incoming datagrams. When an incoming datagram appears, it is converted into a `String` with the same length as the incoming data and printed on `System.out`. As in the input thread, this thread then yields to give other threads an opportunity to execute.

Example 12-14. The ReceiverThread class

```
import java.io.*;
import java.net.*;

class ReceiverThread extends Thread {

  private DatagramSocket socket;
  private volatile boolean stopped = false;

  ReceiverThread(DatagramSocket socket) {
    this.socket = socket;
  }

  public void halt() {
    this.stopped = true;
  }

  @Override
  public void run() {
    byte[] buffer = new byte[65507];
    while (true) {
      if (stopped) return;
      DatagramPacket dp = new DatagramPacket(buffer, buffer.length);
      try {
```

```
        socket.receive(dp);
        String s = new String(dp.getData(), 0, dp.getLength(), "UTF-8");
        System.out.println(s);
        Thread.yield();
      } catch (IOException ex) {
        System.err.println(ex);
      }
    }
  }
}
```

You can run the echo client on one machine and connect to the echo server on a second machine to verify that the network is functioning properly between them.

DatagramChannel

The DatagramChannel class is used for nonblocking UDP applications, in the same way as SocketChannel and ServerSocketChannel are used for nonblocking TCP applications. Like SocketChannel and ServerSocketChannel, DatagramChannel is a subclass of SelectableChannel that can be registered with a Selector. This is useful in servers where one thread can manage communications with multiple clients. However, UDP is by its nature much more asynchronous than TCP so the net effect is smaller. In UDP, a single datagram socket can process requests from multiple clients for both input and output. What the DatagramChannel class adds is the ability to do this in a nonblocking fashion, so methods return quickly if the network isn't immediately ready to receive or send data.

Using DatagramChannel

DatagramChannel is a near-complete alternate API for UDP. In Java 6 and earlier, you still need to use the DatagramSocket class to bind a channel to a port. However, you do not have to use it thereafter, and you don't have to use it all in Java 7 and later. Nor do you ever use DatagramPacket. Instead, you read and write byte buffers, just as you do with a SocketChannel.

Opening a socket

The java.nio.channels.DatagramChannel class does not have any public constructors. Instead, you create a new DatagramChannel object using the static open() method For example:

```
    DatagramChannel channel = DatagramChannel.open();
```

This channel is not initially bound to any port. To bind it, you access the channel's peer DatagramSocket object using the socket() method. For example, this binds a channel to port 3141:

```
  SocketAddress address = new InetSocketAddress(3141);
  DatagramSocket socket = channel.socket();
  socket.bind(address);
```

Java 7 adds a convenient bind() method directly to DatagramChannel, so you don't have to use a DatagramSocket at all. For example:

```
  SocketAddress address = new InetSocketAddress(3141);
  channel.bind(address);
```

Receiving

The receive() method reads one datagram packet from the channel into a ByteBuffer. It returns the address of the host that sent the packet:

```
  public SocketAddress receive(ByteBuffer dst) throws IOException
```

If the channel is blocking (the default), this method will not return until a packet has been read. If the channel is nonblocking, this method will immediately return null if no packet is available to read.

If the datagram packet has more data than the buffer can hold, *the extra data is thrown away with no notification of the problem.* You do not receive a BufferOverflowException or anything similar. Again you see that UDP is unreliable. This behavior introduces an additional layer of unreliability into the system. The data can arrive safely from the network and still be lost inside your own program.

Using this method, you can reimplement the discard server to log the host sending the data as well as the data sent. Example 12-15 demonstrates. It avoids the potential loss of data by using a buffer that's big enough to hold any UDP packet and clearing it before it's used again.

Example 12-15. A UDPDiscardServer based on channels

```
import java.io.*;
import java.net.*;
import java.nio.*;
import java.nio.channels.*;

public class UDPDiscardServerWithChannels {

  public final static int PORT = 9;
  public final static int MAX_PACKET_SIZE = 65507;

  public static void main(String[] args) {

    try {
      DatagramChannel channel = DatagramChannel.open();
      DatagramSocket socket = channel.socket();
      SocketAddress address = new InetSocketAddress(PORT);
      socket.bind(address);
```

```
      ByteBuffer buffer = ByteBuffer.allocateDirect(MAX_PACKET_SIZE);
      while (true) {
        SocketAddress client = channel.receive(buffer);
        buffer.flip();
        System.out.print(client + " says ");
        while (buffer.hasRemaining()) System.out.write(buffer.get());
        System.out.println();
        buffer.clear();
      }
    } catch (IOException ex) {
      System.err.println(ex);
    }
  }
}
```

Sending

The send() method writes one datagram packet into the channel from a ByteBuffer to the address specified as the second argument:

```
    public int send(ByteBuffer src, SocketAddress target) throws IOException
```

The source ByteBuffer can be reused if you want to send the same data to multiple clients. Just don't forget to rewind it first.

The send() method returns the number of bytes written. This will either be the number of bytes that were available in the buffer to be written or zero, nothing in between. It is zero if the channel is in nonblocking mode and the data can't be sent immediately. Otherwise, if the channel is not in nonblocking mode, send() simply waits to return until it can send all the data in the buffer.

Example 12-16 demonstrates with a simple echo server based on channels. Just as it did in Example 12-15, the receive() method reads a packet. However, this time, rather than logging the packet on System.out, it returns the same data to the client that sent it.

Example 12-16. A UDPEchoServer based on channels

```
import java.io.*;
import java.net.*;
import java.nio.*;
import java.nio.channels.*;

public class UDPEchoServerWithChannels {

  public final static int PORT = 7;
  public final static int MAX_PACKET_SIZE = 65507;

  public static void main(String[] args) {

    try {
```

```
    DatagramChannel channel = DatagramChannel.open();
    DatagramSocket socket = channel.socket();
    SocketAddress address = new InetSocketAddress(PORT);
    socket.bind(address);
    ByteBuffer buffer = ByteBuffer.allocateDirect(MAX_PACKET_SIZE);
    while (true) {
      SocketAddress client = channel.receive(buffer);
      buffer.flip();
      channel.send(buffer, client);
      buffer.clear();
    }
  } catch (IOException ex) {
    System.err.println(ex);
  }
 }
}
```

This program is iterative, blocking, and synchronous. This is much less of a problem for UDP-based protocols than for TCP protocols. The unreliable, packet-based, connectionless nature of UDP means that the server at most has to wait for the local buffer to clear. It does not wait for the client to be ready to receive data. There's much less opportunity for one client to get held up behind a slower client.

Connecting

Once you've opened a datagram channel, you connect it to a particular remote address using the connect() method:

```
SocketAddress remote = new InetSocketAddress("time.nist.gov", 37);
channel.connect(remote);
```

The channel will only send data to or receive data from this host. Unlike the connect() method of SocketChannel, this method alone does not send or receive any packets across the network because UDP is a connectionless protocol. It merely establishes the host it will send packets to when there's data ready to be sent. Thus, connect() returns fairly quickly, and doesn't block in any meaningful sense. There's no need here for a finishConnect() or isConnectionPending() method. There is an isConnected() method that returns true if and only if the DatagramSocket is connected:

```
public boolean isConnected()
```

This tells you whether the DatagramChannel is limited to one host. Unlike SocketChannel, a DatagramChannel doesn't have to be connected to transmit or receive data.

Finally, the disconnect() method breaks the connection:

```
public DatagramChannel disconnect() throws IOException
```

This doesn't really close anything because nothing was really open in the first place. It just allows the channel to be connected to a different host in the future.

Reading

Besides the special-purpose `receive()` method, `DatagramChannel` has the usual three `read()` methods:

```
public int read(ByteBuffer dst) throws IOException
public long read(ByteBuffer[] dsts) throws IOException
public long read(ByteBuffer[] dsts, int offset, int length)
    throws IOException
```

However, these methods can only be used on connected channels. That is, before invoking one of these methods, you must invoke `connect()` to glue the channel to a particular remote host. This makes them more suitable for use with clients that know who they'll be talking to than for servers that must accept input from multiple hosts at the same time that are normally not known prior to the arrival of the first packet.

Each of these three methods only reads a single datagram packet from the network. As much data from that datagram as possible is stored in the argument `ByteBuffer`(s). Each method returns the number of bytes read or –1 if the channel has been closed. This method may return 0 for any of several reasons, including:

- The channel is nonblocking and no packet was ready.
- A datagram packet contained no data.
- The buffer is full.

As with the `receive()` method, if the datagram packet has more data than the `Byte Buffer`(s) can hold, *the extra data is thrown away with no notification of the problem.* You do not receive a `BufferOverflowException` or anything similar.

Writing

Naturally, `DatagramChannel` has the three write methods common to all writable, scattering channels, which can be used instead of the `send()` method:

```
public int write(ByteBuffer src) throws IOException
public long write(ByteBuffer[] dsts) throws IOException
public long write(ByteBuffer[] dsts, int offset, int length)
    throws IOException
```

These methods can only be used on connected channels; otherwise, they don't know where to send the packet. Each of these methods sends a single datagram packet over the connection. None of these methods are guaranteed to write the complete contents of the buffer(s). Fortunately, the cursor-based nature of buffers enables you to easily call this method again and again until the buffer is fully drained and the data has been completely sent, possibly using multiple datagram packets. For example:

```
while (buffer.hasRemaining() && channel.write(buffer) != -1) ;
```

You can use the read and write methods to implement a simple UDP echo client. On the client side, it's easy to connect before sending. Because packets may be lost in transit (always remember UDP is unreliable), you don't want to tie up the sending while waiting to receive a packet. Thus, you can take advantage of selectors and nonblocking I/O. These work for UDP pretty much exactly like they worked for TCP in Chapter 11. This time, though, rather than sending text data, let's send one hundred ints from 0 to 99. You'll print out the values returned so it will be easy to figure out if any packets are being lost. Example 12-17 demonstrates.

Example 12-17. A UDP echo client based on channels

```java
import java.io.*;
import java.net.*;
import java.nio.*;
import java.nio.channels.*;
import java.util.*;

public class UDPEchoClientWithChannels {

  public  final static int PORT = 7;
  private final static int LIMIT = 100;

  public static void main(String[] args) {

    SocketAddress remote;
    try {
      remote = new InetSocketAddress(args[0], PORT);
    } catch (RuntimeException ex) {
      System.err.println("Usage: java UDPEchoClientWithChannels host");
      return;
    }

    try (DatagramChannel channel = DatagramChannel.open()) {
      channel.configureBlocking(false);
      channel.connect(remote);

      Selector selector = Selector.open();
      channel.register(selector, SelectionKey.OP_READ | SelectionKey.OP_WRITE);

      ByteBuffer buffer = ByteBuffer.allocate(4);
      int n = 0;
      int numbersRead = 0;
      while (true) {
        if (numbersRead == LIMIT) break;
        // wait one minute for a connection
        selector.select(60000);
```

```
          Set<SelectionKey> readyKeys = selector.selectedKeys();
          if (readyKeys.isEmpty() && n == LIMIT) {
            // All packets have been written and it doesn't look like any
            // more are will arrive from the network
            break;
          }
          else {
            Iterator<SelectionKey> iterator = readyKeys.iterator();
            while (iterator.hasNext()) {
              SelectionKey key = (SelectionKey) iterator.next();
              iterator.remove();
              if (key.isReadable()) {
                buffer.clear();
                channel.read(buffer);
                buffer.flip();
                int echo = buffer.getInt();
                System.out.println("Read: " + echo);
                numbersRead++;
              }
              if (key.isWritable()) {
                buffer.clear();
                buffer.putInt(n);
                buffer.flip();
                channel.write(buffer);
                System.out.println("Wrote: " + n);
                n++;
                if (n == LIMIT) {
                  // All packets have been written; switch to read-only mode
                  key.interestOps(SelectionKey.OP_READ);
                }
              }
            }
          }
        }
        System.out.println("Echoed " + numbersRead + " out of " + LIMIT +
                                                          " sent");
        System.out.println("Success rate: " + 100.0 * numbersRead / LIMIT +
                                                          "%");
    } catch (IOException ex) {
      System.err.println(ex);
    }
  }
}
```

There is one major difference between selecting TCP channels and selecting datagram channels. Because datagram channels are truly connectionless (despite the connect() method), you need to notice when the data transfer is complete and shut down. In this example, you assume the data is finished when all packets have been sent and one minute has passed since the last packet was received. Any expected packets that have not been received by this point are assumed to be lost in the ether.

A typical run produced output like this:

```
Wrote: 0
Read: 0
Wrote: 1
Wrote: 2
Read: 1
Wrote: 3
Read: 2
Wrote: 4
Wrote: 5
Wrote: 6
Wrote: 7
Wrote: 8
Wrote: 9
Wrote: 10
Wrote: 11
Wrote: 12
Wrote: 13
Wrote: 14
Wrote: 15
Wrote: 16
Wrote: 17
Wrote: 18
Wrote: 19
Wrote: 20
Wrote: 21
Wrote: 22
Read: 3
Wrote: 23
...
Wrote: 97
Read: 72
Wrote: 98
Read: 73
Wrote: 99
Read: 75
Read: 76
...
Read: 97
Read: 98
Read: 99
Echoed 92 out of 100 sent
Success rate: 92.0%
```

Connecting to a remote server a couple of miles and seven hops away (according to traceroute), I saw between 90% and 98% of the packets make the round trip.

Closing

Just as with regular datagram sockets, a channel should be closed when you're done with it to free up the port and any other resources it may be using:

```
public void close() throws IOException
```

Closing an already closed channel has no effect. Attempting to write data to or read data from a closed channel throws an exception. If you're uncertain whether a channel has been closed, check with isOpen():

```
public boolean isOpen()
```

This returns false if the channel is closed, true if it's open.

Like all channels, in Java 7 DatagramChannel implements AutoCloseable so you can use it in try-with-resources statements. Prior to Java 7, close it in a finally block if you can. By now the pattern should be quite familiar. In Java 6 and earlier:

```
DatagramChannel channel = null;
try {
  channel = DatagramChannel.open();
  // Use the channel...
} catch (IOException ex) {
  // handle exceptions...
} finally {
  if (channel != null) {
    try {
      channel.close();
    } catch (IOException ex) {
      // ignore
    }
  }
}
```

and in Java 7 and later:

```
try (DatagramChannel channel = DatagramChannel.open()) {
  // Use the channel...
} catch (IOException ex) {
  // handle exceptions...
}
```

Socket Options // Java 7

In Java 7 and later, DatagramChannel supports eight socket options listed in Table 12-1.

Table 12-1. Socket options supported by datagram sockets

Option	Type	Constant	Purpose
SO_SNDBUF	StandardSocketOptions.	Integer	Size of the buffer used for sending datagram packets
SO_RCVBUF	StandardSocketOp tions.SO_RCVBUF	Integer	Size of the buffer used for receiving datagram packets
SO_REUSEADDR	StandardSocketOptions.SO_RE USEADDR	Boolean	Enable/disable address reuse
SO_BROADCAST	StandardSocketOp tions.SO_BROADCAST	Boolean	Enable/disable broadcast messages
IP_TOS	StandardSocketOptions.IP_TOS	Integer	Traffic class
IP_MULTICAST_IF	StandardSocketOptions.IP_MUL TICAST_IF	NetworkInter face	Local network interface to use for multicast
IP_MULTICAST_TTL	StandardSocketOptions.IP_MUL TICAST_TTL	Integer	Time-to-live value for multicast datagrams
IP_MULTICAST_LOOP	StandardSocketOptions.IP_MUL TICAST_LOOP	Boolean	Enable/disable loopback of multicast datagrams

The first five options have the same meanings as they do for datagram sockets as described in "Socket Options" on page 421. The last three are used by multicast sockets, which we'll take up in Chapter 13.

These are inspected and configured by just three methods:

```
public <T> DatagramChannel setOption(SocketOption<T> name, T value)
    throws IOException
public <T> T getOption(SocketOption<T> name) throws IOException
public Set<SocketOption<?>> supportedOptions()
```

The supportedOptions() method lists the available socket options. The getOption() method tells you the current value of any of these. And setOption() lets you change the value. For example, suppose you want to send a broadcast message. SO_BROADCAST is usually turned off by default, but you can switch it on like so:

```
try (DatagramChannel channel = DatagramChannel.open()) {
  channel.setOption(StandardSocketOptions.SO_BROADCAST, true);
  // Send the broadcast message...
} catch (IOException ex) {
  // handle exceptions...
}
```

Example 12-18 opens a channel just to check the default values of these options.

Example 12-18. Default socket option values

```
import java.io.IOException;
import java.net.SocketOption;
import java.nio.channels.DatagramChannel;
```

```
public class DefaultSocketOptionValues {

  public static void main(String[] args) {
    try (DatagramChannel channel = DatagramChannel.open()) {
      for (SocketOption<?> option : channel.supportedOptions()) {
        System.out.println(option.name() + ": " + channel.getOption(option));
      }
    } catch (IOException ex) {
      ex.printStackTrace();
    }
  }
}
```

Here's the output I got on my Mac:

```
IP_MULTICAST_TTL: 1
SO_BROADCAST: false
SO_REUSEADDR: false
SO_RCVBUF: 196724
IP_MULTICAST_LOOP: true
SO_SNDBUF: 9216
IP_MULTICAST_IF: null
IP_TOS: 0
```

It's a bit surprising that my send buffer is so much larger than my receive buffer.

CHAPTER 13

IP Multicast

The sockets in the previous chapters are *unicast*: they provide point-to-point communication. Unicast sockets create a connection with two well-defined endpoints; there is one sender and one receiver and, although they may switch roles, at any given time it is easy to tell which is which. However, although point-to-point communications serve many, if not most needs (people have engaged in one-on-one conversations for millennia), many tasks require a different model. For example, a television station broadcasts data from one location to every point within range of its transmitter. The signal reaches every television set, whether or not it's turned on and whether or not it's tuned to that particular station. Indeed, the signal even reaches homes with cable boxes instead of antennas and homes that don't have a television. This is the classic example of broadcasting. It's indiscriminate and quite wasteful of both the electromagnetic spectrum and power.

Videoconferencing, by contrast, sends an audio-video feed to a select group of people. Usenet news is posted at one site and distributed around the world to hundreds of thousands of people. DNS router updates travel from the site, announcing a change to many other routers. However, the sender relies on the intermediate sites to copy and relay the message to downstream sites. The sender does not address its message to every host that will eventually receive it. These are examples of multicasting, although they're implemented with additional application layer protocols on top of TCP or UDP. These protocols require fairly detailed configuration and intervention by human beings. For instance, to join Usenet you have to find a site willing to send news to you and relay your outgoing news to the rest of the world. To add you to the Usenet feed, the news administrator of the news relay has to specifically add your site to their news config files. However, recent developments with the network software in most major operating systems as well as Internet routers have opened up a new possibility—true multicasting, in which the routers decide how to efficiently move a message to individual hosts. In particular, the initial router sends only one copy of the message to a router near the receiving hosts, which then makes multiple copies for different recipients at or closer to the destinations. Internet multicasting is built on top of UDP. Multicasting in Java uses the `DatagramPacket` class introduced in Chapter 12, along with a new `Multicast Socket` class.

Multicasting

Multicasting is broader than unicast, point-to-point communication but narrower and more targeted than broadcast communication. Multicasting sends data from one host to many different hosts, but not to everyone; the data only goes to clients that have expressed an interest by joining a particular multicast group. In a way, this is like a public meeting. People can come and go as they please, leaving when the discussion no longer interests them. Before they arrive and after they have left, they don't need to process the information at all: it just doesn't reach them. On the Internet, such "public meetings" are best implemented using a multicast socket that sends a copy of the data to a location (or a group of locations) close to the parties that have declared an interest in the data. In the best case, the data is duplicated only when it reaches the local network serving the interested clients: the data crosses the Internet only once. More realistically, several identical copies of the data traverse the Internet; but, by carefully choosing the points at which the streams are duplicated, the load on the network is minimized. The good news is that programmers and network administrators aren't responsible for choosing the points where the data is duplicated or even for sending multiple copies; the Internet's routers handle all that.

IP also supports broadcasting, but the use of broadcasts is strictly limited. Protocols require broadcasts only when there is no alternative; and routers limit broadcasts to the local network or subnet, preventing broadcasts from reaching the Internet at large. Even a few small global broadcasts could bring the Internet to its knees. Broadcasting high-bandwidth data such as audio, video, or even text and still images is out of the question. A single email spam that goes to millions of addresses is bad enough. Imagine what would happen if a real-time video feed were copied to all billion+ Internet users, whether they wanted to watch it or not.

However, there's a middle ground between point-to-point communications and broadcasts to the whole world. There's no reason to send a video feed to hosts that aren't interested in it; we need a technology that sends data to the hosts that want it, without bothering the rest of the world. One way to do this is to use many unicast streams. If 1,000 clients want to watch a BBC live stream, the data is sent a thousand times. This is inefficient, since it duplicates data needlessly, but it's orders-of-magnitude more efficient than broadcasting the data to every host on the Internet. Still, if the number of interested clients is large enough, you will eventually run out of bandwidth or CPU power—probably sooner rather than later.

Another approach to the problem is to create static *connection trees*. This is the solution employed by Usenet news and some conferencing systems. Data is fed from the originating site to other servers, which replicate it to still other servers, which eventually replicate it to clients. Each client connects to the nearest server. This is more efficient than sending everything to all interested clients via multiple unicasts, but the scheme is kludgy and beginning to show its age. New sites need to find a place to hook into the tree manually. The tree does not necessarily reflect the best possible topology at any one time, and servers still need to maintain many point-to-point connections to their clients, sending the same data to each one. It would be better to allow the routers in the Internet to dynamically determine the best possible routes for transmitting distributed information and to replicate data only when absolutely necessary. This is where multicasting comes in.

For example, if you're multicasting video from New York and 20 people attached to one LAN are watching the show in Los Angeles, the feed will be sent to that LAN only once. If 50 more people are watching in San Francisco, the data stream will be duplicated somewhere (let's say Fresno) and sent to the two cities. If a hundred more people are watching in Houston, another data stream will be sent there (perhaps from St. Louis); see Figure 13-1. The data has crossed the Internet only three times—not the 170 times that would be required by point-to-point connections, or the millions of times that would be required by a true broadcast. Multicasting is halfway between the point-to-point communication common to the Internet and the broadcast model of television and it's more efficient than either. When a packet is multicast, it is addressed to a multicast group and sent to each host belonging to the group. It does not go to a single host (as in unicasting), nor does it go to every host (as in broadcasting). Either would be too inefficient.

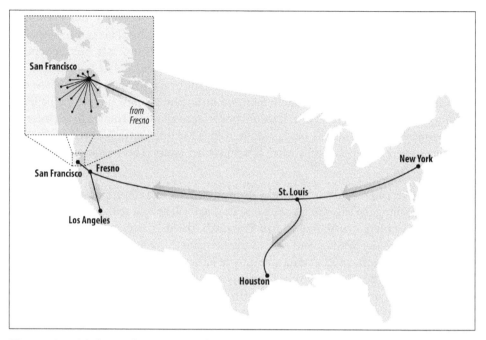

Figure 13-1. Multicast from New York to San Francisco, Los Angeles, and Houston

When people talk about multicasting, audio and video are the first applications that come to mind. Indeed, the BBC has been running a multicast trial (*http://www.bbc.co.uk/multicast/*) covering both TV and radio for several years now, though ISP participation has been regrettably limited. However, audio and video are only the tip of the iceberg. Other possibilities include multiplayer games, distributed filesystems, massively parallel computing, multiperson conferencing, database replication, content delivery networks, and more. Multicasting can be used to implement name services and directory services that don't require the client to know a server's address in advance; to look up a name, a host could multicast its request to some well-known address and wait until a response is received from the nearest server. Apple's Bonjour (a.k.a. Zeroconf) and Apache's River (*https://river.apache.org/*) both use IP multicasting to dynamically discover services on the local network.

Multicasting has been designed to fit into the Internet as seamlessly as possible. Most of the work is done by routers and should be transparent to application programmers. An application simply sends datagram packets to a multicast address, which isn't fundamentally different from any other IP address. The routers make sure the packet is delivered to all the hosts in the multicast group. The biggest problem is that multicast routers are not yet ubiquitous; therefore, you need to know enough about them to find out whether multicasting is supported on your network. For instance, although the BBC has been multicasting for several years now, their multicast streams are only accessible to subscribers of about a dozen relatively small British ISPs. In practice, multicasting is much more commonly used behind the firewall within a single organization than across the global Internet.

As far as the application itself, you need to pay attention to an additional header field in the datagrams called the Time-To-Live (TTL) value. The TTL is the maximum number of routers that the datagram is allowed to cross. Once the packet has crossed that many routers, it is discarded. Multicasting uses the TTL as an ad hoc way to limit how far a packet can travel. For example, you don't want packets for a friendly on-campus game of Dogfight reaching routers on the other side of the world. Figure 13-2 shows how TTLs limit a packet's spread.

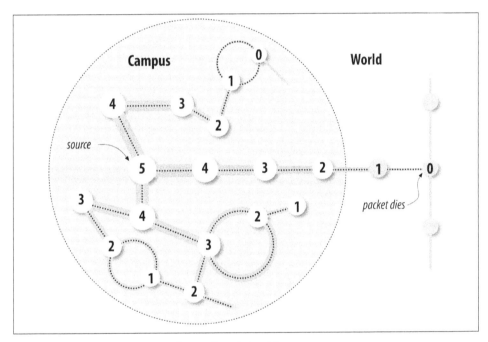

Figure 13-2. Coverage of a packet with a TTL of five

Multicast Addresses and Groups

A *multicast address* is the shared address of a group of hosts called a *multicast group*. We'll talk about the address first. IPv4 multicast addresses are IP addresses in the CIDR group 224.0.0.0/4 (i.e., they range from 224.0.0.0 to 239.255.255.255). All addresses in this range have the binary digits 1110 as their first four bits. IPv6 multicast addresses are in the CIDR group ff00::/8 (i.e., they all start with the byte 0xFF, or 11111111 in binary).

Like any IP address, a multicast address can have a hostname. For example, the multicast address 224.0.1.1 (the address of the Network Time Protocol distributed service) is assigned the name *ntp.mcast.net*.

A multicast group is a set of Internet hosts that share a multicast address. Any data sent to the multicast address is relayed to all the members of the group. Membership in a multicast group is open; hosts can enter or leave the group at any time. Groups can be either permanent or transient. Permanent groups have assigned addresses that remain constant, whether or not there are any members in the group. However, most multicast groups are transient and exist only as long as they have members. All you have to do to create a new multicast group is pick a random address from 225.0.0.0 to 238.255.255.255, construct an `InetAddress` object for that address, and start sending it data.

The IANA is responsible for handing out permanent multicast addresses as needed. So far, a few hundred have been specifically assigned. *Link-local* multicast addresses begin with 224.0.0 (i.e., addresses from 224.0.0.0 to 224.0.0.255) and are reserved for routing protocols and other low-level activities, such as gateway discovery and group membership reporting. For example, *all-systems.mcast.net*, 224.0.0.1, is a multicast group that includes all systems on the local subnet. Multicast routers never forward datagrams with destinations in this range. Table 13-1 lists a few of these assigned addresses.

Table 13-1. Link-local multicast addresses

Domain name	IP address	Purpose
BASE-ADDRESS.MCAST.NET	224.0.0.0	The reserved base address. This is never assigned to any multicast group.
ALL-SYSTEMS.MCAST.NET	224.0.0.1	All systems on the local subnet.
ALL-ROUTERS.MCAST.NET	224.0.0.2	All routers on the local subnet.
DVMRP.MCAST.NET	224.0.0.4	All Distance Vector Multicast Routing Protocol (DVMRP) routers on this subnet.
MOBILE-AGENTS.MCAST.NET	224.0.0.11	Mobile agents on the local subnet.
DHCP-AGENTS.MCAST.NET	224.0.0.12	This multicast group allows a client to locate a Dynamic Host Configuration Protocol (DHCP) server or relay agent on the local subnet.
RSVP-ENCAPSULATION.MCAST.NET	224.0.0.14	RSVP encapsulation on this subnet. RSVP stands for Resource reSerVation setup Protocol, an effort to allow people to reserve a guaranteed amount of Internet bandwidth in advance for an event.
VRRP.MCAST.NET	224.0.0.18	Virtual Router Redundancy Protocol (VRRP) Routers
	224.0.0.35	DXCluster (*http://www.dxcluster.org/*) is used to announce foreign amateur (DX) stations.
	224.0.0.36	Digital Transmission Content Protection (DTCP), a digital restrictions management (DRM) technology that encrypts interconnections between DVD players, televisions, and similar devices.
	224.0.0.37–224.0.0.68	zeroconf addressing
	224.0.0.106	Multicast Router Discovery (*http://bit.ly/17EaPLL*)

Domain name	IP address	Purpose
	224.0.0.112	Multipath Management Agent Device Discovery
	224.0.0.113	Qualcomm's AllJoyn
	224.0.0.114	Inter RFID Reader Protocol
	224.0.0.251	Multicast DNS (*https://tools.ietf.org/html/rfc6762*) self assigns and resolves host names for multicast addresses.
	224.0.0.252	Link-local Multicast Name Resolution (*http://bit.ly/1djewsm*), a precursor of mDNS, allows nodes ot self-assign domain names strictly for the local network, and to resolve such domain names on the local network.
	224.0.0.253	Teredo (*http://bit.ly/19Y00nU*) is used to tunnel IPv6 over IPv4. Other Teredo clients on the same IPv4 subnet respond to this multicast address.
	224.0.0.254	Reserved for experimentation.

Permanently assigned multicast addresses that extend beyond the local subnet begin with 224.1. or 224.2. Table 13-2 lists a few of these permanent addresses. A few blocks of addresses ranging in size from a few dozen to a few thousand addresses have also been reserved for particular purposes. The complete list is available from iana.org (*http://bit.ly/multicast-registry*), though you should note that it contains many now defunct services, protocols, and companies. The remaining 248 million multicast addresses can be used on a temporary basis by anyone who needs them. Multicast routers (*mrouters* for short) are responsible for making sure that two different systems don't try to use the same address at the same time.

Table 13-2. Common permanent multicast addresses

Domain name	IP address	Purpose
NTP.MCAST.NET	224.0.1.1	The Network Time Protocol.
NSS.MCAST.NET	224.0.1.6	The Name Service Server.
AUDIONEWS.MCAST.NET	224.0.1.7	Audio news multicast.
MTP.MCAST.NET	224.0.1.9	The Multicast Transport Protocol.
IETF-1-LOW-AUDIO.MCAST.NET	224.0.1.10	Channel 1 of low-quality audio from IETF meetings.
IETF-1-AUDIO.MCAST.NET	224.0.1.11	Channel 1 of high-quality audio from IETF meetings.
IETF-1-VIDEO.MCAST.NET	224.0.1.12	Channel 1 of video from IETF meetings.
IETF-2-LOW-AUDIO.MCAST.NET	224.0.1.13	Channel 2 of low-quality audio from IETF meetings.
IETF-2-AUDIO.MCAST.NET	224.0.1.14	Channel 2 of high-quality audio from IETF meetings.
IETF-2-VIDEO.MCAST.NET	224.0.1.15	Channel 2 of video from IETF meetings.
MLOADD.MCAST.NET	224.0.1.19	MLOADD measures the traffic load through one or more network interfaces over a number of seconds. Multicasting is used to communicate between the different interfaces being measured.
EXPERIMENT.MCAST.NET	224.0.1.20	Experiments.

Domain name	IP address	Purpose
	224.0.23.178	JDP Java Discovery Protocol, used to find manageable JVMs on the network.
MICROSOFT.MCAST.NET	224.0.1.24	Used by Windows Internet Name Service (WINS) servers to locate one another.
MTRACE.MCAST.NET	224.0.1.32	A multicast version of traceroute.
JINI-ANNOUNCEMENT.MCAST.NET	224.0.1.84	JINI announcements.
JINI-REQUEST.MCAST.NET	224.0.1.85	JINI requests.
	224.0.1.143	Emergency Managers Weather Information Network.
	224.2.0.0-224.2.255.255	The Multicast Backbone on the Internet (MBONE) addresses are reserved for multimedia conference calls (i.e., audio, video, whiteboard, and shared web browsing between many people).
	224.2.2.2	Port 9875 on this address is used to broadcast the currently available MBONE programming. You can look at this with the X Window utility sdr or the Windows/Unix multikit program.
	239.0.0.0-239.255.255.255	Organization local scope, in contrast to TTL scope, uses different ranges of multicast addresses to constrain multicast traffic to a particular region or group of routers. For example, when a Universal Plug and Play (UPnP) device joins a network, it sends an HTTPU (HTTP over UDP) message to the multicast address 239.255.255.250 on port 1900. The idea is to allow the possible group membership to be established in advance without relying on less-than-reliable TTL values.

Clients and Servers

When a host wants to send data to a multicast group, it puts that data in multicast datagrams, which are nothing more than UDP datagrams addressed to a multicast group. Multicast data is sent via UDP, which, though unreliable, can be as much as three times faster than data sent via connection-oriented TCP. (If you think about it, multicast over TCP would be next to impossible. TCP requires hosts to acknowledge that they have received packets; handling acknowledgments in a multicast situation would be a nightmare.) If you're developing a multicast application that can't tolerate data loss, it's your responsibility to determine whether data was damaged in transit and how to handle missing data. For example, if you are building a distributed cache system, you might simply decide to leave any files that don't arrive intact out of the cache.

Earlier, I said that from an application programmer's standpoint, the primary difference between multicasting and using regular UDP sockets is that you have to worry about the TTL value. This is a single byte in the IP header that takes values from 1 to 255; it is interpreted roughly as the number of routers through which a packet can pass before it is discarded. Each time the packet passes through a router, its TTL field is decremented by at least one; some routers may decrement the TTL by two or more. When the TTL reaches zero, the packet is discarded. The TTL field was originally designed to prevent routing loops by guaranteeing that all packets would eventually be discarded. It prevents misconfigured routers from sending packets back and forth to each other indefinitely. In IP multicasting, the TTL limits the multicast geographically. For example, a TTL value of 16 limits the packet to the local area, generally one organization or perhaps an organization and its immediate upstream and downstream neighbors. A TTL of 127, however, sends the packet around the world. Intermediate values are also possible. However, there is no precise way to map TTLs to geographical distance. Generally, the farther away a site is, the more routers a packet has to pass through before reaching it. Packets with small TTL values won't travel as far as packets with large TTL values. Table 13-3 provides some rough estimates relating TTL values to geographical reach. Packets addressed to a multicast group from 224.0.0.0 to 224.0.0.255 are never forwarded beyond the local subnet, regardless of the TTL values used.

Table 13-3. Estimated TTL values for datagrams originating in the continental United States

Destinations	TTL value
The local host	0
The local subnet	1
The local campus—that is, the same side of the nearest Internet router—but on possibly different LANs	16
High-bandwidth sites in the same country, generally those fairly close to the backbone	32
All sites in the same country	48
All sites on the same continent	64
High-bandwidth sites worldwide	128
All sites worldwide	255

Once the data has been stuffed into one or more datagrams, the sending host launches the datagrams onto the Internet. This is just like sending regular (unicast) UDP data. The sending host begins by transmitting a multicast datagram to the local network. This packet immediately reaches all members of the multicast group in the same subnet. If the Time-To-Live field of the packet is greater than 1, multicast routers on the local network forward the packet to other networks that have members of the destination group. When the packet arrives at one of the final destinations, the multicast router on the foreign network transmits the packet to each host it serves that is a member of the multicast group. If necessary, the multicast router also retransmits the packet to the next routers in the paths between the current router and all its eventual destinations.

When data arrives at a host in a multicast group, the host receives it as it receives any other UDP datagram—even though the packet's destination address doesn't match the receiving host. The host recognizes that the datagram is intended for it because it belongs to the multicast group to which the datagram is addressed, much as most of us accept mail addressed to "Occupant," even though none of us are named Mr. or Ms. Occupant.

The receiving host must be listening on the proper port, ready to process the datagram when it arrives.

Routers and Routing

Figure 13-3 shows one of the simplest possible multicast configurations: a single server sending the same data to four clients served by the same router. A multicast socket sends one stream of data over the Internet to the clients' router; the router duplicates the stream and sends it to each of the clients. Without multicast sockets, the server would have to send four separate but identical streams of data to the router, which would route each stream to a client. Using the same stream to send the same data to multiple clients significantly reduces the bandwidth required on the Internet backbone.

Of course, real-world routes can be much more complex, involving multiple hierarchies of redundant routers. However, the goal of multicast sockets is simple: no matter how complex the network, the same data should never be sent more than once over any given network segment. Fortunately, you don't need to worry about routing issues. Just create a `MulticastSocket`, have the socket join a multicast group, and stuff the address of the multicast group in the `DatagramPacket` you want to send. The routers and the `MulticastSocket` class take care of the rest.

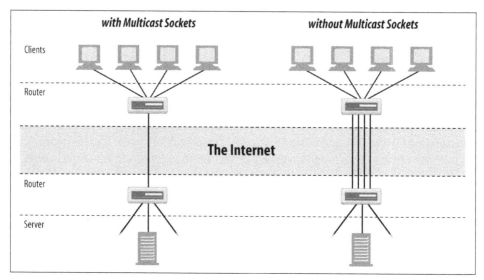

Figure 13-3. With and without multicast sockets

The biggest restriction on multicasting is the availability of special multicast routers (mrouters). Mrouters are reconfigured Internet routers or workstations that support the IP multicast extensions. Many consumer-oriented ISPs quite deliberately do not enable multicasting in their routers. In 2013, it is still possible to find hosts between which no multicast route exists (i.e., there is no route between the hosts that travels exclusively over mrouters).

To send and receive multicast data beyond the local subnet, you need a multicast router. Check with your network administrator to see whether your routers support multicasting. You can also try pinging *all-routers.mcast.net*. If any router responds, then your network is hooked up to a multicast router:

```
% ping all-routers.mcast.net
all-routers.mcast.net is alive
```

This still may not allow you to send to or receive from every multicast-capable host on the Internet. For your packets to reach any given host, there must be a path of multicast-capable routers between your host and the remote host. Alternatively, some sites may be connected by special multicast tunnel software that transmits multicast data over unicast UDP that all routers understand. If you have trouble getting the examples in this chapter to produce the expected results, check with your local network administrator or ISP to see whether multicasting is actually supported by your routers.

Working with Multicast Sockets

Enough theory. In Java, you multicast data using the `java.net.MulticastSocket` class, a subclass of `java.net.DatagramSocket`:

```
public class MulticastSocket extends DatagramSocket
    implements Closeable, AutoCloseable
```

As you would expect, `MulticastSocket`'s behavior is very similar to `DatagramSocket`'s: you put your data in `DatagramPacket` objects that you send and receive with the `MulticastSocket`. Therefore, I won't repeat the basics; this discussion assumes that you already know how to work with datagrams. If you're jumping around in this book rather than reading it cover to cover, now might be a good time to go back and read Chapter 12.

To receive data that is being multicast from a remote site, first create a `MulticastSocket` with the `MulticastSocket()` constructor. As with other kinds of sockets, you need to know the port to listen on. This code fragment opens a `MulticastSocket` that listens on port 2300:

```
MulticastSocket ms = new MulticastSocket(2300);
```

Next, join a multicast group using the `MulticastSocket`'s `joinGroup()` method:

```
InetAddress group = InetAddress.getByName("224.2.2.2");
ms.joinGroup(group);
```

This signals the routers in the path between you and the server to start sending data your way and tells the local host that it should pass you IP packets addressed to the multicast group.

Once you've joined the multicast group, you receive UDP data just as you would with a DatagramSocket. You create a DatagramPacket with a byte array that serves as a buffer for data and enter a loop in which you receive the data by calling the receive() method inherited from the DatagramSocket class:

```
byte[] buffer = new byte[8192];
DatagramPacket dp = new DatagramPacket(buffer, buffer.length);
ms.receive(dp);
```

When you no longer want to receive data, leave the multicast group by invoking the socket's leaveGroup() method. You can then close the socket with the close() method inherited from DatagramSocket:

```
ms.leaveGroup(group);
ms.close();
```

Sending data to a multicast address is similar to sending UDP data to a unicast address. You do not need to join a multicast group to send data to it. You create a new Datagram Packet, stuff the data and the address of the multicast group into the packet, and pass it to the send() method:

```
InetAddress ia = InetAddress.getByName("experiment.mcast.net");
byte[] data = "Here's some multicast data\r\n".getBytes("UTF-8");
int port = 4000;
DatagramPacket dp = new DatagramPacket(data, data.length, ia, port);
MulticastSocket ms = new MulticastSocket();
ms.send(dp);
```

There is one caveat to all this: multicast sockets are a security hole big enough to drive a small truck through. Consequently, untrusted code running under the control of a SecurityManager is not allowed to do anything involving multicast sockets. Remotely loaded code is normally only allowed to send datagrams to or receive datagrams from the host it was downloaded from. However, multicast sockets don't allow this sort of restriction to be placed on the packets they send or receive. Once you send data to a multicast socket, you have very limited and unreliable control over which hosts receive that data. Consequently, most environments that execute remote code take the conservative approach of disallowing all multicasting.

The Constructors

The constructors are simple. You can either pick a port to listen on or let Java assign an anonymous port for you:

```
public MulticastSocket() throws SocketException
public MulticastSocket(int port) throws SocketException
public MulticastSocket(SocketAddress bindAddress) throws IOException
```

For example:

```
MulticastSocket ms1 = new MulticastSocket();
MulticastSocket ms2 = new MulticastSocket(4000);
SocketAddress address = new InetSocketAddress("192.168.254.32", 4000);
MulticastSocket ms3 = new MulticastSocket(address);
```

All three constructors throw a SocketException if the Socket can't be created. If you don't have sufficient privileges to bind to the port or if the port you're trying to bind to is already in use, then a Socket cannot be created. Note that because a multicast socket is a datagram socket as far as the operating system is concerned, a MulticastSocket cannot occupy a port already occupied by a DatagramSocket, and vice versa.

You can pass null to the constructor to create an unbound socket, which will be connected later with the bind() method. This is useful when setting socket options that can only be set before the socket is bound. For example, this code fragment creates a multicast socket with SO_REUSEADDR disabled (that option is normally enabled by default for multicast sockets):

```
MulticastSocket ms = new MulticastSocket(null);
ms.setReuseAddress(false);
SocketAddress address = new InetSocketAddress(4000);
ms.bind(address);
```

Communicating with a Multicast Group

Once a MulticastSocket has been created, it can perform four key operations:

1. Join a multicast group.
2. Send data to the members of the group.
3. Receive data from the group.
4. Leave the multicast group.

The MulticastSocket class has methods for operations 1 and 4. No new methods are required to send or receive data. The send() and receive() methods of the superclass, DatagramSocket, suffice for those operations. You can perform these operations in any order, with the exception that you must join a group before you can receive data from it. You do not need to join a group to send data to it, and you can freely intermix sending and receiving data.

Joining groups

To join a group, pass an InetAddress or a SocketAddress for the multicast group to the joinGroup() method:

```
public void joinGroup(InetAddress address) throws IOException
public void joinGroup(SocketAddress address, NetworkInterface interface)
    throws IOException
```

Once you've joined a multicast group, you receive datagrams exactly as you receive unicast datagrams, as shown in the previous chapter. That is, you set up a `Datagram Packet` as a buffer and pass it into this socket's `receive()` method. For example:

```
try {
  MulticastSocket ms = new MulticastSocket(4000);
  InetAddress ia = InetAddress.getByName("224.2.2.2");
  ms.joinGroup(ia);
  byte[] buffer = new byte[8192];
  while (true) {
    DatagramPacket dp = new DatagramPacket(buffer, buffer.length);
    ms.receive(dp);
    String s = new String(dp.getData(), "8859_1");
    System.out.println(s);
  }
} catch (IOException ex) {
  System.err.println(ex);
}
```

If the address that you try to join is not a multicast address (if it is not between 224.0.0.0 and 239.255.255.255), the `joinGroup()` method throws an `IOException`.

A single `MulticastSocket` can join multiple multicast groups. Information about membership in multicast groups is stored in multicast routers, not in the object. In this case, you'd use the address stored in the incoming datagram to determine which address a packet was intended for.

Multiple multicast sockets on the same machine and even in the same Java program can all join the same group. If so, each socket receives a complete copy of the data addressed to that group that arrives at the local host.

A second argument allows you to join a multicast group only on a specified local network interface. For example, this code fragment attempts to join the group with IP address 224.2.2.2 on the network interface named "eth0", if such an interface exists. If no such interface exists, then it joins on all available network interfaces:

```
MulticastSocket ms = new MulticastSocket();
SocketAddress group = new InetSocketAddress("224.2.2.2", 40);
NetworkInterface ni = NetworkInterface.getByName("eth0");
if (ni != null) {
  ms.joinGroup(group, ni);
} else {
  ms.joinGroup(group);
}
```

Other than the extra argument specifying the network interface to listen from, this behaves pretty much like the single-argument `joinGroup()` method. For instance, passing a `SocketAddress` object that does not represent a multicast group as the first argument throws an `IOException`.

Leaving groups and closing the connection

Call the leaveGroup() method when you no longer want to receive datagrams from the specified multicast group, on either all or a specified network interface:

```
public void leaveGroup(InetAddress address) throws IOException
public void leaveGroup(SocketAddress multicastAddress,
NetworkInterface interface)
    throws IOException
```

It signals the local multicast router, telling it to stop sending you datagrams. If the address you try to leave is not a multicast address (if it is not between 224.0.0.0 and 239.255.255.255), the method throws an IOException. However, no exception occurs if you leave a multicast group you never joined.

Pretty much all the methods in MulticastSocket can throw an IOException, so you'll usually wrap all this in a try block. In Java 7, DatagramSocket implements Autocloseable so you can use try-with-resources:

```
try (MulticastSocket socket = new MulticastSocket()) {
  // connect to the server...
} catch (IOException ex) {
  ex.printStackTrace();
}
```

In Java 6 and earlier, you'll want to explicitly close the socket in a finally block to release resources the socket holds:

```
MulticastSocket socket = null;
try {
  socket = new MulticastSocket();
  // connect to the server...
} catch (IOException ex) {
  ex.printStackTrace();
} finally {
  if (socket != null) {
    try {
      socket.close();
    } catch (IOException ex) {
      // ignore
    }
  }
}
```

Sending multicast data

Sending data with a MulticastSocket is similar to sending data with a DatagramSock et. Stuff your data into a DatagramPacket object and send it off using the send() method inherited from DatagramSocket. The data is sent to every host that belongs to the multicast group to which the packet is addressed. For example:

```
try {
  InetAddress ia = InetAddress.getByName("experiment.mcast.net");
  byte[] data = "Here's some multicast data\r\n".getBytes();
  int port = 4000;
  DatagramPacket dp = new DatagramPacket(data, data.length, ia, port);
  MulticastSocket ms = new MulticastSocket();
  ms.send(dp);
} catch (IOException ex) {
  System.err.println(ex);
}
```

By default, multicast sockets uses a TTL of 1 (that is, packets don't travel outside the local subnet). However, you can change this setting for an individual packet by passing an integer from 0 to 255 as the first argument to the constructor.

The setTimeToLive() method sets the default TTL value used for packets sent from the socket using the send(DatagramPacket dp) method inherited from DatagramSock et (as opposed to the send(DatagramPacket dp, byte ttl) method in Multicast Socket). The getTimeToLive() method returns the default TTL value of the Multi castSocket:

```
public void setTimeToLive(int ttl) throws IOException
public int getTimeToLive() throws IOException
```

For example, this code fragment sets a TTL of 64:

```
try {
  InetAddress ia = InetAddress.getByName("experiment.mcast.net");
  byte[] data = "Here's some multicast data\r\n".getBytes();
  int port = 4000;
  DatagramPacket dp = new DatagramPacket(data, data.length, ia, port);
  MulticastSocket ms = new MulticastSocket();
  ms.setTimeToLive(64);
  ms.send(dp);
} catch (IOException ex) {
  System.err.println(ex);
}
```

Loopback mode

Whether or not a host receives the multicast packets it sends is platform dependent—that is, whether or not they loop back. Passing true to setLoopback() indicates you don't want to receive the packets you send. Passing false indicates you do want to receive the packets you send:

```
public void setLoopbackMode(boolean disable) throws SocketException
public boolean getLoopbackMode() throws SocketException
```

However, this is only a hint. Implementations are not required to do as you request. Because loopback mode may not be followed on all systems, it's important to check what the loopback mode is if you're both sending and receiving packets. The getLoopback

Mode() method returns true if packets are not looped back and false if they are. (This feels backward to me. I suspect this method was written by a programmer following the ill-advised convention that defaults should always be true.)

If the system is looping packets back and you don't want it to, you'll need to recognize the packets somehow and discard them. If the system is not looping the packets back and you do want it to, store copies of the packets you send and inject them into your internal data structures manually at the same time you send them. You can ask for the behavior you want with setLoopback(), but you can't count on it.

Network interfaces

On a multihomed host, the setInterface() and setNetworkInterface() methods choose the network interface used for multicast sending and receiving:

```
public void setInterface(InetAddress address) throws SocketException
public InetAddress getInterface() throws SocketException
public void setNetworkInterface(NetworkInterface interface) throws
        SocketException
public NetworkInterface getNetworkInterface() throws SocketException
```

The setter methods throw a SocketException if the argument is not the address of a network interface on the local machine. It is unclear why the network interface is immutably set in the constructor for unicast Socket and DatagramSocket objects but is variable and set with a separate method for MulticastSocket objects. To be safe, set the interface immediately after constructing a MulticastSocket and don't change it thereafter. Here's how you might use setInterface():

```
try {
  InetAddress ia = InetAddress.getByName("www.ibiblio.org");
  MulticastSocket ms = new MulticastSocket(2048);
  ms.setInterface(ia);
  // send and receive data...
} catch (UnknownHostException ue) {
  System.err.println(ue);
} catch (SocketException se) {
  System.err.println(se);
}
```

The setNetworkInterface() method serves the same purpose as the setInterface() method; that is, it chooses the network interface used for multicast sending and receiving. However, it does so based on the local name of a network interface such as "eth0" (as encapsulated in a NetworkInterface object) rather than on the IP address bound to that network interface (as encapsulated in an InetAddress object). setNetworkInterface() throws a SocketException if the NetworkInterface passed as an argument is not a network interface on the local machine.

The getNetworkInterface() method returns a NetworkInterface object representing the network interface on which this MulticastSocket is listening for data. If no network interface has been explicitly set in the constructor or with setNetworkInterface(), it returns a placeholder object with the address "0.0.0.0" and the index –1. For example, this code fragment prints the network interface used by a socket:

```
NetworkInterface intf = ms.getNetworkInterface();
System.out.println(intf.getName());
```

Two Simple Examples

Most multicast servers are indiscriminate about who they will talk to. Therefore, it's easy to join a group and watch the data that's being sent to it. Example 13-1 is a MulticastS niffer class that reads the name of a multicast group from the command line, constructs an InetAddress from that hostname, and creates a MulticastSocket, which attempts to join the multicast group at that hostname. If the attempt succeeds, MulticastSniff er receives datagrams from the socket and prints their contents on System.out. This program is useful primarily to verify that you are receiving multicast data at a particular host. Most multicast data is binary and won't be intelligible when printed as text.

Example 13-1. Multicast sniffer

```
import java.io.*;
import java.net.*;

public class MulticastSniffer {

  public static void main(String[] args) {

    InetAddress group = null;
    int port = 0;

    // read the address from the command line
    try {
      group = InetAddress.getByName(args[0]);
      port = Integer.parseInt(args[1]);
    } catch (ArrayIndexOutOfBoundsException | NumberFormatException
        | UnknownHostException ex) {
      System.err.println(
          "Usage: java MulticastSniffer multicast_address port");
      System.exit(1);
    }

    MulticastSocket ms = null;
    try {
      ms = new MulticastSocket(port);
      ms.joinGroup(group);

      byte[] buffer = new byte[8192];
```

```
      while (true) {
        DatagramPacket dp = new DatagramPacket(buffer, buffer.length);
        ms.receive(dp);
        String s = new String(dp.getData(), "8859_1");
        System.out.println(s);
      }
    } catch (IOFxception ex) {
      System.err.println(ex);
    } finally {
      if (ms != null) {
        try {
          ms.leaveGroup(group);
          ms.close();
        } catch (IOException ex) {}
      }
    }
  }
}
```

The program begins by reading the name and port of the multicast group from the first two command-line arguments. Next, it creates a new MulticastSocket ms on the specified port. This socket joins the multicast group at the specified InetAddress. Then it enters a loop in which it waits for packets to arrive. As each packet arrives, the program reads its data, converts the data to an ISO Latin-1 String, and prints it on Sys tem.out. Finally, when the user interrupts the program or an exception is thrown, the socket leaves the group and closes itself.

When a Universal Plug and Play (UPnP) device joins a network, it sends an HTTPU (HTTP over UDP) message to the multicast address 239.255.255.250 on port 1900. You can use this program to listen to those messages. If such a device is broadcasting, you should see a message pop through within the first minute or two. In fact, you'll probably see a lot more. I collected about a megabyte and a half of announcements within the first couple of minutes I had this program running. I show only the first two here:

```
$ java MulticastSniffer 239.255.255.250 1900
NOTIFY * HTTP/1.1
HOST: 239.255.255.250:1900
CACHE-CONTROL: max-age=1800
LOCATION: http://192.168.1.2:23519/Ircc.xml
NT: upnp:rootdevice
NTS: ssdp:alive
SERVER: Android/3.2 UPnP/1.0 Internet TV Box NSZ-GT1/1.0
USN: uuid:34567890-1234-1010-8000-544249cb49fd::upnp:rootdevice
X-AV-Server-Info: av=5.0; hn=""; cn="Sony Corporation";
mn="Internet TV Box NSZ-GT1"; mv="1.0";

NOTIFY * HTTP/1.1
HOST: 239.255.255.250:1900
CACHE-CONTROL: max-age=1800
LOCATION: http://192.168.1.2:23519/Ircc.xml
```

```
NT: uuid:34567890-1234-1010-8000-544249cb49fd
NTS: ssdp:alive
SERVER: Android/3.2 UPnP/1.0 Internet TV Box NSZ-GT1/1.0
USN: uuid:34567890-1234-1010-8000-544249cb49fd
X-AV-Server-Info: av=5.0; hn=""; cn="Sony Corporation";
mn="Internet TV Box NSZ-GT1"; mv="1.0";
```

It appears that my Google TV is very chatty, sending an announcement about once a second. Most devices only announce when they're first connected to the network, or when they're queried by another device.

Now let's consider sending multicast data. Example 13-2 is a `MulticastSender` class that reads input from the command line and sends it to a multicast group. It's fairly simple, overall.

Example 13-2. MulticastSender

```
import java.io.*;
import java.net.*;

public class MulticastSender {

  public static void main(String[] args) {

    InetAddress ia = null;
    int port = 0;
    byte ttl = (byte) 1;

    // read the address from the command line
    try {
      ia = InetAddress.getByName(args[0]);
      port = Integer.parseInt(args[1]);
      if (args.length > 2) ttl = (byte) Integer.parseInt(args[2]);
    } catch (NumberFormatException | IndexOutOfBoundsException
        | UnknownHostException ex)  {
      System.err.println(ex);
      System.err.println(
          "Usage: java MulticastSender multicast_address port ttl");
      System.exit(1);
    }

    byte[] data = "Here's some multicast data\r\n".getBytes();
    DatagramPacket dp = new DatagramPacket(data, data.length, ia, port);

    try (MulticastSocket ms = new MulticastSocket()) {
      ms.setTimeToLive(ttl);
      ms.joinGroup(ia);
      for (int i = 1; i < 10; i++) {
        ms.send(dp);
      }
      ms.leaveGroup(ia);
    } catch (SocketException ex) {
```

```
        System.err.println(ex);
    } catch (IOException ex) {
        System.err.println(ex);
    }
  }
}
```

Example 13-2 reads the address of a multicast group, a port number, and an optional TTL from the command line. It then stuffs the string "Here's some multicast data \r\n" into the byte array data using the getBytes() method of java.lang.String, and places this array in the DatagramPacket dp. Next, it constructs the MulticastSocket ms, which joins the group ia. Once it has joined the group, ms sends the datagram packet dp to the group ia 10 times. The TTL value is set to one to make sure that this data doesn't go beyond the local subnet. Having sent the data, ms leaves the group and closes itself.

Run MulticastSniffer on one machine in your local subnet. Listen to the group *all-systems.mcast.net* on port 4000, like this:

> **% java MulticastSniffer all-systems.mcast.net 4000**

Next, send data to that group by running MulticastSender on another machine in your local subnet. You can also run it in a different window on the same machine, although that option is not as exciting. However, you must start running the MulticastSniff er before you start running the MulticastSender. Send to the group *all-systems.mcast.net* on port 4000, like this:

> **% java MulticastSender all-systems.mcast.net 4000**

Back on the first machine, you should see this output:

```
Here's some multicast data
Here's some multicast data
Here's some multicast data
Here's some multicast data
Here's some multicast data
Here's some multicast data
Here's some multicast data
Here's some multicast data
Here's some multicast data
```

For this to work beyond the local subnet, the two subnets must each have multicast routers, and the routers in between them need to have multicast enabled.

Index

We'd like to hear your suggestions for improving our indexes. Send email to index@oreilly.com.

About the Author

Elliotte Rusty Harold is originally from New Orleans, and he returns there periodically in search of a decent bowl of gumbo. However, he currently resides in the Prospect Heights neighborhood of Brooklyn with his wife, Beth, and dog, Thor. He's a frequent speaker at industry conferences including Software Development, Dr. Dobb's Architecture & Design World, JavaZone, JAOO, SD Best Practices, Extreme Markup Languages, and too many user groups to count. His open source projects include the XOM Library for processing XML with Java and the Amateur media player.

Colophon

The animal on the cover of *Java Network Programming*, Fourth Edition, is a North American river otter (*Lutra canadensis*). These small carnivores are found in all major waterways of the United States and Canada, and in almost every habitat except the tundra and the hot, dry regions of the southwestern United States. They weigh about 20 pounds and are approximately two and a half feet long, and females tend to be about a third smaller than males. Their diet consists mainly of aquatic animals like fish and frogs, but since they spend about two-thirds of their time on land, they also eat the occasional bird or rodent. Two layers of fur—a coarse outer coat and a thick, dense inner coat—protect a river otter from the cold, and, in fact, they seem to enjoy playing in snow and ice. When diving, a river otter's pulse rate slows to only 20 beats per minute from its normal 170, conserving oxygen and allowing the otter to stay underwater longer. These animals are sociable and domesticated easily, and in Europe, a related species was once trained to catch fish for people to eat.

The cover image is from the Dover Pictorial Archive. The cover font is Adobe ITC Garamond. The text font is Adobe Minion Pro; the heading font is Adobe Myriad Condensed; and the code font is Dalton Maag's Ubuntu Mono.

Get even more for your money.

Join the O'Reilly Community, and register the O'Reilly books you own. It's free, and you'll get:

- $4.99 ebook upgrade offer
- 40% upgrade offer on O'Reilly print books
- Membership discounts on books and events
- Free lifetime updates to ebooks and videos
- Multiple ebook formats, DRM FREE
- Participation in the O'Reilly community
- Newsletters
- Account management
- 100% Satisfaction Guarantee

Signing up is easy:

1. Go to: oreilly.com/go/register
2. Create an O'Reilly login.
3. Provide your address.
4. Register your books.

Note: English-language books only

To order books online:
oreilly.com/store

For questions about products or an order:
orders@oreilly.com

To sign up to get topic-specific email announcements and/or news about upcoming books, conferences, special offers, and new technologies:
elists@oreilly.com

For technical questions about book content:
booktech@oreilly.com

To submit new book proposals to our editors:
proposals@oreilly.com

O'Reilly books are available in multiple DRM-free ebook formats. For more information:
oreilly.com/ebooks

9 781449 357672